CHRONICLES OF THE CURSED SWORD

Volume 16

Story by
YEO BEOP-RYONG
Art by
PARK HUI-JIN

HAMBURG // LONDON // LOS ANGELES // TOKYO

Chronicles of the Cursed Sword Vol. 16
Written by Yeo Beop-Ryong
Illustrated by Park Hui-Jin

Translation - Youngju Ryu
English Adaptation - Matt Varosky
Copy Editor - Stephanie Duchin
Retouch and Lettering - Chastain Riggs
Production Artist - L.B.
Cover Design - Fawn Lau

Editor - Hope Donovan
Digital Imaging Manager - Chris Buford
Managing Editor - Vy Nguyen
Production Manager - Elisabeth Brizzi
VP of Production - Ron Klamert
Publisher - Mike Kiley
Editor-In-Chief - Rob Tokar
President and C.O.O. - John Parker
C.E.O. and Chief Creative Officer - Stuart Levy

A  Manga

TOKYOPOP Inc.
5900 Wilshire Blvd. Suite 2000
Los Angeles, CA 90036

E-mail: info@TOKYOPOP.com
Come visit us online at www.TOKYOPOP.com

ISBN: 1-59532-648-0

First TOKYOPOP printing: September 2006
10 9 8 7 6 5 4 3 2 1
Printed in the USA

Chronicles

CHRONICLES OF THE CURSED SWORD

the cast of characters

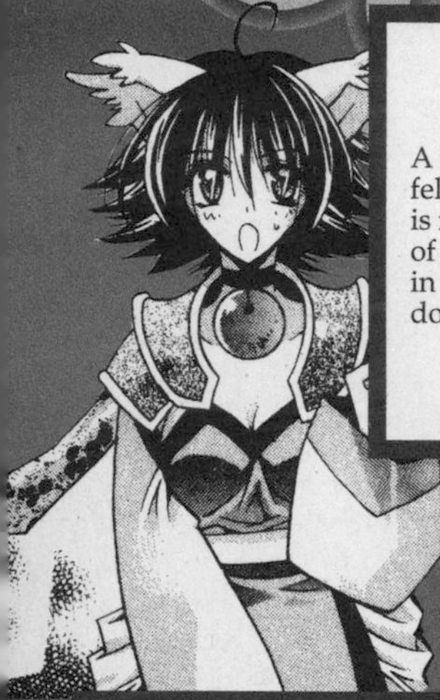

MINGLING

A lesser demon with feline qualities, Mingling is now the loyal follower of Shyao Lin. She lives in fear of Rey, who still doesn't trust her.

THE PASA SWORD

A living sword that hungers for demon blood. It grants its user incredible power, but at a great cost—it can take over the user's body and, in time, his soul.

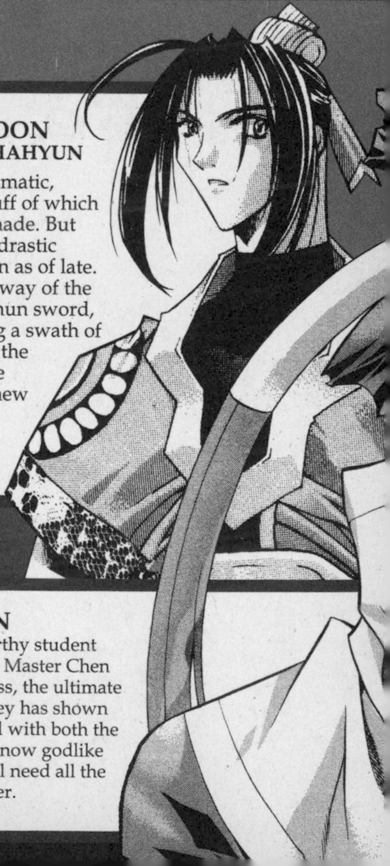

JARYOON
KING OF HAHYUN

Noble and charismatic, Jaryoon is the stuff of which great kings are made. But there has been a drastic change in Jaryoon as of late. Now under the sway of the spirit of the PaChun sword, Jaryoon is cutting a swath of humanity across the countryside as he searches for his new prey: Rey.

SHYAO LIN

A sorceress, previously Rey's traveling companion and greatest ally. Shyao has recently discovered that she is, in fact, one of the Eight Sages of the Azure Pavilion, sent to gather information in the Human Realm. Much to her dismay, she has been told that she must now kill Rey Yan.

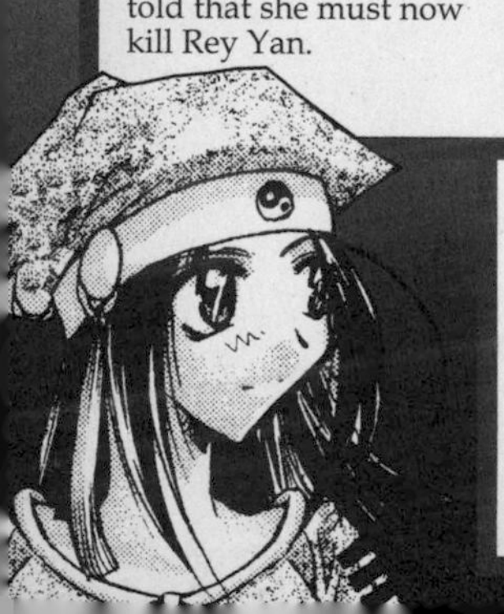

REY YAN

Rey has proven to be a worthy student of the wise and diminutive Master Chen Kaihu. At the Mujin Fortress, the ultimate warrior testing grounds, Rey has shown his martial arts mettle. And with both the possessed Jaryoon and the now godlike Shyao after his blood—he'll need all the survival skills he can muster.

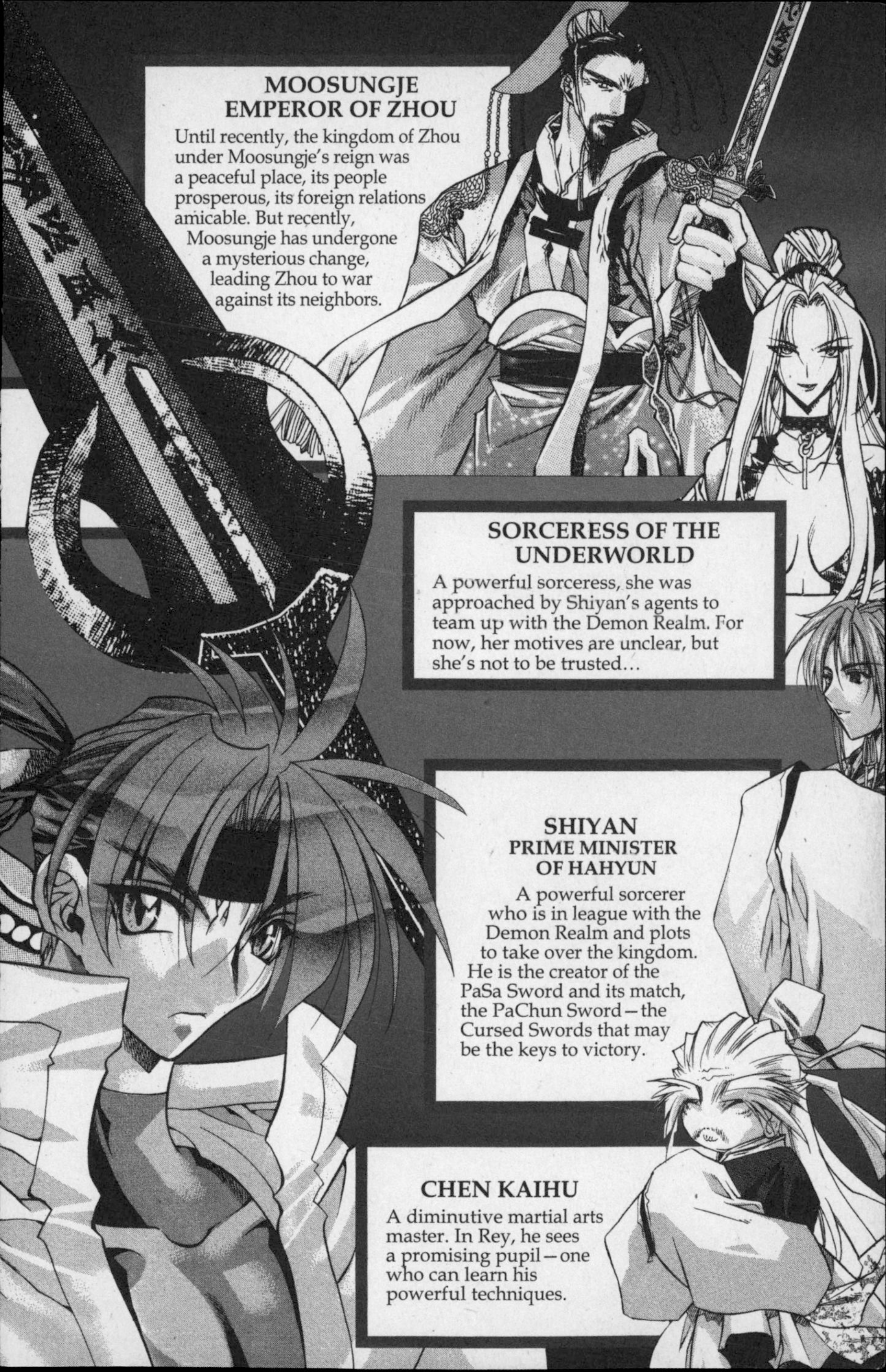

MOOSUNGJE
EMPEROR OF ZHOU

Until recently, the kingdom of Zhou under Moosungje's reign was a peaceful place, its people prosperous, its foreign relations amicable. But recently, Moosungje has undergone a mysterious change, leading Zhou to war against its neighbors.

SORCERESS OF THE UNDERWORLD

A powerful sorceress, she was approached by Shiyan's agents to team up with the Demon Realm. For now, her motives are unclear, but she's not to be trusted...

SHIYAN
PRIME MINISTER OF HAHYUN

A powerful sorcerer who is in league with the Demon Realm and plots to take over the kingdom. He is the creator of the PaSa Sword and its match, the PaChun Sword—the Cursed Swords that may be the keys to victory.

CHEN KAIHU

A diminutive martial arts master. In Rey, he sees a promising pupil—one who can learn his powerful techniques.

Thus Far In...

CHRONICLES OF THE
CURSED SWORD

In an era of warring states, warlords become kings, dynasties crumble, and heroes can rise from the most unlikely places. Rey Yan was an orphan with no home, no skills and no purpose. But when he comes upon the PaSa sword, a cursed blade made from the bones of the Demon Emperor, he suddenly finds himself with the power to be a great hero…

Rey and an unlikely company of demons, sages and warriors are on a journey to the Great Azure Pavilion, the home of the Eight Great Sages, where they hope to thwart an invasion from the Demon Realm. However, King Jaryoon, under the possession of the evil PaChun sword, may beat them there…

Chapter 63: Forbidden Love

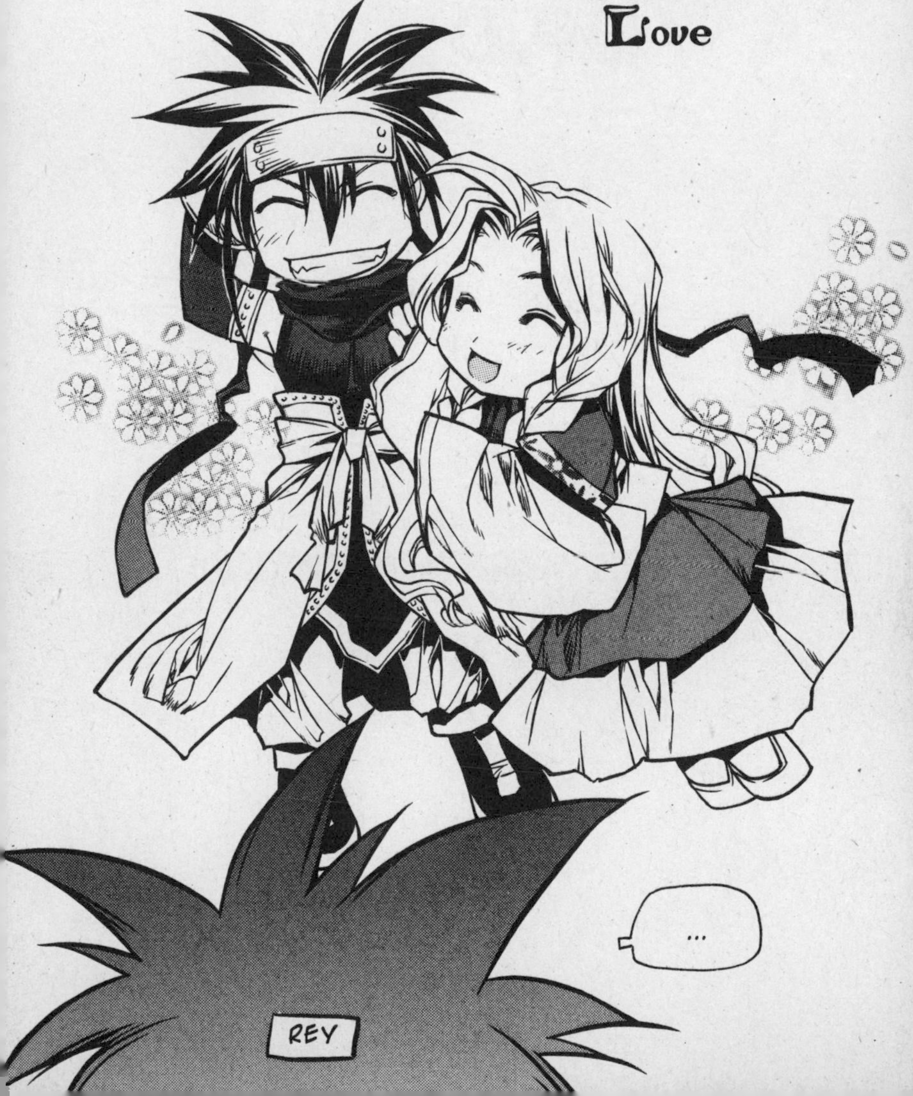
...
REY

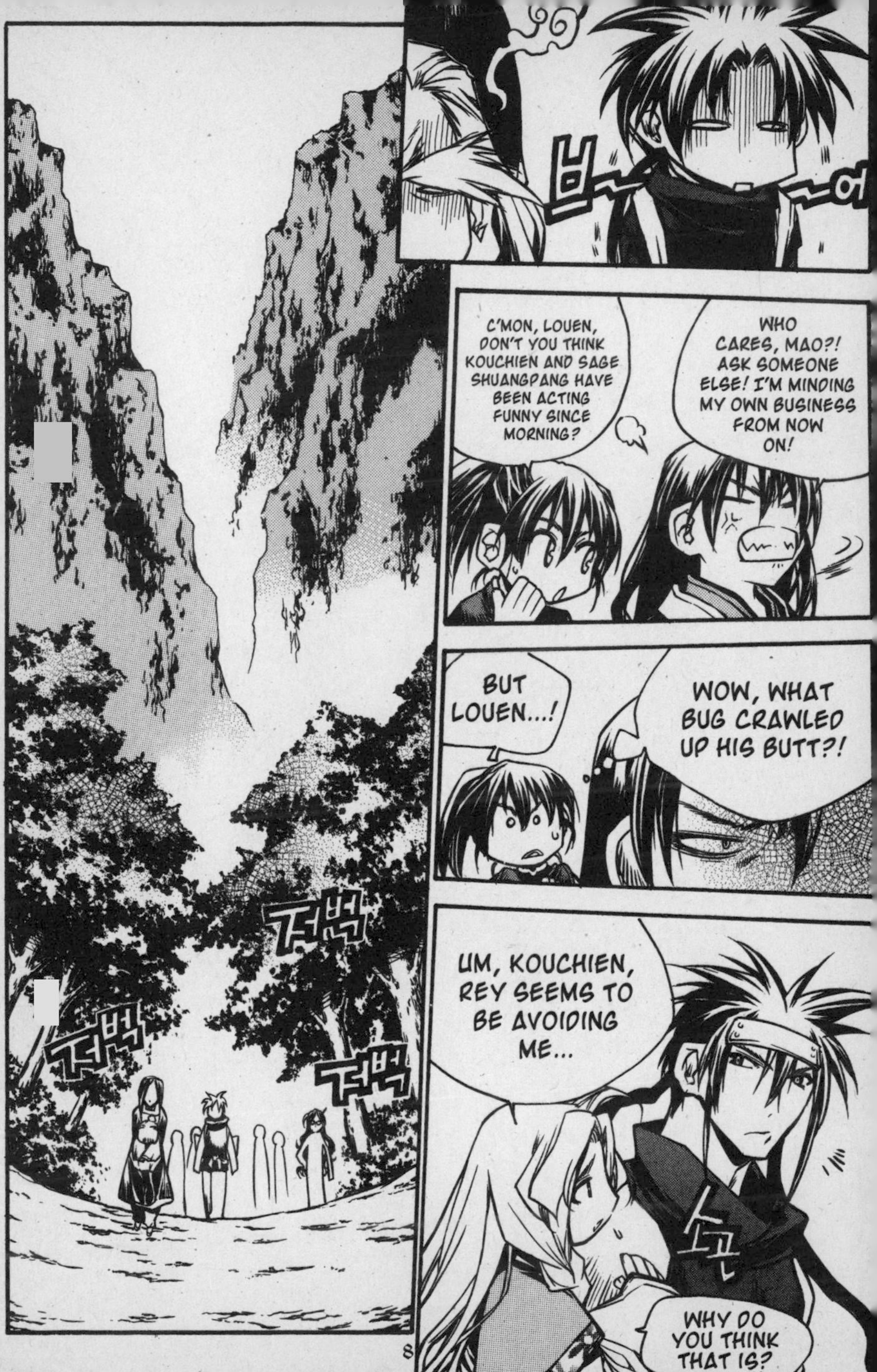
저벅
저벅
저벅
C'MON, LOUEN, DON'T YOU THINK KOUCHIEN AND SAGE SHUANGPANG HAVE BEEN ACTING FUNNY SINCE MORNING?
WHO CARES, MAO?! ASK SOMEONE ELSE! I'M MINDING MY OWN BUSINESS FROM NOW ON!
BUT LOUEN...!
WOW, WHAT BUG CRAWLED UP HIS BUTT?!
UM, KOUCHIEN, REY SEEMS TO BE AVOIDING ME...
WHY DO YOU THINK THAT IS?

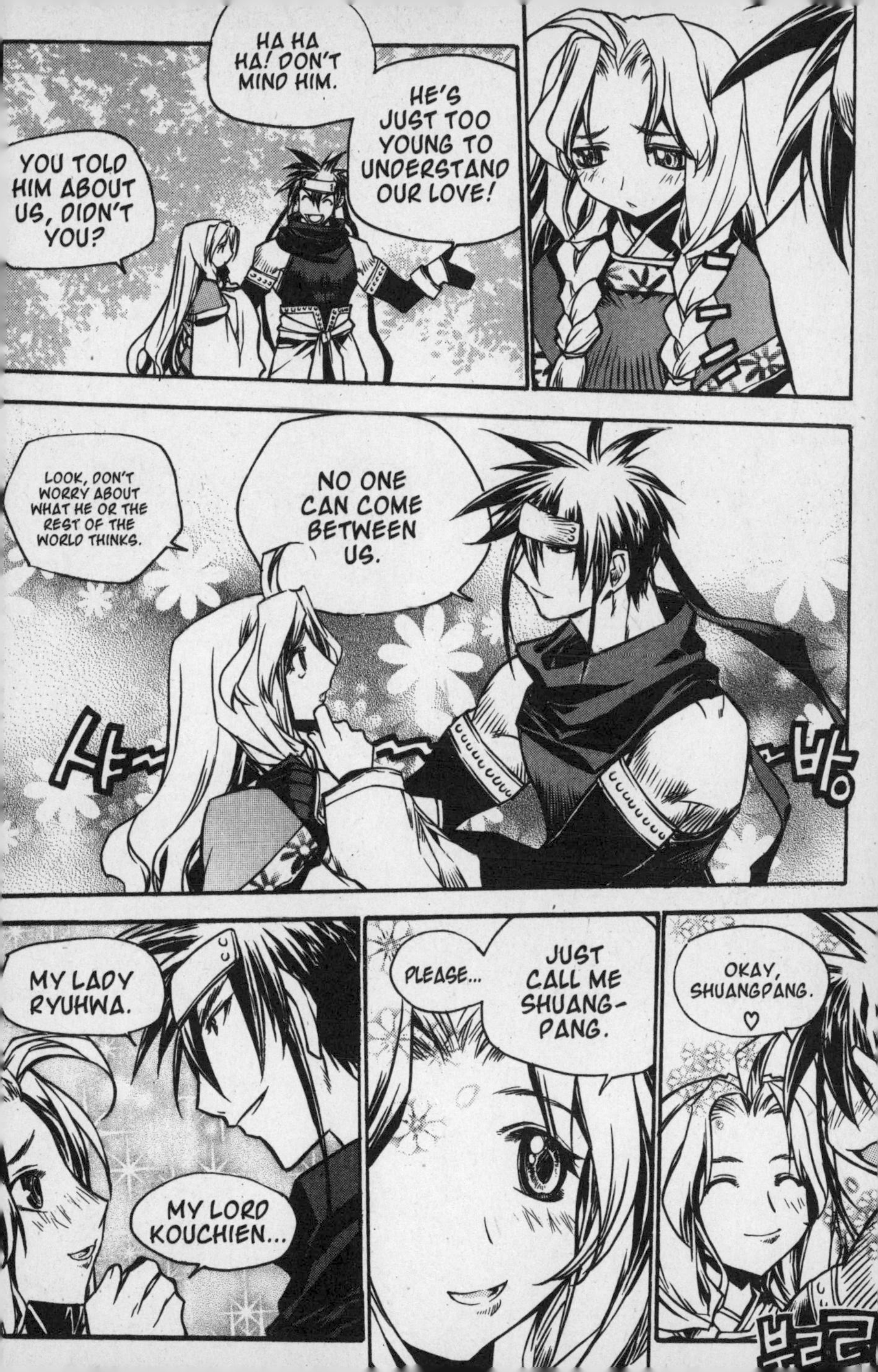
YOU TOLD HIM ABOUT US, DIDN'T YOU?
HA HA HA! DON'T MIND HIM.
HE'S JUST TOO YOUNG TO UNDERSTAND OUR LOVE!
LOOK, DON'T WORRY ABOUT WHAT HE OR THE REST OF THE WORLD THINKS.
NO ONE CAN COME BETWEEN US.
MY LADY RYUHWA.
MY LORD KOUCHIEN...
PLEASE...
JUST CALL ME SHUANG-PANG.
OKAY, SHUANGPANG. ♡

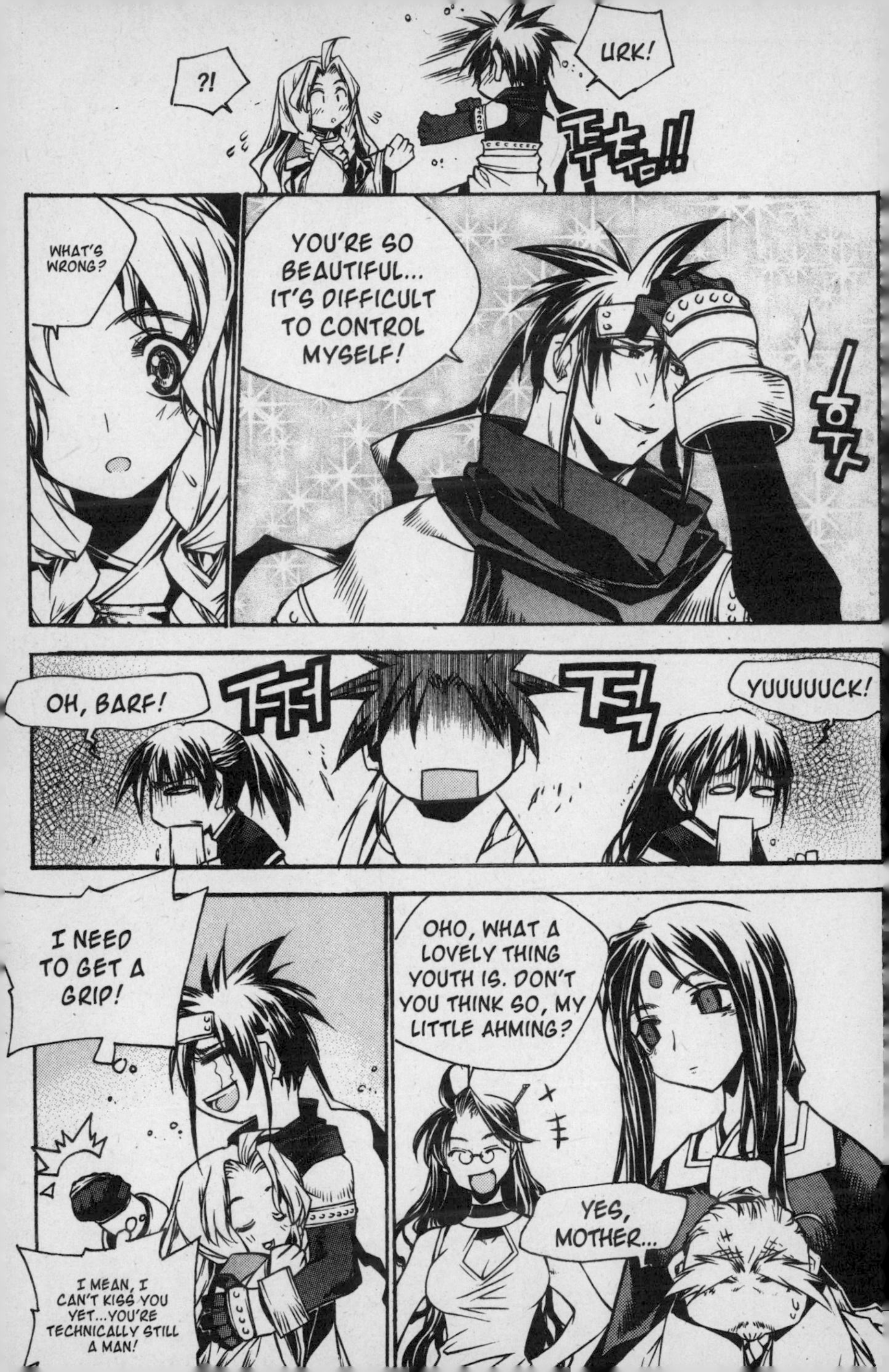
?!
URK!
WHAT'S WRONG?
YOU'RE SO BEAUTIFUL... IT'S DIFFICULT TO CONTROL MYSELF!
OH, BARF!
YUUUUUCK!
I NEED TO GET A GRIP!
I MEAN, I CAN'T KISS YOU YET...YOU'RE TECHNICALLY STILL A MAN!
OHO, WHAT A LOVELY THING YOUTH IS. DON'T YOU THINK SO, MY LITTLE AHMING?
YES, MOTHER...

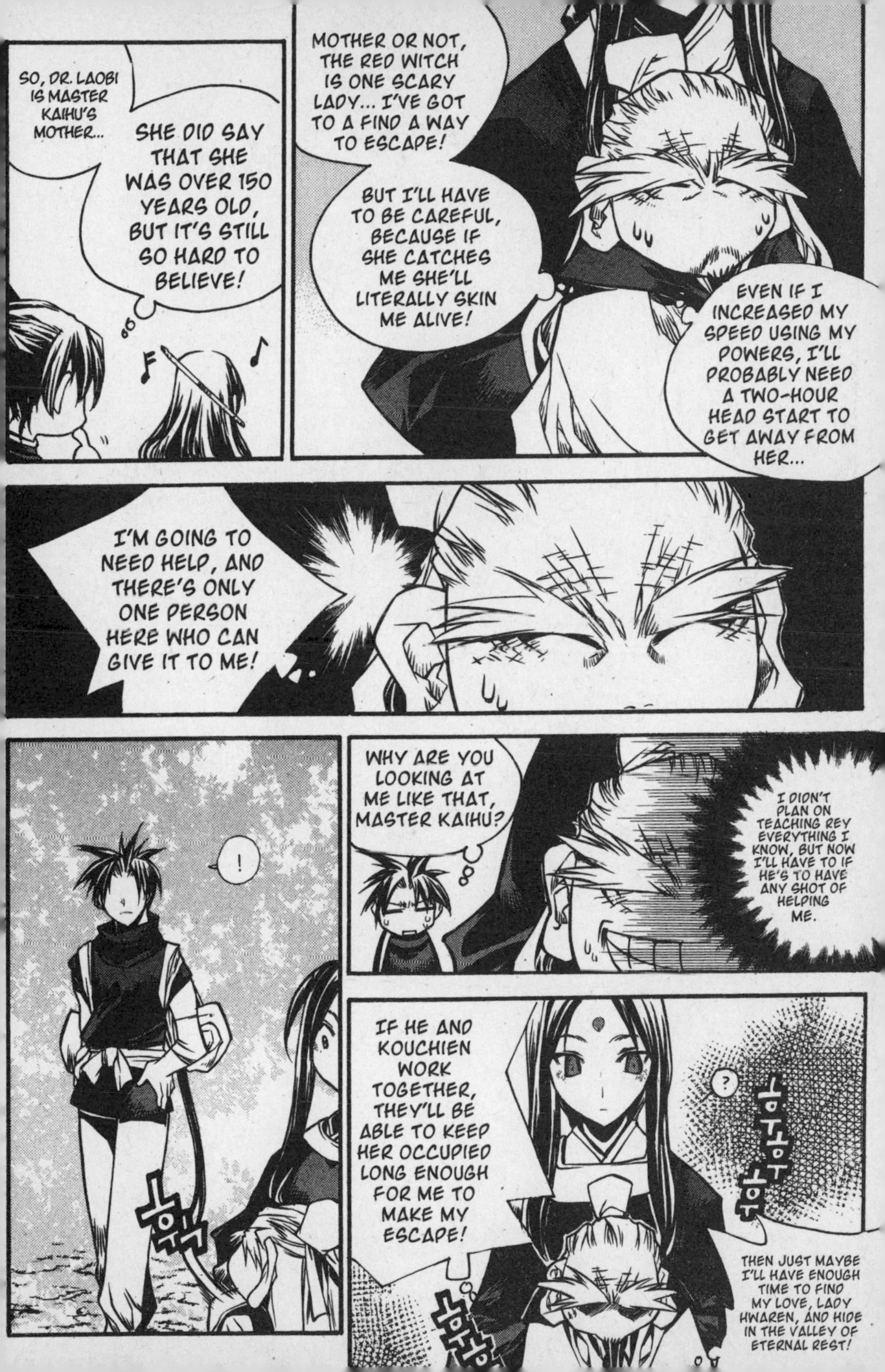

SO, DR. LAOBI IS MASTER KAIHU'S MOTHER...
SHE DID SAY THAT SHE WAS OVER 150 YEARS OLD, BUT IT'S STILL SO HARD TO BELIEVE!
MOTHER OR NOT, THE RED WITCH IS ONE SCARY LADY... I'VE GOT TO A FIND A WAY TO ESCAPE!
BUT I'LL HAVE TO BE CAREFUL, BECAUSE IF SHE CATCHES ME SHE'LL LITERALLY SKIN ME ALIVE!
EVEN IF I INCREASED MY SPEED USING MY POWERS, I'LL PROBABLY NEED A TWO-HOUR HEAD START TO GET AWAY FROM HER...
I'M GOING TO NEED HELP, AND THERE'S ONLY ONE PERSON HERE WHO CAN GIVE IT TO ME!
!
WHY ARE YOU LOOKING AT ME LIKE THAT, MASTER KAIHU?
I DIDN'T PLAN ON TEACHING REY EVERYTHING I KNOW, BUT NOW I'LL HAVE TO IF HE'S TO HAVE ANY SHOT OF HELPING ME.
IF HE AND KOUCHIEN WORK TOGETHER, THEY'LL BE ABLE TO KEEP HER OCCUPIED LONG ENOUGH FOR ME TO MAKE MY ESCAPE!
?
THEN JUST MAYBE I'LL HAVE ENOUGH TIME TO FIND MY LOVE, LADY HWAREN, AND HIDE IN THE VALLEY OF ETERNAL REST!

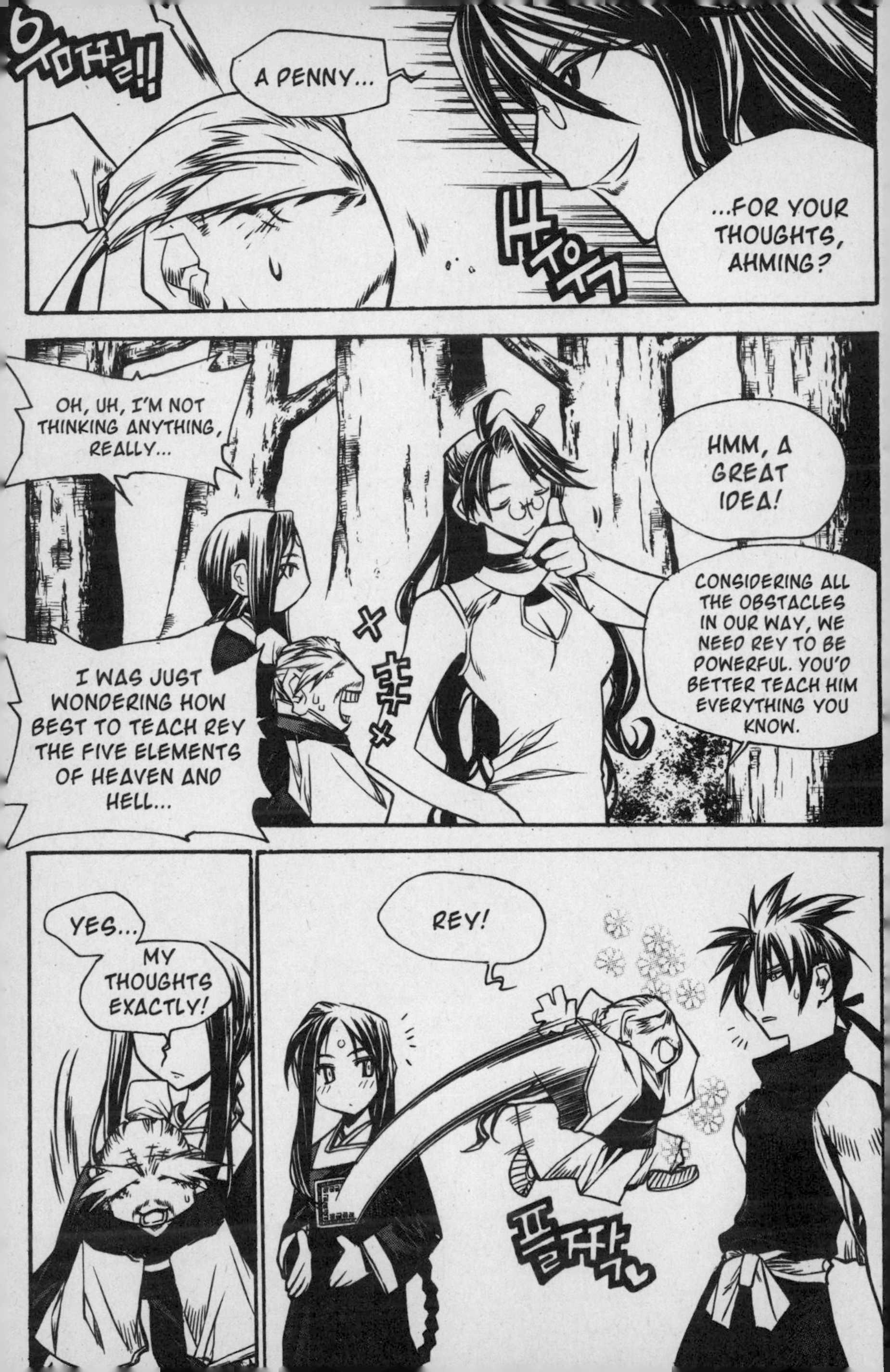
A PENNY...
...FOR YOUR THOUGHTS, AHMING?
OH, UH, I'M NOT THINKING ANYTHING, REALLY...
I WAS JUST WONDERING HOW BEST TO TEACH REY THE FIVE ELEMENTS OF HEAVEN AND HELL...
HMM, A GREAT IDEA!
CONSIDERING ALL THE OBSTACLES IN OUR WAY, WE NEED REY TO BE POWERFUL. YOU'D BETTER TEACH HIM EVERYTHING YOU KNOW.
YES... MY THOUGHTS EXACTLY!
REY!

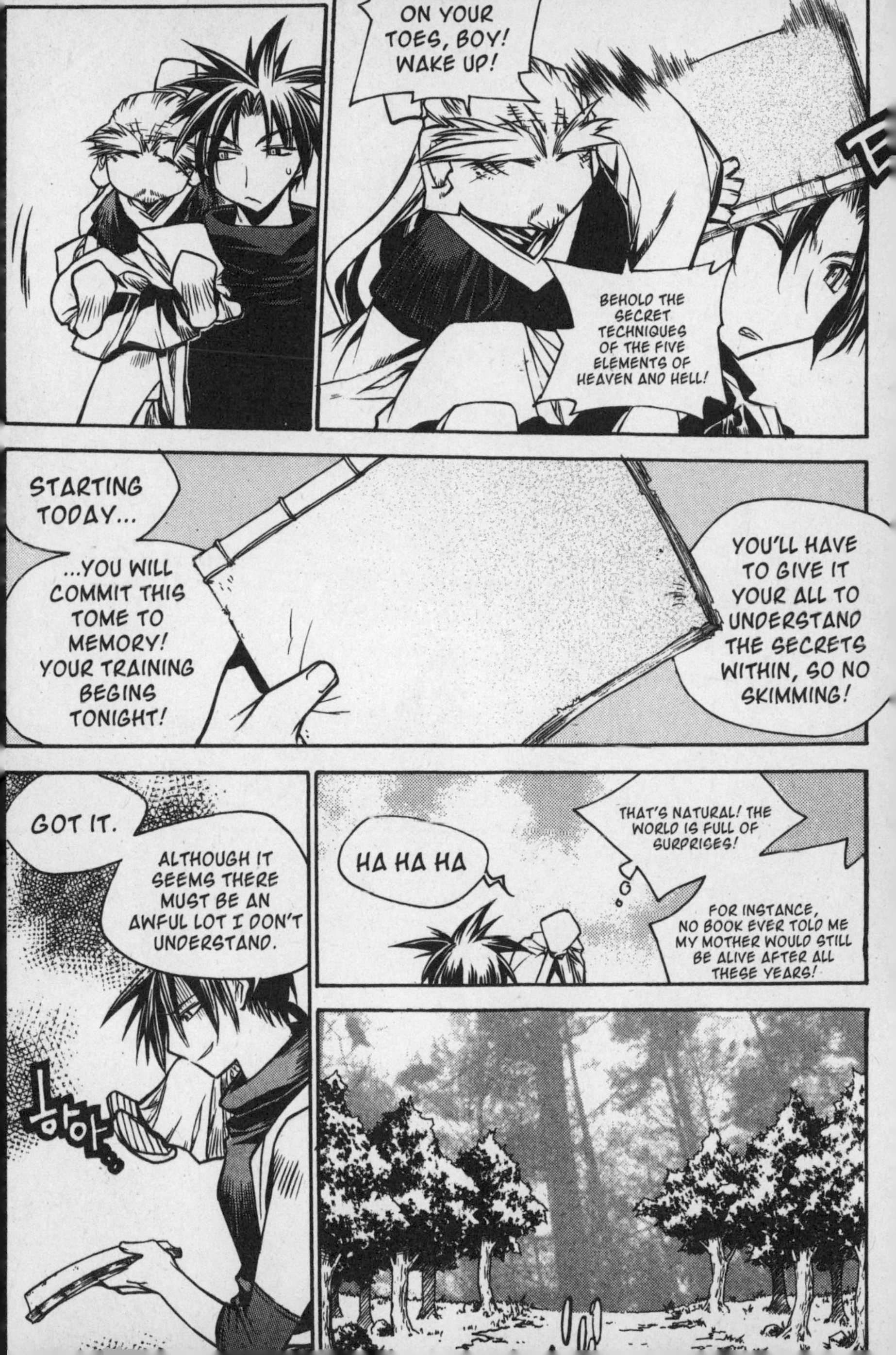
ON YOUR TOES, BOY! WAKE UP!
BEHOLD THE SECRET TECHNIQUES OF THE FIVE ELEMENTS OF HEAVEN AND HELL!
STARTING TODAY...
...YOU WILL COMMIT THIS TOME TO MEMORY! YOUR TRAINING BEGINS TONIGHT!
YOU'LL HAVE TO GIVE IT YOUR ALL TO UNDERSTAND THE SECRETS WITHIN, SO NO SKIMMING!
GOT IT.
ALTHOUGH IT SEEMS THERE MUST BE AN AWFUL LOT I DON'T UNDERSTAND.
HA HA HA
THAT'S NATURAL! THE WORLD IS FULL OF SURPRISES!
FOR INSTANCE, NO BOOK EVER TOLD ME MY MOTHER WOULD STILL BE ALIVE AFTER ALL THESE YEARS!

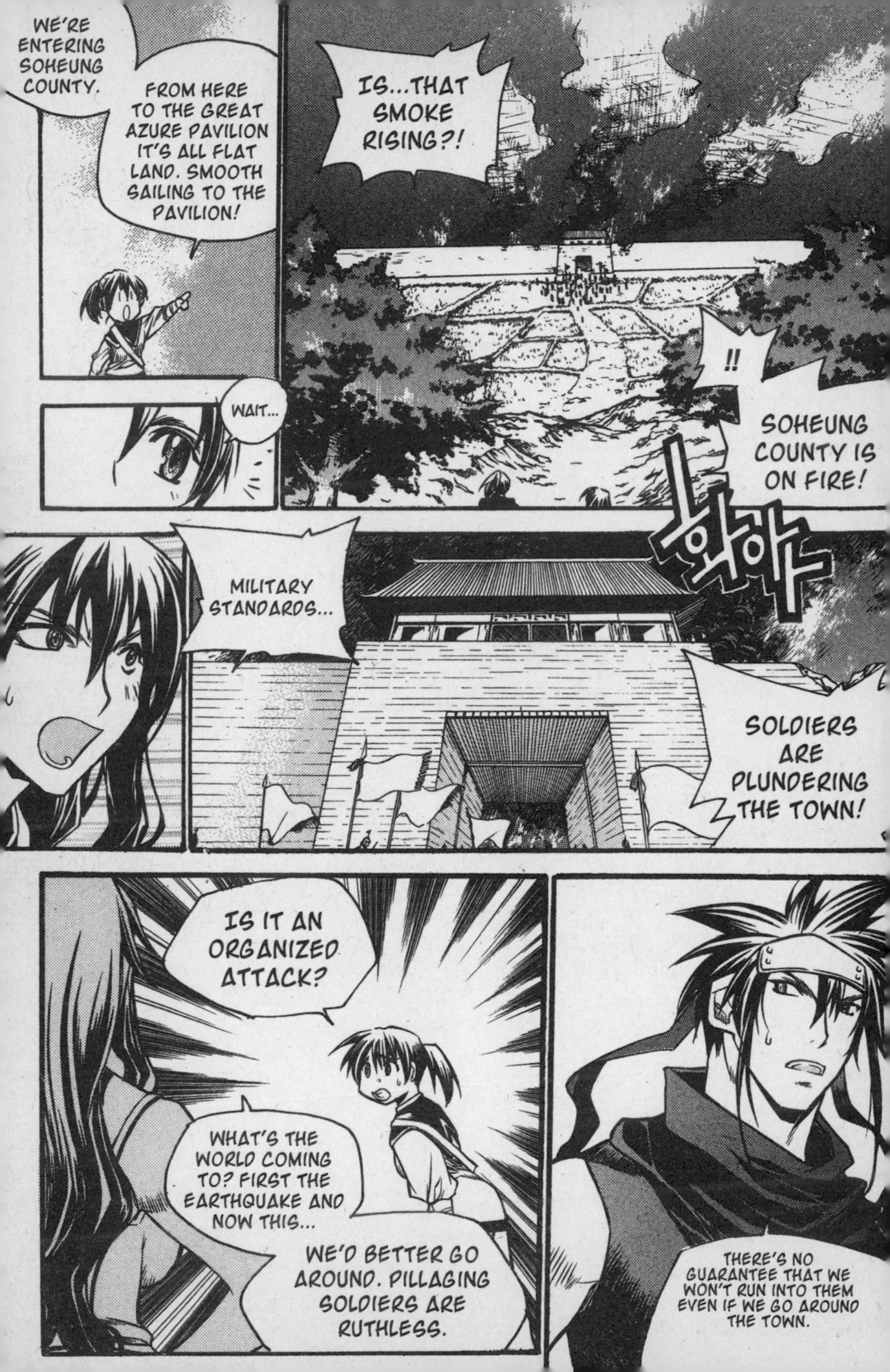

WE'RE ENTERING SOHEUNG COUNTY.
FROM HERE TO THE GREAT AZURE PAVILION IT'S ALL FLAT LAND. SMOOTH SAILING TO THE PAVILION!
WAIT...
IS...THAT SMOKE RISING?!
!!
SOHEUNG COUNTY IS ON FIRE!
와아
MILITARY STANDARDS...
SOLDIERS ARE PLUNDERING THE TOWN!
IS IT AN ORGANIZED ATTACK?
WHAT'S THE WORLD COMING TO? FIRST THE EARTHQUAKE AND NOW THIS...
WE'D BETTER GO AROUND. PILLAGING SOLDIERS ARE RUTHLESS.
THERE'S NO GUARANTEE THAT WE WON'T RUN INTO THEM EVEN IF WE GO AROUND THE TOWN.

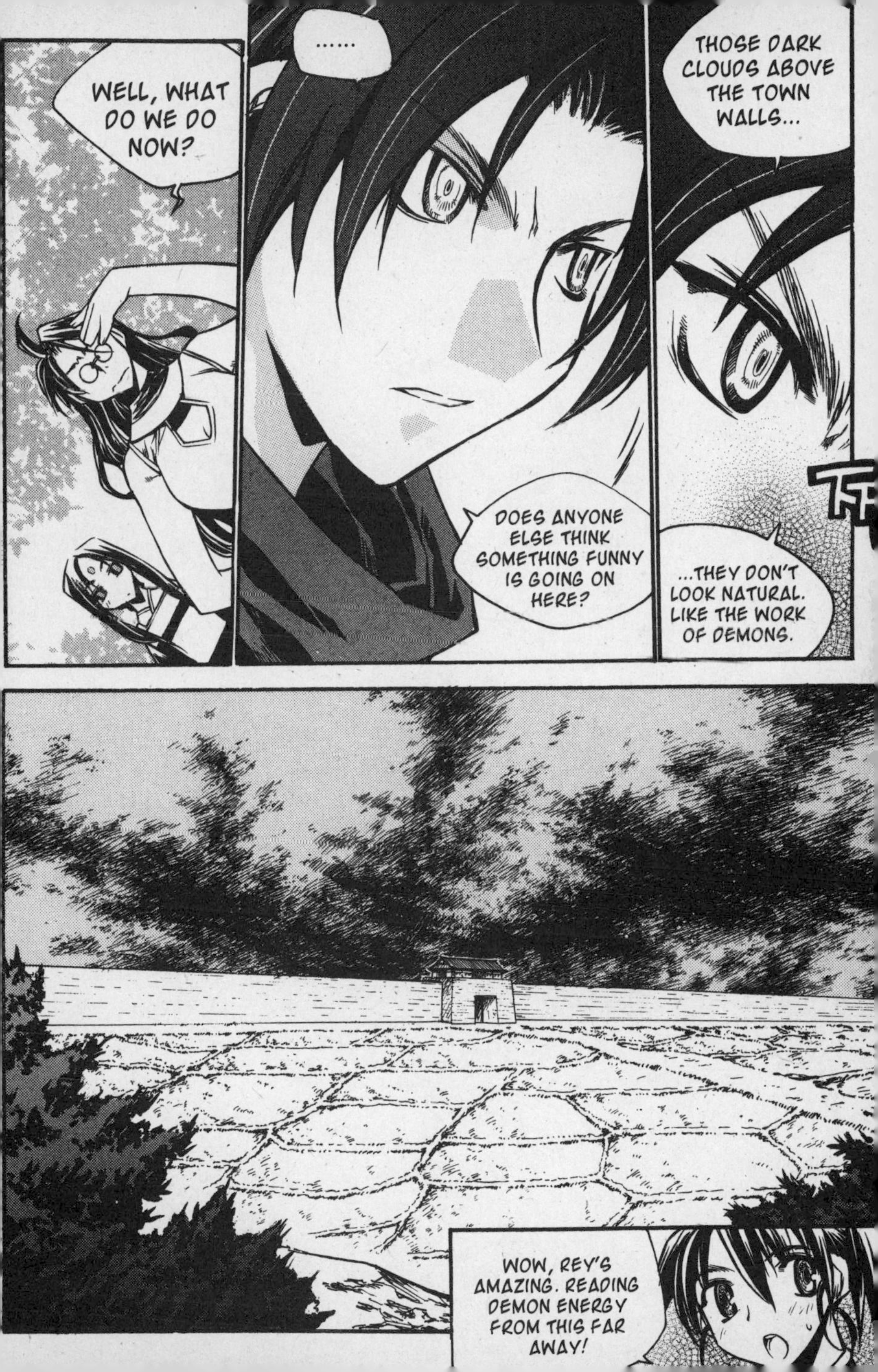
WELL, WHAT DO WE DO NOW?
......
DOES ANYONE ELSE THINK SOMETHING FUNNY IS GOING ON HERE?
THOSE DARK CLOUDS ABOVE THE TOWN WALLS...
...THEY DON'T LOOK NATURAL. LIKE THE WORK OF DEMONS.
WOW, REY'S AMAZING. READING DEMON ENERGY FROM THIS FAR AWAY!

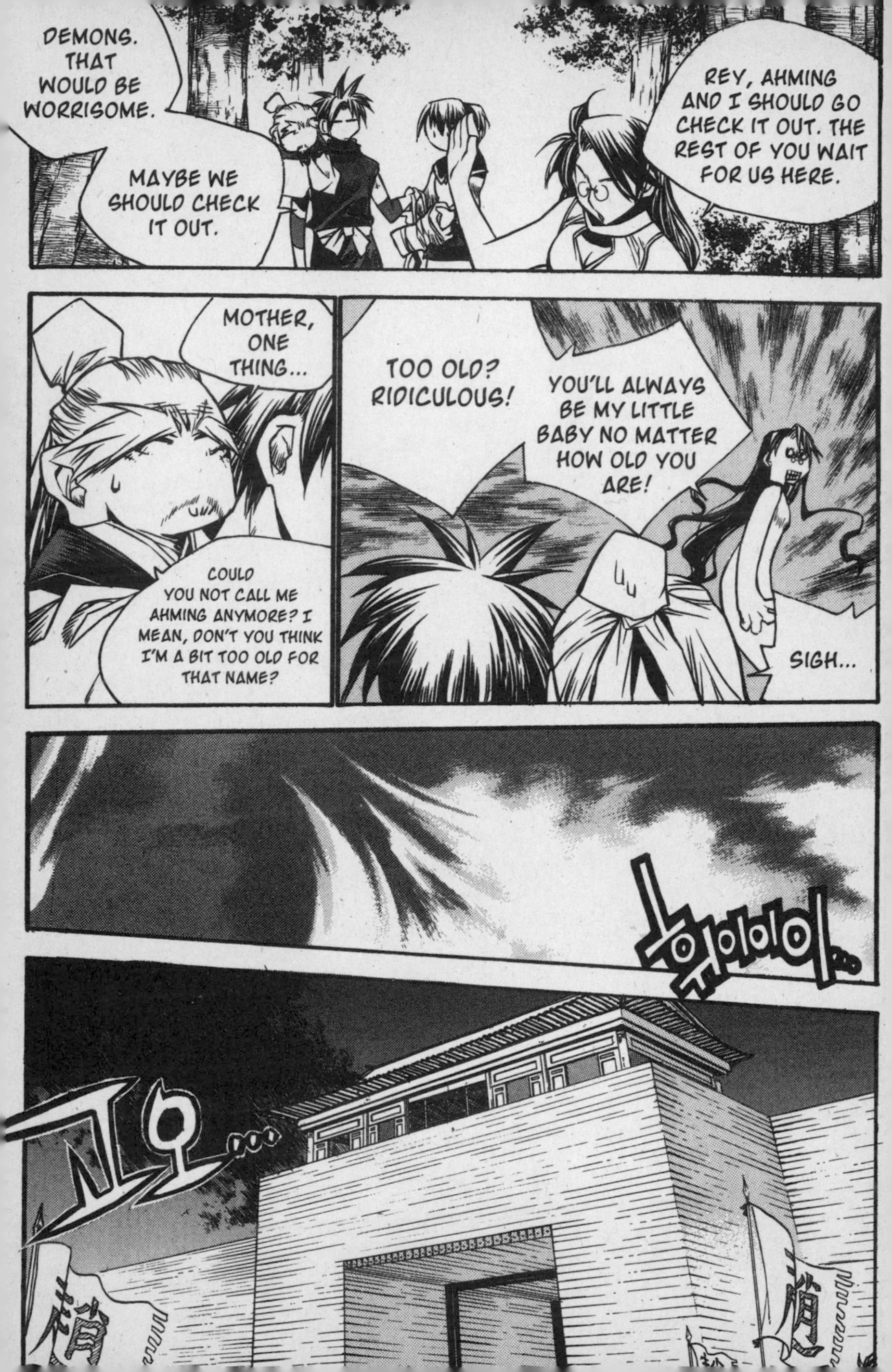
DEMONS. THAT WOULD BE WORRISOME.
MAYBE WE SHOULD CHECK IT OUT.
REY, AHMING AND I SHOULD GO CHECK IT OUT. THE REST OF YOU WAIT FOR US HERE.
MOTHER, ONE THING...
COULD YOU NOT CALL ME AHMING ANYMORE? I MEAN, DON'T YOU THINK I'M A BIT TOO OLD FOR THAT NAME?
TOO OLD? RIDICULOUS!
YOU'LL ALWAYS BE MY LITTLE BABY NO MATTER HOW OLD YOU ARE!
SIGH...

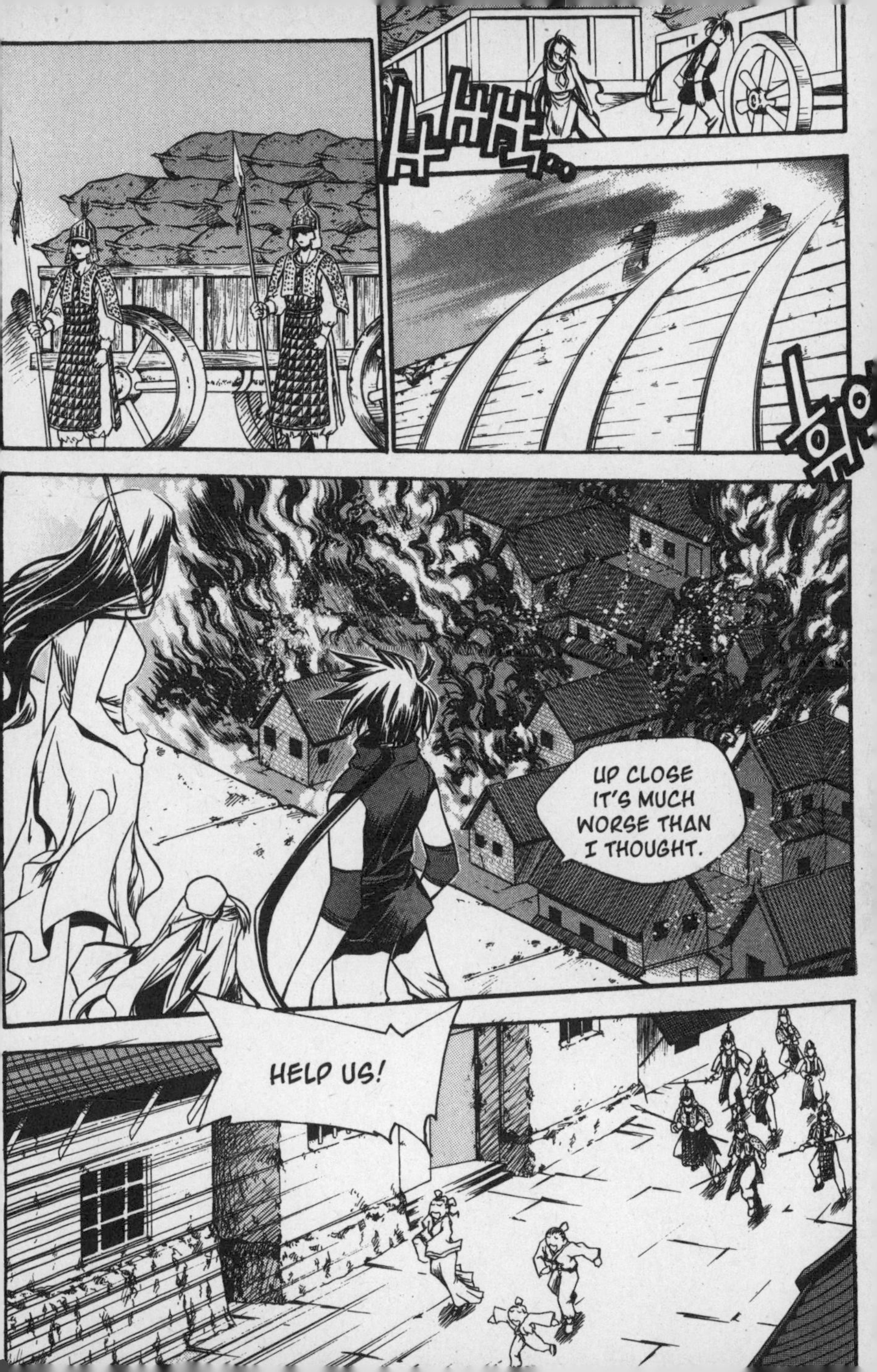
UP CLOSE IT'S MUCH WORSE THAN I THOUGHT.
HELP US!

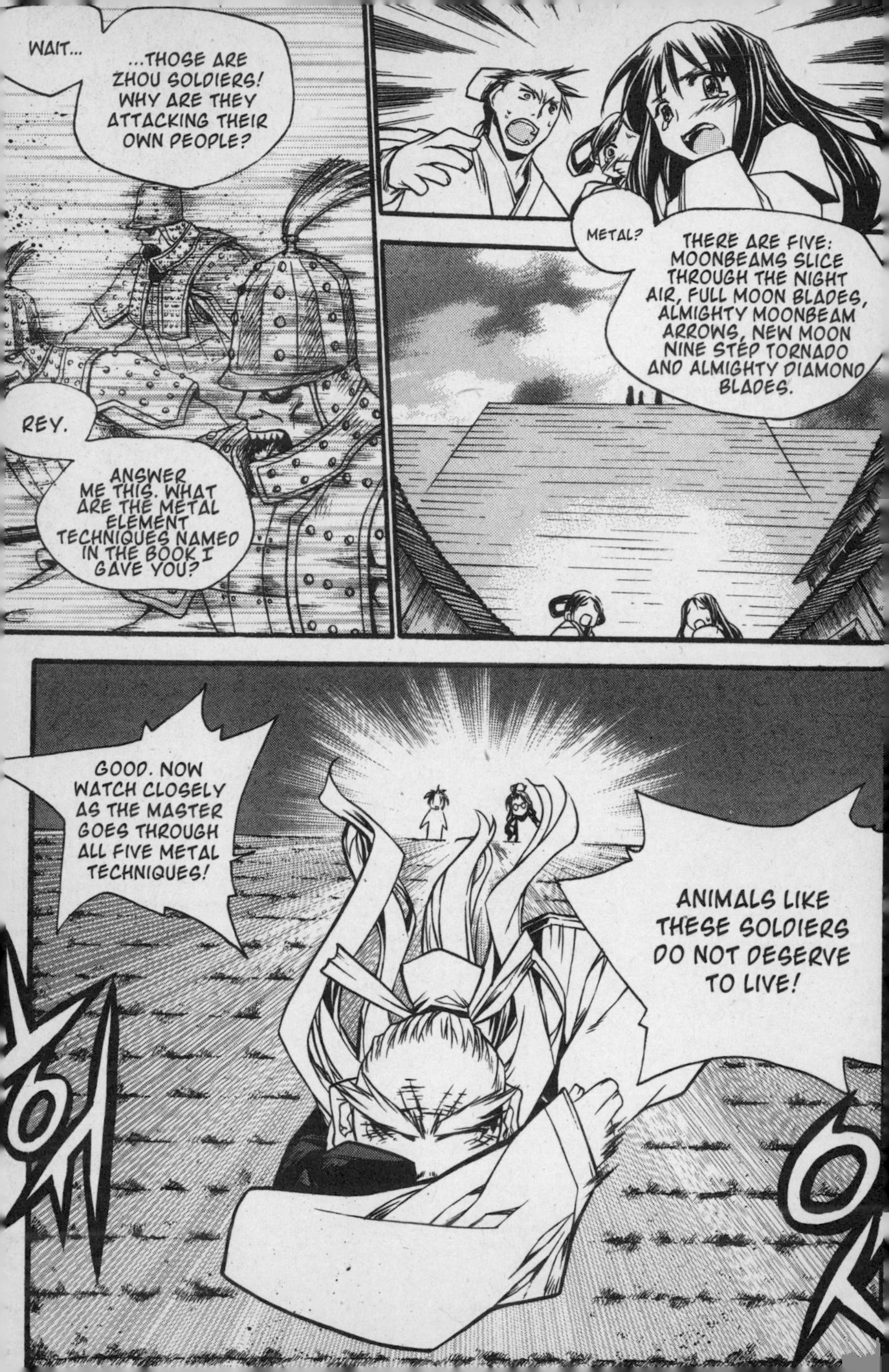
WAIT...
...THOSE ARE ZHOU SOLDIERS! WHY ARE THEY ATTACKING THEIR OWN PEOPLE?
REY.
ANSWER ME THIS. WHAT ARE THE METAL ELEMENT TECHNIQUES NAMED IN THE BOOK I GAVE YOU?
METAL?
THERE ARE FIVE: MOONBEAMS SLICE THROUGH THE NIGHT AIR, FULL MOON BLADES, ALMIGHTY MOONBEAM ARROWS, NEW MOON NINE STEP TORNADO AND ALMIGHTY DIAMOND BLADES.
GOOD. NOW WATCH CLOSELY AS THE MASTER GOES THROUGH ALL FIVE METAL TECHNIQUES!
ANIMALS LIKE THESE SOLDIERS DO NOT DESERVE TO LIVE!

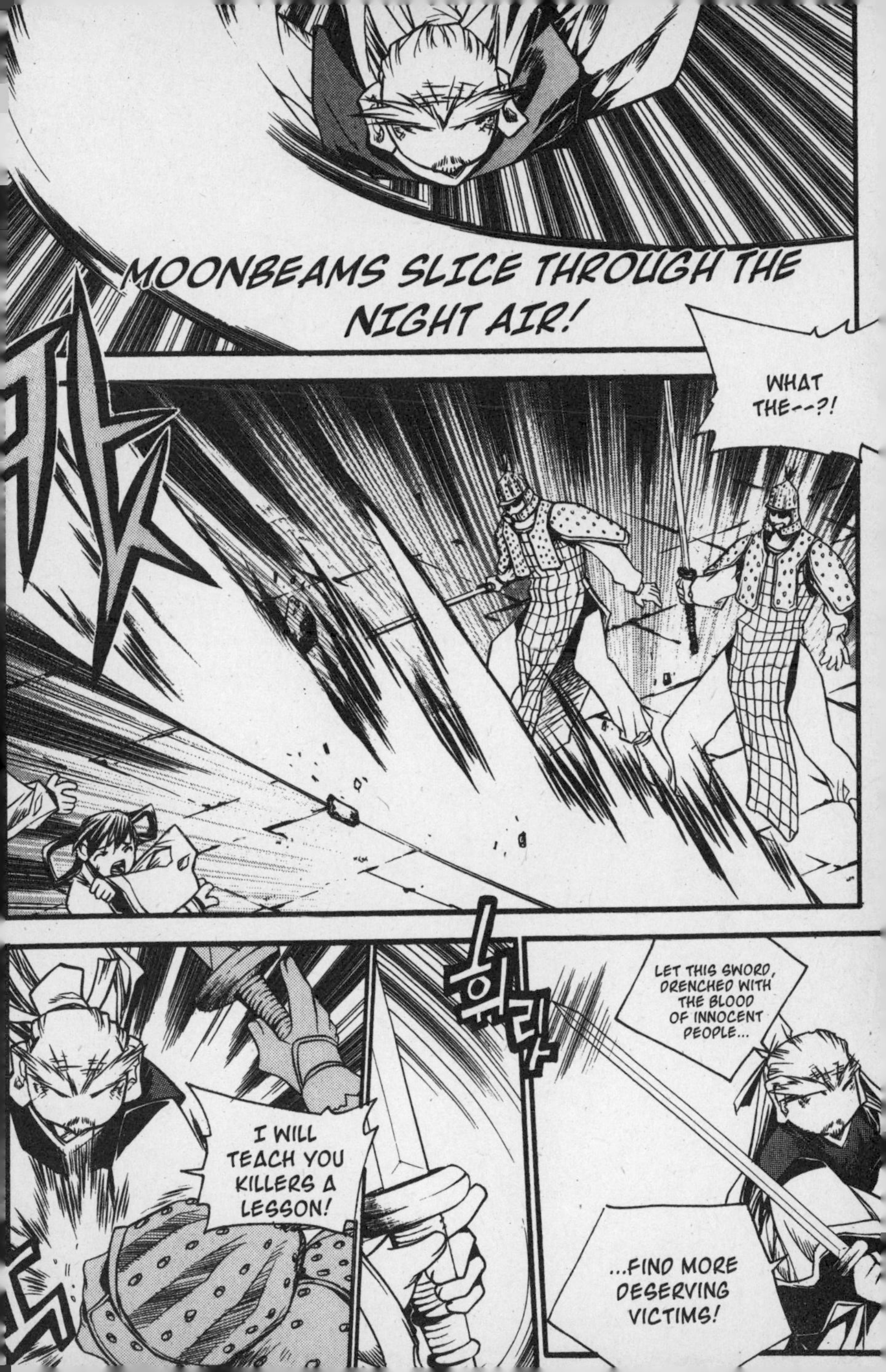
MOONBEAMS SLICE THROUGH THE NIGHT AIR!
WHAT THE--?!
I WILL TEACH YOU KILLERS A LESSON!
LET THIS SWORD, DRENCHED WITH THE BLOOD OF INNOCENT PEOPLE...
...FIND MORE DESERVING VICTIMS!

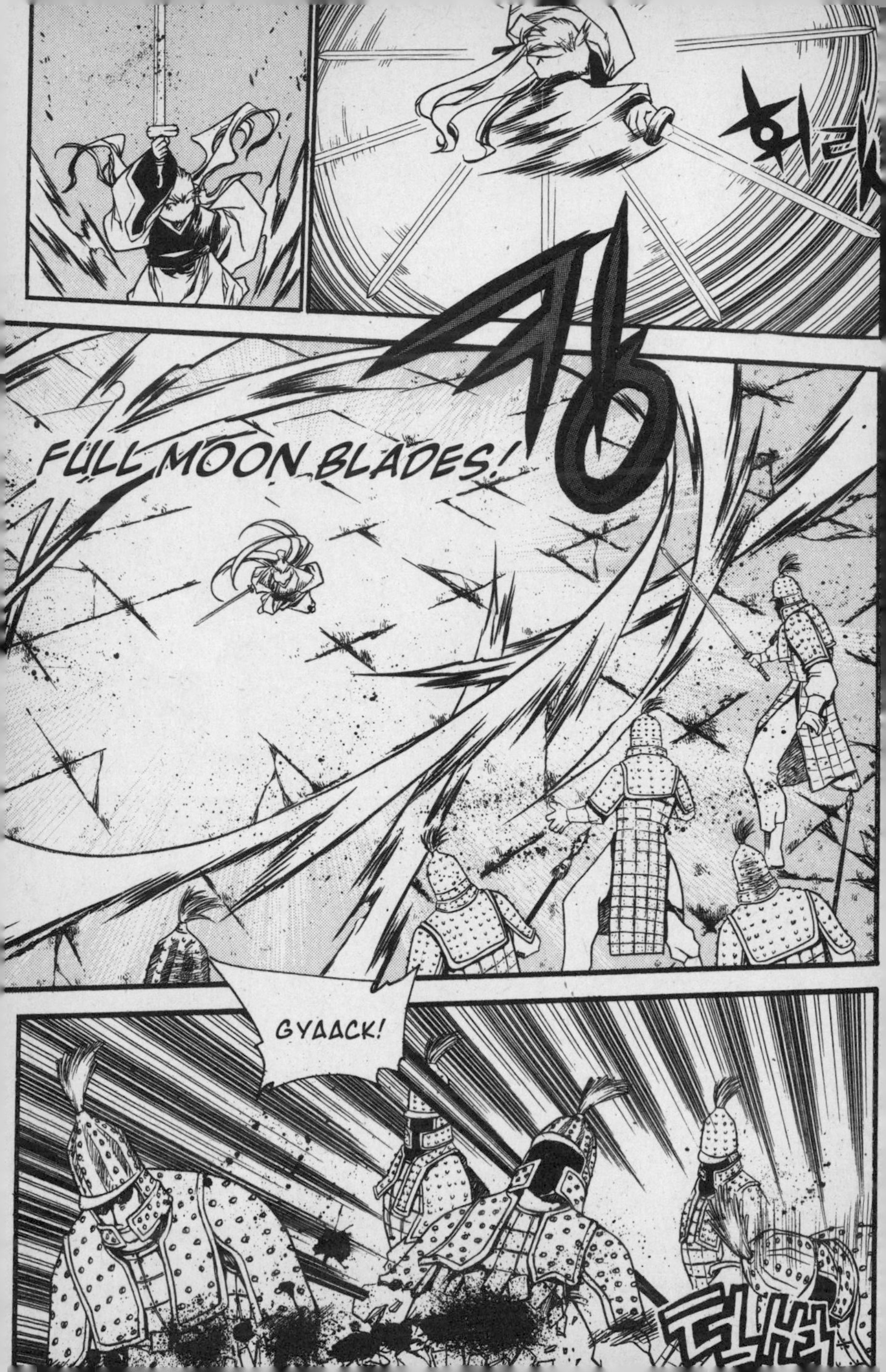
FULL MOON BLADES!
GYAACK!

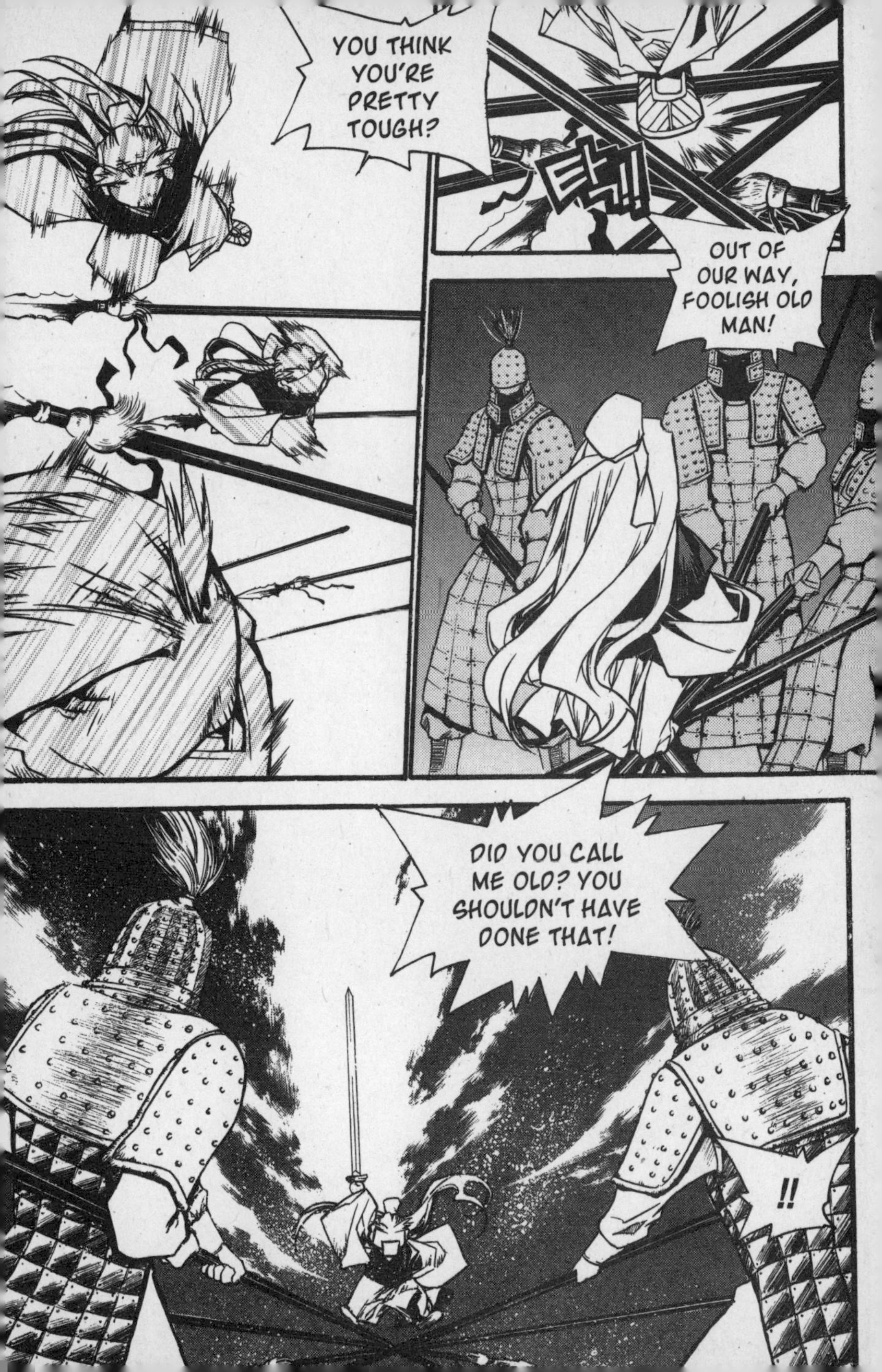
YOU THINK YOU'RE PRETTY TOUGH?
탁!!
OUT OF OUR WAY, FOOLISH OLD MAN!
DID YOU CALL ME OLD? YOU SHOULDN'T HAVE DONE THAT!
!!

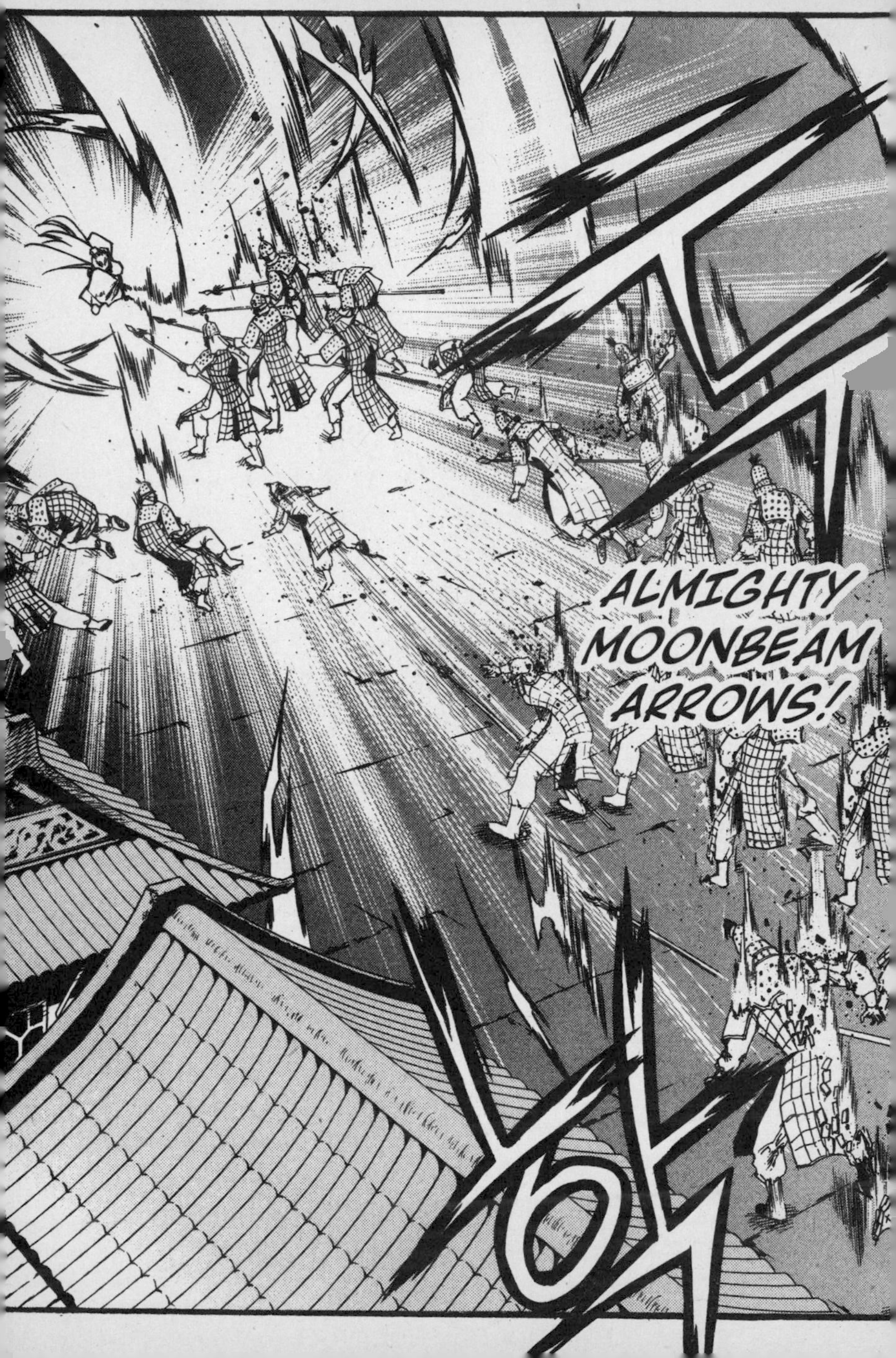
ALMIGHTY MOONBEAM ARROWS!

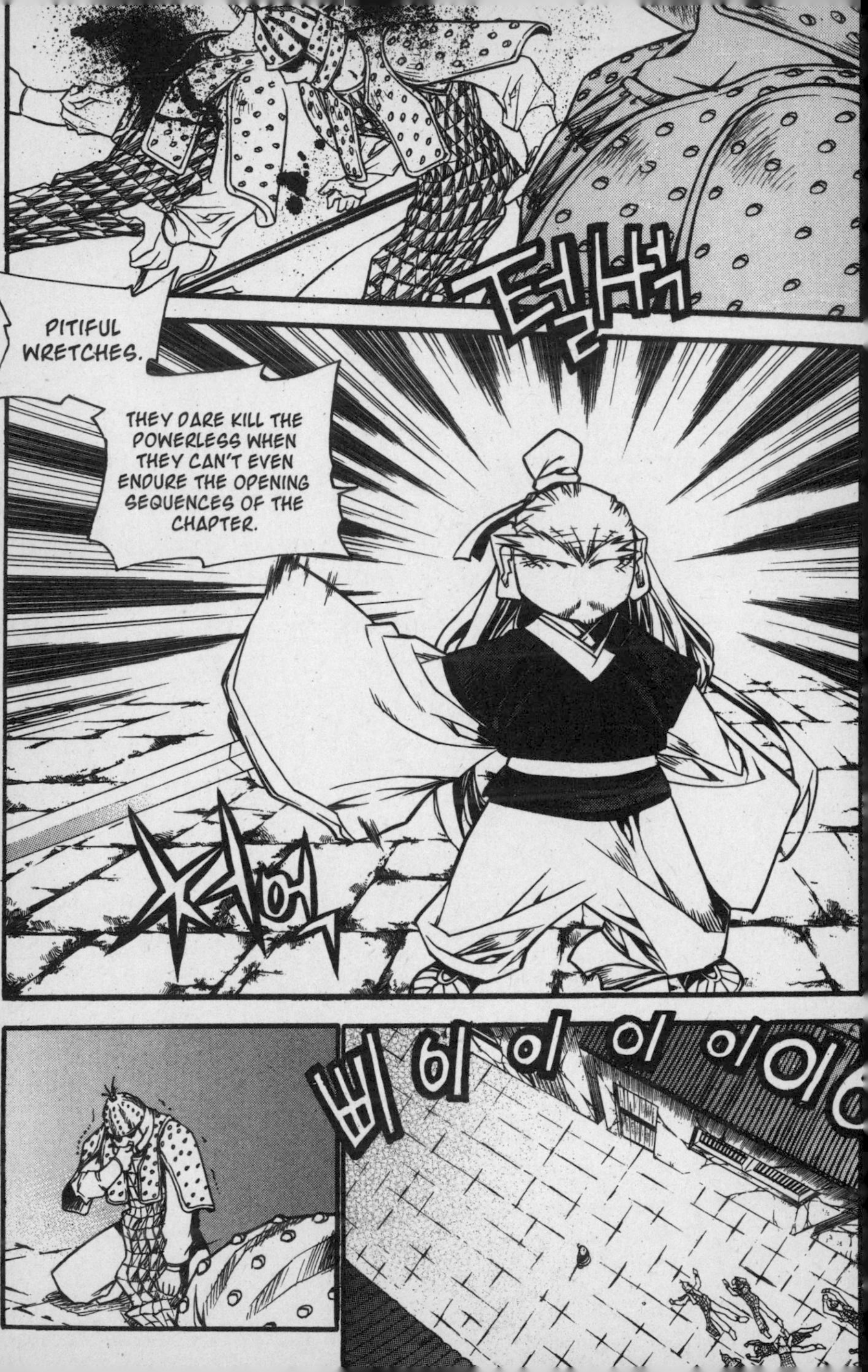
털썩
PITIFUL WRETCHES.
THEY DARE KILL THE POWERLESS WHEN THEY CAN'T EVEN ENDURE THE OPENING SEQUENCES OF THE CHAPTER.
삐히이이이이이이

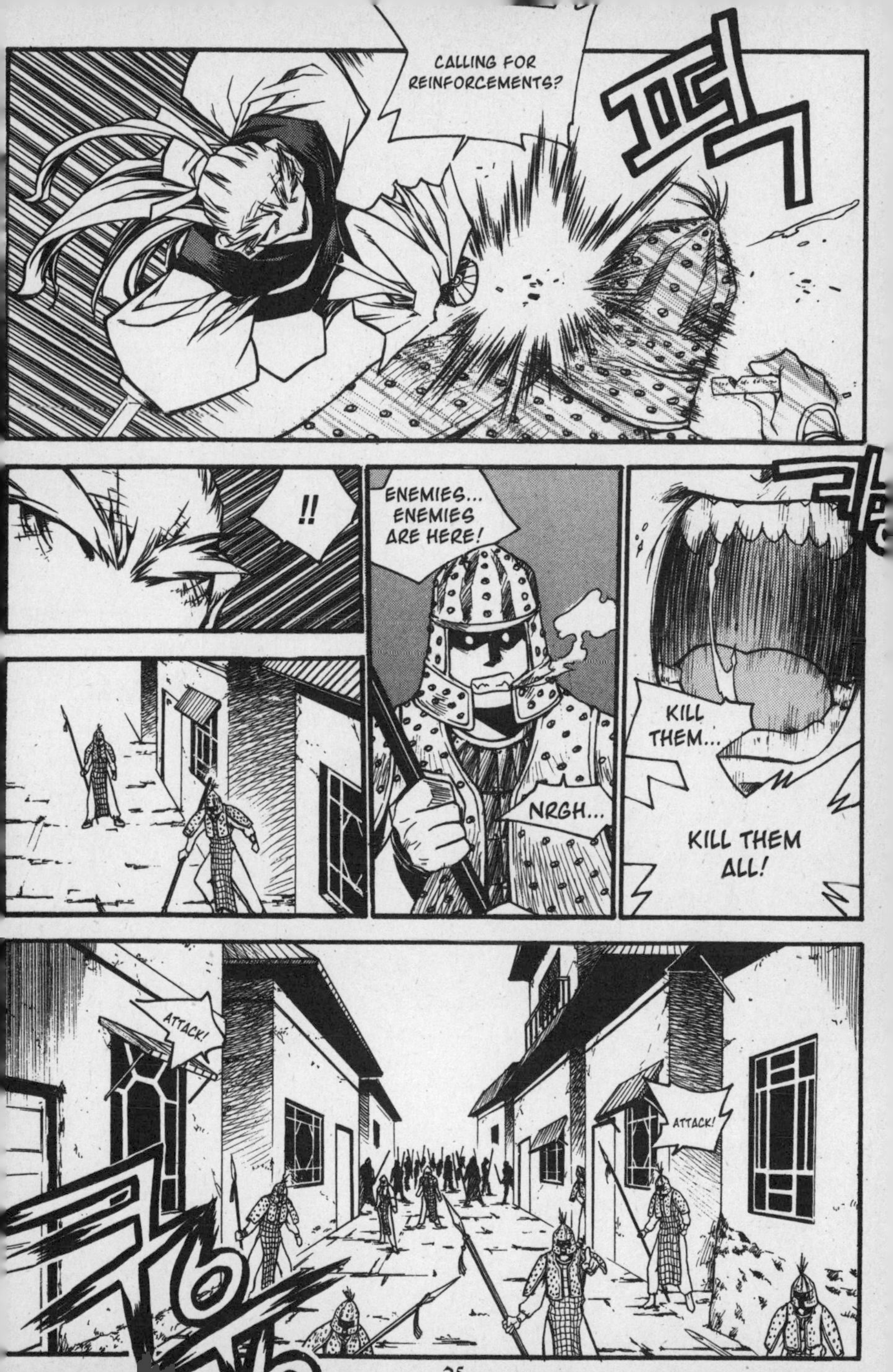
CALLING FOR REINFORCEMENTS?
!!
ENEMIES... ENEMIES ARE HERE!
NRGH...
KILL THEM...
KILL THEM ALL!
ATTACK!
ATTACK!

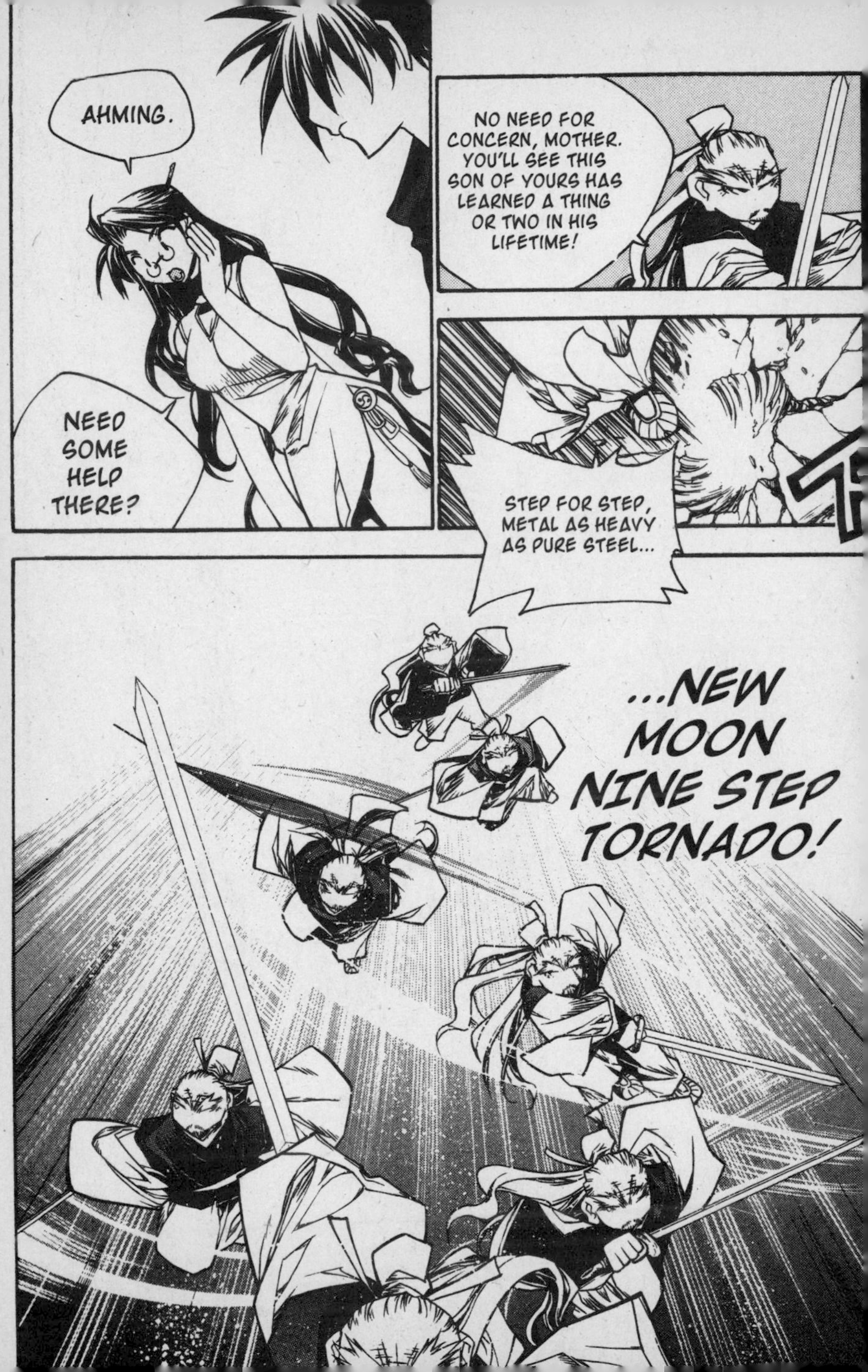
AHMING.
NEED SOME HELP THERE?
NO NEED FOR CONCERN, MOTHER. YOU'LL SEE THIS SON OF YOURS HAS LEARNED A THING OR TWO IN HIS LIFETIME!
STEP FOR STEP, METAL AS HEAVY AS PURE STEEL...
...NEW MOON NINE STEP TORNADO!

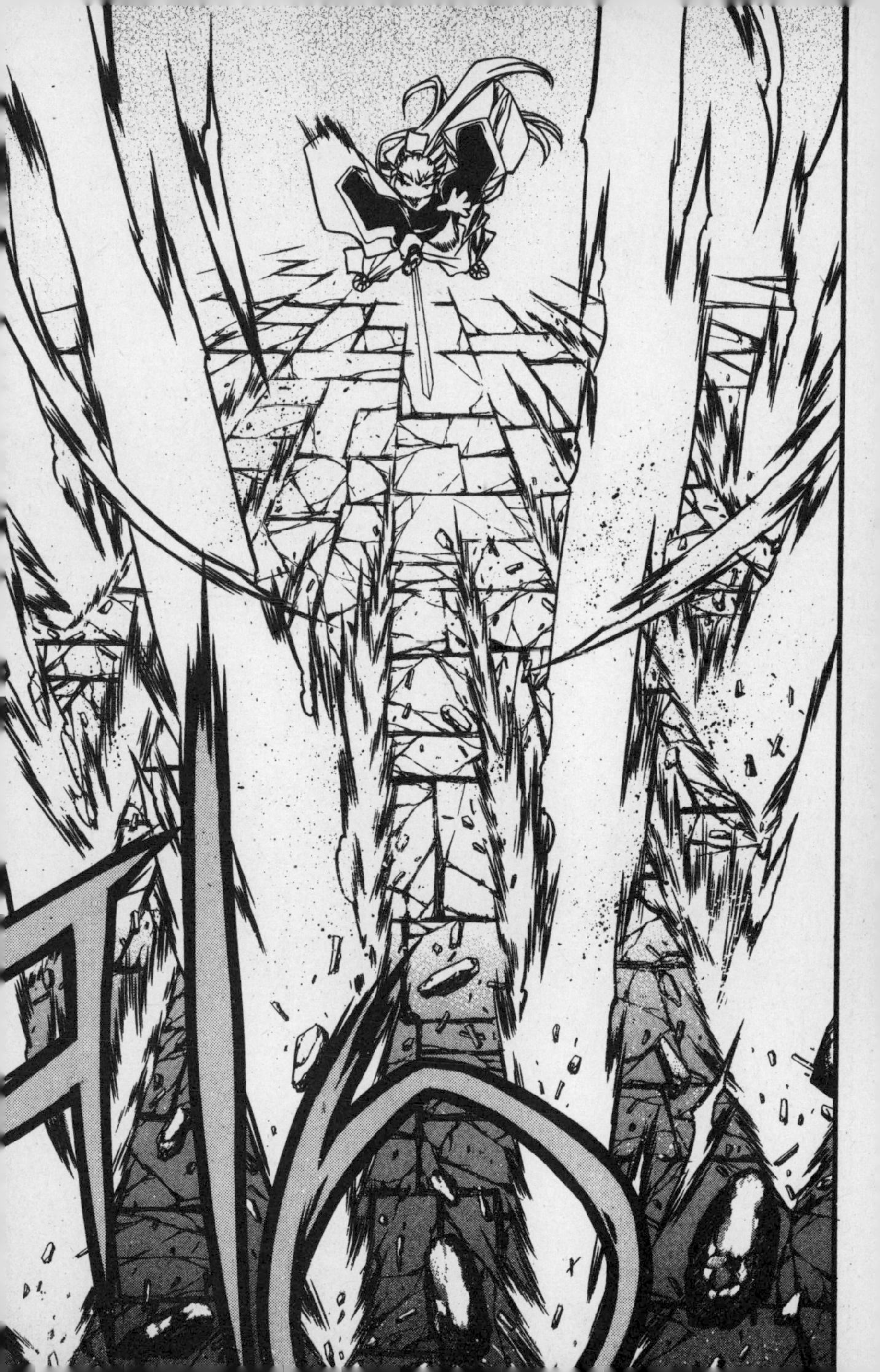

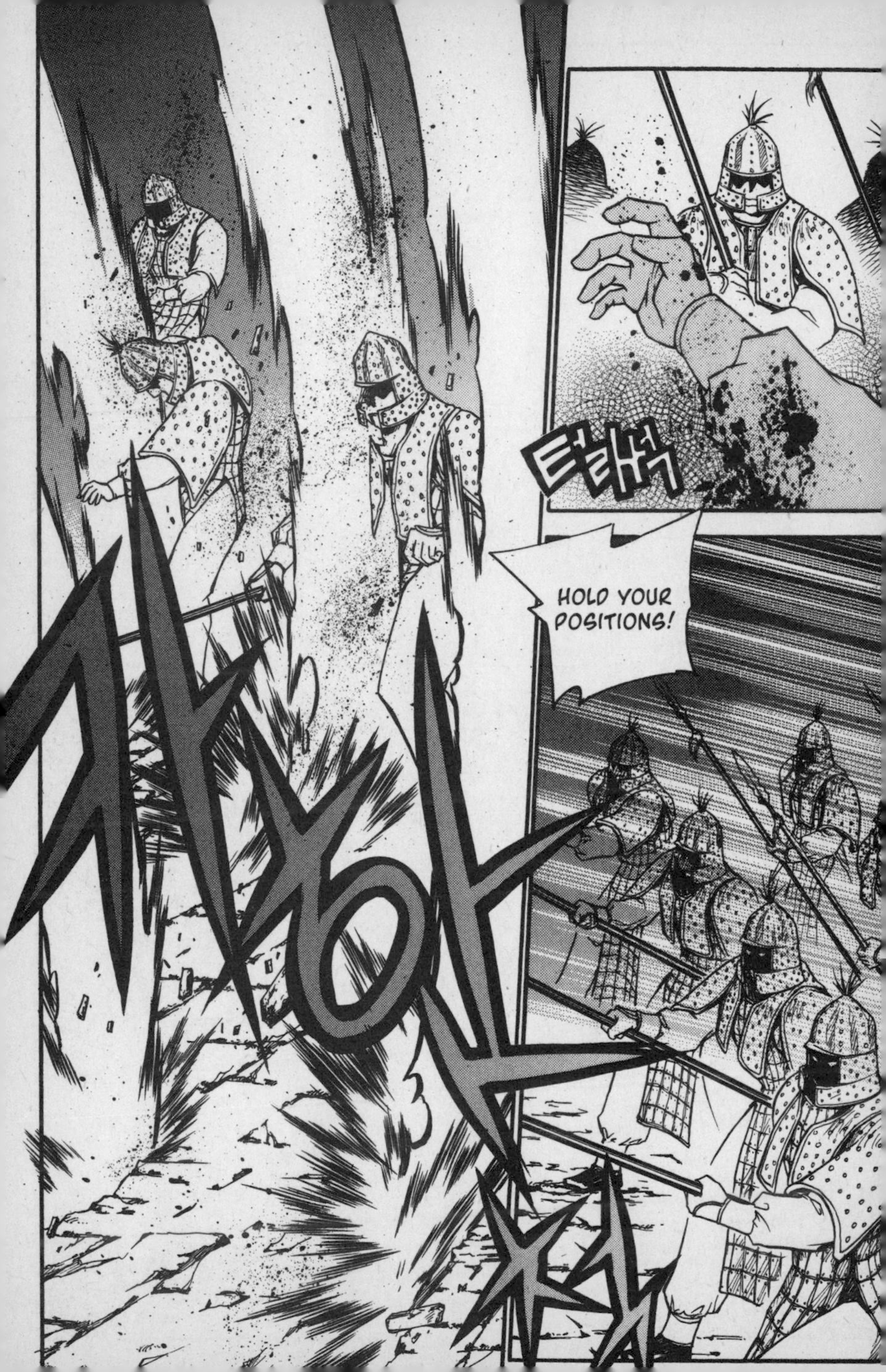

터ㄹ래셕
HOLD YOUR POSITIONS!

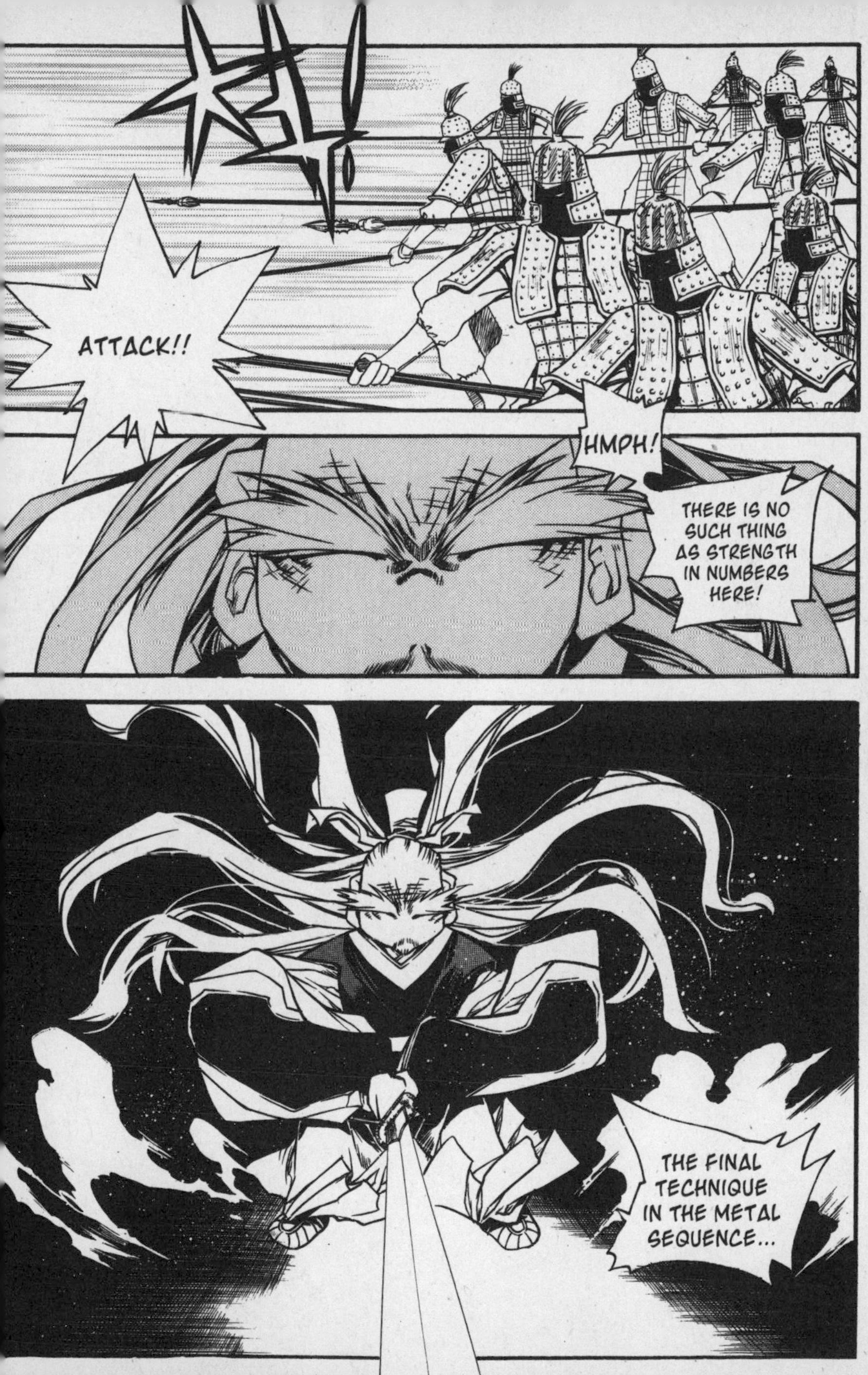
ATTACK!!
HMPH!
THERE IS NO SUCH THING AS STRENGTH IN NUMBERS HERE!
THE FINAL TECHNIQUE IN THE METAL SEQUENCE...

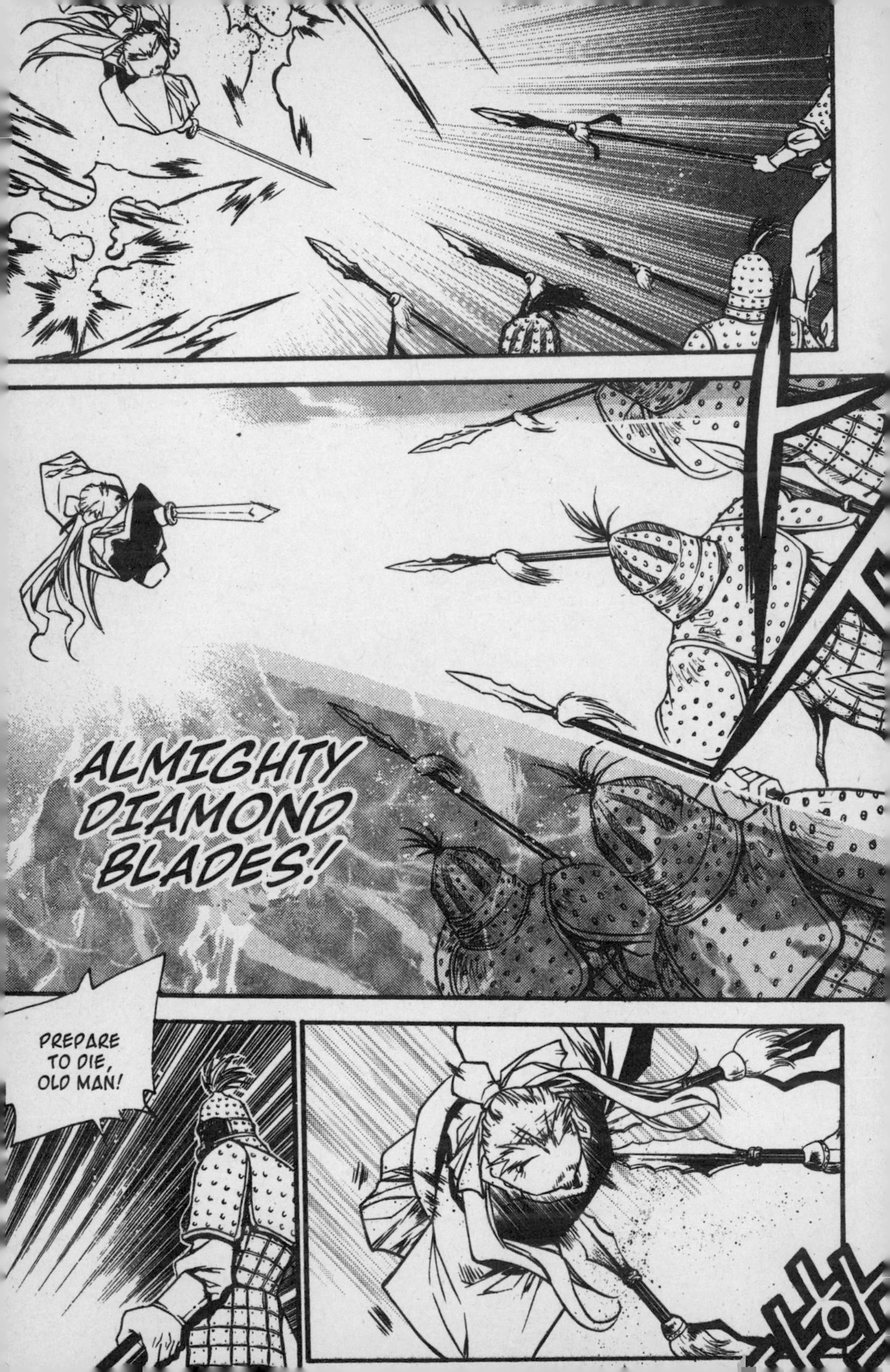
ALMIGHTY DIAMOND BLADES!
PREPARE TO DIE, OLD MAN!

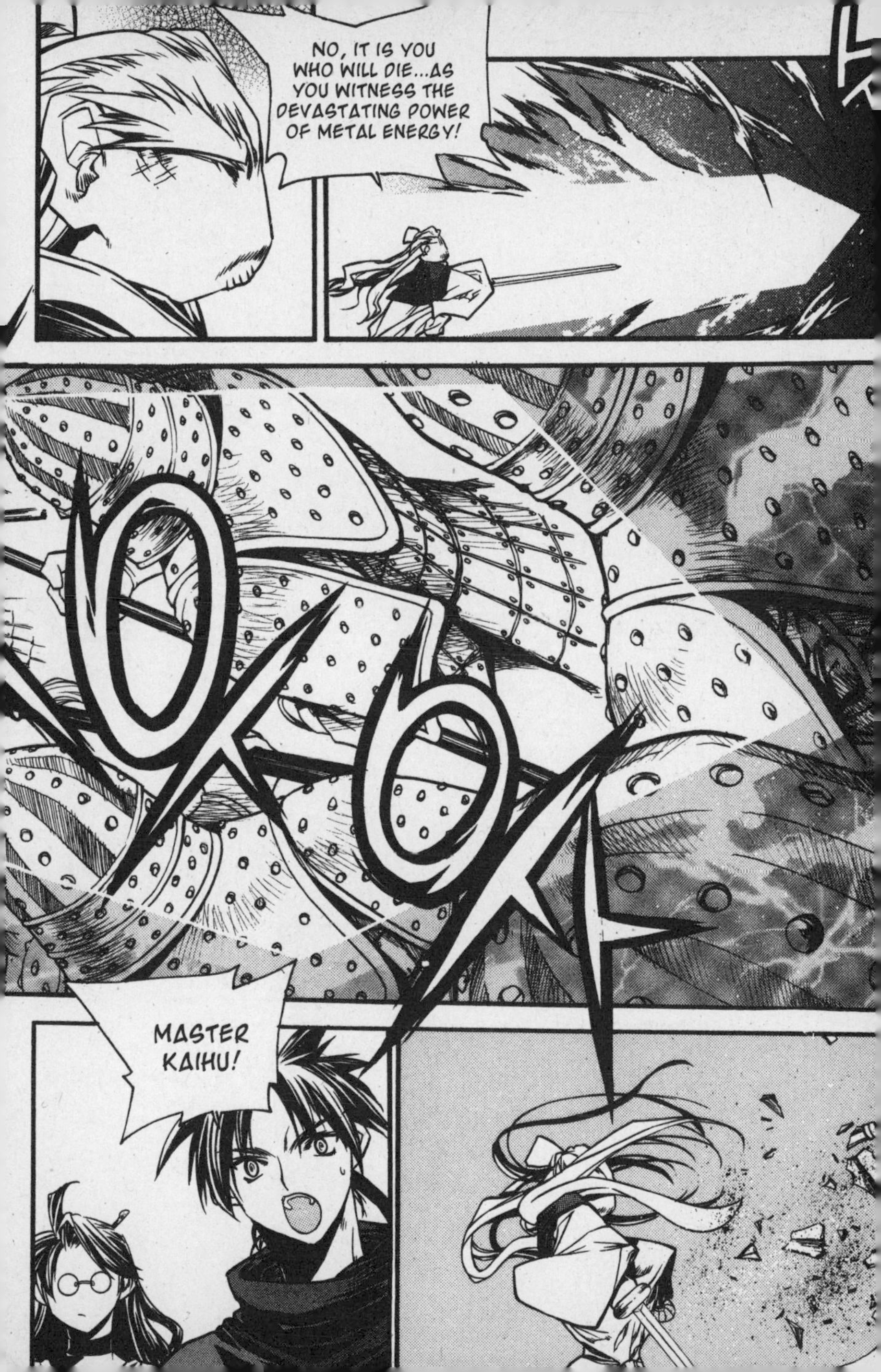
NO, IT IS YOU WHO WILL DIE...AS YOU WITNESS THE DEVASTATING POWER OF METAL ENERGY!
MASTER KAIHU!

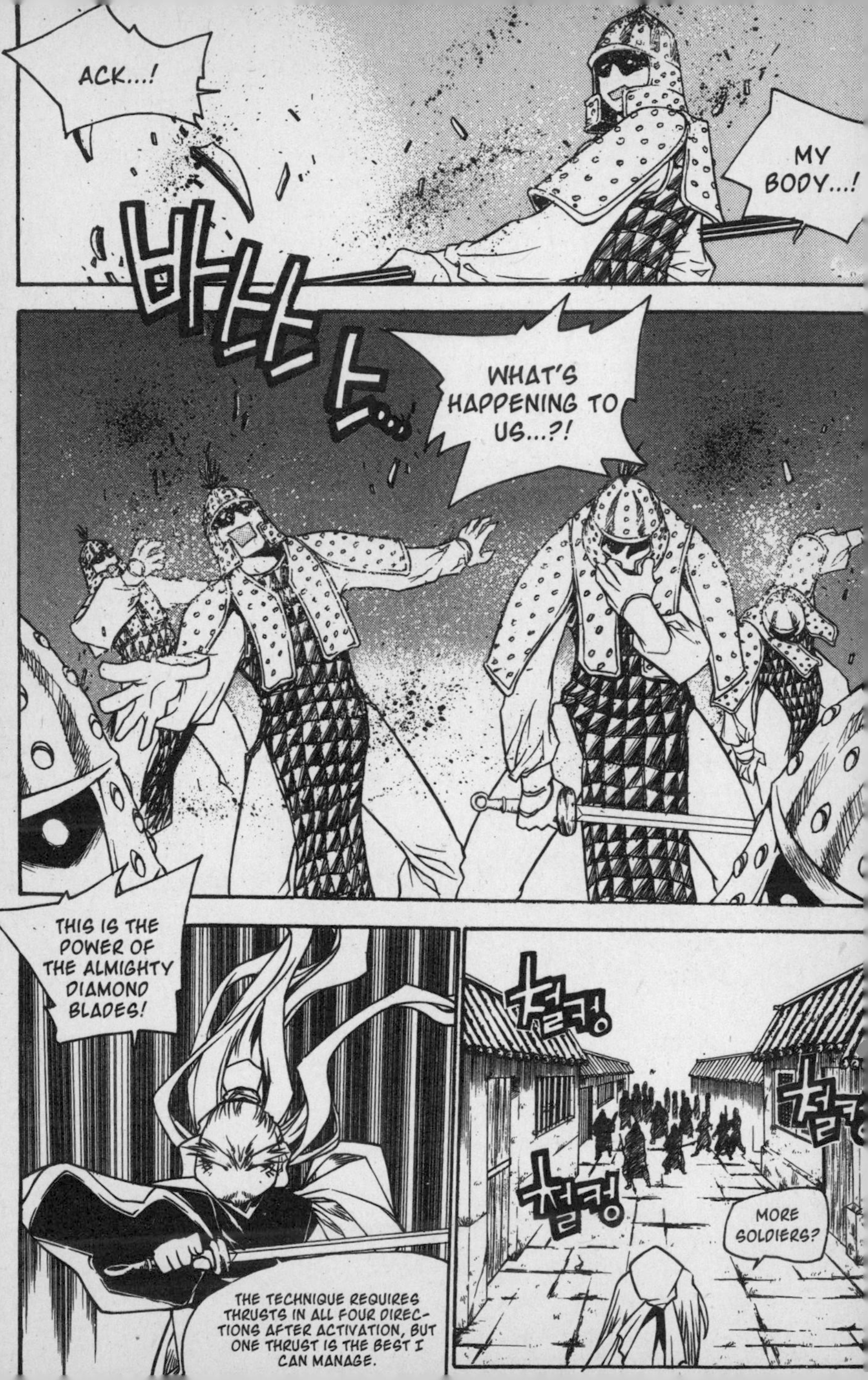
ACK...!
MY BODY...!
WHAT'S HAPPENING TO US...?!
THIS IS THE POWER OF THE ALMIGHTY DIAMOND BLADES!
THE TECHNIQUE REQUIRES THRUSTS IN ALL FOUR DIRECTIONS AFTER ACTIVATION, BUT ONE THRUST IS THE BEST I CAN MANAGE.
철컥!
철컥!
철컥!
MORE SOLDIERS?

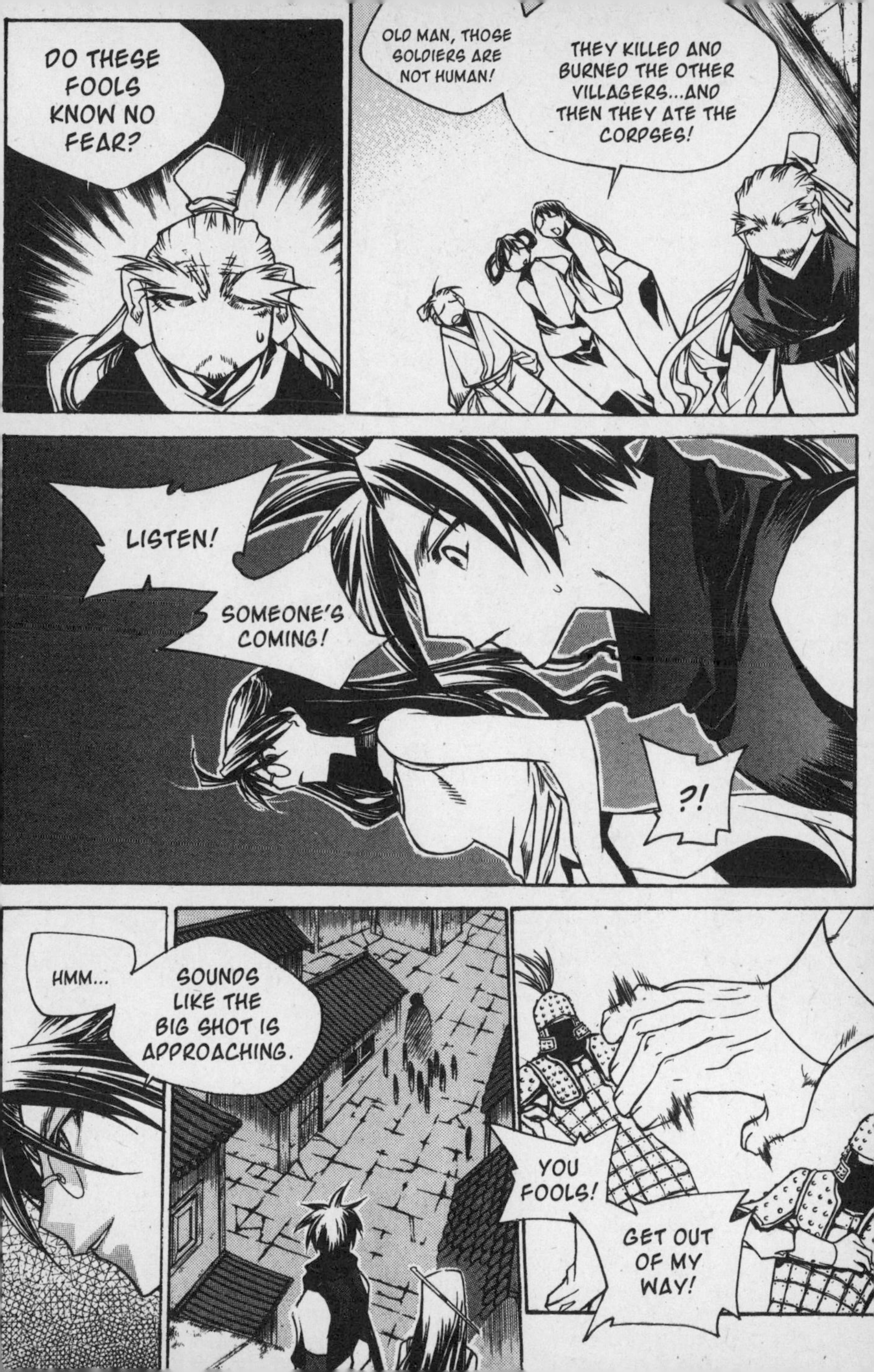
DO THESE FOOLS KNOW NO FEAR?
OLD MAN, THOSE SOLDIERS ARE NOT HUMAN!
THEY KILLED AND BURNED THE OTHER VILLAGERS...AND THEN THEY ATE THE CORPSES!
LISTEN!
SOMEONE'S COMING!
?!
HMM...
SOUNDS LIKE THE BIG SHOT IS APPROACHING.
YOU FOOLS!
GET OUT OF MY WAY!

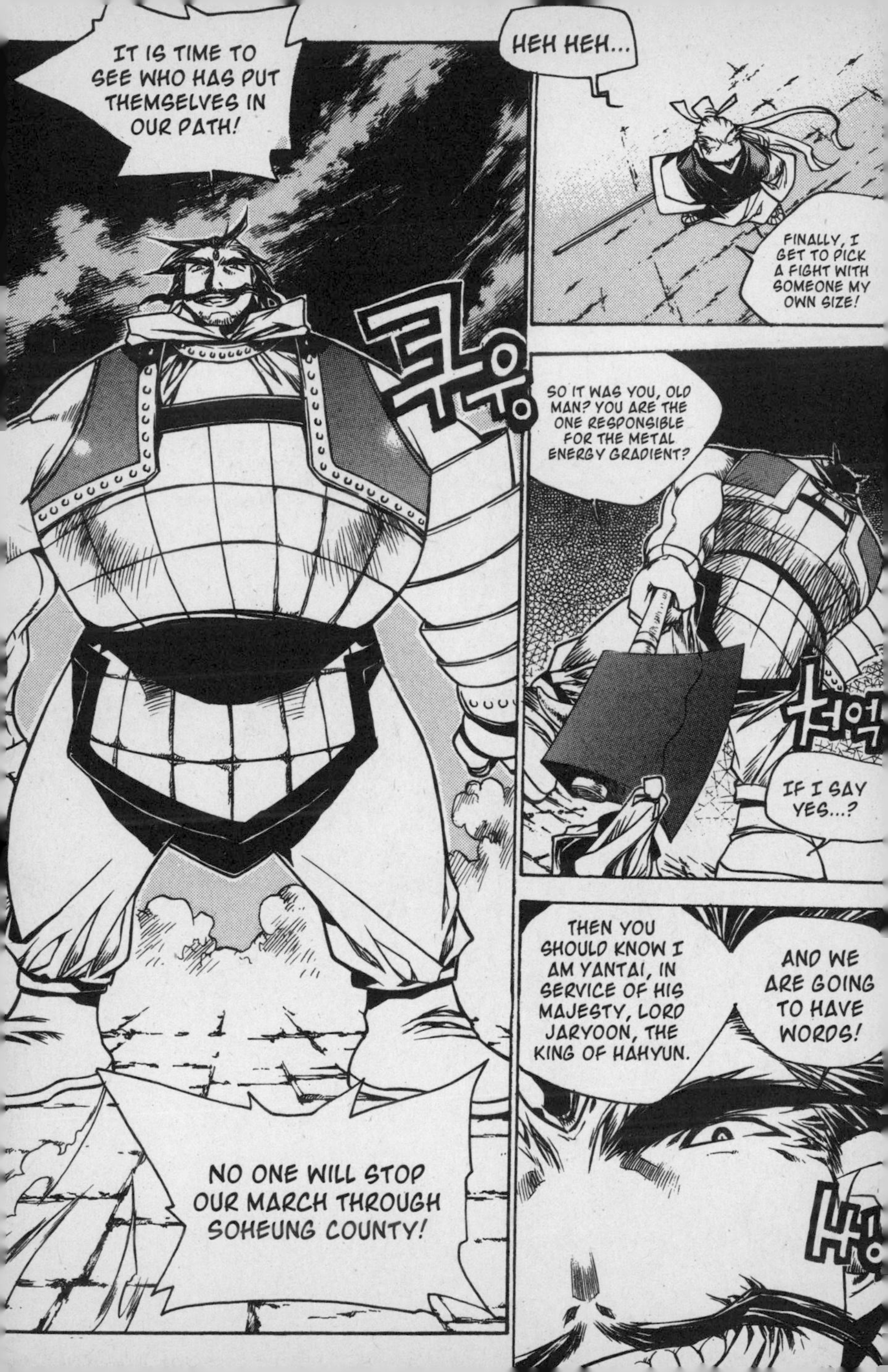
IT IS TIME TO SEE WHO HAS PUT THEMSELVES IN OUR PATH!
NO ONE WILL STOP OUR MARCH THROUGH SOHEUNG COUNTY!
HEH HEH...
FINALLY, I GET TO PICK A FIGHT WITH SOMEONE MY OWN SIZE!
SO IT WAS YOU, OLD MAN? YOU ARE THE ONE RESPONSIBLE FOR THE METAL ENERGY GRADIENT?
IF I SAY YES...?
THEN YOU SHOULD KNOW I AM YANTAI, IN SERVICE OF HIS MAJESTY, LORD JARYOON, THE KING OF HAHYUN.
AND WE ARE GOING TO HAVE WORDS!

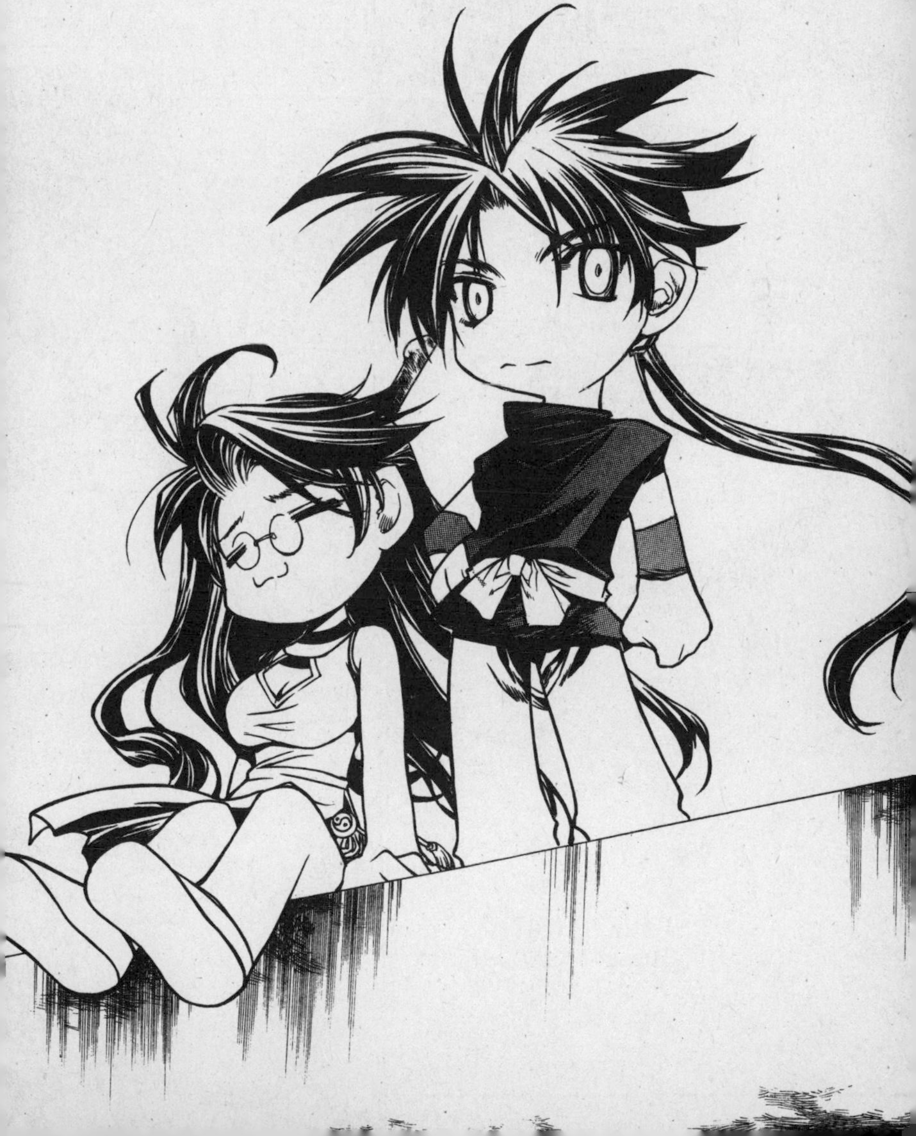

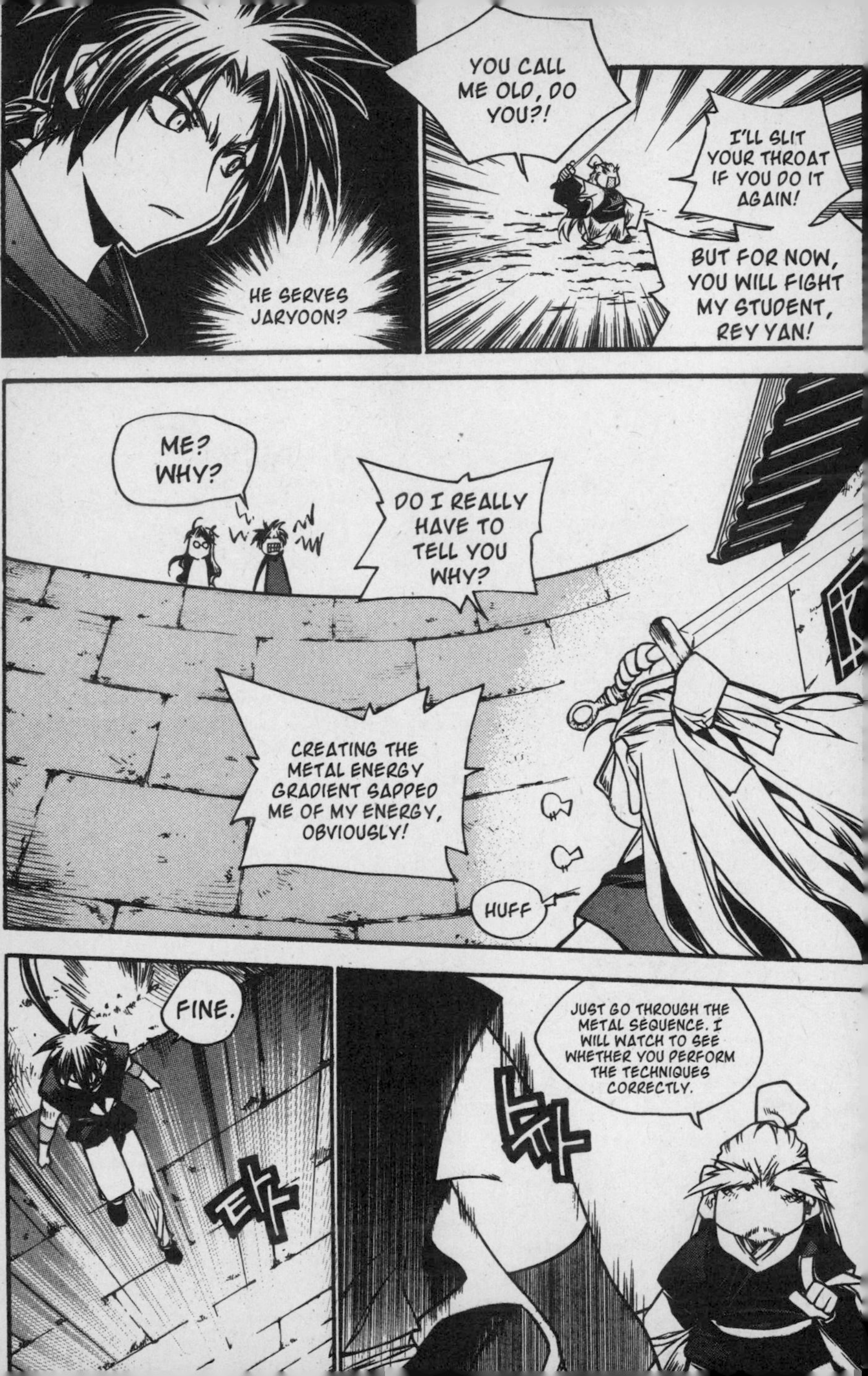
HE SERVES JARYOON?
YOU CALL ME OLD, DO YOU?!
I'LL SLIT YOUR THROAT IF YOU DO IT AGAIN!
BUT FOR NOW, YOU WILL FIGHT MY STUDENT, REY YAN!
ME? WHY?
DO I REALLY HAVE TO TELL YOU WHY?
CREATING THE METAL ENERGY GRADIENT SAPPED ME OF MY ENERGY, OBVIOUSLY!
HUFF
FINE.
JUST GO THROUGH THE METAL SEQUENCE. I WILL WATCH TO SEE WHETHER YOU PERFORM THE TECHNIQUES CORRECTLY.

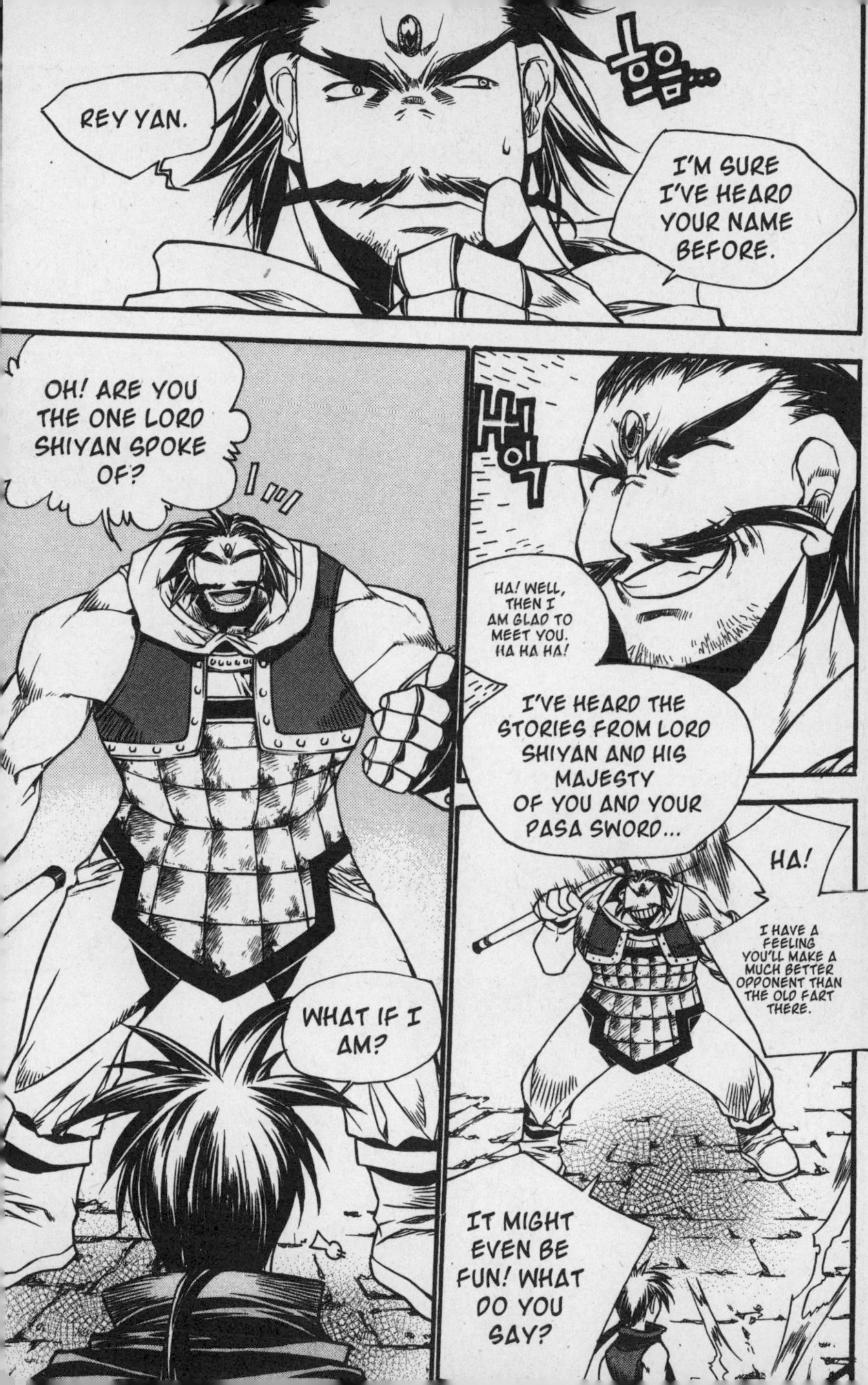
REY YAN.
I'M SURE I'VE HEARD YOUR NAME BEFORE.
OH! ARE YOU THE ONE LORD SHIYAN SPOKE OF?
WHAT IF I AM?
HA! WELL, THEN I AM GLAD TO MEET YOU. HA HA HA!
I'VE HEARD THE STORIES FROM LORD SHIYAN AND HIS MAJESTY OF YOU AND YOUR PASA SWORD...
HA!
I HAVE A FEELING YOU'LL MAKE A MUCH BETTER OPPONENT THAN THE OLD FART THERE.
IT MIGHT EVEN BE FUN! WHAT DO YOU SAY?

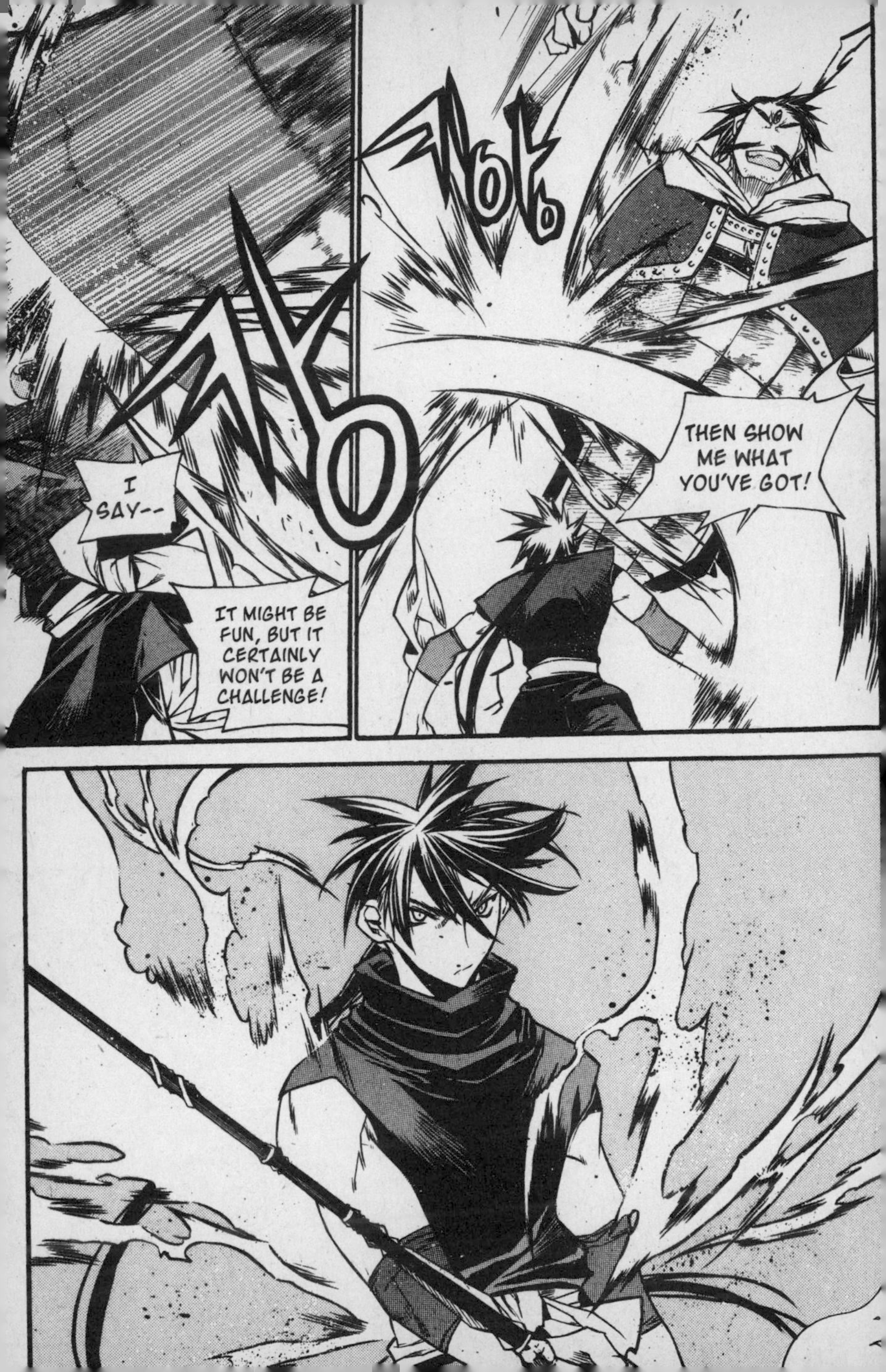
I SAY--
IT MIGHT BE FUN, BUT IT CERTAINLY WON'T BE A CHALLENGE!
THEN SHOW ME WHAT YOU'VE GOT!

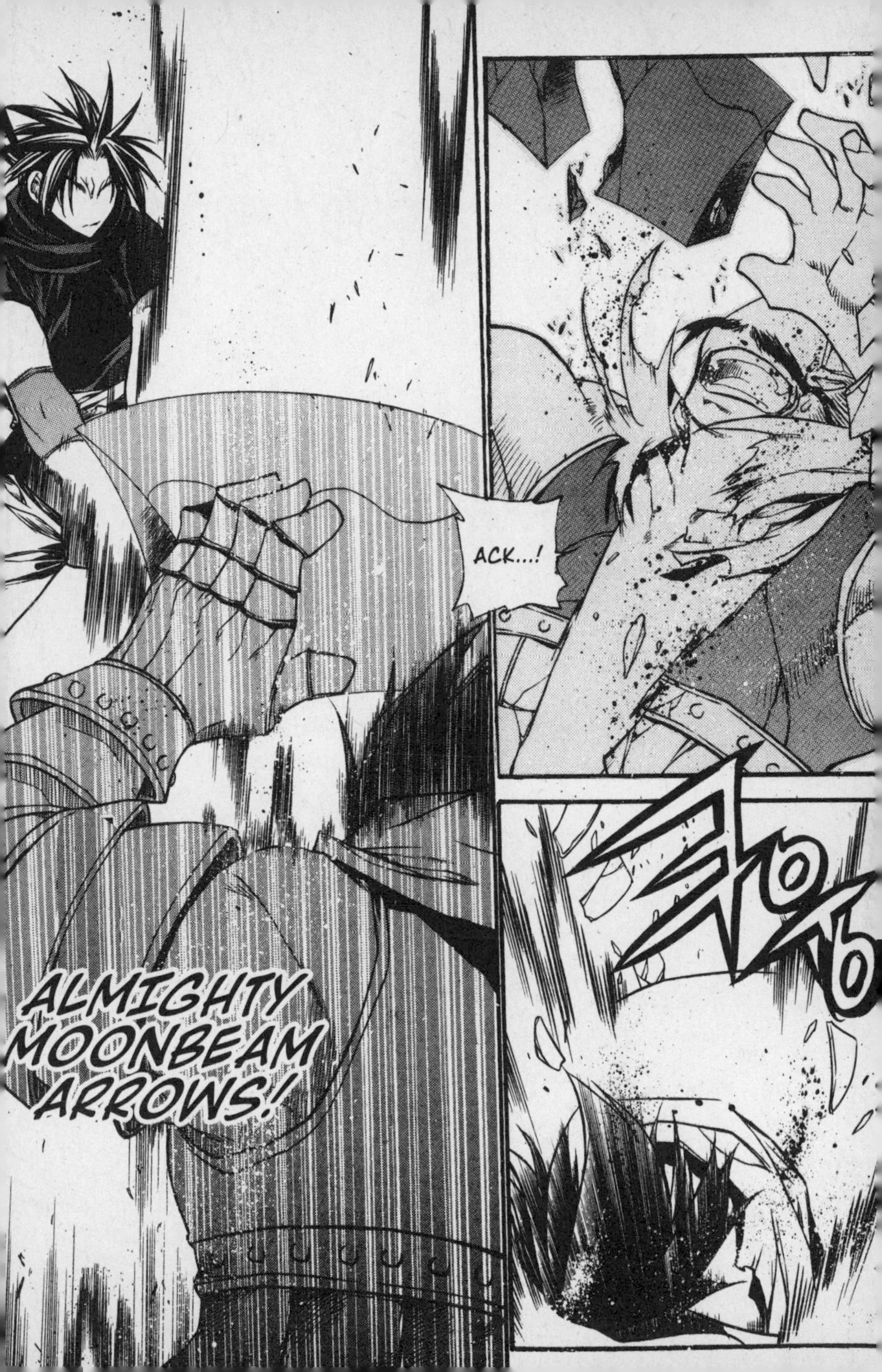
ALMIGHTY MOONBEAM ARROWS!
ACK...!

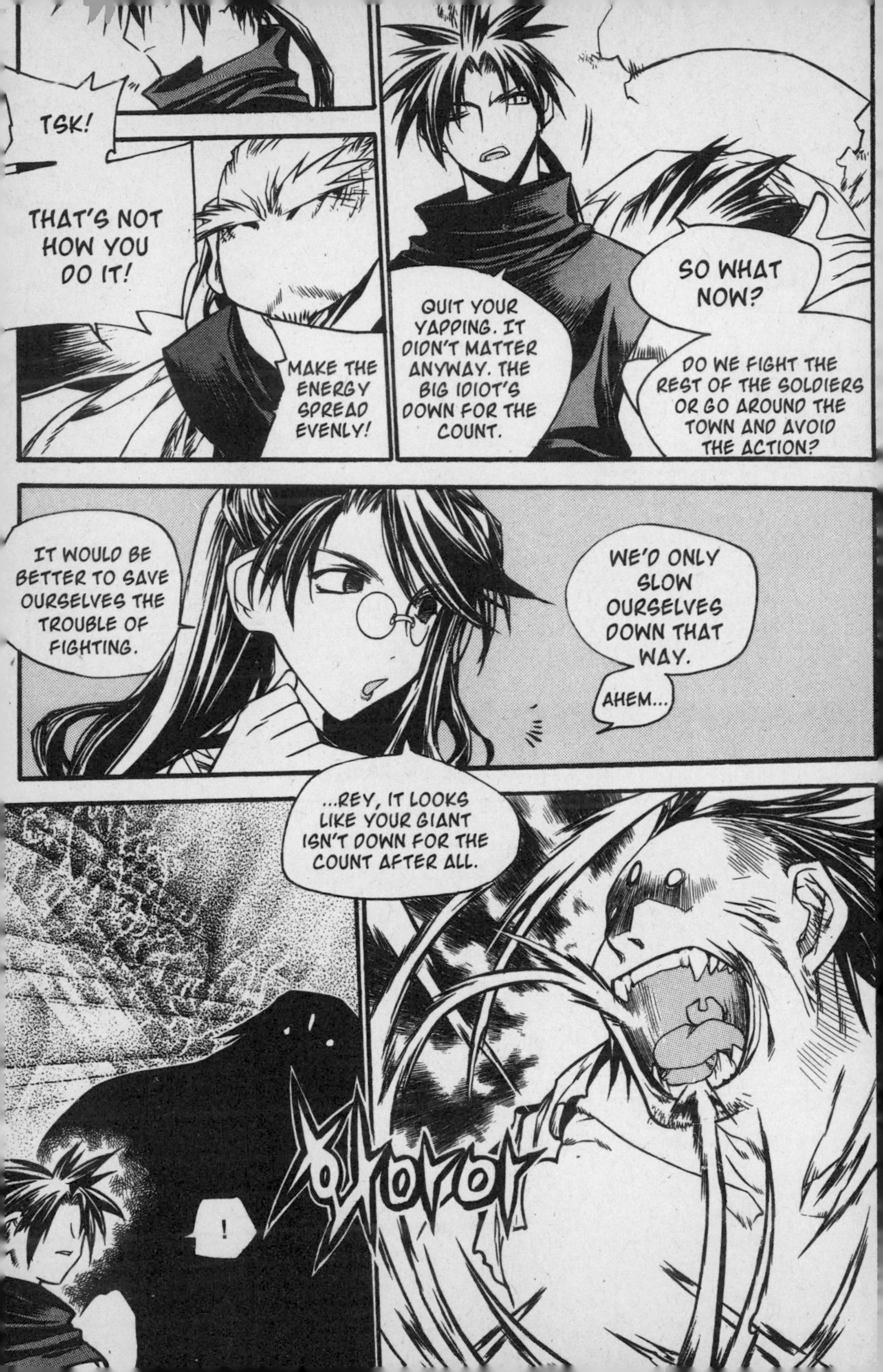
TSK!
THAT'S NOT HOW YOU DO IT!
MAKE THE ENERGY SPREAD EVENLY!
QUIT YOUR YAPPING. IT DIDN'T MATTER ANYWAY. THE BIG IDIOT'S DOWN FOR THE COUNT.
SO WHAT NOW?
DO WE FIGHT THE REST OF THE SOLDIERS OR GO AROUND THE TOWN AND AVOID THE ACTION?
IT WOULD BE BETTER TO SAVE OURSELVES THE TROUBLE OF FIGHTING.
WE'D ONLY SLOW OURSELVES DOWN THAT WAY.
AHEM...
...REY, IT LOOKS LIKE YOUR GIANT ISN'T DOWN FOR THE COUNT AFTER ALL.
!

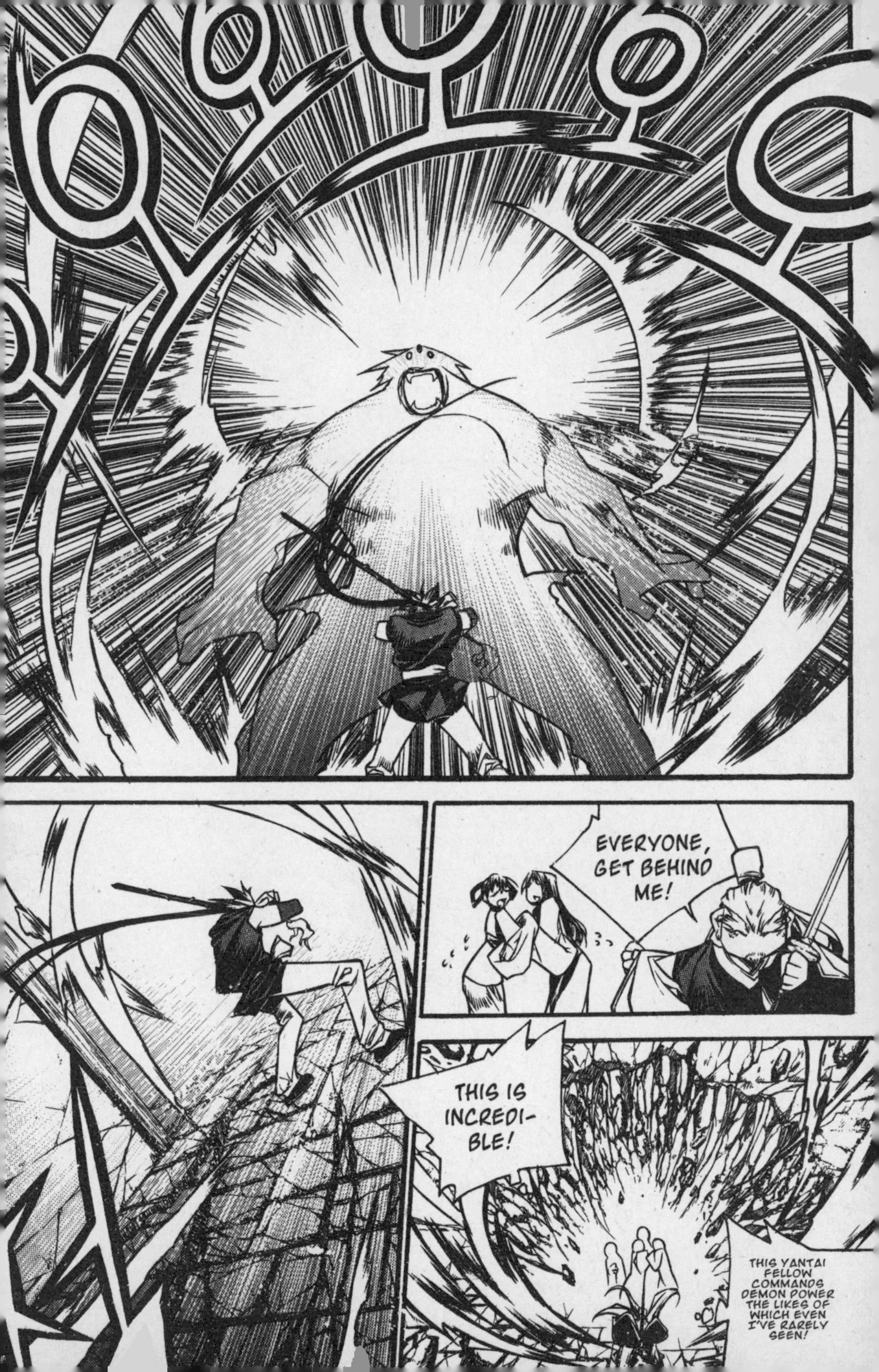
EVERYONE, GET BEHIND ME!
THIS IS INCREDI-BLE!
THIS YANTAI FELLOW COMMANDS DEMON POWER THE LIKES OF WHICH EVEN I'VE RARELY SEEN!

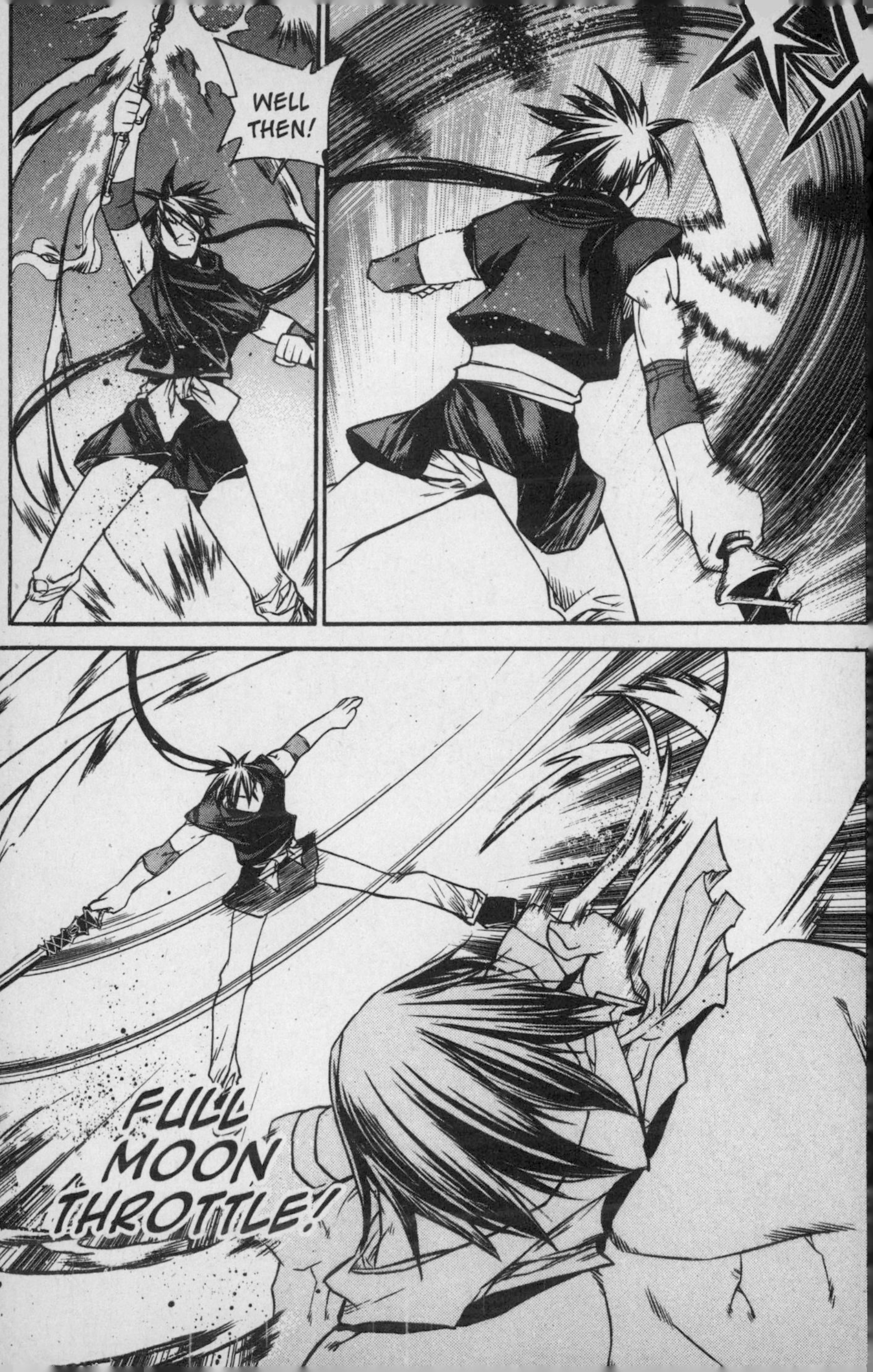
WELL THEN!
FULL MOON THROTTLE!

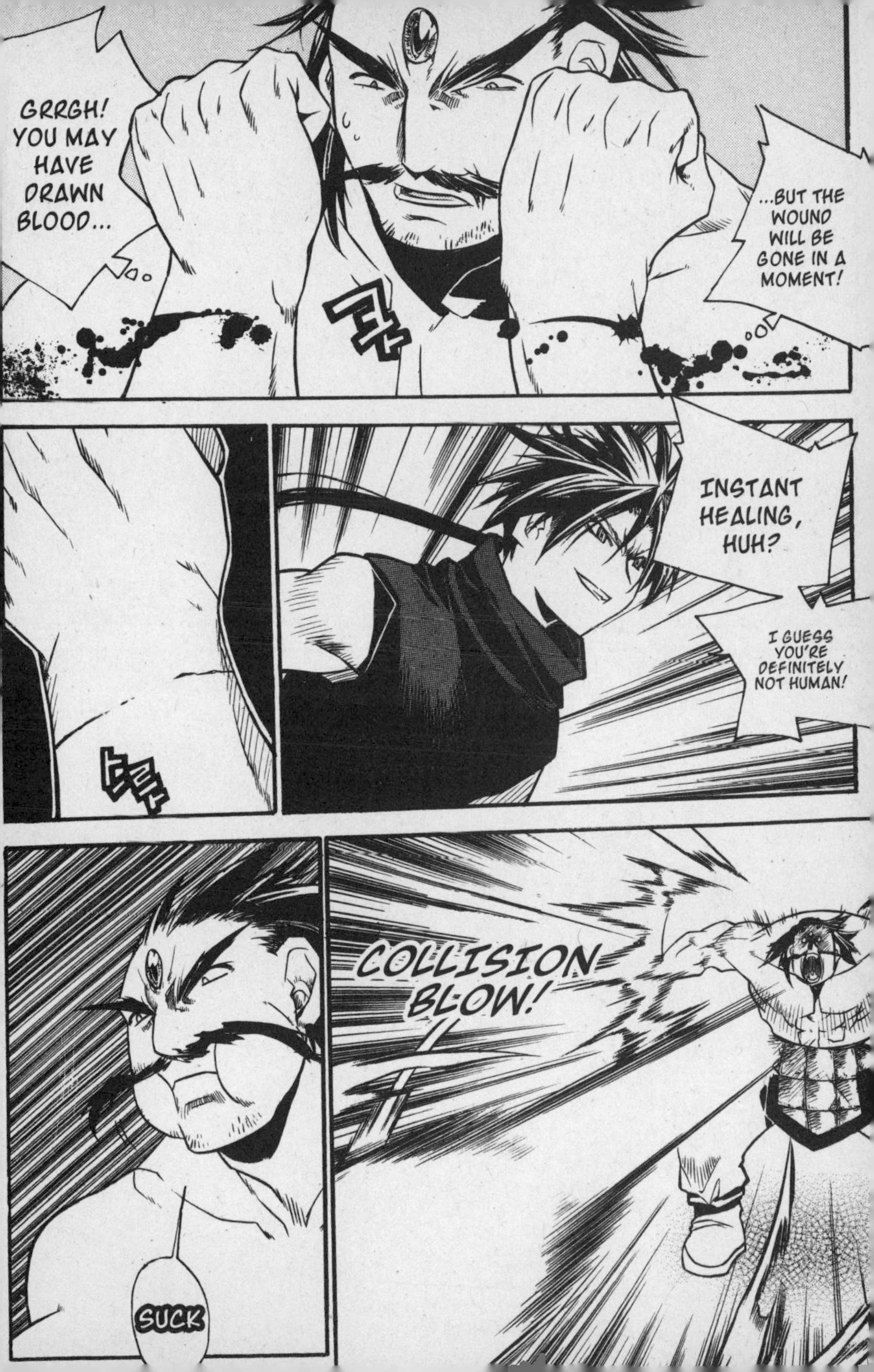
GRRGH! YOU MAY HAVE DRAWN BLOOD...
...BUT THE WOUND WILL BE GONE IN A MOMENT!
INSTANT HEALING, HUH?
I GUESS YOU'RE DEFINITELY NOT HUMAN!
SUCK
COLLISION BLOW!

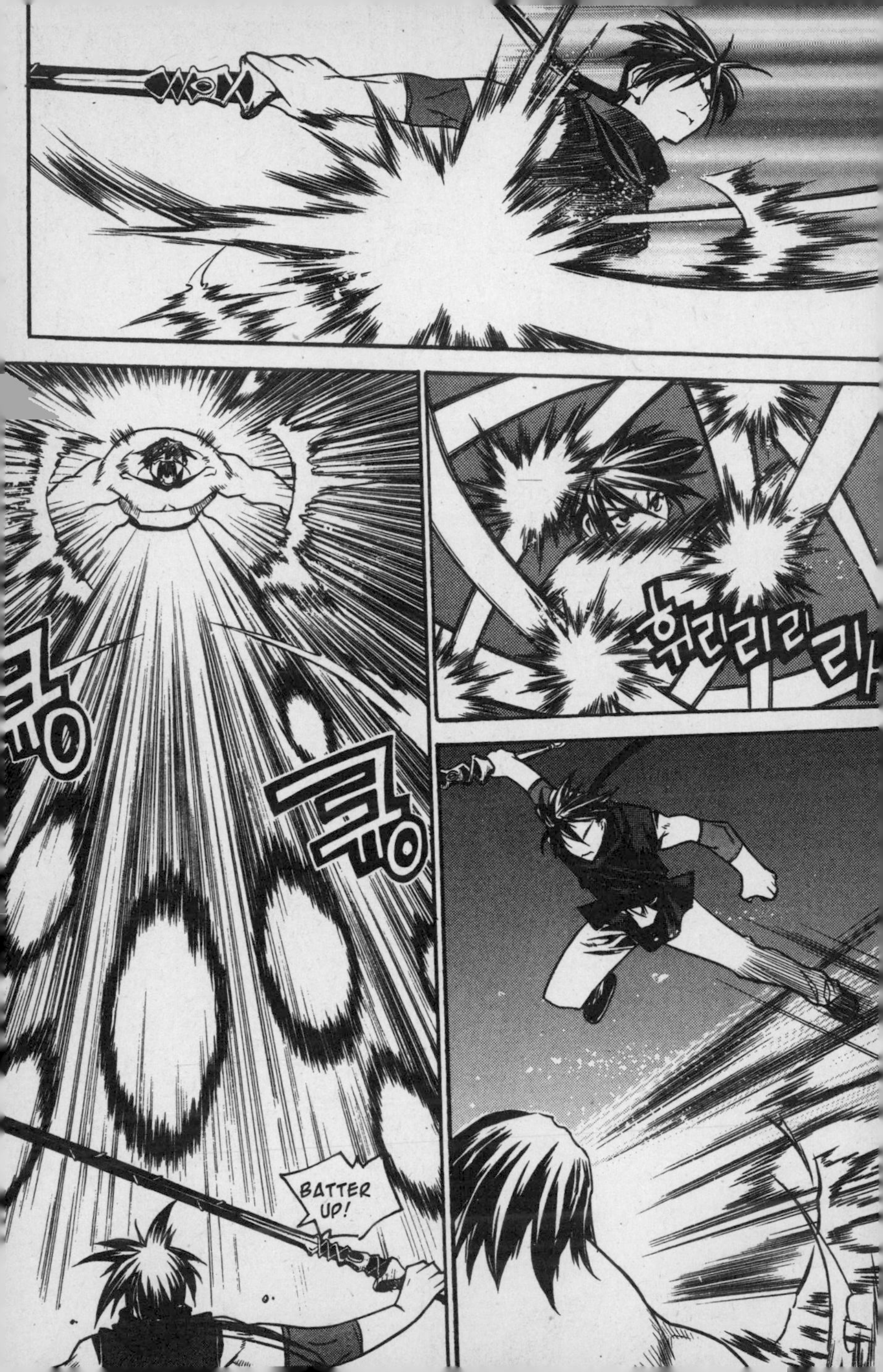
쿵
쿵
BATTER UP!
휴리리리 리

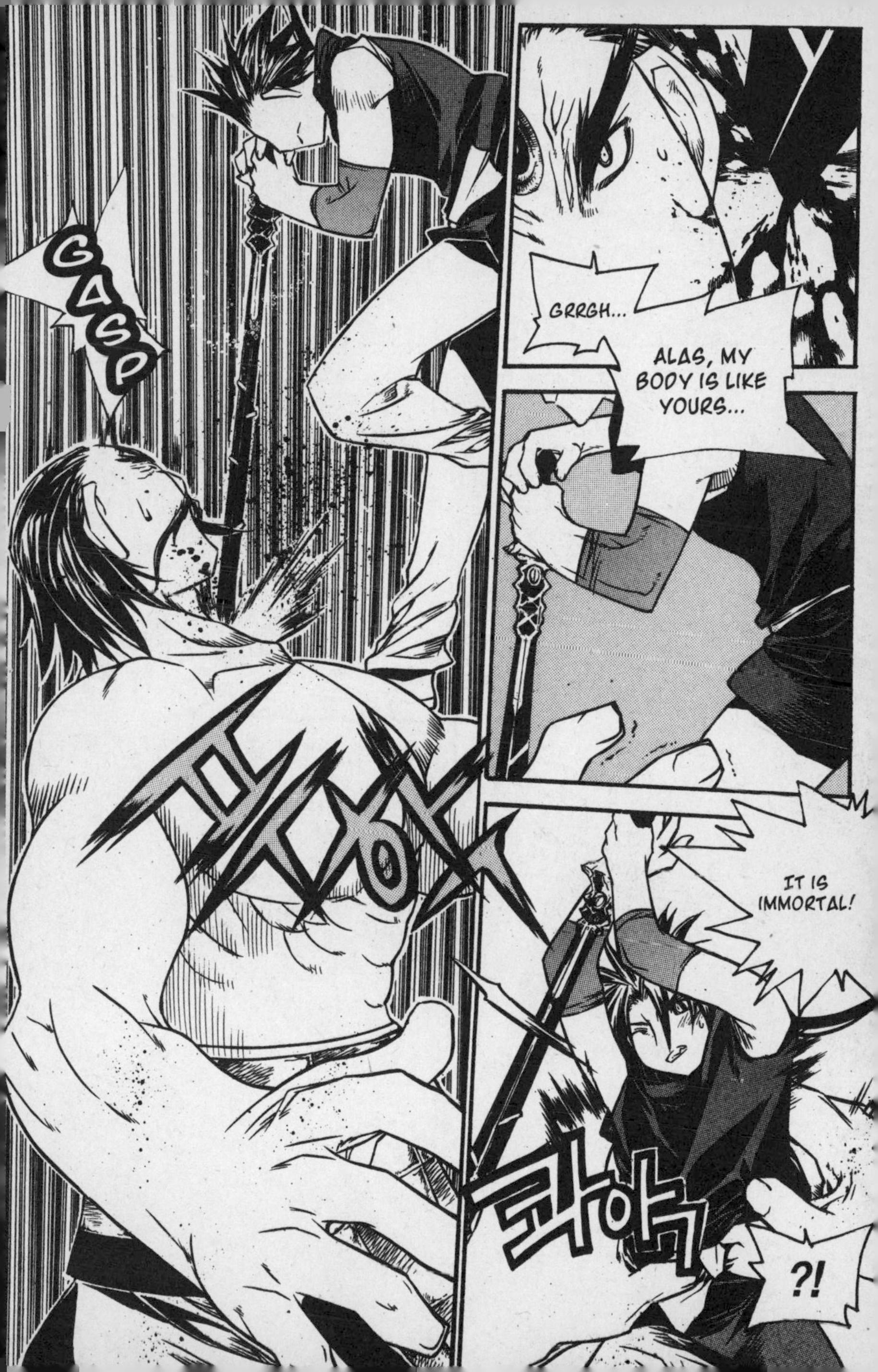
GASP
GRRGH...
ALAS, MY BODY IS LIKE YOURS...
IT IS IMMORTAL!
?!

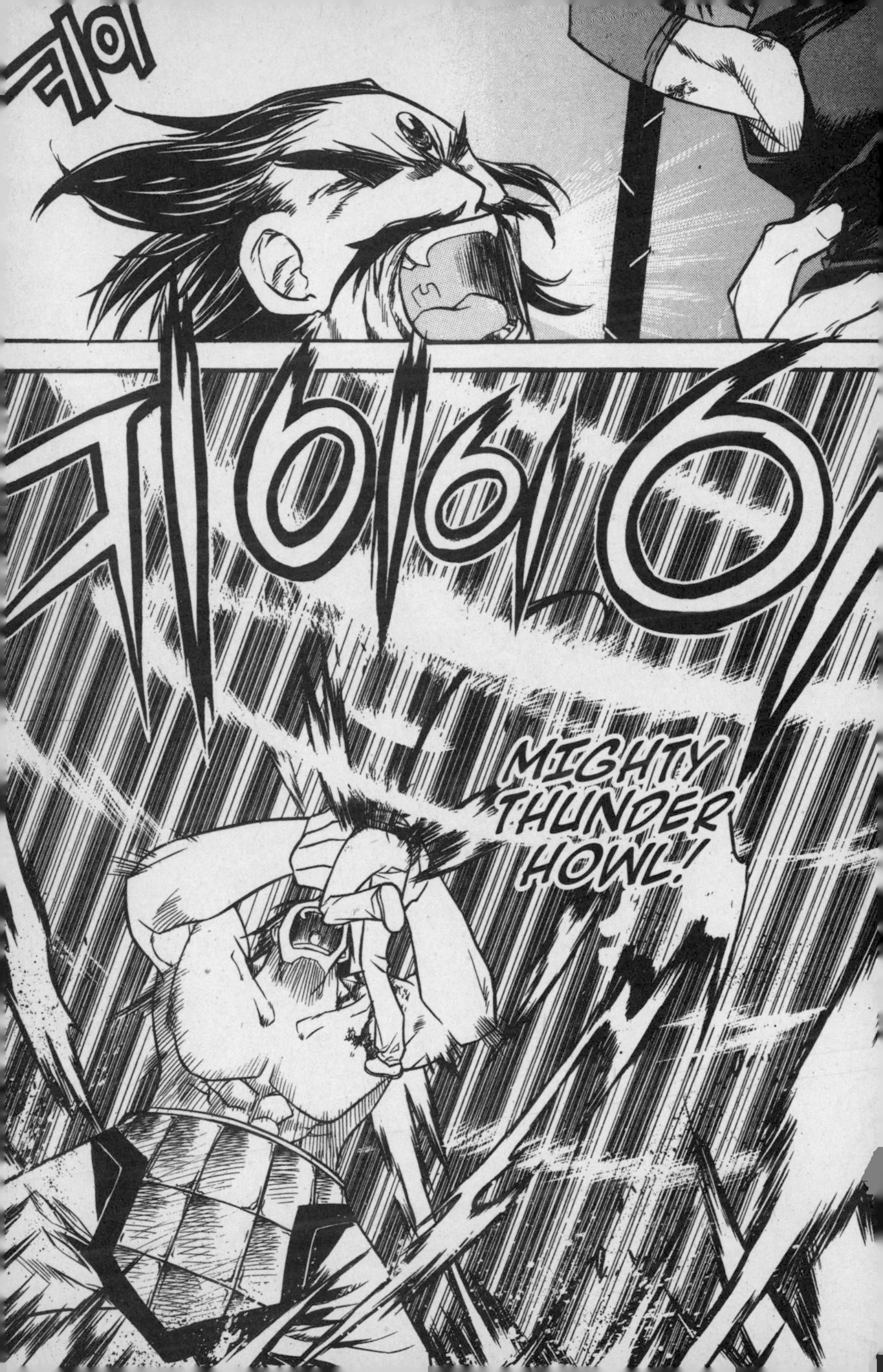
MIGHTY THUNDER HOWL!

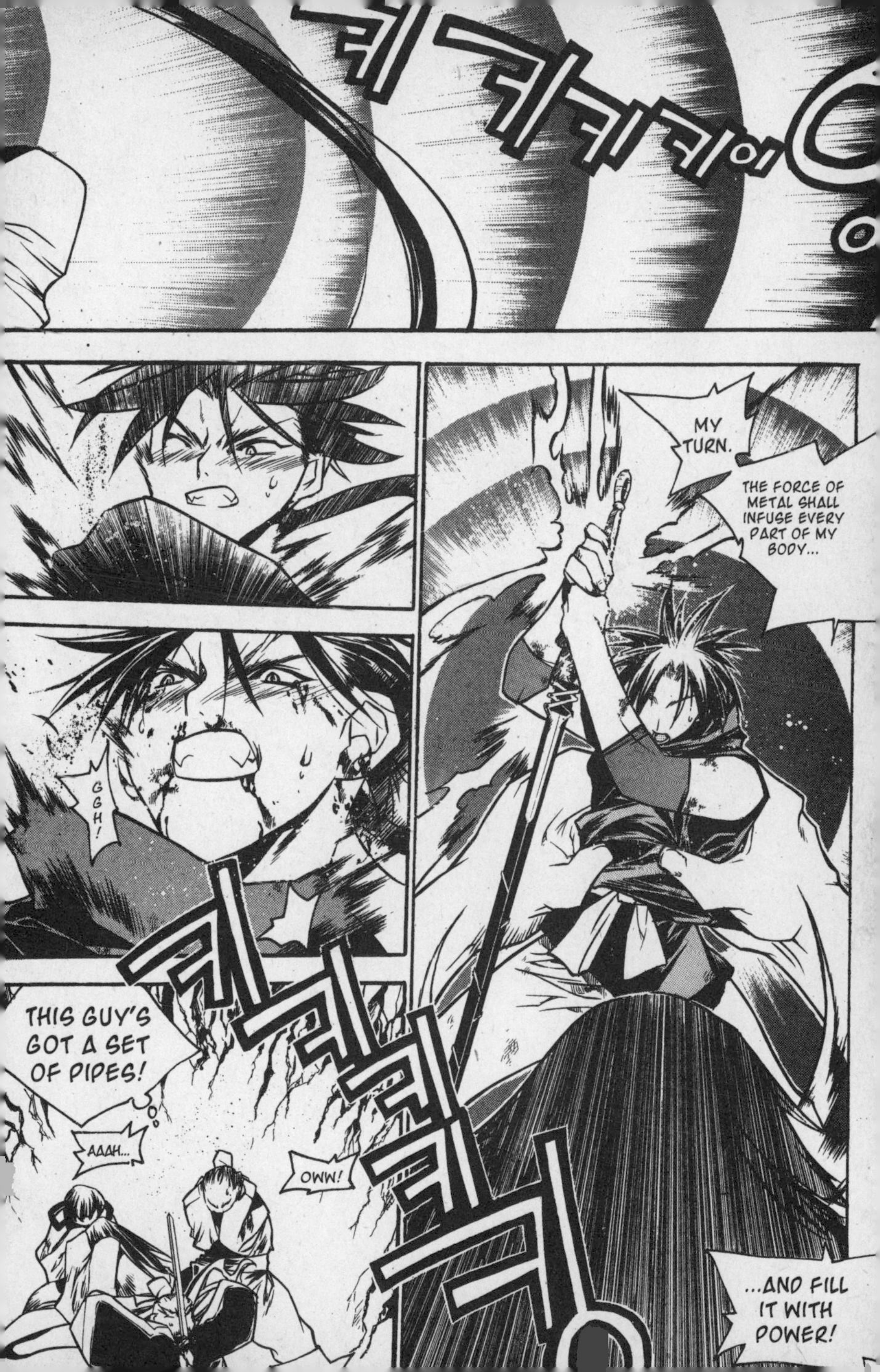
GGH!
MY TURN.
THE FORCE OF METAL SHALL INFUSE EVERY PART OF MY BODY...
THIS GUY'S GOT A SET OF PIPES!
AAAH...
OWW!
...AND FILL IT WITH POWER!

GRAH!

KWAAAAAAA!!

GET OFF
OF ME!

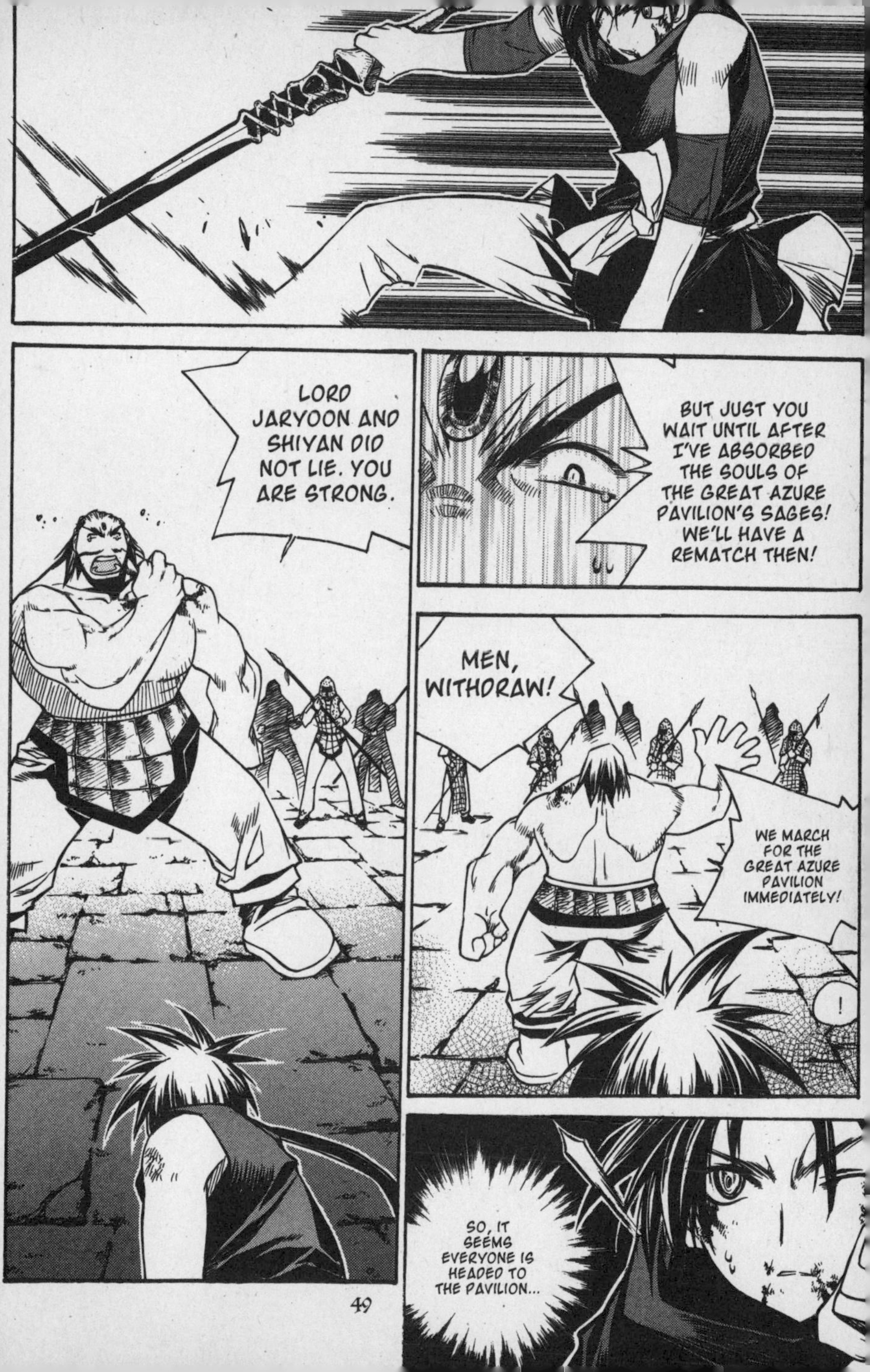
LORD JARYOON AND SHIYAN DID NOT LIE. YOU ARE STRONG.
BUT JUST YOU WAIT UNTIL AFTER I'VE ABSORBED THE SOULS OF THE GREAT AZURE PAVILION'S SAGES! WE'LL HAVE A REMATCH THEN!
MEN, WITHDRAW!
WE MARCH FOR THE GREAT AZURE PAVILION IMMEDIATELY!
!
SO, IT SEEMS EVERYONE IS HEADED TO THE PAVILION...

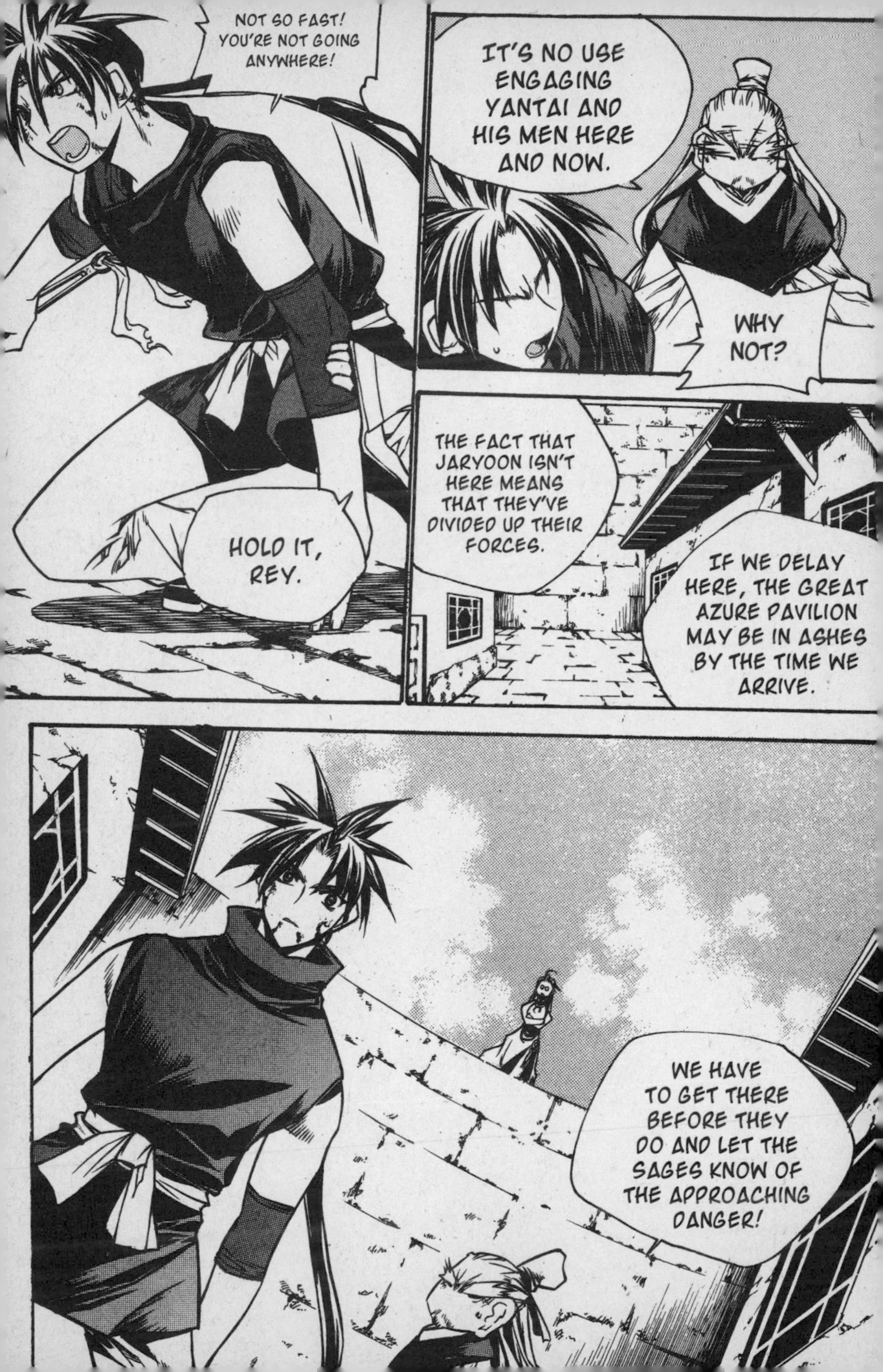
NOT SO FAST! YOU'RE NOT GOING ANYWHERE!
HOLD IT, REY.
IT'S NO USE ENGAGING YANTAI AND HIS MEN HERE AND NOW.
WHY NOT?
THE FACT THAT JARYOON ISN'T HERE MEANS THAT THEY'VE DIVIDED UP THEIR FORCES.
IF WE DELAY HERE, THE GREAT AZURE PAVILION MAY BE IN ASHES BY THE TIME WE ARRIVE.
WE HAVE TO GET THERE BEFORE THEY DO AND LET THE SAGES KNOW OF THE APPROACHING DANGER!

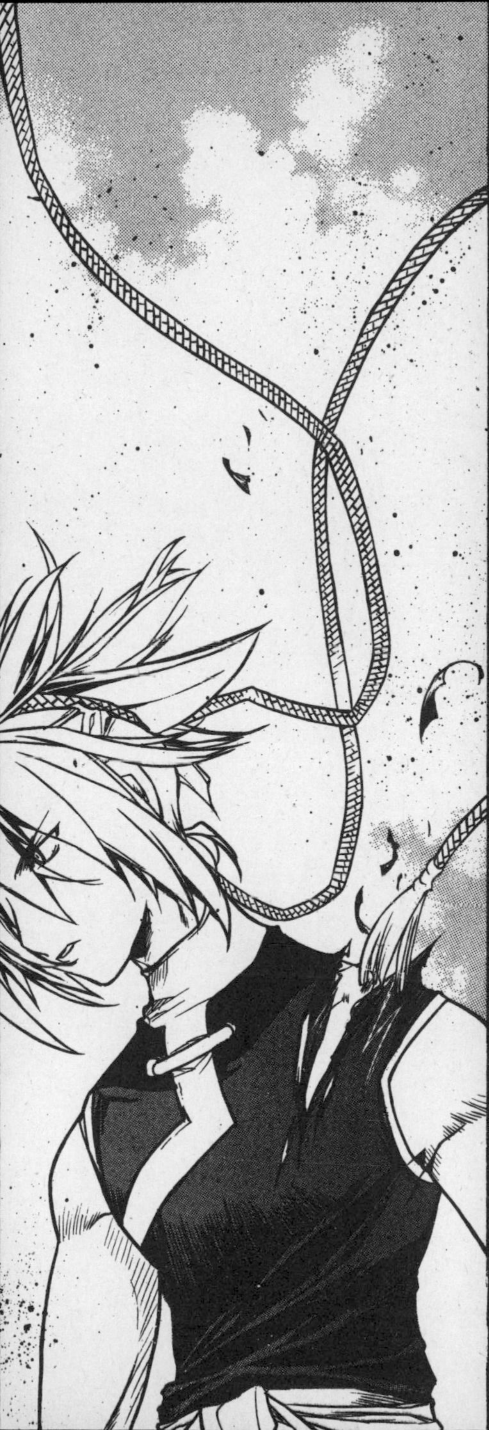

Chapter 64: The Battle for the Great Azure Pavilion

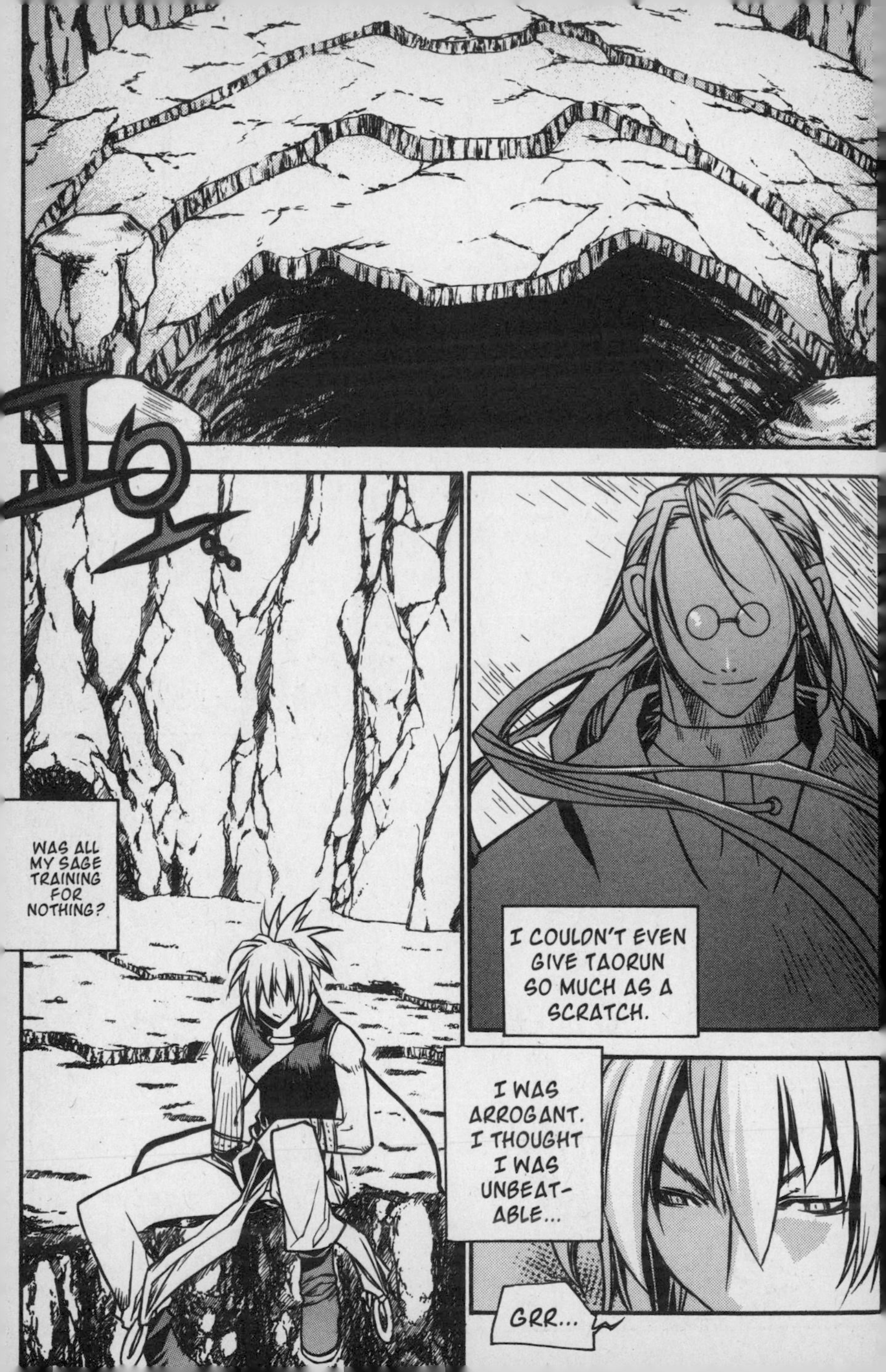
WAS ALL MY SAGE TRAINING FOR NOTHING?
I COULDN'T EVEN GIVE TAORUN SO MUCH AS A SCRATCH.
I WAS ARROGANT. I THOUGHT I WAS UNBEAT-ABLE...
GRR...

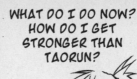

......

WHAT DO I DO NOW?
HOW DO I GET
STRONGER THAN
TAORUN?

SIGH...

SHOUREN!

YOU SHOULD
BE GETTING
REST!

YOUR INTERNAL
INJURIES WILL
TAKE TIME TO
HEAL.

턱

턱

ANY NEWS
FROM LORD
HEIAN AND
LADY SOHWA?

NOPE...

ㅋㅋ응

THEY'RE
GONE
WITHOUT A
TRACE.

53

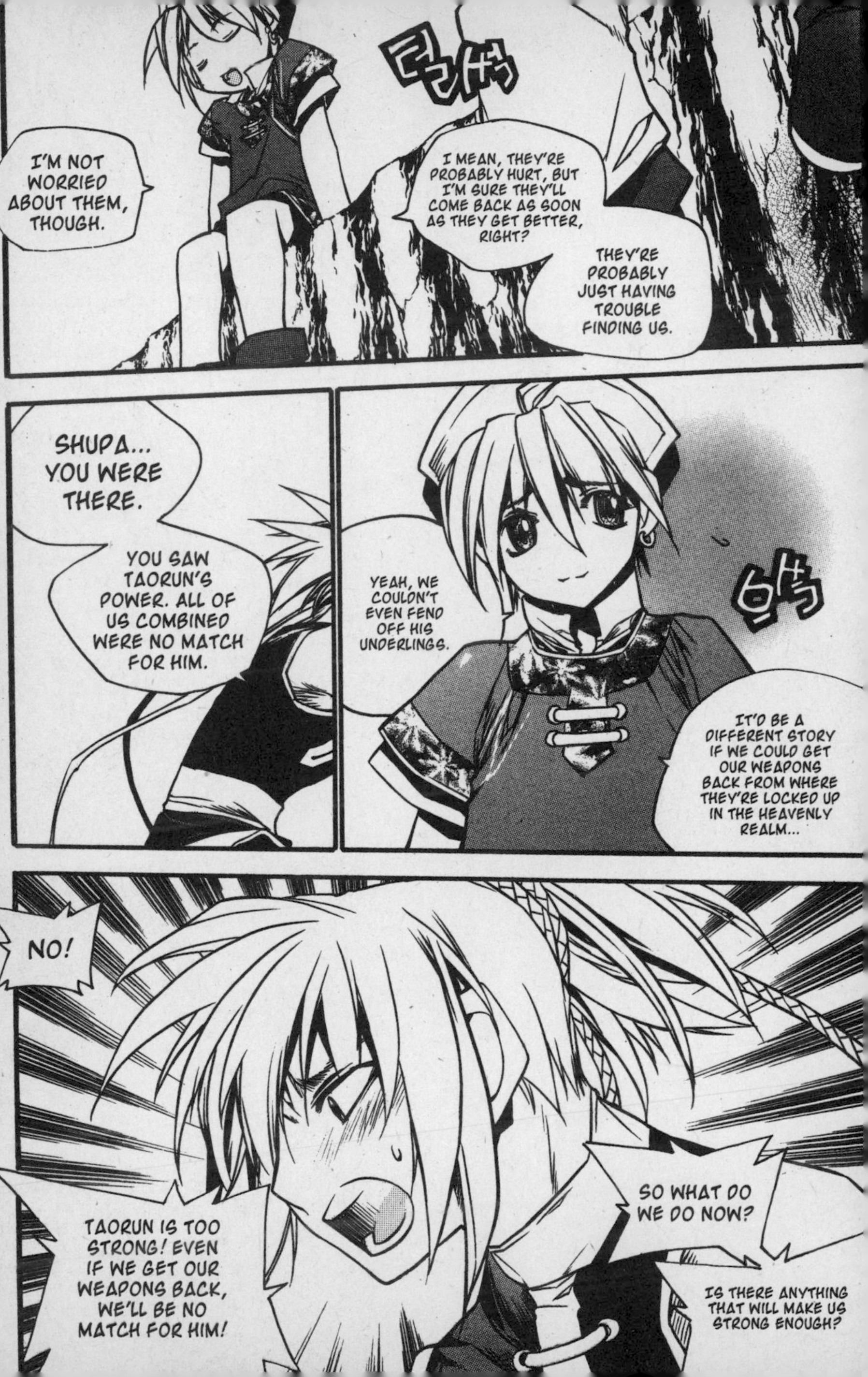
I'M NOT WORRIED ABOUT THEM, THOUGH.
I MEAN, THEY'RE PROBABLY HURT, BUT I'M SURE THEY'LL COME BACK AS SOON AS THEY GET BETTER, RIGHT?
THEY'RE PROBABLY JUST HAVING TROUBLE FINDING US.
SHUPA... YOU WERE THERE.
YOU SAW TAORUN'S POWER. ALL OF US COMBINED WERE NO MATCH FOR HIM.
YEAH, WE COULDN'T EVEN FEND OFF HIS UNDERLINGS.
IT'D BE A DIFFERENT STORY IF WE COULD GET OUR WEAPONS BACK FROM WHERE THEY'RE LOCKED UP IN THE HEAVENLY REALM...
NO!
TAORUN IS TOO STRONG! EVEN IF WE GET OUR WEAPONS BACK, WE'LL BE NO MATCH FOR HIM!
SO WHAT DO WE DO NOW?
IS THERE ANYTHING THAT WILL MAKE US STRONG ENOUGH?

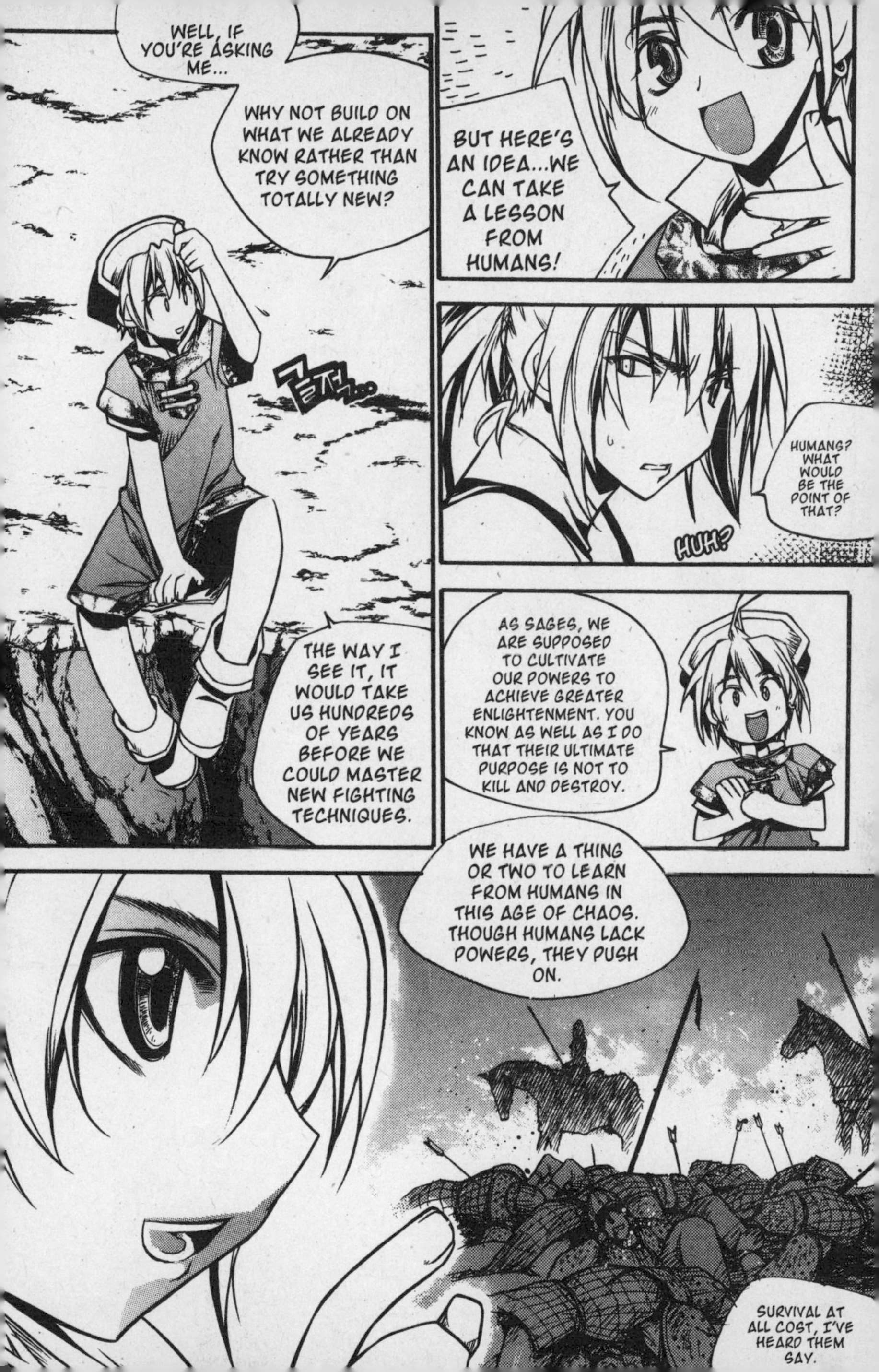
WELL, IF YOU'RE ASKING ME...
WHY NOT BUILD ON WHAT WE ALREADY KNOW RATHER THAN TRY SOMETHING TOTALLY NEW?
THE WAY I SEE IT, IT WOULD TAKE US HUNDREDS OF YEARS BEFORE WE COULD MASTER NEW FIGHTING TECHNIQUES.
BUT HERE'S AN IDEA...WE CAN TAKE A LESSON FROM HUMANS!
HUMANS? WHAT WOULD BE THE POINT OF THAT?
HUH?
AS SAGES, WE ARE SUPPOSED TO CULTIVATE OUR POWERS TO ACHIEVE GREATER ENLIGHTENMENT. YOU KNOW AS WELL AS I DO THAT THEIR ULTIMATE PURPOSE IS NOT TO KILL AND DESTROY.
WE HAVE A THING OR TWO TO LEARN FROM HUMANS IN THIS AGE OF CHAOS. THOUGH HUMANS LACK POWERS, THEY PUSH ON.
SURVIVAL AT ALL COST, I'VE HEARD THEM SAY.

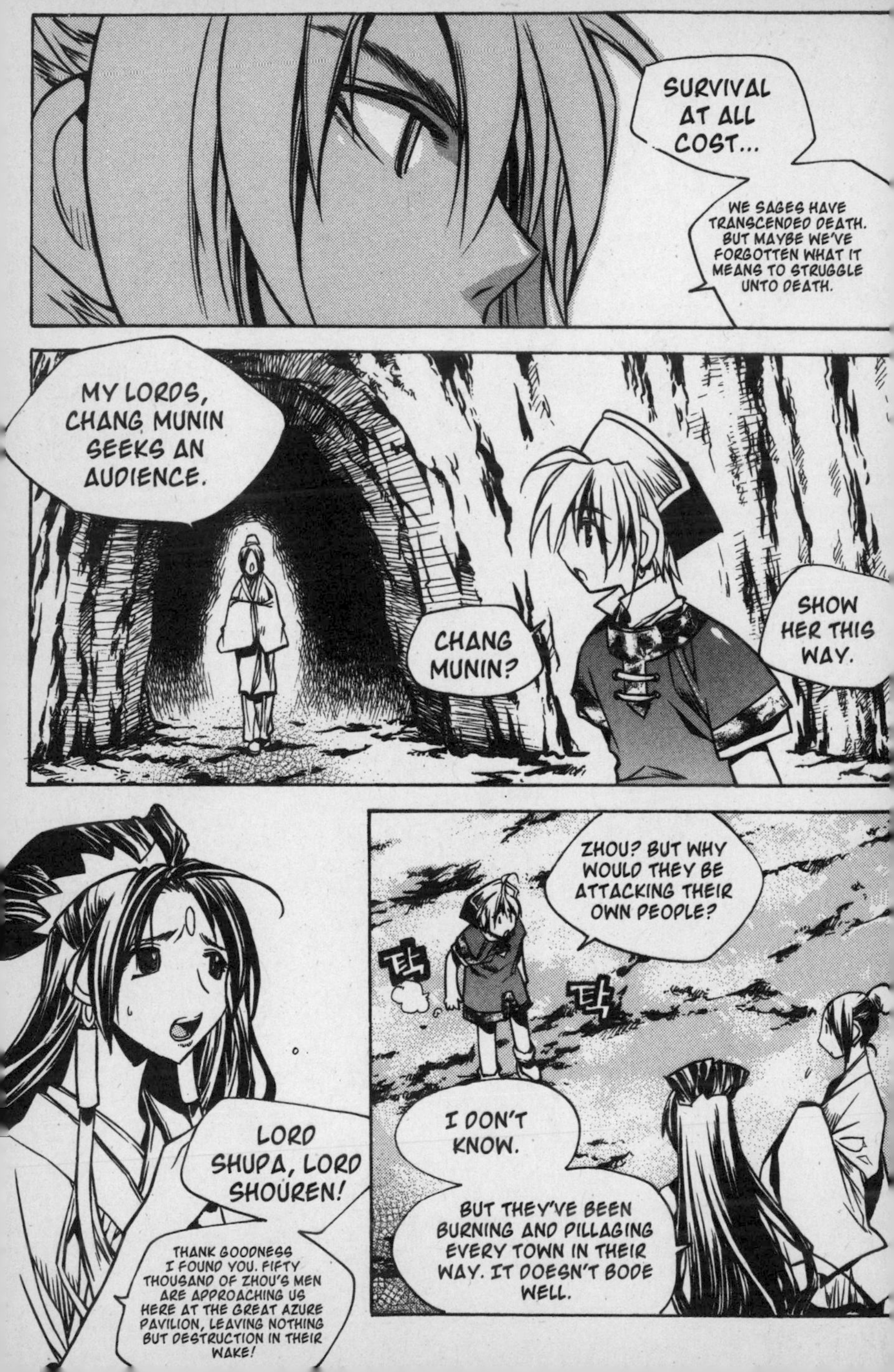
SURVIVAL AT ALL COST...
WE SAGES HAVE TRANSCENDED DEATH. BUT MAYBE WE'VE FORGOTTEN WHAT IT MEANS TO STRUGGLE UNTO DEATH.
MY LORDS, CHANG MUNIN SEEKS AN AUDIENCE.
CHANG MUNIN?
SHOW HER THIS WAY.
LORD SHUPA, LORD SHOUREN!
THANK GOODNESS I FOUND YOU. FIFTY THOUSAND OF ZHOU'S MEN ARE APPROACHING US HERE AT THE GREAT AZURE PAVILION, LEAVING NOTHING BUT DESTRUCTION IN THEIR WAKE!
ZHOU? BUT WHY WOULD THEY BE ATTACKING THEIR OWN PEOPLE?
탁
탁
I DON'T KNOW.
BUT THEY'VE BEEN BURNING AND PILLAGING EVERY TOWN IN THEIR WAY. IT DOESN'T BODE WELL.

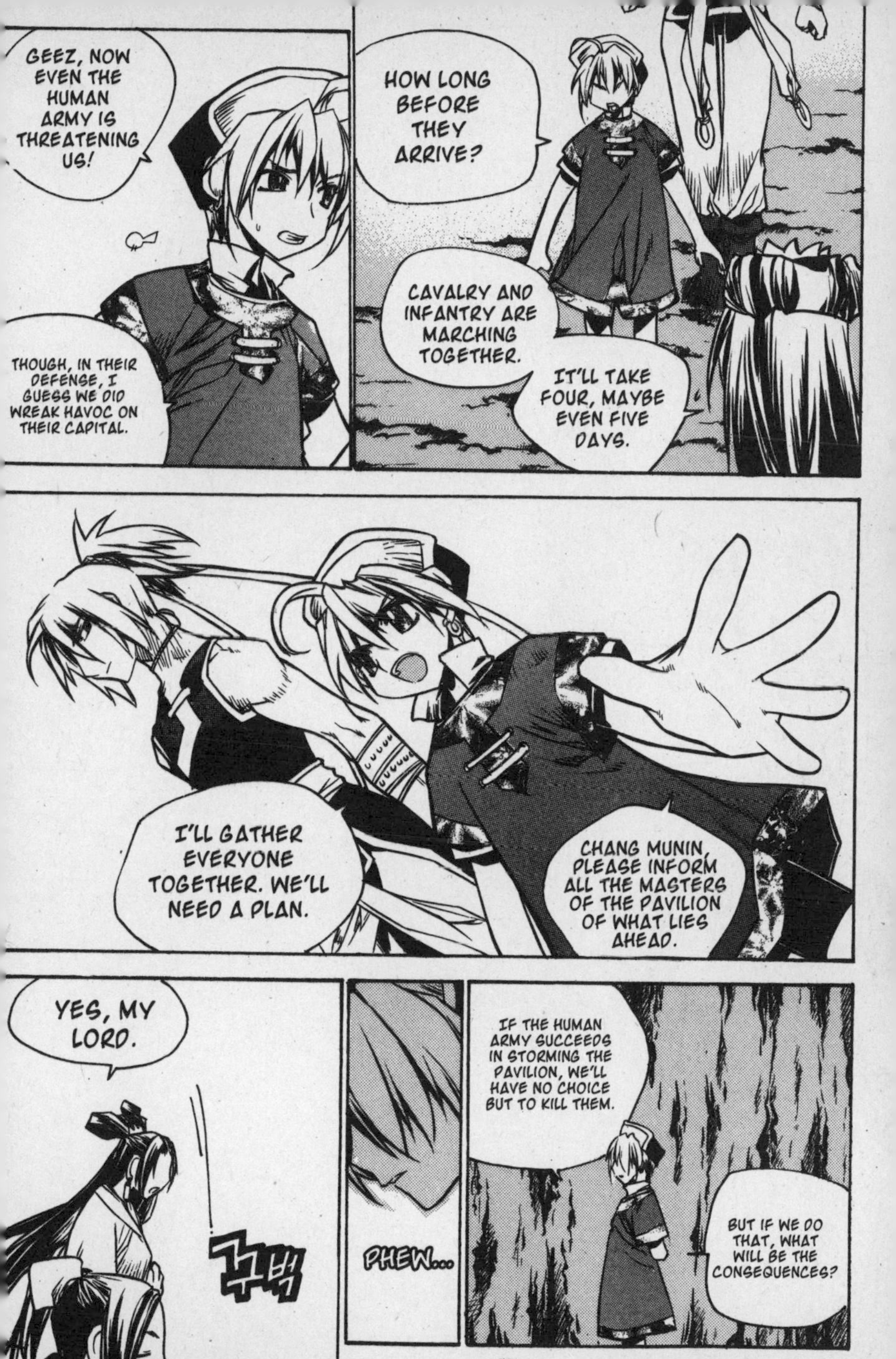
GEEZ, NOW EVEN THE HUMAN ARMY IS THREATENING US!
THOUGH, IN THEIR DEFENSE, I GUESS WE DID WREAK HAVOC ON THEIR CAPITAL.
HOW LONG BEFORE THEY ARRIVE?
CAVALRY AND INFANTRY ARE MARCHING TOGETHER.
IT'LL TAKE FOUR, MAYBE EVEN FIVE DAYS.
I'LL GATHER EVERYONE TOGETHER. WE'LL NEED A PLAN.
CHANG MUNIN, PLEASE INFORM ALL THE MASTERS OF THE PAVILION OF WHAT LIES AHEAD.
YES, MY LORD.
꾸벅
PHEW...
IF THE HUMAN ARMY SUCCEEDS IN STORMING THE PAVILION, WE'LL HAVE NO CHOICE BUT TO KILL THEM.
BUT IF WE DO THAT, WHAT WILL BE THE CONSEQUENCES?

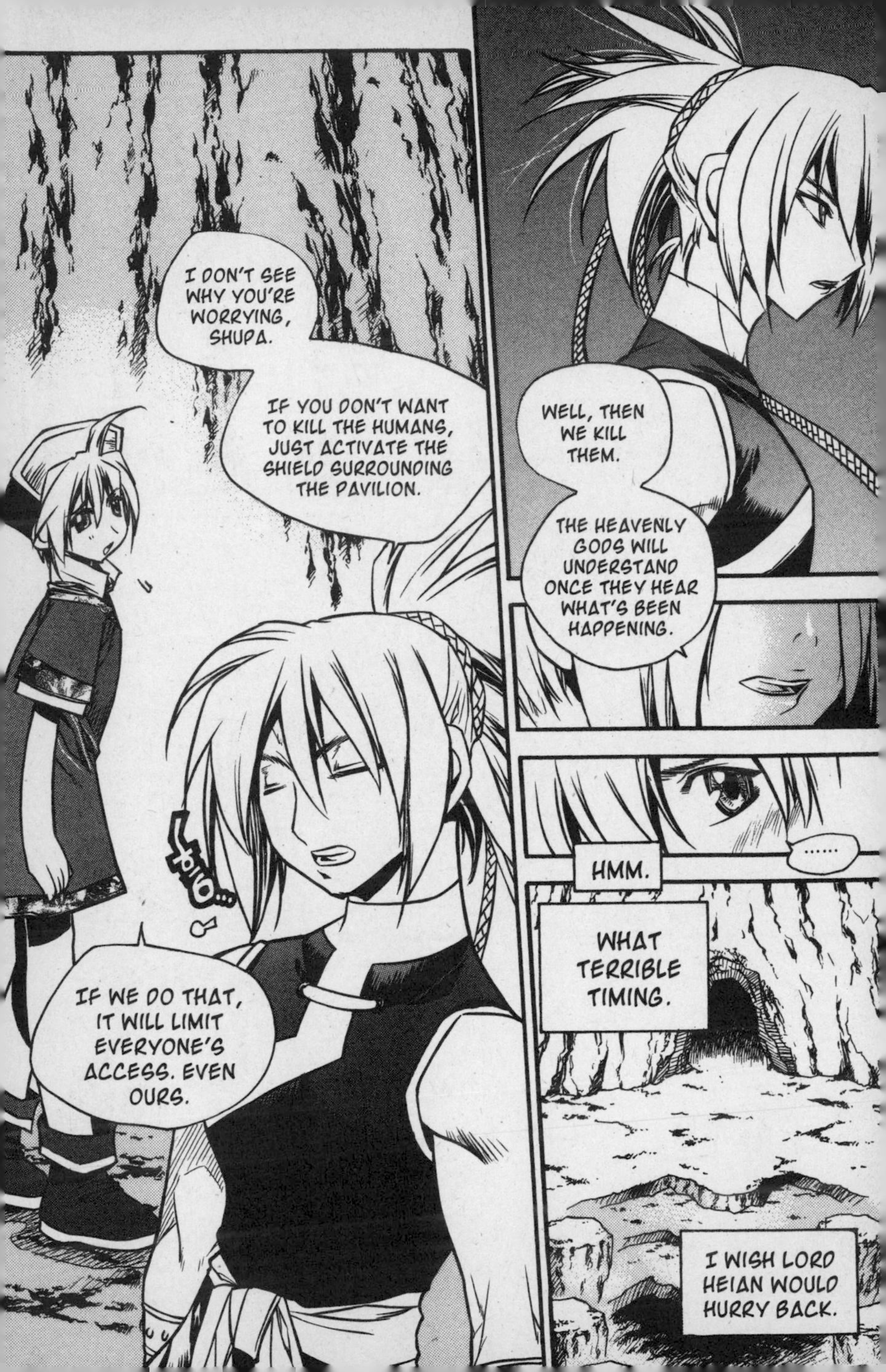
I DON'T SEE WHY YOU'RE WORRYING, SHUPA.
IF YOU DON'T WANT TO KILL THE HUMANS, JUST ACTIVATE THE SHIELD SURROUNDING THE PAVILION.
IF WE DO THAT, IT WILL LIMIT EVERYONE'S ACCESS. EVEN OURS.
WELL, THEN WE KILL THEM.
THE HEAVENLY GODS WILL UNDERSTAND ONCE THEY HEAR WHAT'S BEEN HAPPENING.
HMM.
......
WHAT TERRIBLE TIMING.
I WISH LORD HEIAN WOULD HURRY BACK.

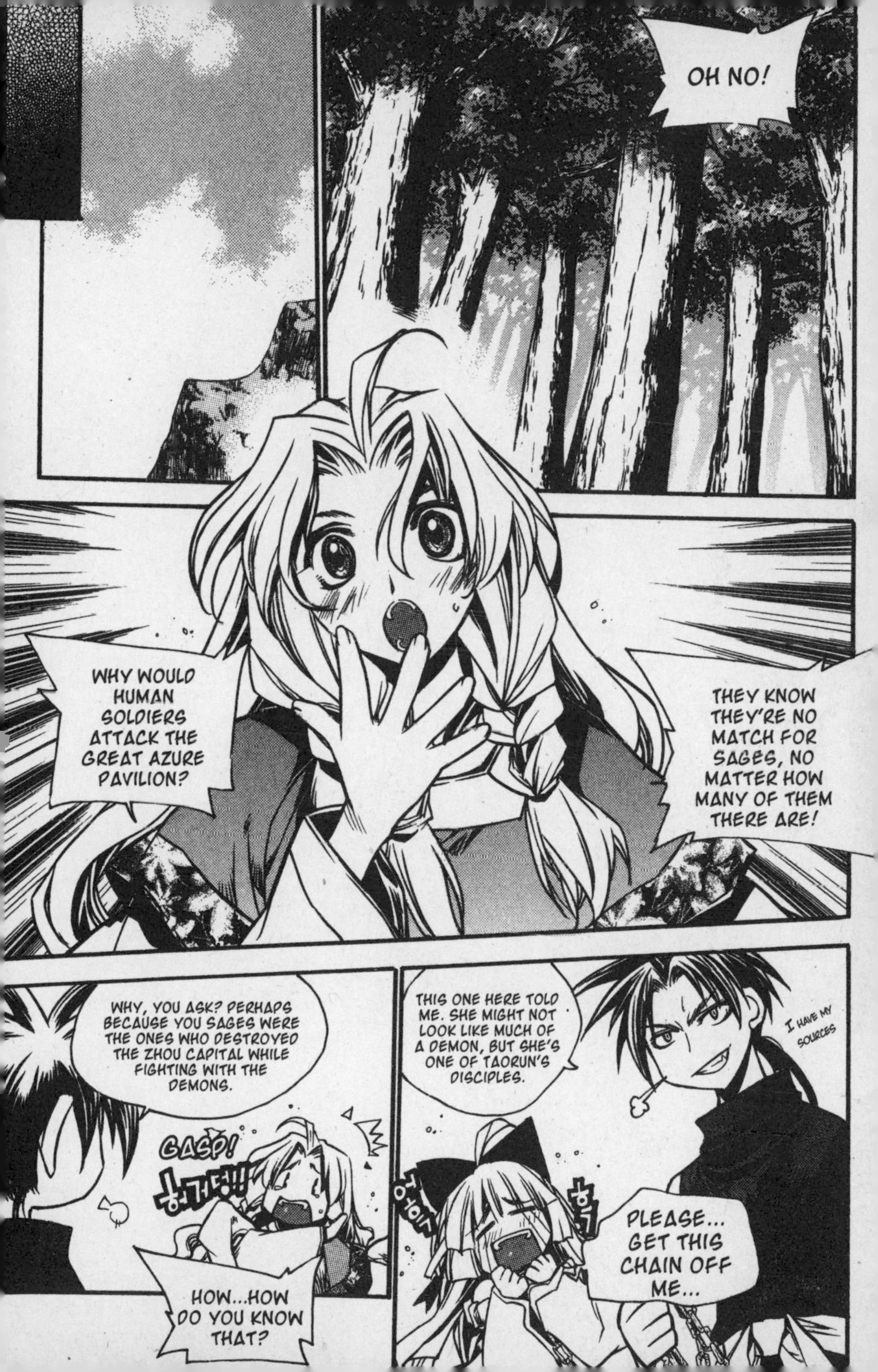
OH NO!
WHY WOULD HUMAN SOLDIERS ATTACK THE GREAT AZURE PAVILION?
THEY KNOW THEY'RE NO MATCH FOR SAGES, NO MATTER HOW MANY OF THEM THERE ARE!
WHY, YOU ASK? PERHAPS BECAUSE YOU SAGES WERE THE ONES WHO DESTROYED THE ZHOU CAPITAL WHILE FIGHTING WITH THE DEMONS.
GASP!
HOW...HOW DO YOU KNOW THAT?
THIS ONE HERE TOLD ME. SHE MIGHT NOT LOOK LIKE MUCH OF A DEMON, BUT SHE'S ONE OF TAORUN'S DISCIPLES.
I HAVE MY SOURCES
PLEASE... GET THIS CHAIN OFF ME...

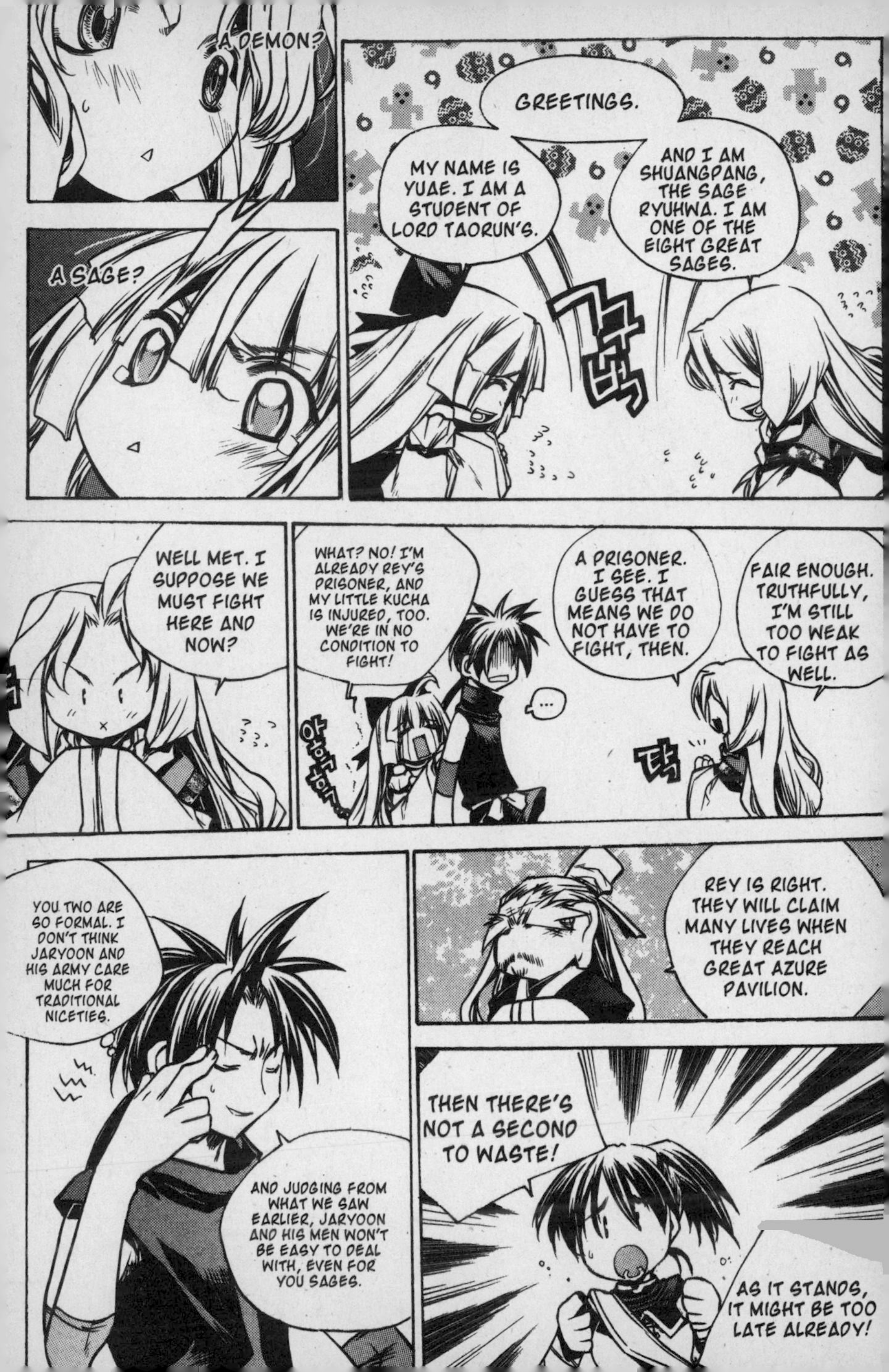

A DEMON?
A SAGE?
GREETINGS.
MY NAME IS YUAE. I AM A STUDENT OF LORD TAORUN'S.
AND I AM SHUANGPANG, THE SAGE RYUHWA. I AM ONE OF THE EIGHT GREAT SAGES.
WELL MET. I SUPPOSE WE MUST FIGHT HERE AND NOW?
WHAT? NO! I'M ALREADY REY'S PRISONER, AND MY LITTLE KUCHA IS INJURED, TOO. WE'RE IN NO CONDITION TO FIGHT!
...
A PRISONER. I SEE. I GUESS THAT MEANS WE DO NOT HAVE TO FIGHT, THEN.
FAIR ENOUGH. TRUTHFULLY, I'M STILL TOO WEAK TO FIGHT AS WELL.
YOU TWO ARE SO FORMAL. I DON'T THINK JARYOON AND HIS ARMY CARE MUCH FOR TRADITIONAL NICETIES.
AND JUDGING FROM WHAT WE SAW EARLIER, JARYOON AND HIS MEN WON'T BE EASY TO DEAL WITH, EVEN FOR YOU SAGES.
REY IS RIGHT. THEY WILL CLAIM MANY LIVES WHEN THEY REACH GREAT AZURE PAVILION.
THEN THERE'S NOT A SECOND TO WASTE!
AS IT STANDS, IT MIGHT BE TOO LATE ALREADY!

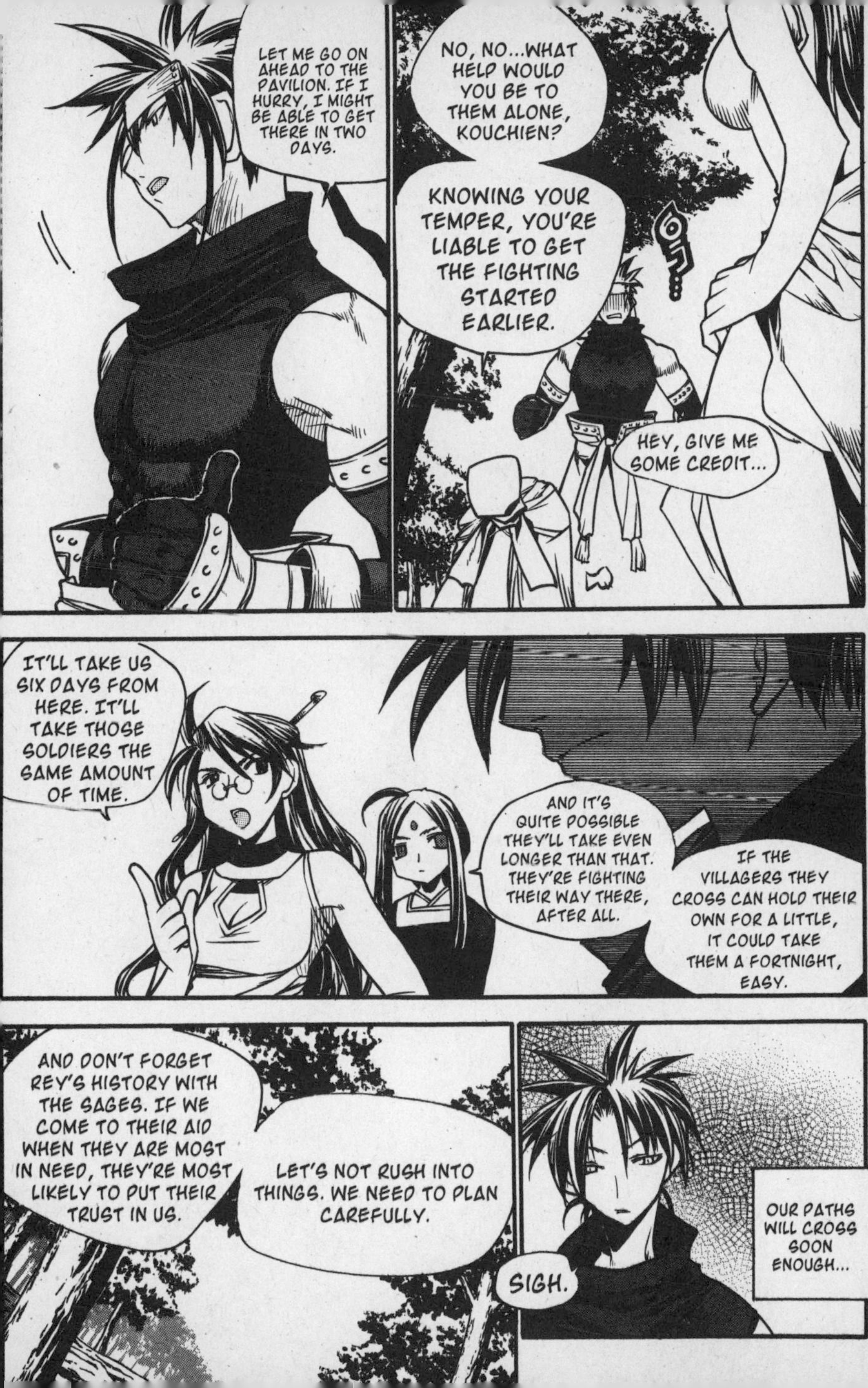
LET ME GO ON AHEAD TO THE PAVILION. IF I HURRY, I MIGHT BE ABLE TO GET THERE IN TWO DAYS.
NO, NO...WHAT HELP WOULD YOU BE TO THEM ALONE, KOUCHIEN?
KNOWING YOUR TEMPER, YOU'RE LIABLE TO GET THE FIGHTING STARTED EARLIER.
HEY, GIVE ME SOME CREDIT...
IT'LL TAKE US SIX DAYS FROM HERE. IT'LL TAKE THOSE SOLDIERS THE SAME AMOUNT OF TIME.
AND IT'S QUITE POSSIBLE THEY'LL TAKE EVEN LONGER THAN THAT. THEY'RE FIGHTING THEIR WAY THERE, AFTER ALL.
IF THE VILLAGERS THEY CROSS CAN HOLD THEIR OWN FOR A LITTLE, IT COULD TAKE THEM A FORTNIGHT, EASY.
AND DON'T FORGET REY'S HISTORY WITH THE SAGES. IF WE COME TO THEIR AID WHEN THEY ARE MOST IN NEED, THEY'RE MOST LIKELY TO PUT THEIR TRUST IN US.
LET'S NOT RUSH INTO THINGS. WE NEED TO PLAN CAREFULLY.
SIGH.
OUR PATHS WILL CROSS SOON ENOUGH...

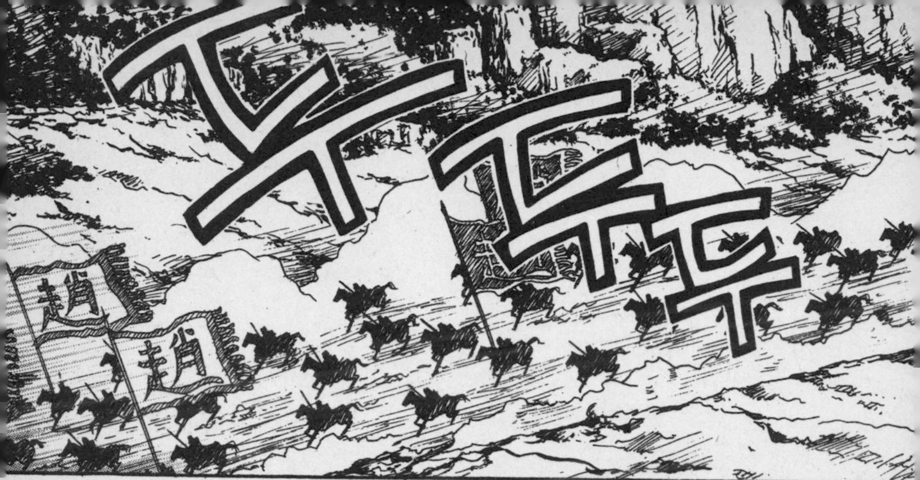

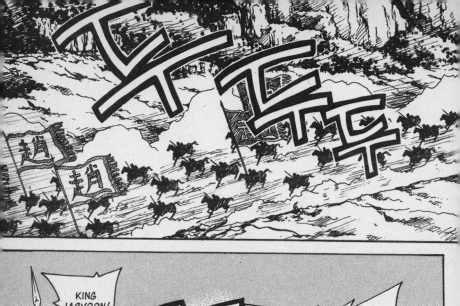

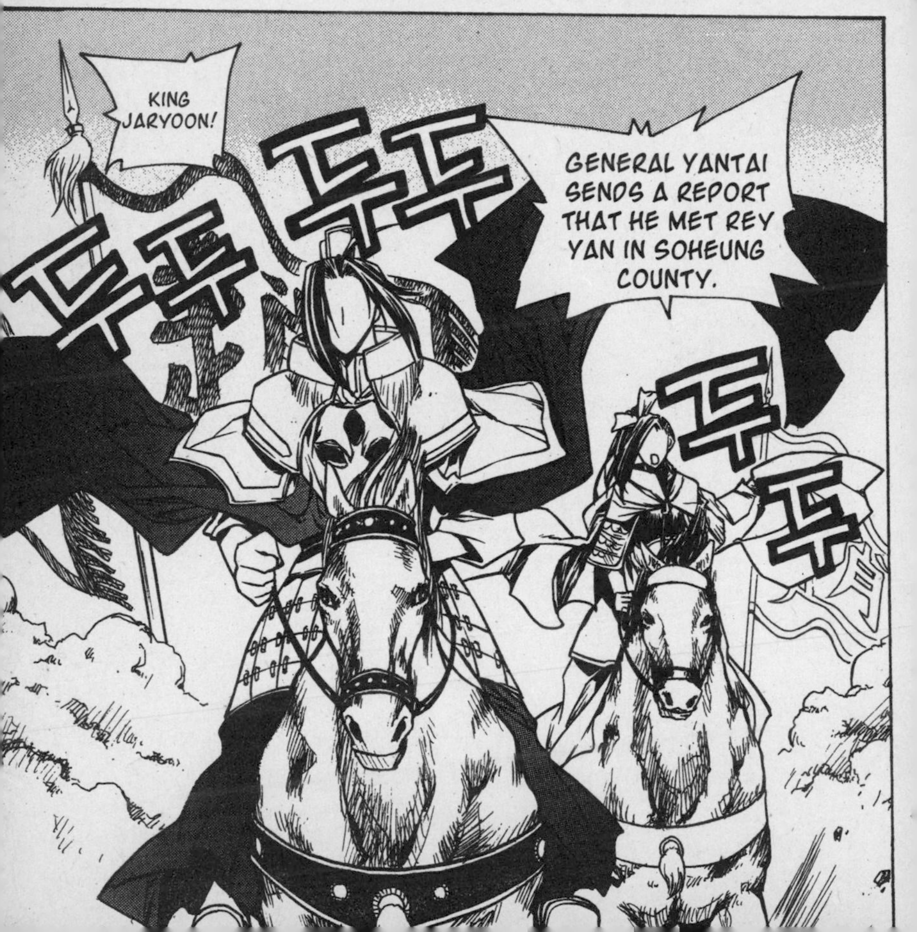
KING JARYOON!
GENERAL YANTAI SENDS A REPORT THAT HE MET REY YAN IN SOHEUNG COUNTY.

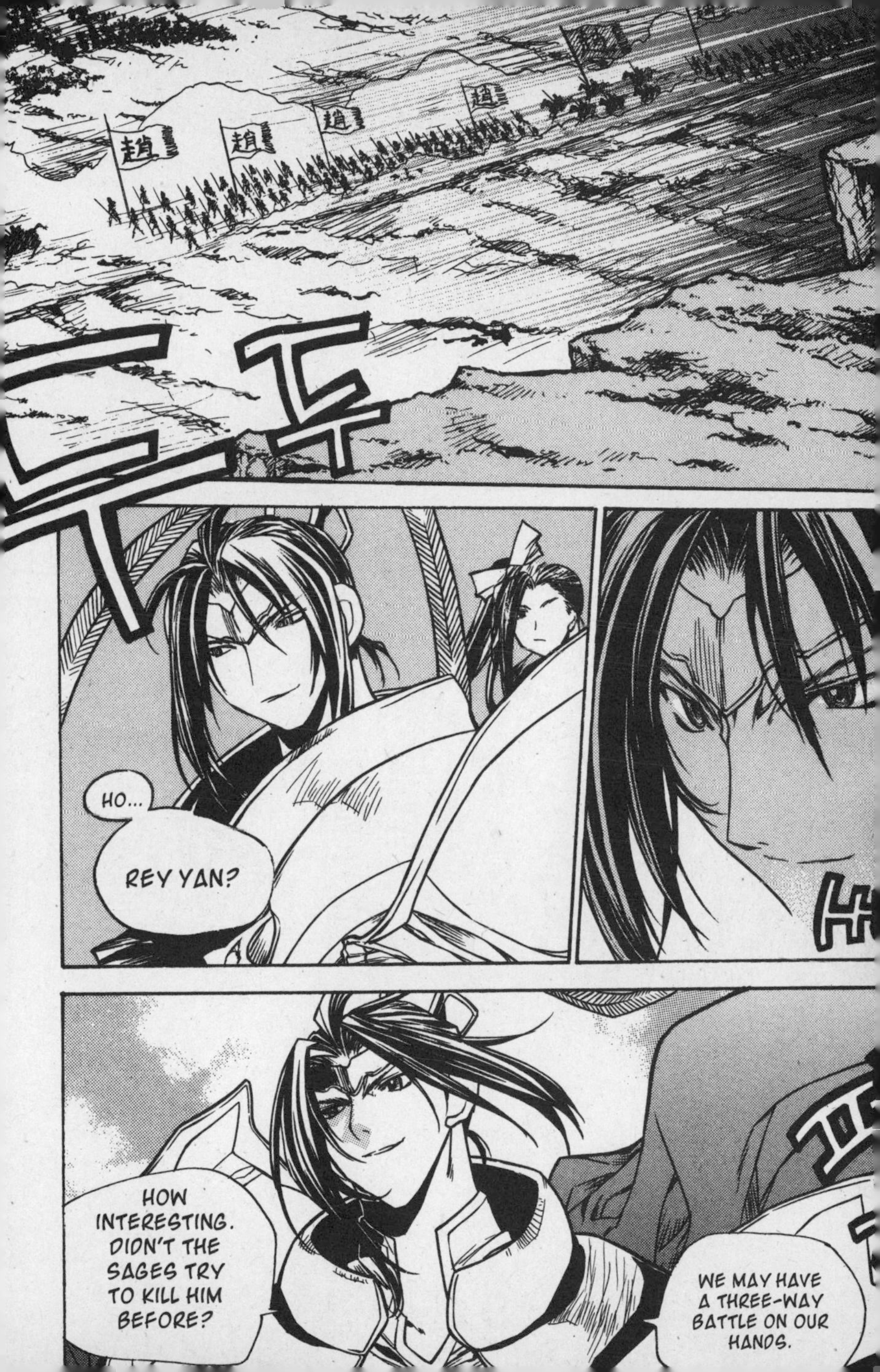
HO...
REY YAN?
HOW INTERESTING. DIDN'T THE SAGES TRY TO KILL HIM BEFORE?
WE MAY HAVE A THREE-WAY BATTLE ON OUR HANDS.

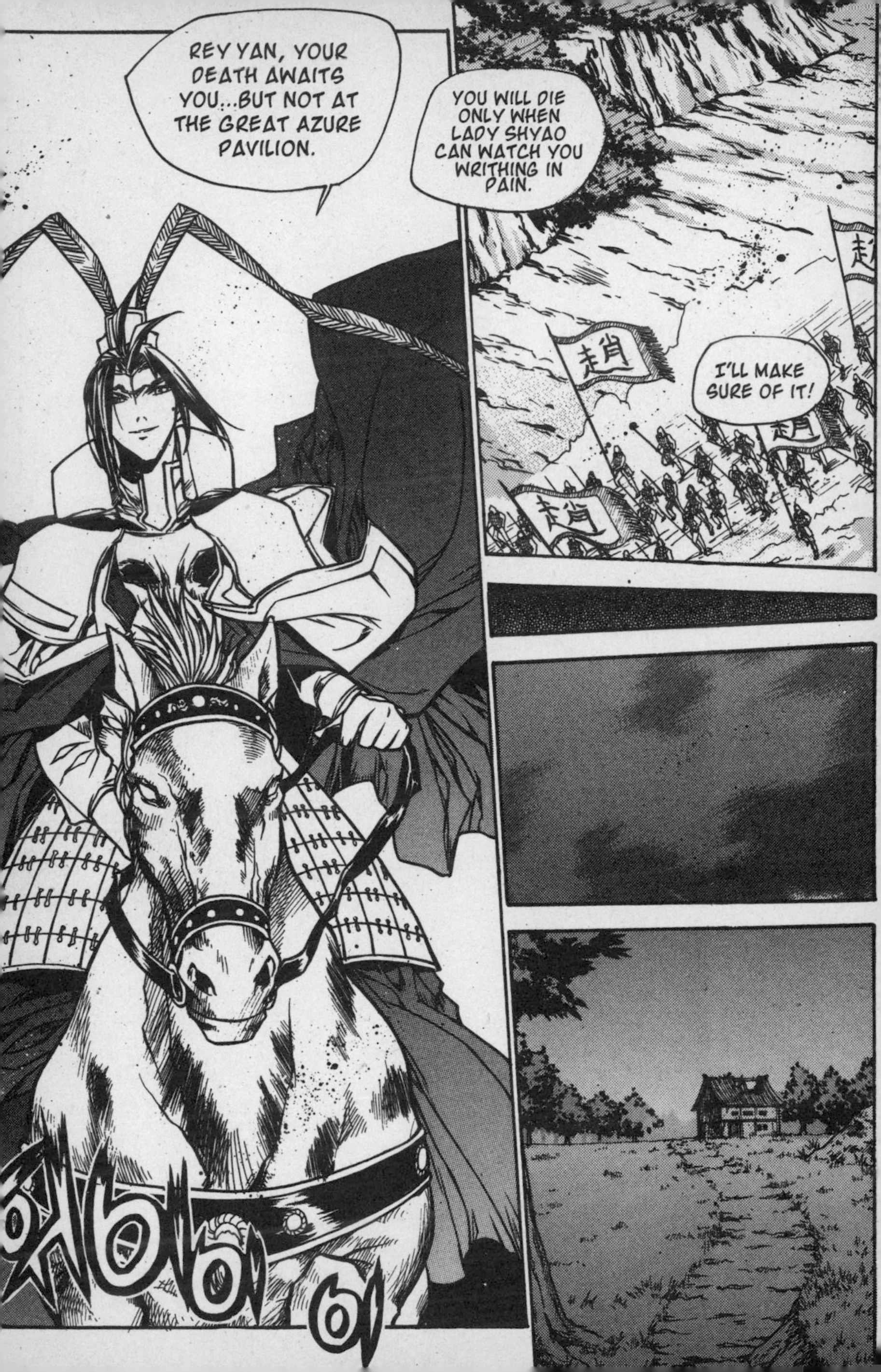
REY YAN, YOUR DEATH AWAITS YOU...BUT NOT AT THE GREAT AZURE PAVILION.
YOU WILL DIE ONLY WHEN LADY SHYAO CAN WATCH YOU WRITHING IN PAIN.
I'LL MAKE SURE OF IT!

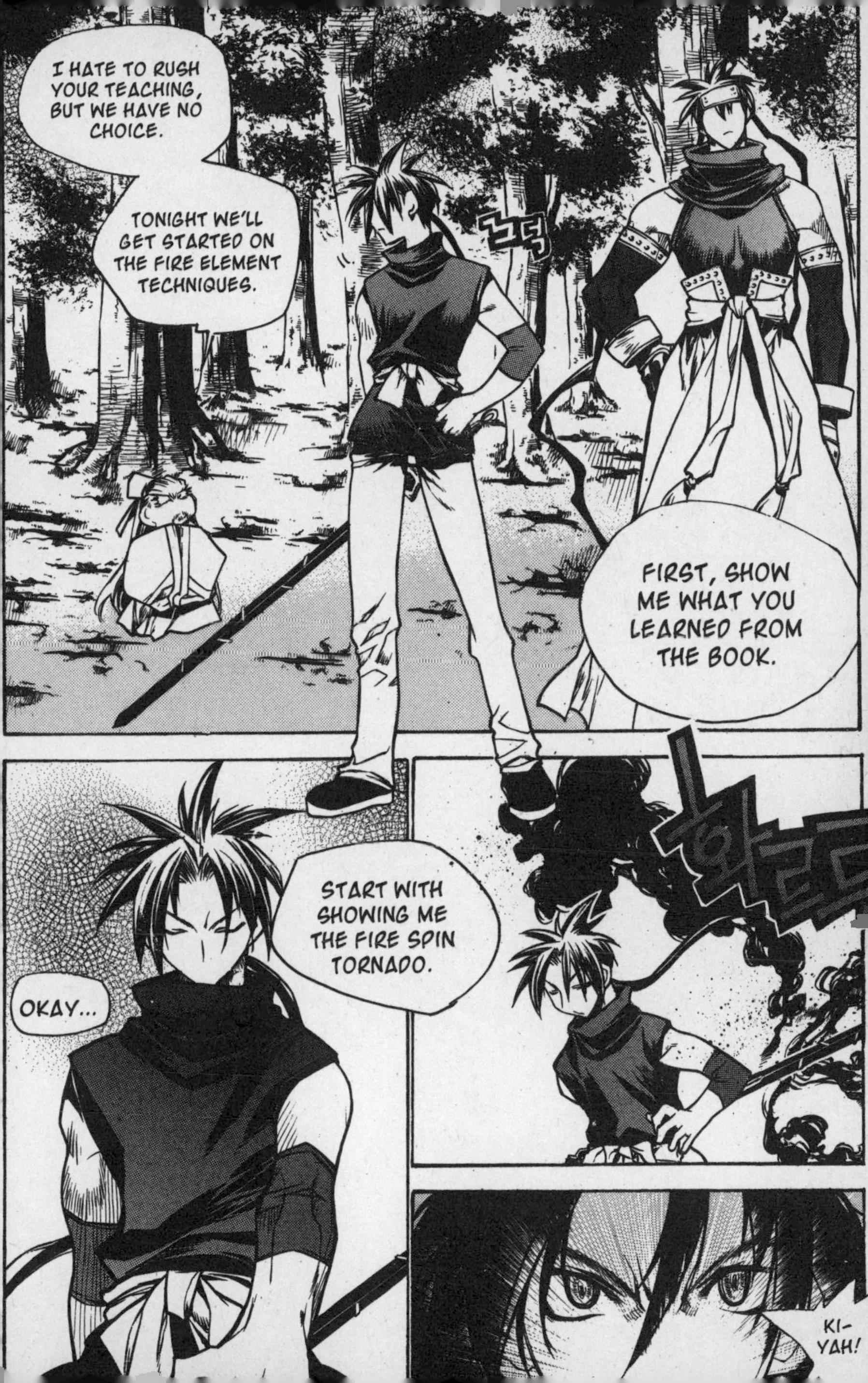
I HATE TO RUSH YOUR TEACHING, BUT WE HAVE NO CHOICE.
TONIGHT WE'LL GET STARTED ON THE FIRE ELEMENT TECHNIQUES.
FIRST, SHOW ME WHAT YOU LEARNED FROM THE BOOK.
START WITH SHOWING ME THE FIRE SPIN TORNADO.
OKAY...
KI-YAH!

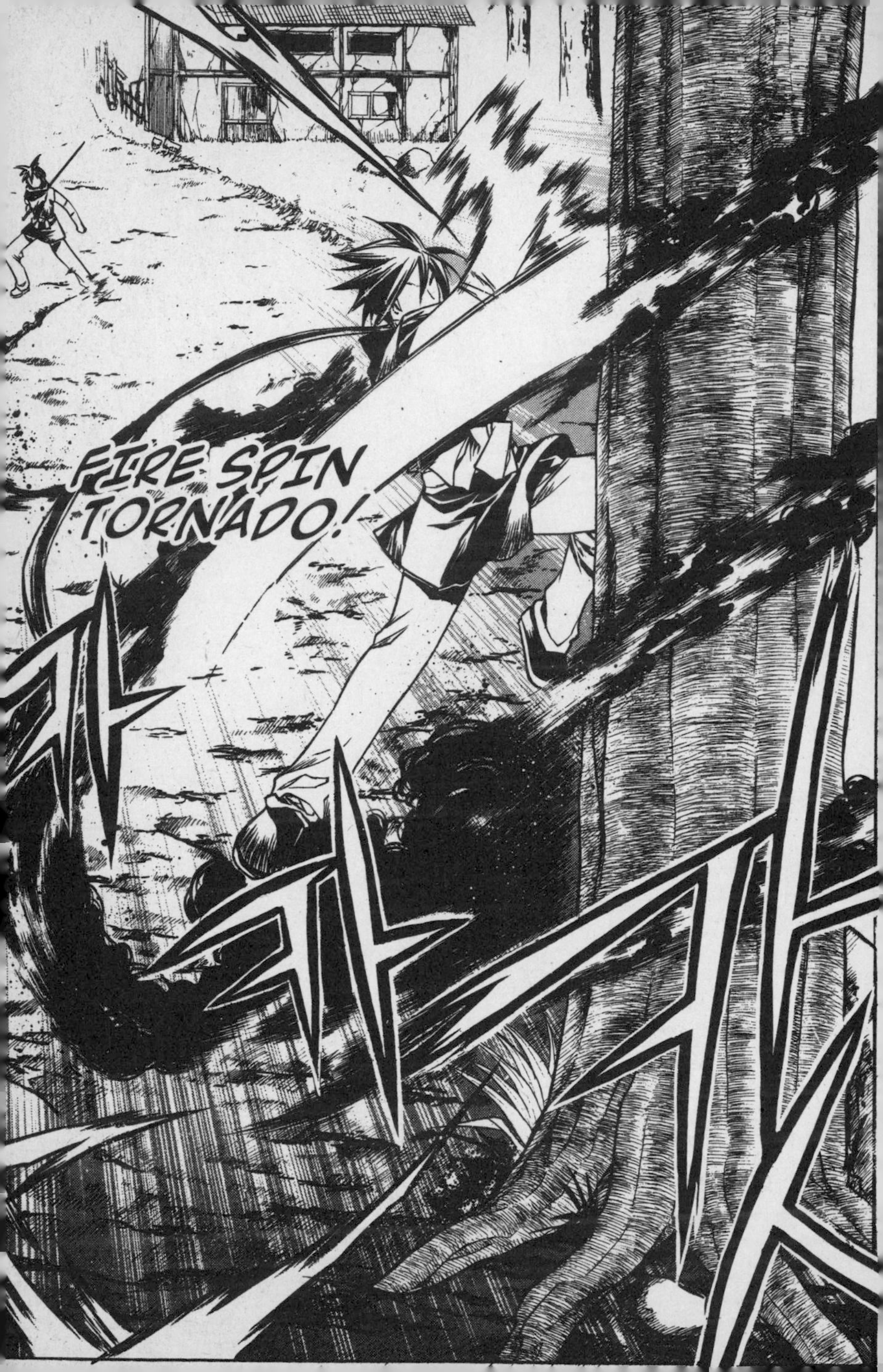
FIRE SPIN TORNADO!

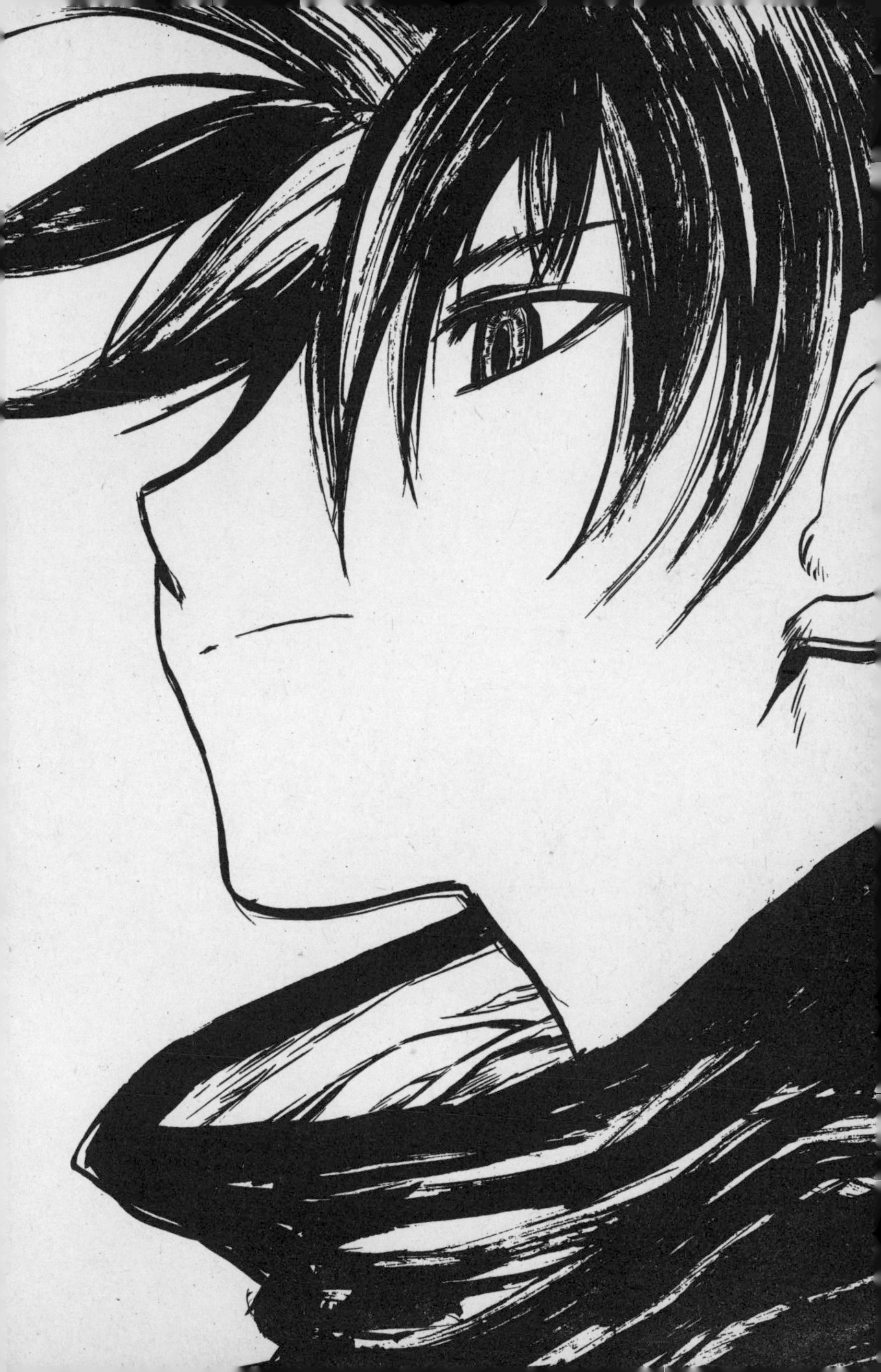

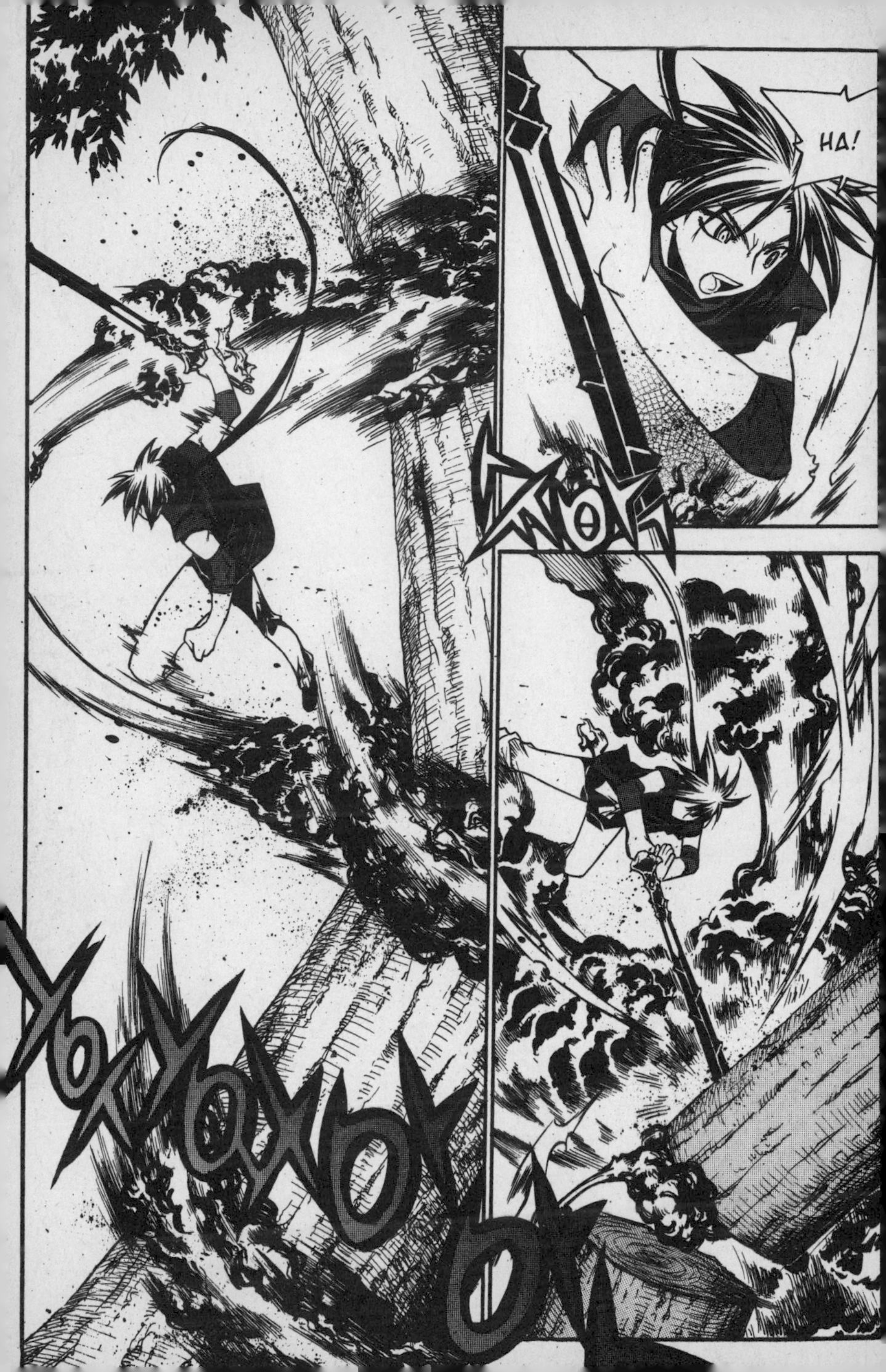
HA!

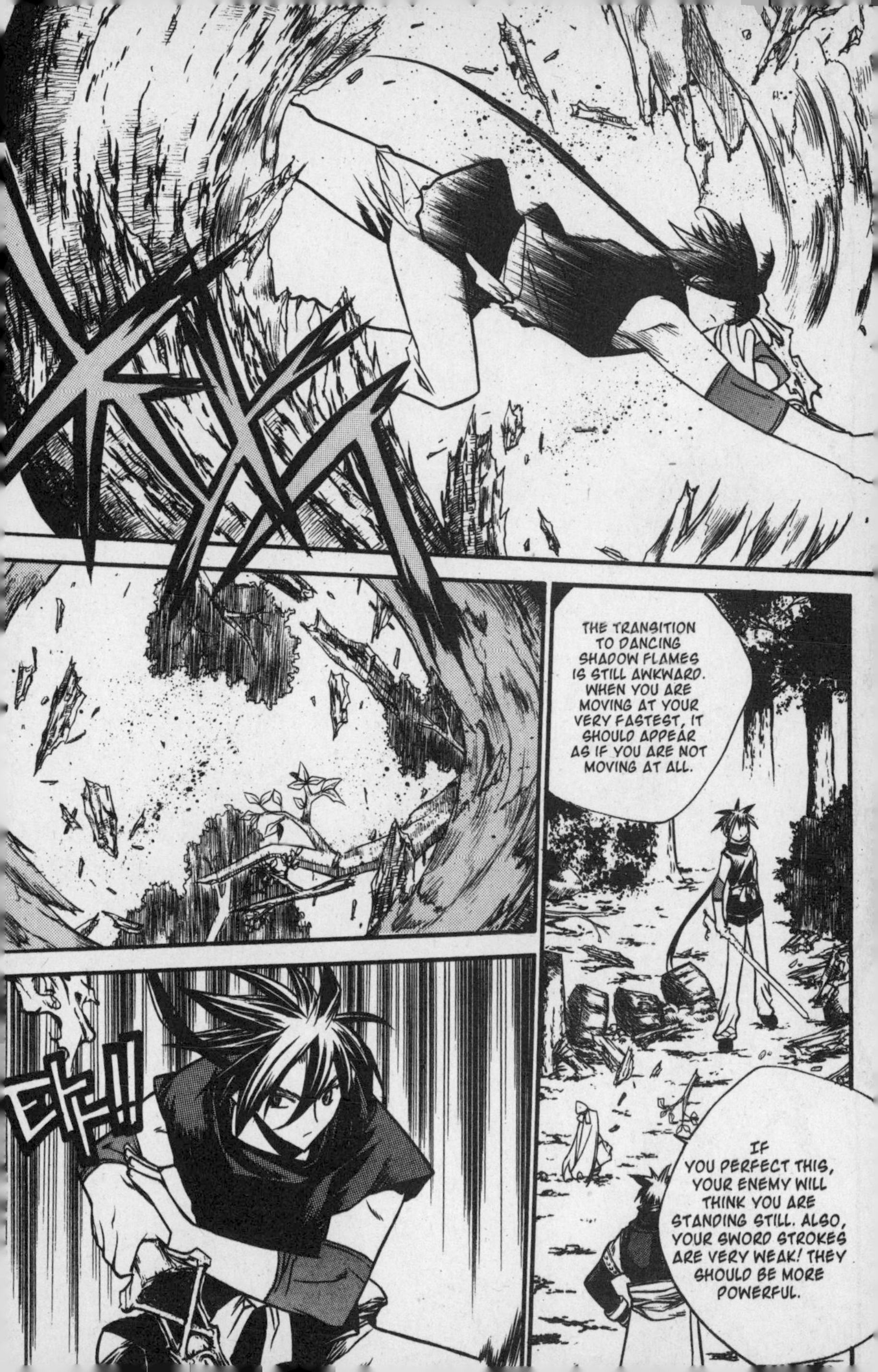
THE TRANSITION TO DANCING SHADOW FLAMES IS STILL AWKWARD. WHEN YOU ARE MOVING AT YOUR VERY FASTEST, IT SHOULD APPEAR AS IF YOU ARE NOT MOVING AT ALL.
IF YOU PERFECT THIS, YOUR ENEMY WILL THINK YOU ARE STANDING STILL. ALSO, YOUR SWORD STROKES ARE VERY WEAK! THEY SHOULD BE MORE POWERFUL.

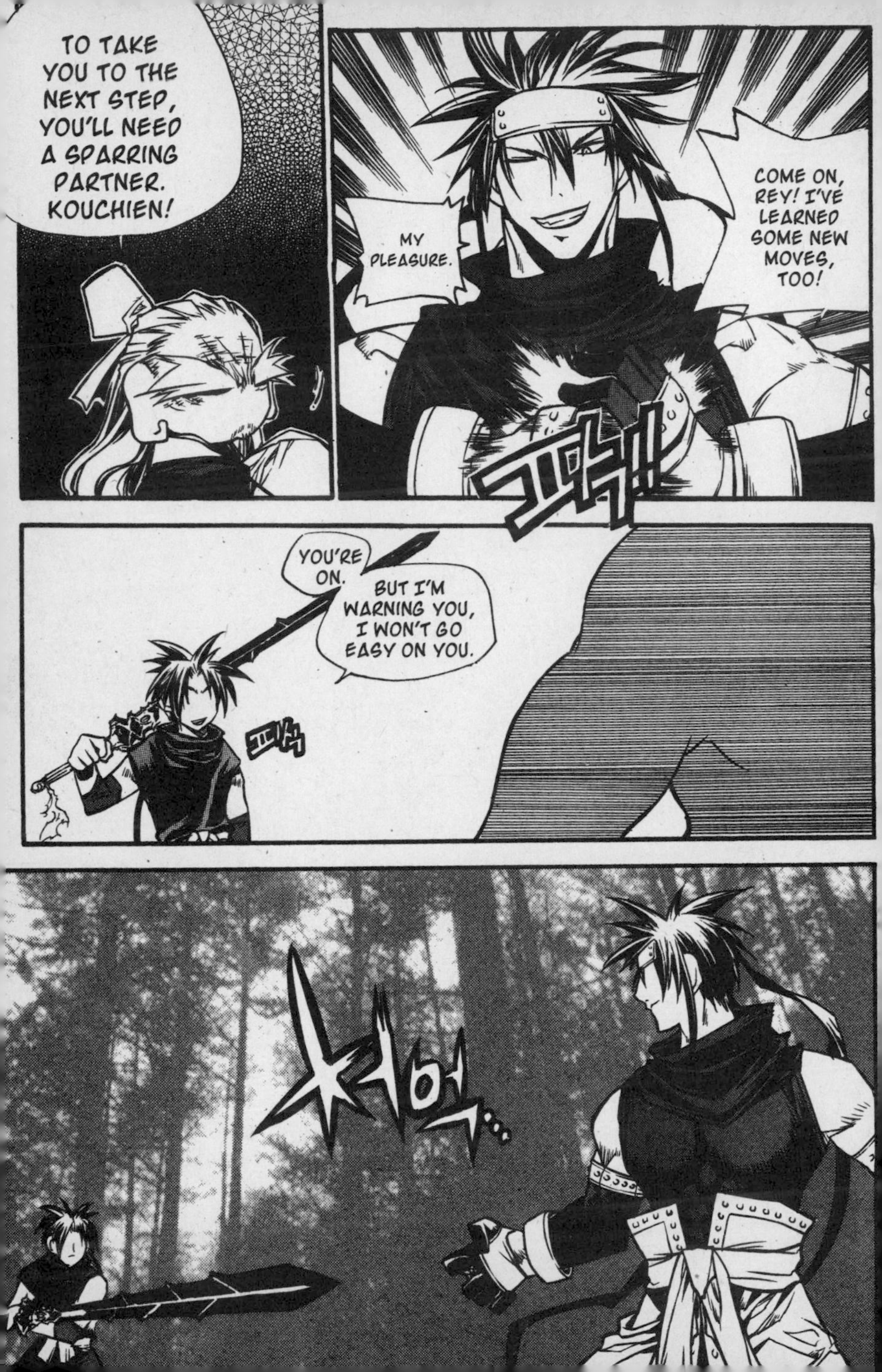
TO TAKE YOU TO THE NEXT STEP, YOU'LL NEED A SPARRING PARTNER. KOUCHIEN!
MY PLEASURE.
COME ON, REY! I'VE LEARNED SOME NEW MOVES, TOO!
YOU'RE ON.
BUT I'M WARNING YOU, I WON'T GO EASY ON YOU.

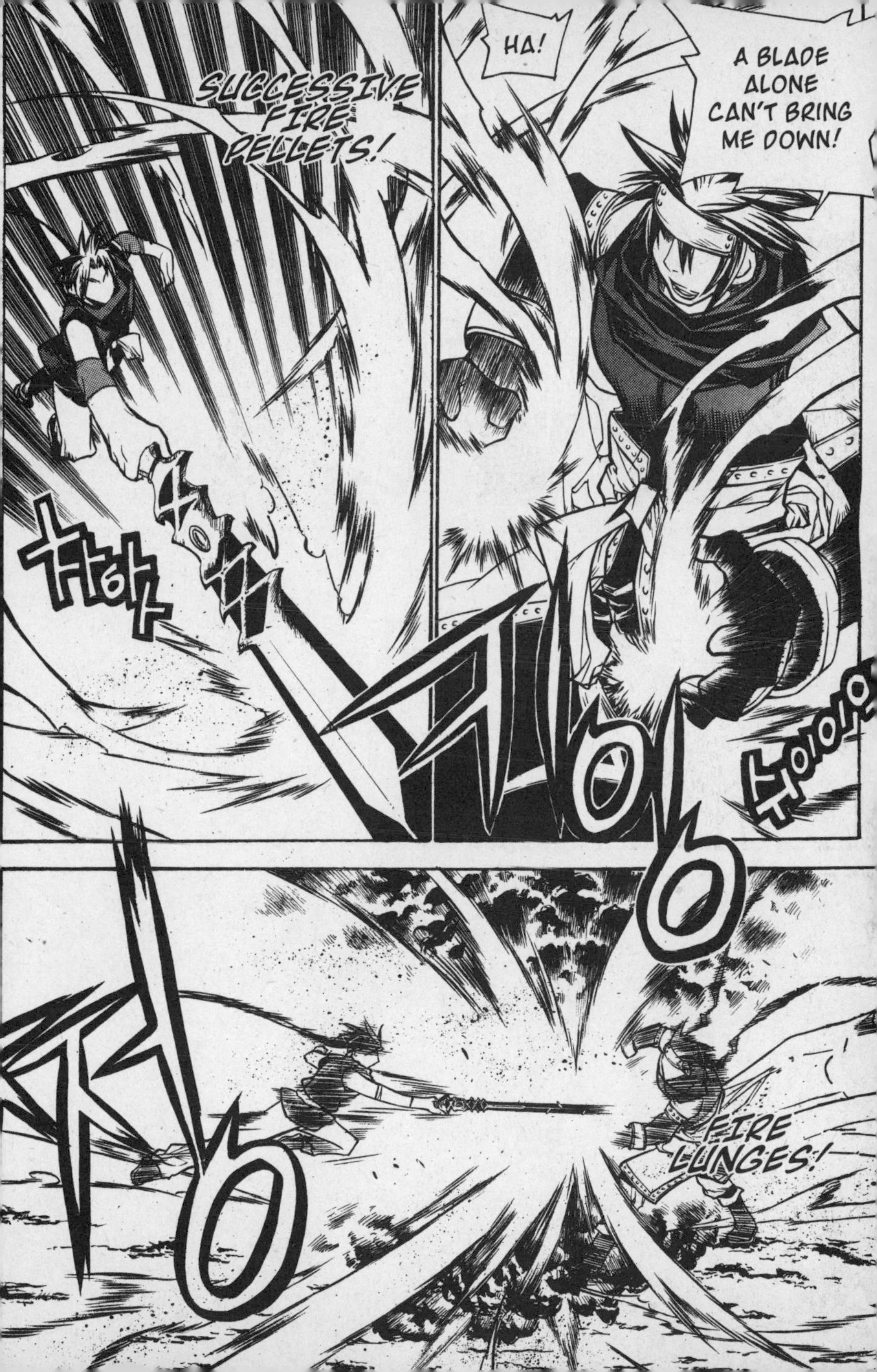
SUCCESSIVE FIRE PELLETS!
HA!
A BLADE ALONE CAN'T BRING ME DOWN!
FIRE LUNGES!

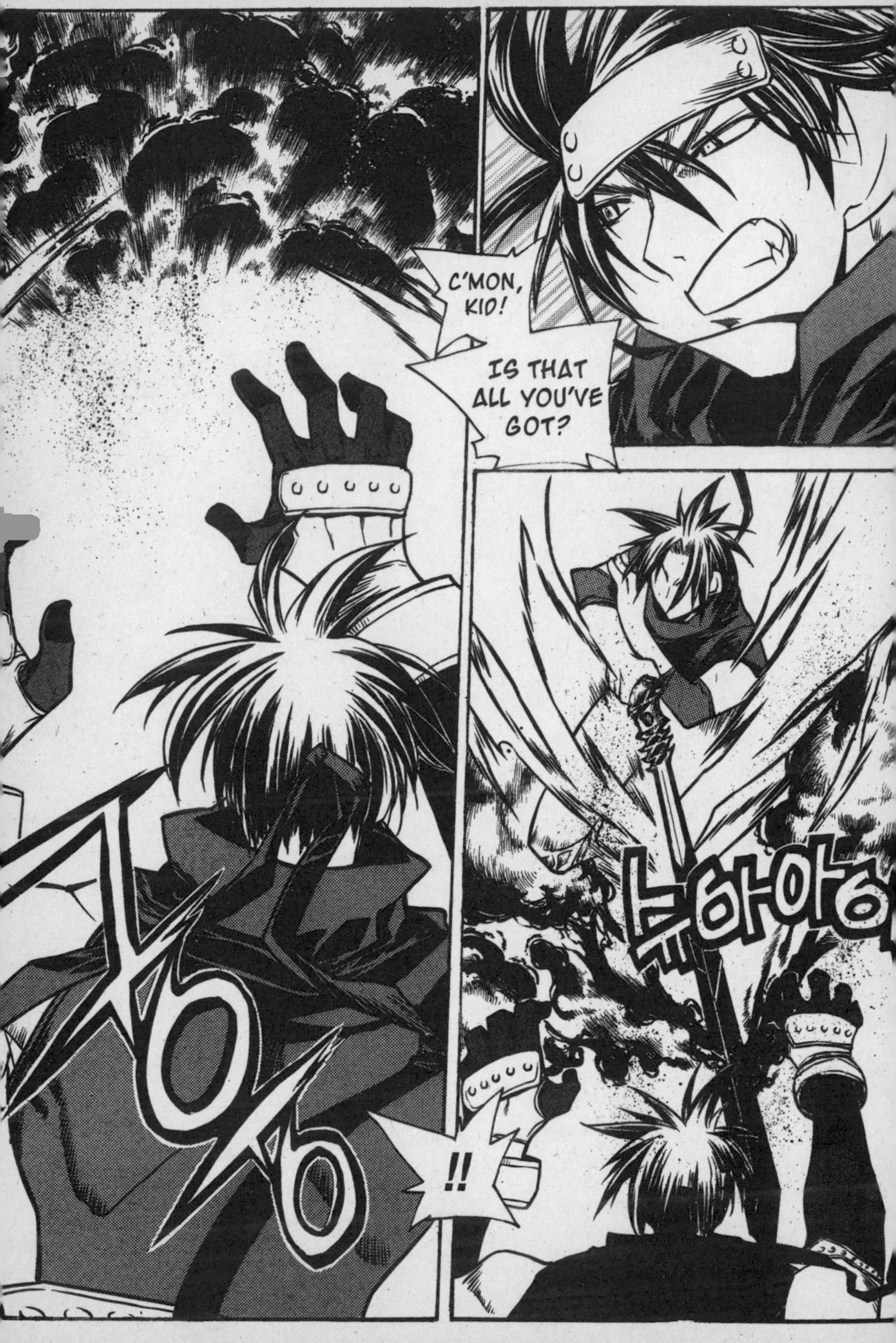

C'MON, KID!
IS THAT ALL YOU'VE GOT?
!!

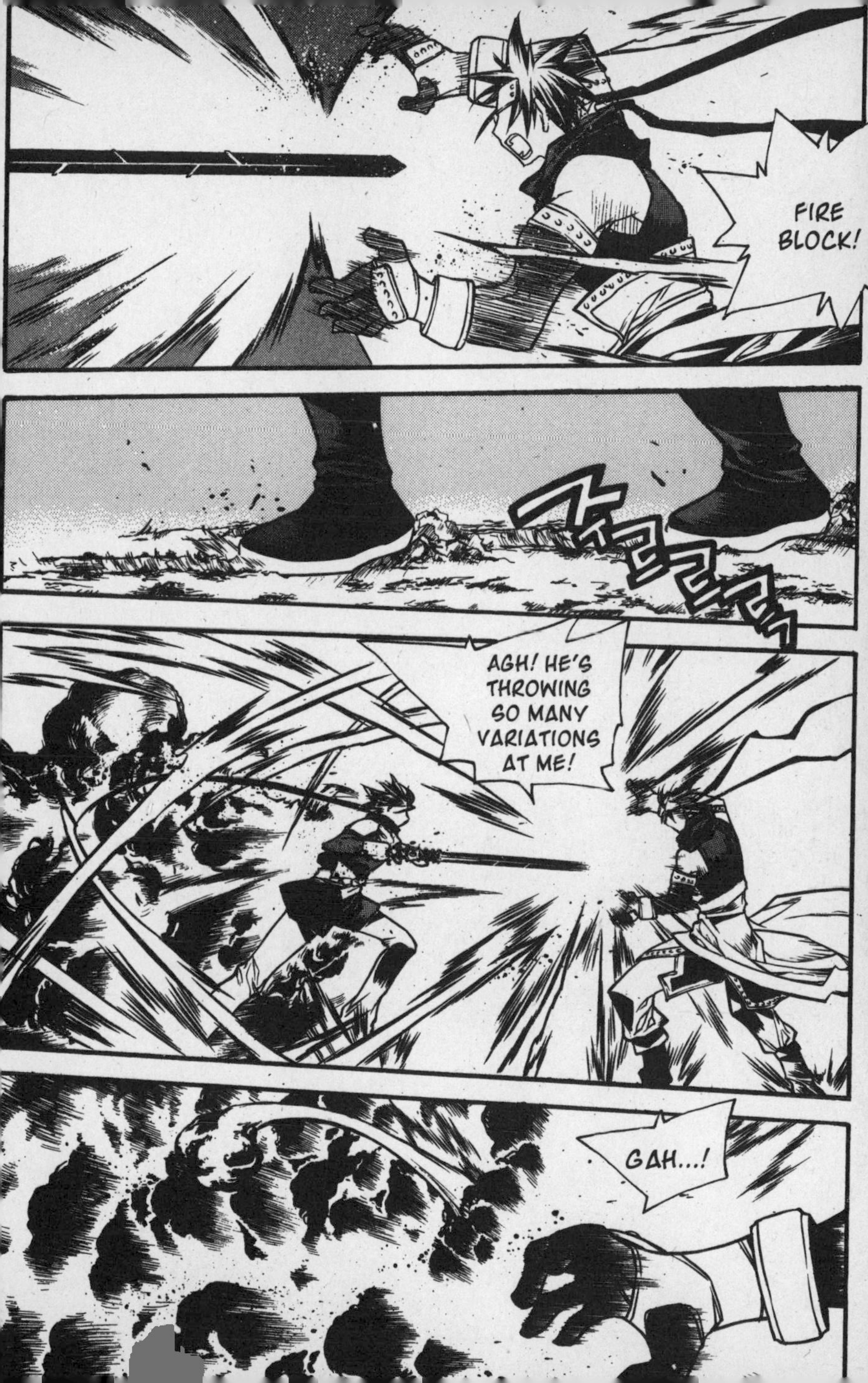
FIRE BLOCK!
AGH! HE'S THROWING SO MANY VARIATIONS AT ME!
GAH...!

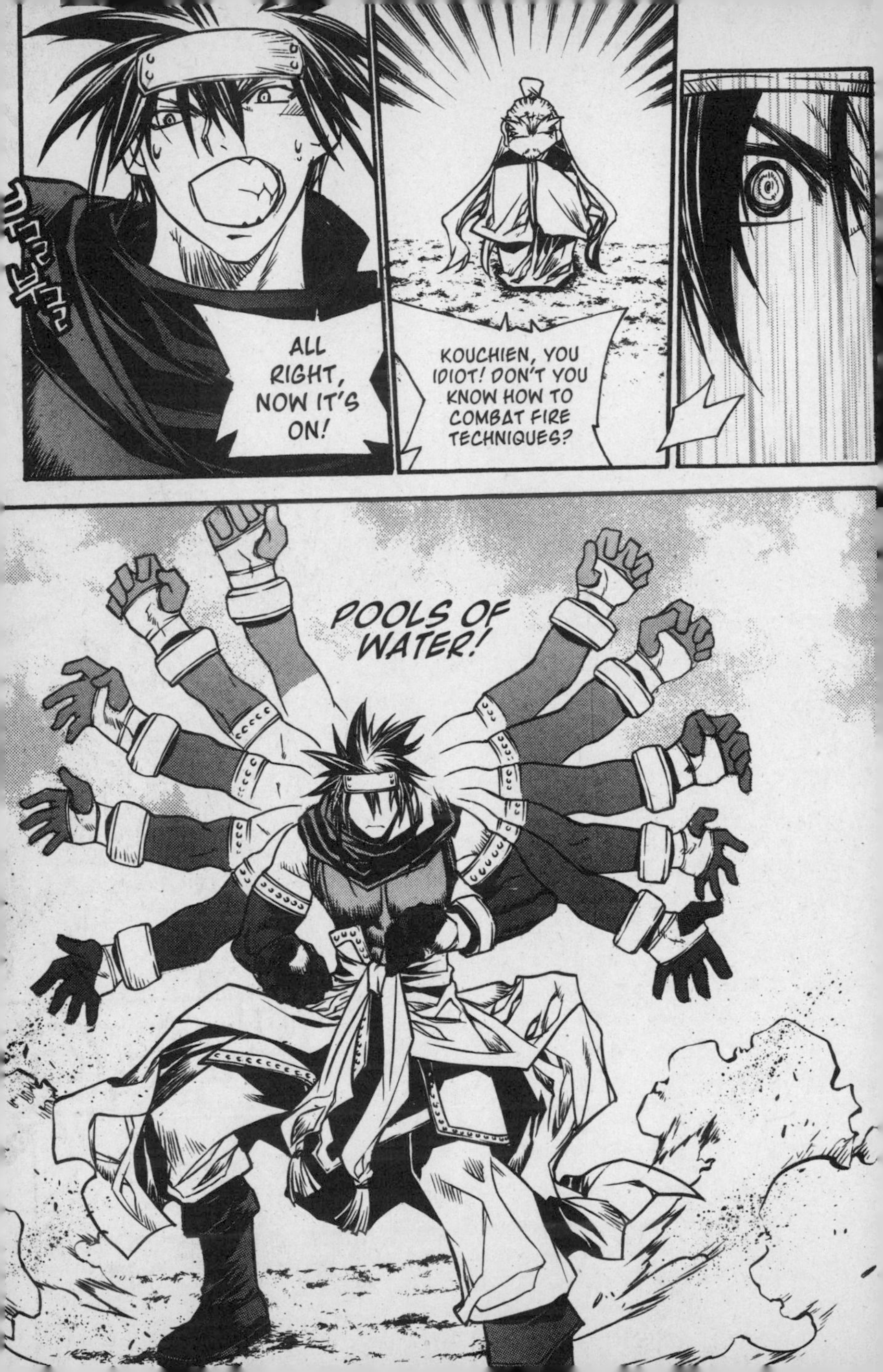
ALL RIGHT, NOW IT'S ON!
KOUCHIEN, YOU IDIOT! DON'T YOU KNOW HOW TO COMBAT FIRE TECHNIQUES?
POOLS OF WATER!

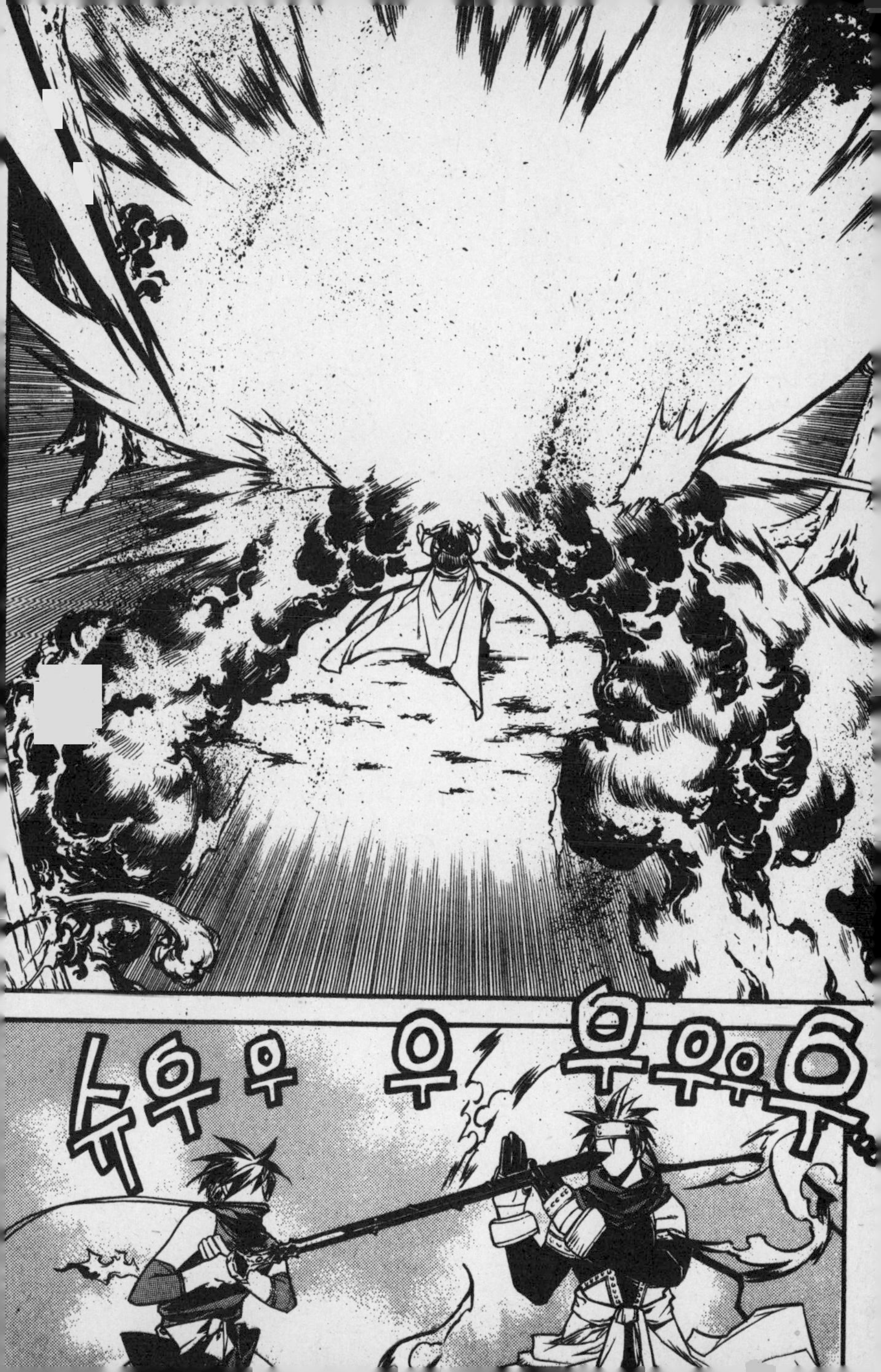
뉴우우 우 후우우우…

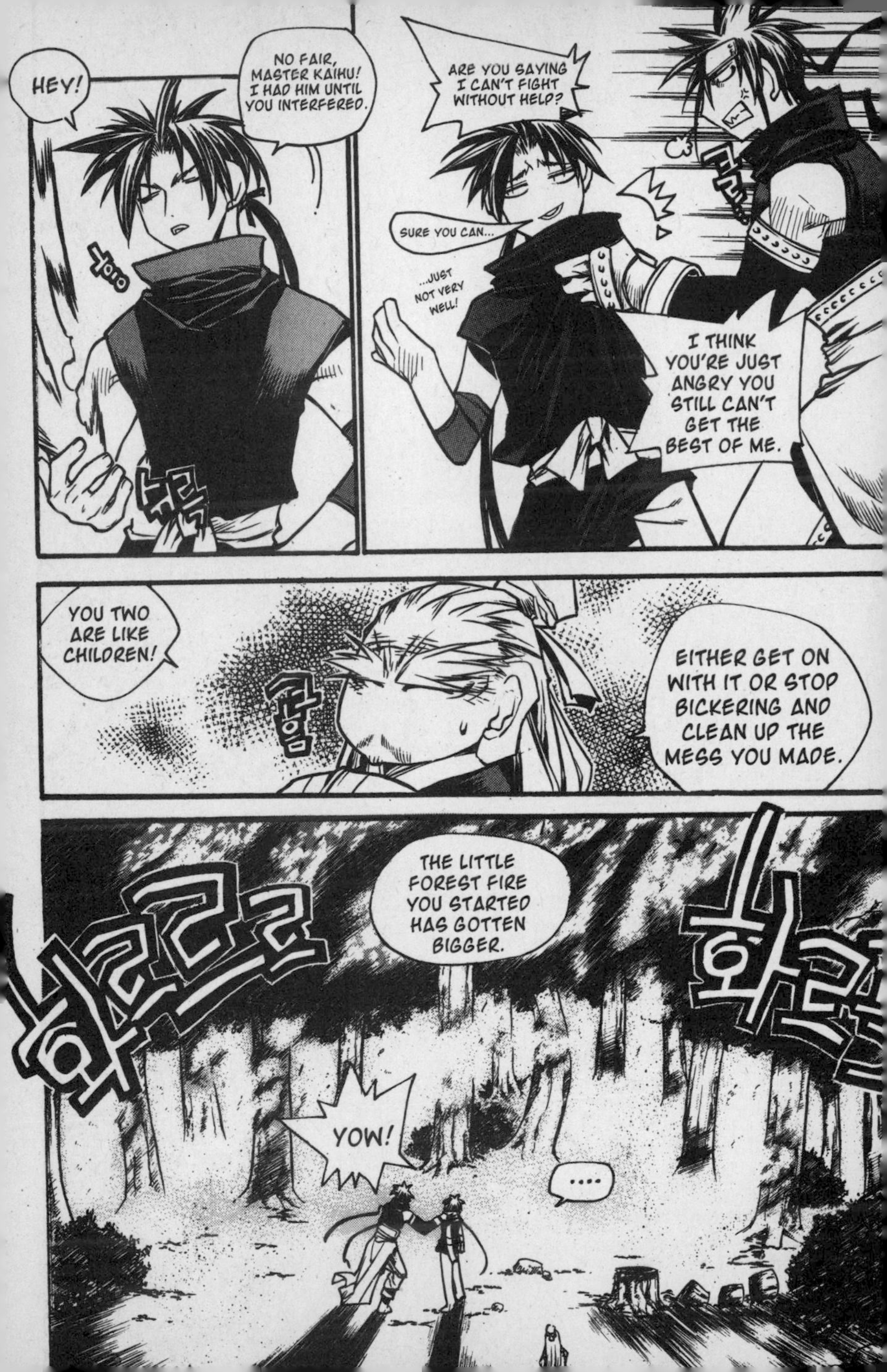
HEY!
NO FAIR, MASTER KAIHU! I HAD HIM UNTIL YOU INTERFERED.
ARE YOU SAYING I CAN'T FIGHT WITHOUT HELP?
SURE YOU CAN...
...JUST NOT VERY WELL!
I THINK YOU'RE JUST ANGRY YOU STILL CAN'T GET THE BEST OF ME.
YOU TWO ARE LIKE CHILDREN!
EITHER GET ON WITH IT OR STOP BICKERING AND CLEAN UP THE MESS YOU MADE.
THE LITTLE FOREST FIRE YOU STARTED HAS GOTTEN BIGGER.
YOW!
....

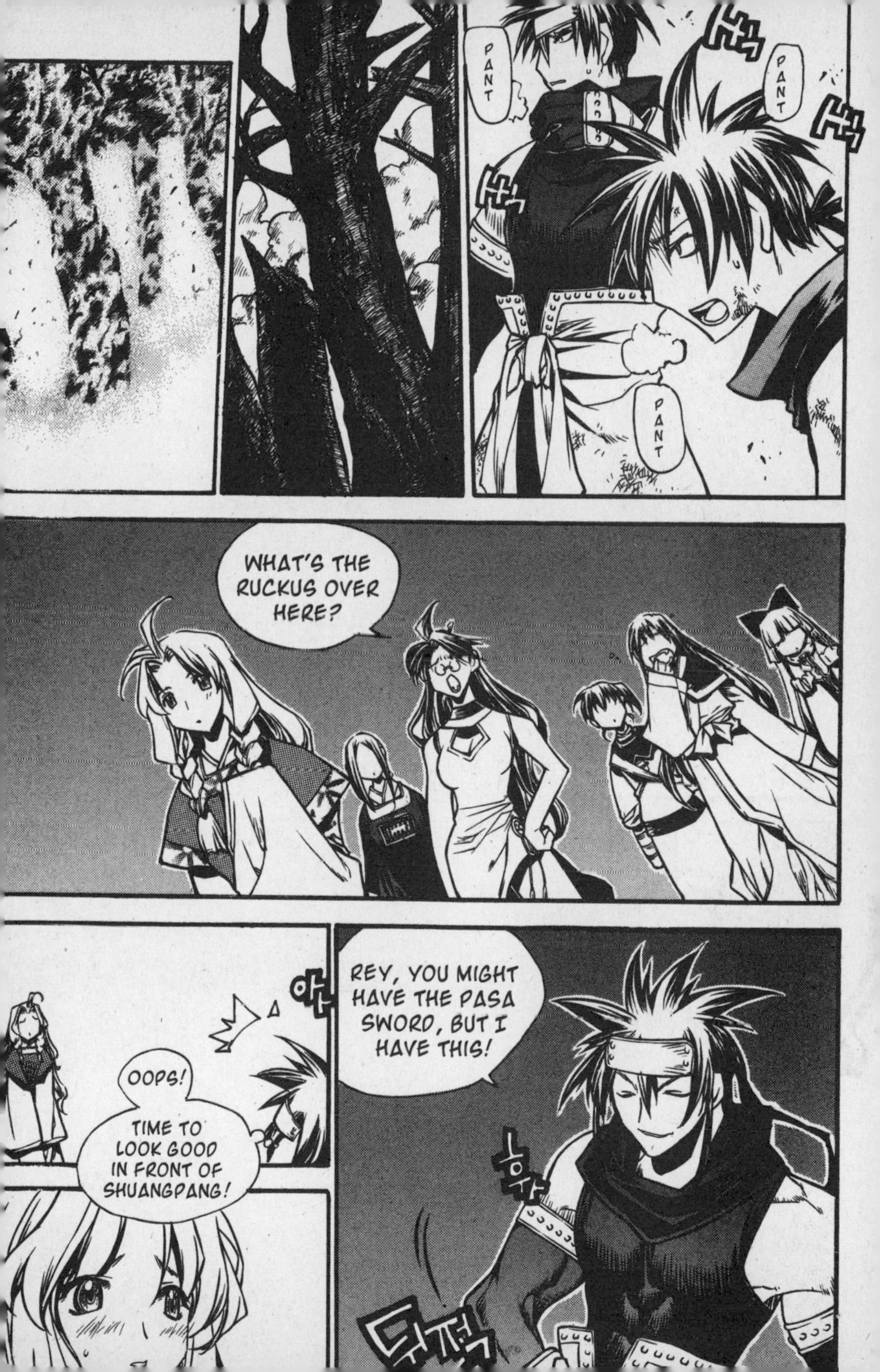
PANT
PANT
PANT
WHAT'S THE RUCKUS OVER HERE?
OOPS!
TIME TO LOOK GOOD IN FRONT OF SHUANGPANG!
REY, YOU MIGHT HAVE THE PASA SWORD, BUT I HAVE THIS!

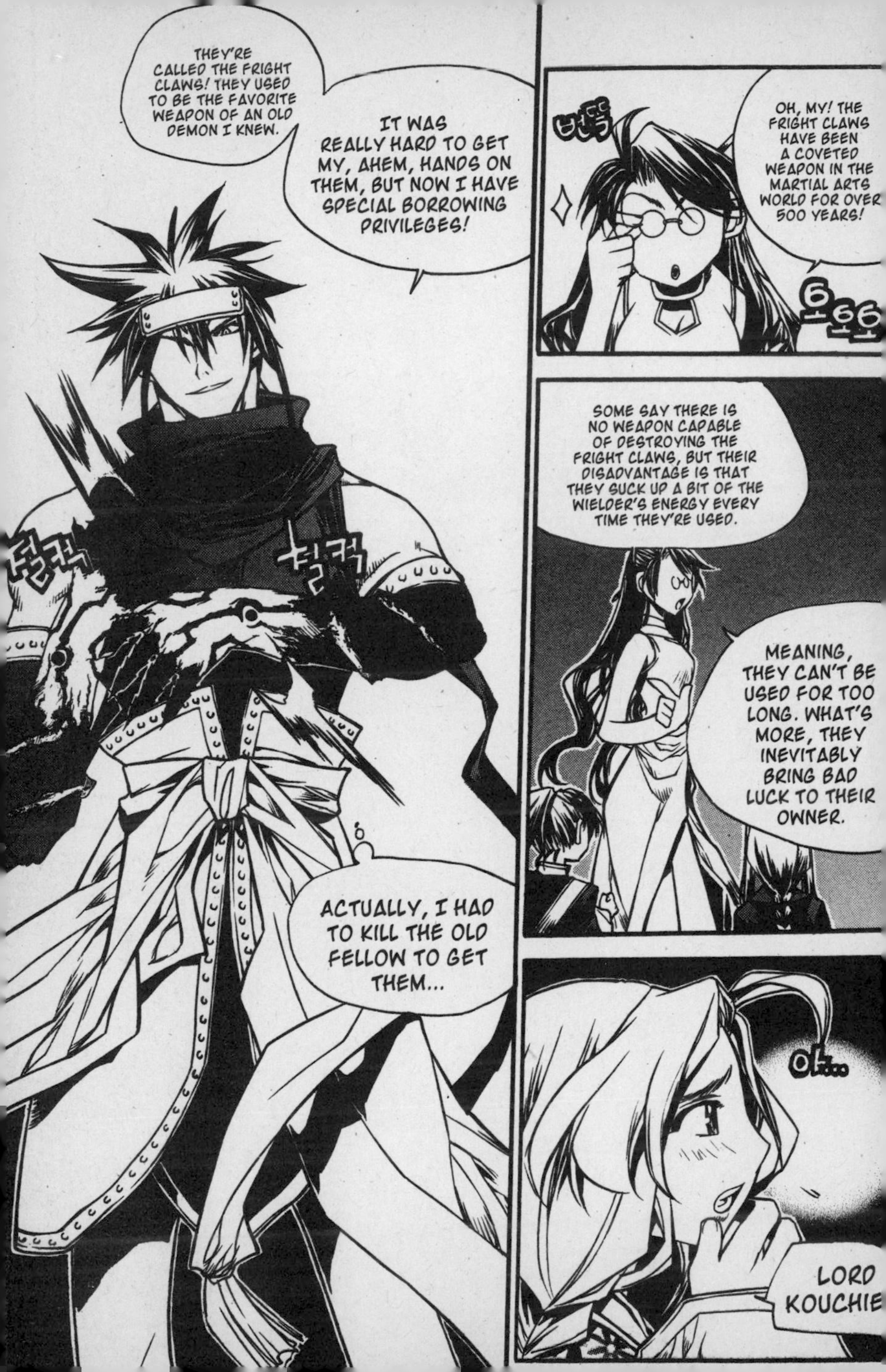
THEY'RE CALLED THE FRIGHT CLAWS! THEY USED TO BE THE FAVORITE WEAPON OF AN OLD DEMON I KNEW.
IT WAS REALLY HARD TO GET MY, AHEM, HANDS ON THEM, BUT NOW I HAVE SPECIAL BORROWING PRIVILEGES!
ACTUALLY, I HAD TO KILL THE OLD FELLOW TO GET THEM...
OH, MY! THE FRIGHT CLAWS HAVE BEEN A COVETED WEAPON IN THE MARTIAL ARTS WORLD FOR OVER 500 YEARS!
SOME SAY THERE IS NO WEAPON CAPABLE OF DESTROYING THE FRIGHT CLAWS, BUT THEIR DISADVANTAGE IS THAT THEY SUCK UP A BIT OF THE WIELDER'S ENERGY EVERY TIME THEY'RE USED.
MEANING, THEY CAN'T BE USED FOR TOO LONG. WHAT'S MORE, THEY INEVITABLY BRING BAD LUCK TO THEIR OWNER.
LORD KOUCHIE

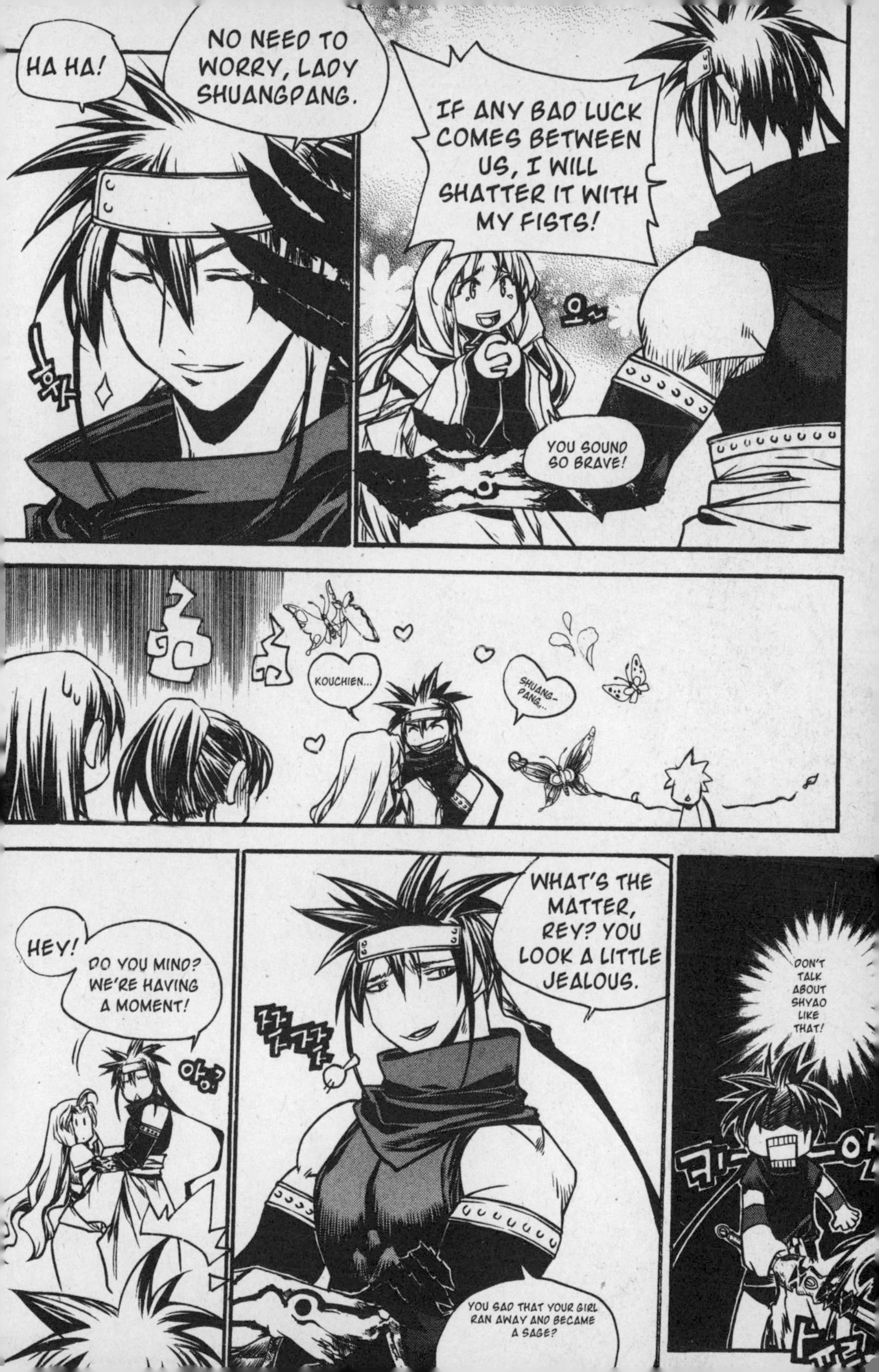
HA HA!
NO NEED TO WORRY, LADY SHUANGPANG.
IF ANY BAD LUCK COMES BETWEEN US, I WILL SHATTER IT WITH MY FISTS!
YOU SOUND SO BRAVE!
KOUCHIEN...
SHUANG-PANG...
HEY!
DO YOU MIND? WE'RE HAVING A MOMENT!
WHAT'S THE MATTER, REY? YOU LOOK A LITTLE JEALOUS.
YOU SAID THAT YOUR GIRL RAN AWAY AND BECAME A SAGE?
DON'T TALK ABOUT SHYAO LIKE THAT!

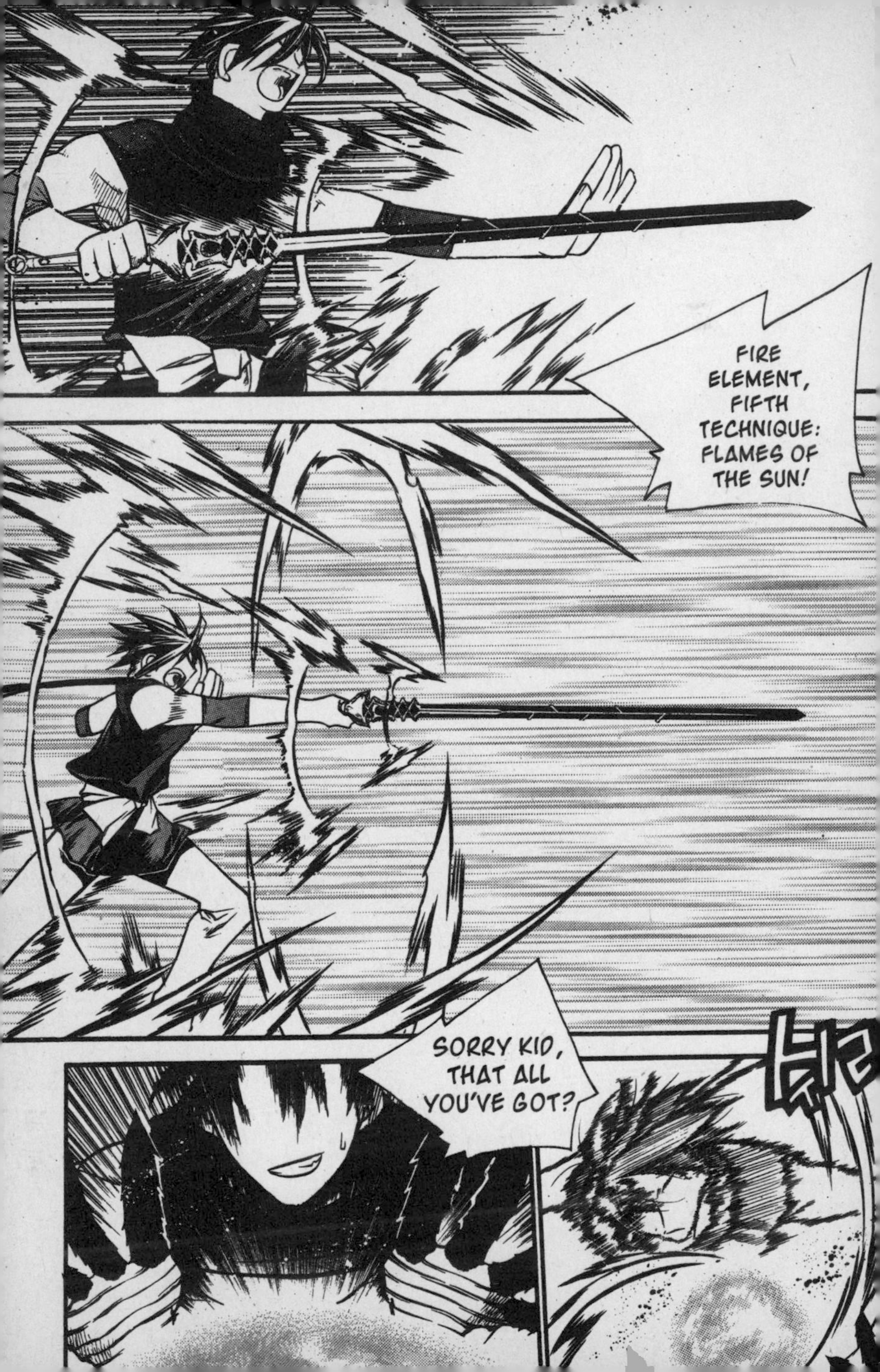
FIRE ELEMENT, FIFTH TECHNIQUE: FLAMES OF THE SUN!
SORRY KID, THAT ALL YOU'VE GOT?

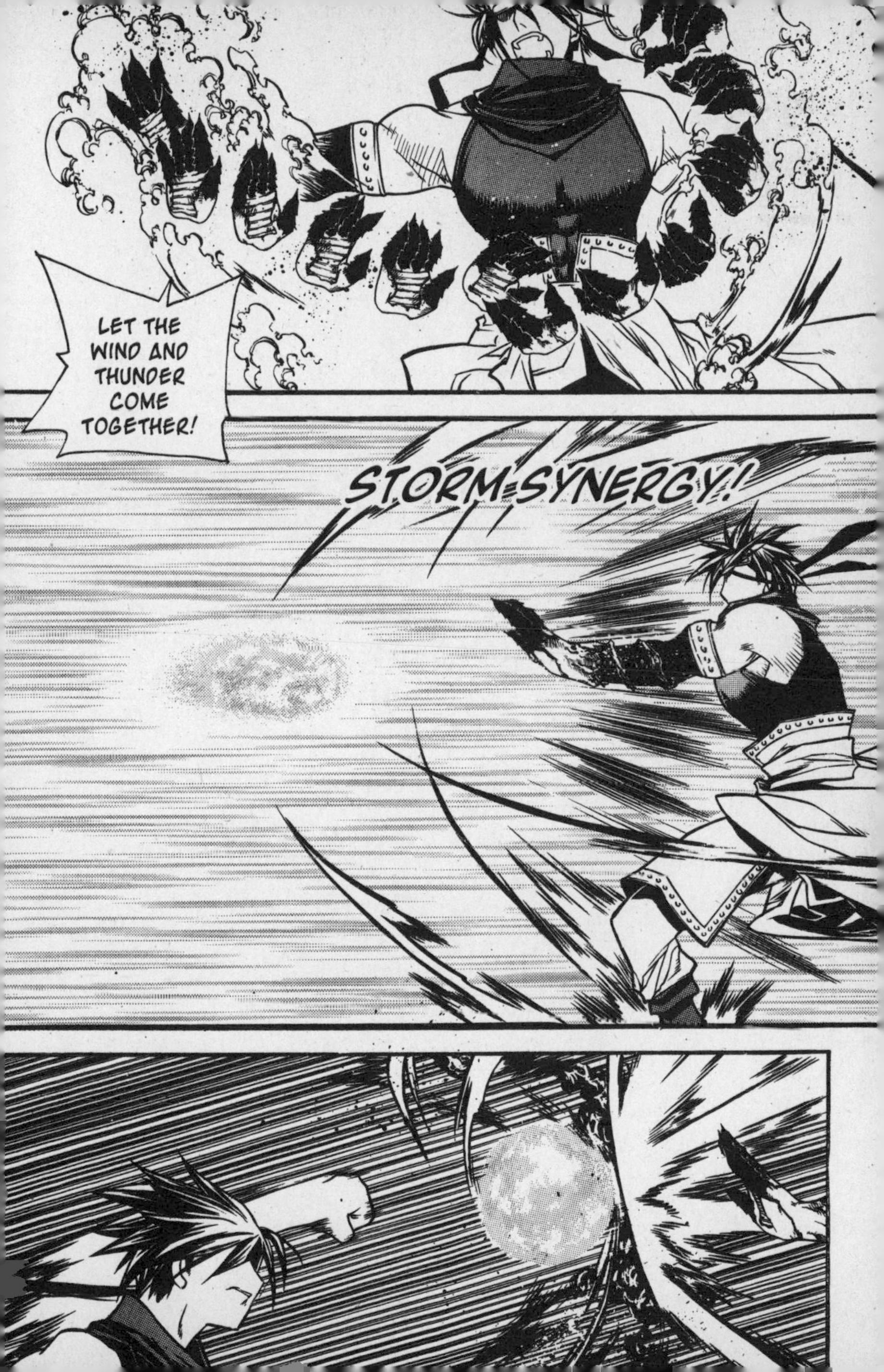
LET THE WIND AND THUNDER COME TOGETHER!
STORM SYNERGY!

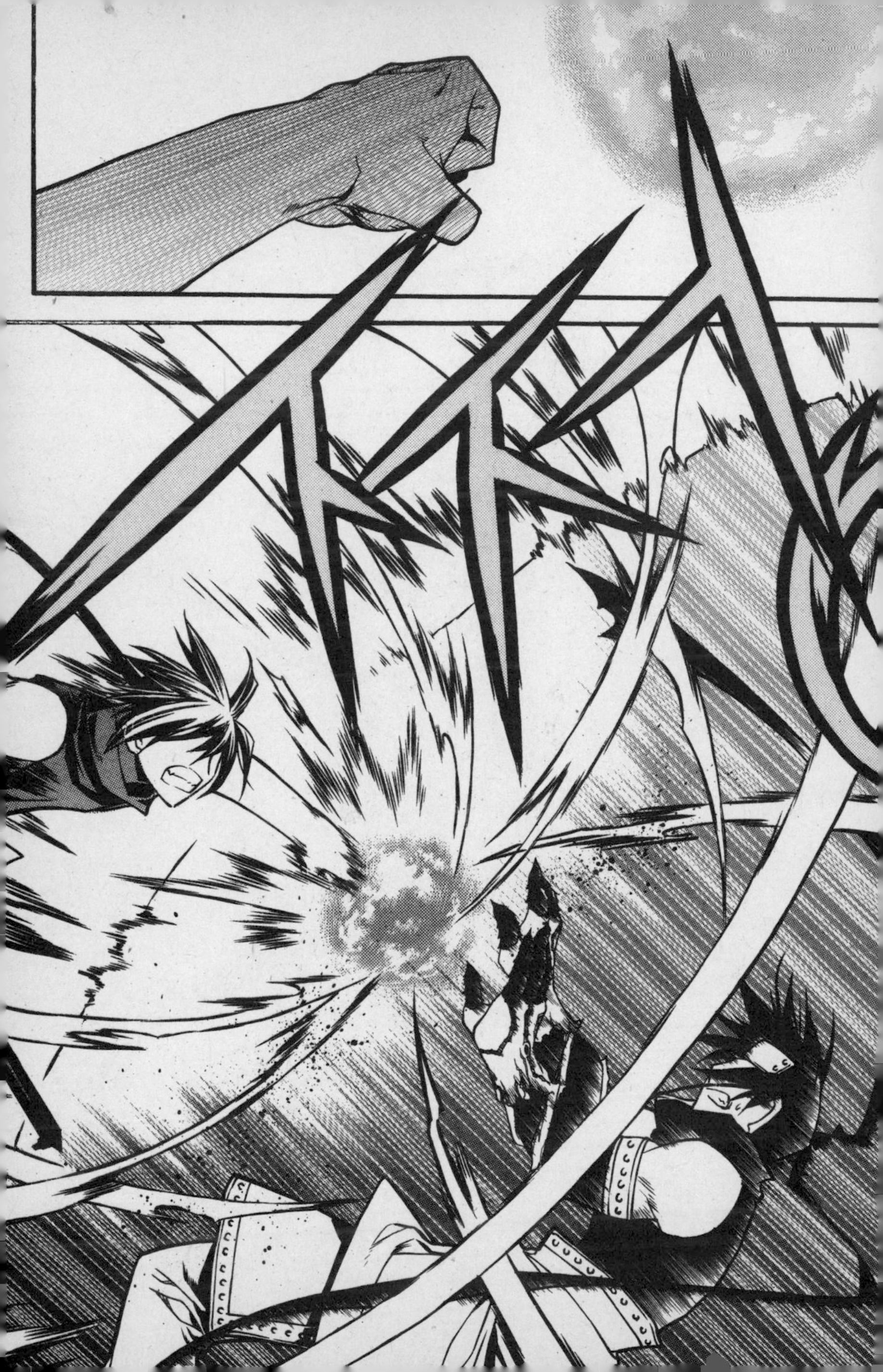

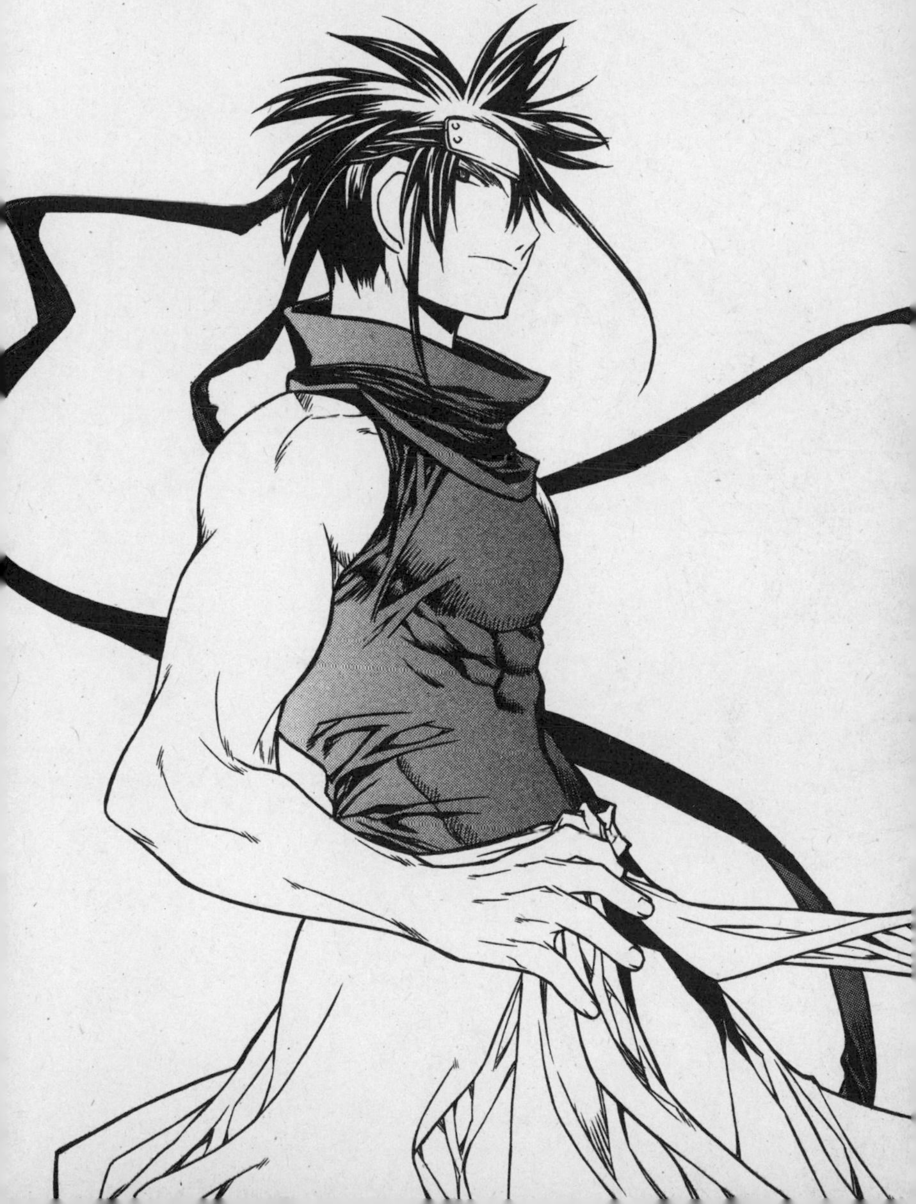

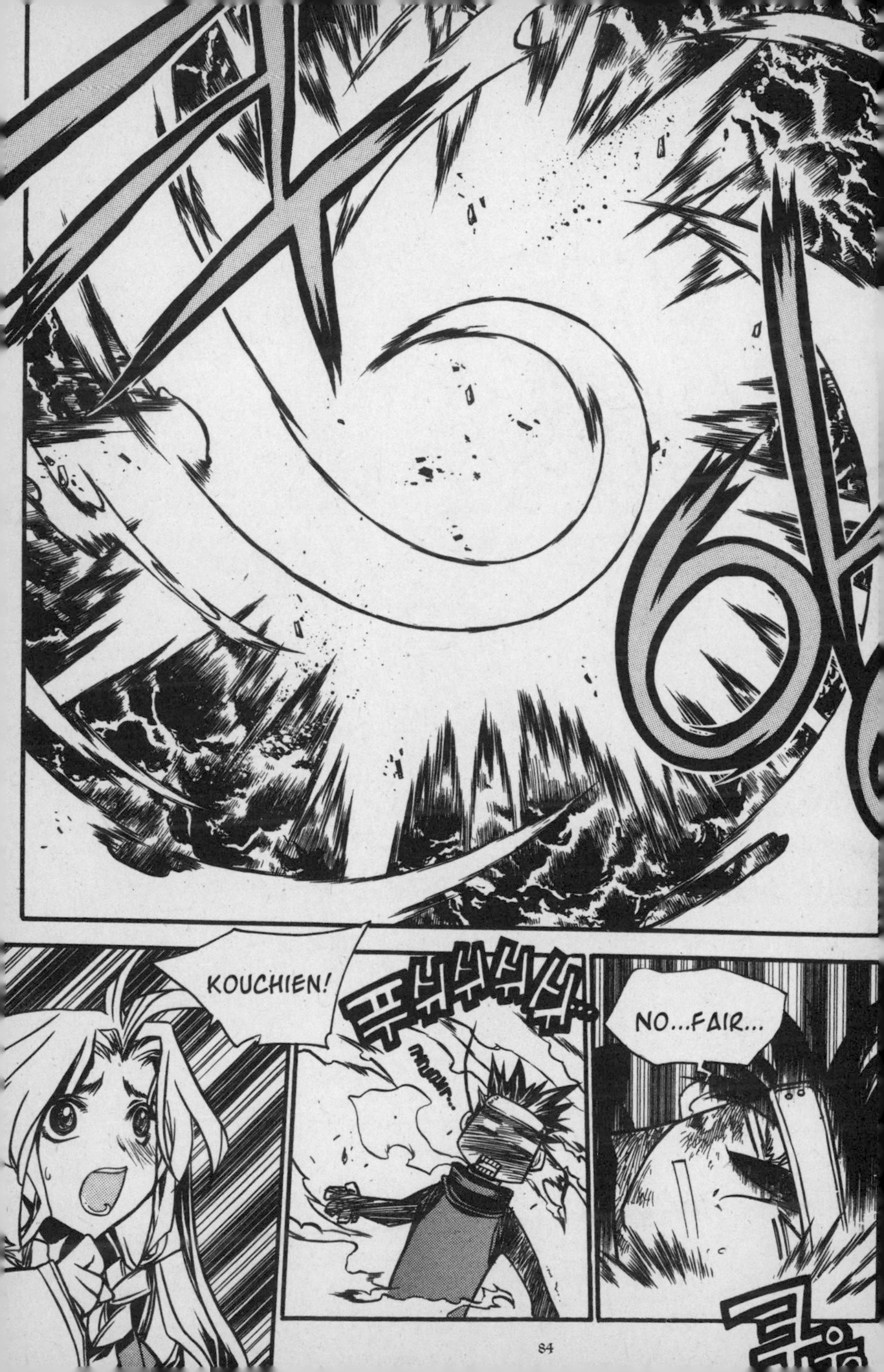
KOUCHIEN!
NO...FAIR...

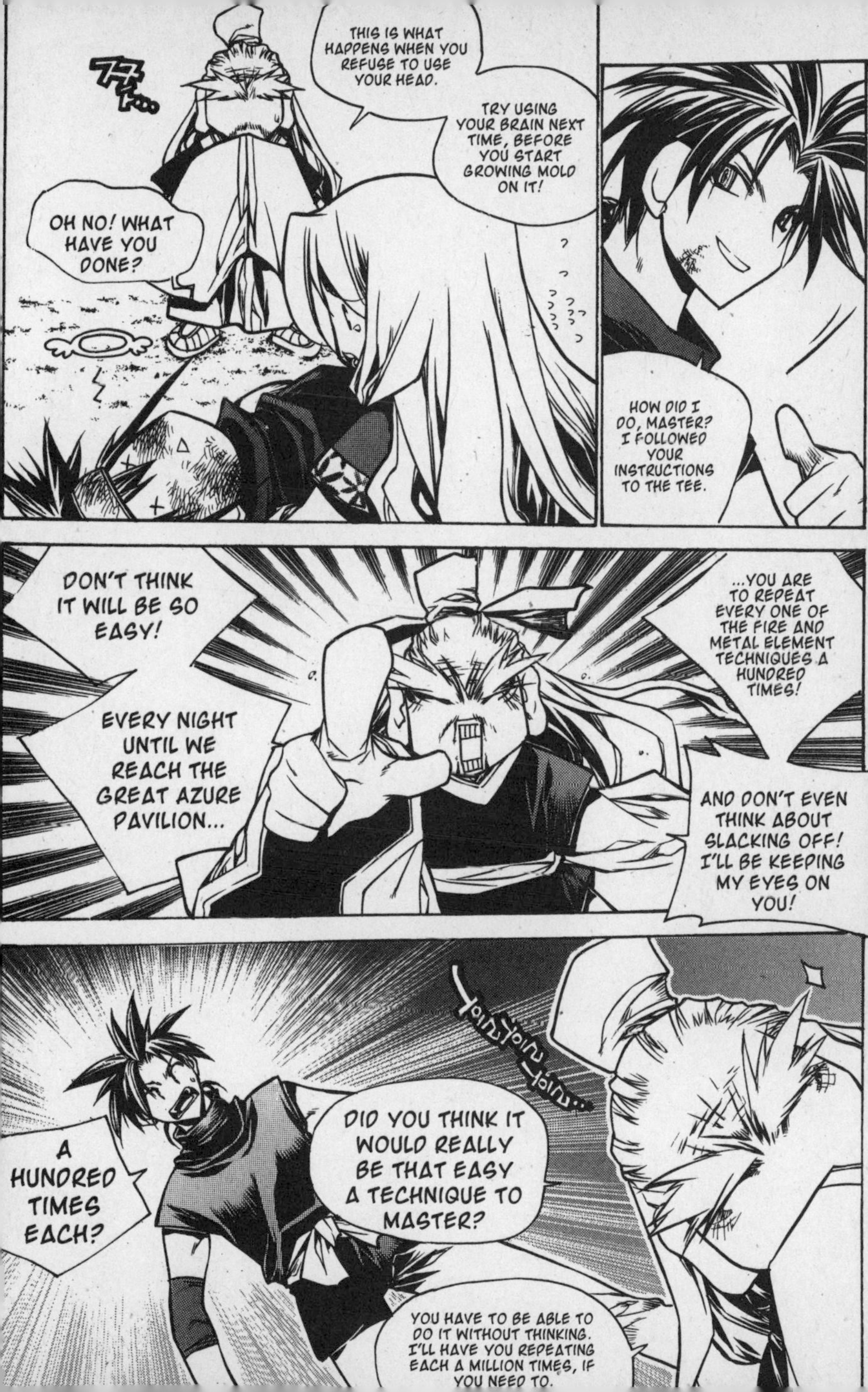
HOW DID I DO, MASTER? I FOLLOWED YOUR INSTRUCTIONS TO THE TEE.
THIS IS WHAT HAPPENS WHEN YOU REFUSE TO USE YOUR HEAD.
TRY USING YOUR BRAIN NEXT TIME, BEFORE YOU START GROWING MOLD ON IT!
OH NO! WHAT HAVE YOU DONE?
DON'T THINK IT WILL BE SO EASY!
EVERY NIGHT UNTIL WE REACH THE GREAT AZURE PAVILION...
...YOU ARE TO REPEAT EVERY ONE OF THE FIRE AND METAL ELEMENT TECHNIQUES A HUNDRED TIMES!
AND DON'T EVEN THINK ABOUT SLACKING OFF! I'LL BE KEEPING MY EYES ON YOU!
A HUNDRED TIMES EACH?
DID YOU THINK IT WOULD REALLY BE THAT EASY A TECHNIQUE TO MASTER?
YOU HAVE TO BE ABLE TO DO IT WITHOUT THINKING. I'LL HAVE YOU REPEATING EACH A MILLION TIMES, IF YOU NEED TO.

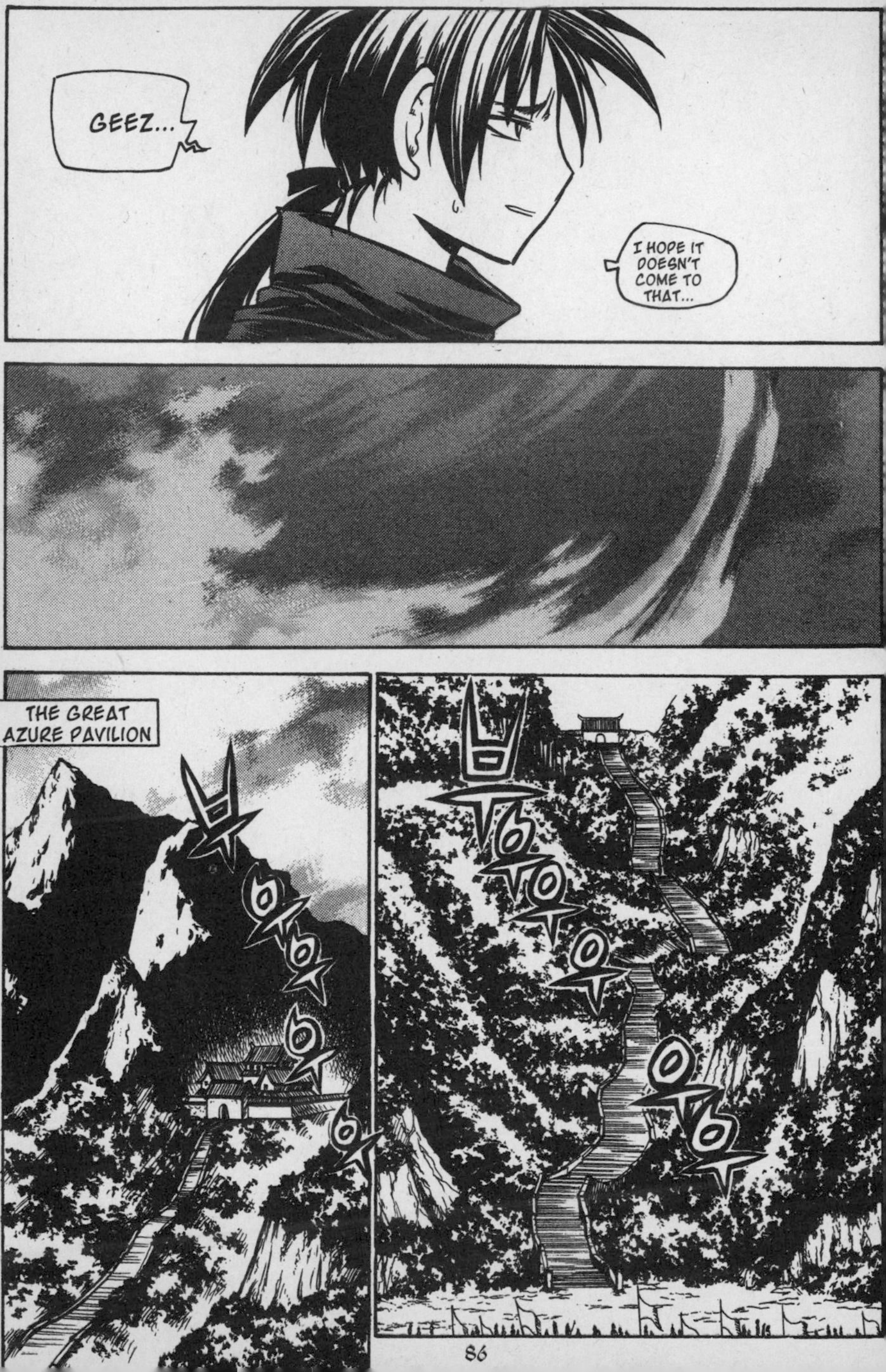
GEEZ...
I HOPE IT DOESN'T COME TO THAT...
THE GREAT AZURE PAVILION

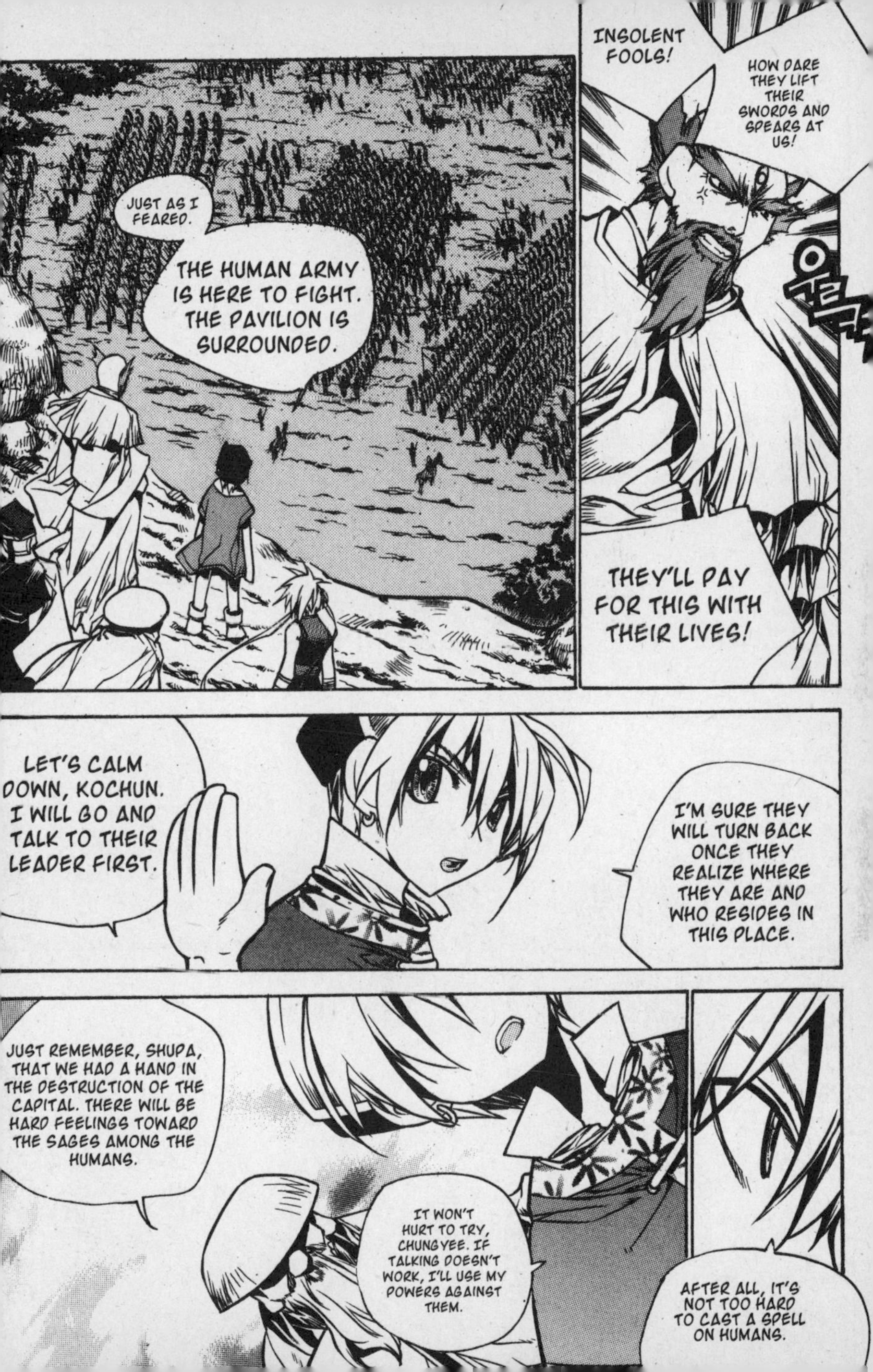
JUST AS I FEARED.
THE HUMAN ARMY IS HERE TO FIGHT. THE PAVILION IS SURROUNDED.
INSOLENT FOOLS!
HOW DARE THEY LIFT THEIR SWORDS AND SPEARS AT US!
THEY'LL PAY FOR THIS WITH THEIR LIVES!
LET'S CALM DOWN, KOCHUN. I WILL GO AND TALK TO THEIR LEADER FIRST.
I'M SURE THEY WILL TURN BACK ONCE THEY REALIZE WHERE THEY ARE AND WHO RESIDES IN THIS PLACE.
JUST REMEMBER, SHUPA, THAT WE HAD A HAND IN THE DESTRUCTION OF THE CAPITAL. THERE WILL BE HARD FEELINGS TOWARD THE SAGES AMONG THE HUMANS.
IT WON'T HURT TO TRY, CHUNGYEE. IF TALKING DOESN'T WORK, I'LL USE MY POWERS AGAINST THEM.
AFTER ALL, IT'S NOT TOO HARD TO CAST A SPELL ON HUMANS.

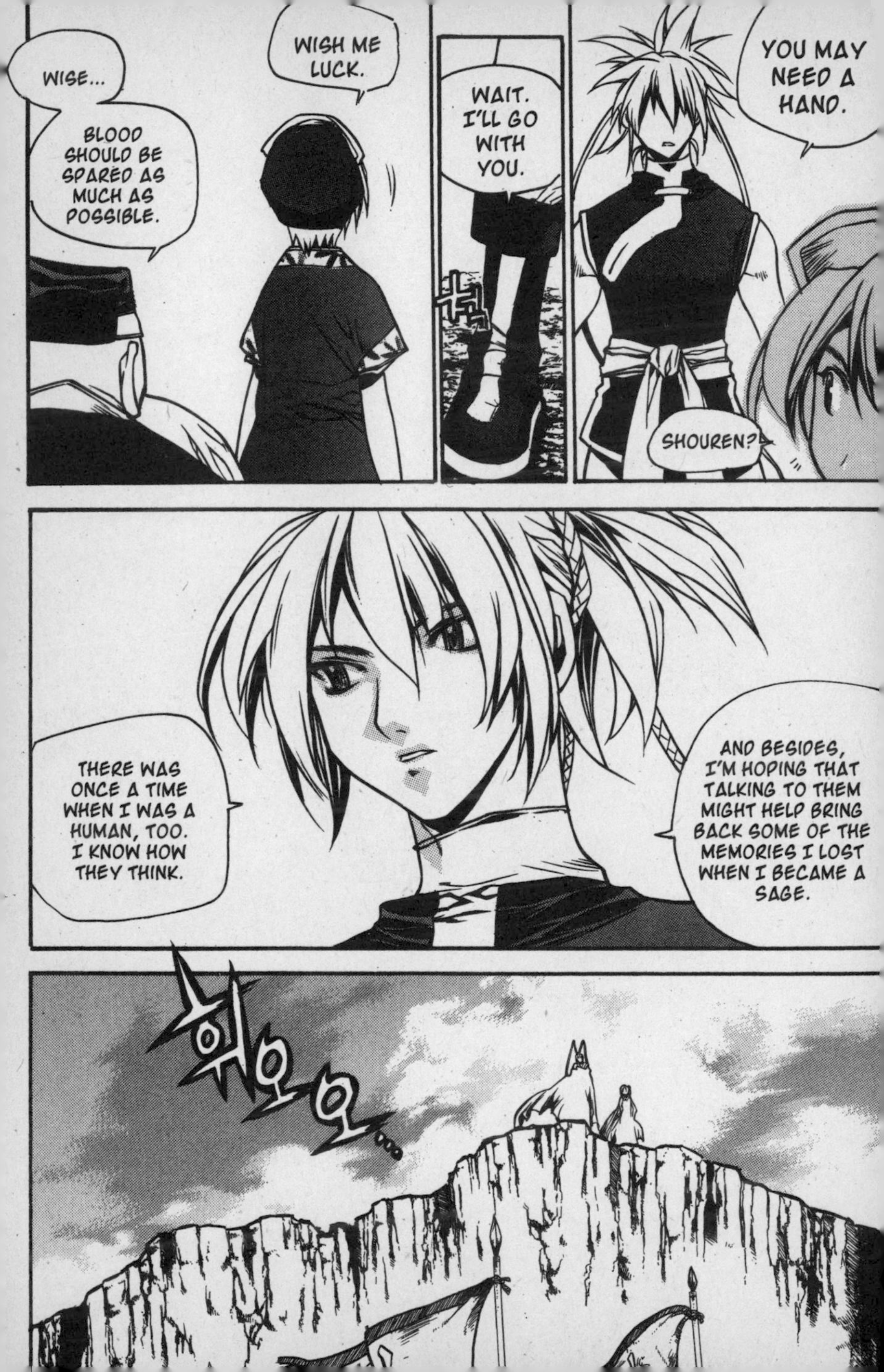
WISE...
BLOOD SHOULD BE SPARED AS MUCH AS POSSIBLE.
WISH ME LUCK.
WAIT. I'LL GO WITH YOU.
YOU MAY NEED A HAND.
SHOUREN?
THERE WAS ONCE A TIME WHEN I WAS A HUMAN, TOO. I KNOW HOW THEY THINK.
AND BESIDES, I'M HOPING THAT TALKING TO THEM MIGHT HELP BRING BACK SOME OF THE MEMORIES I LOST WHEN I BECAME A SAGE.
히오오...

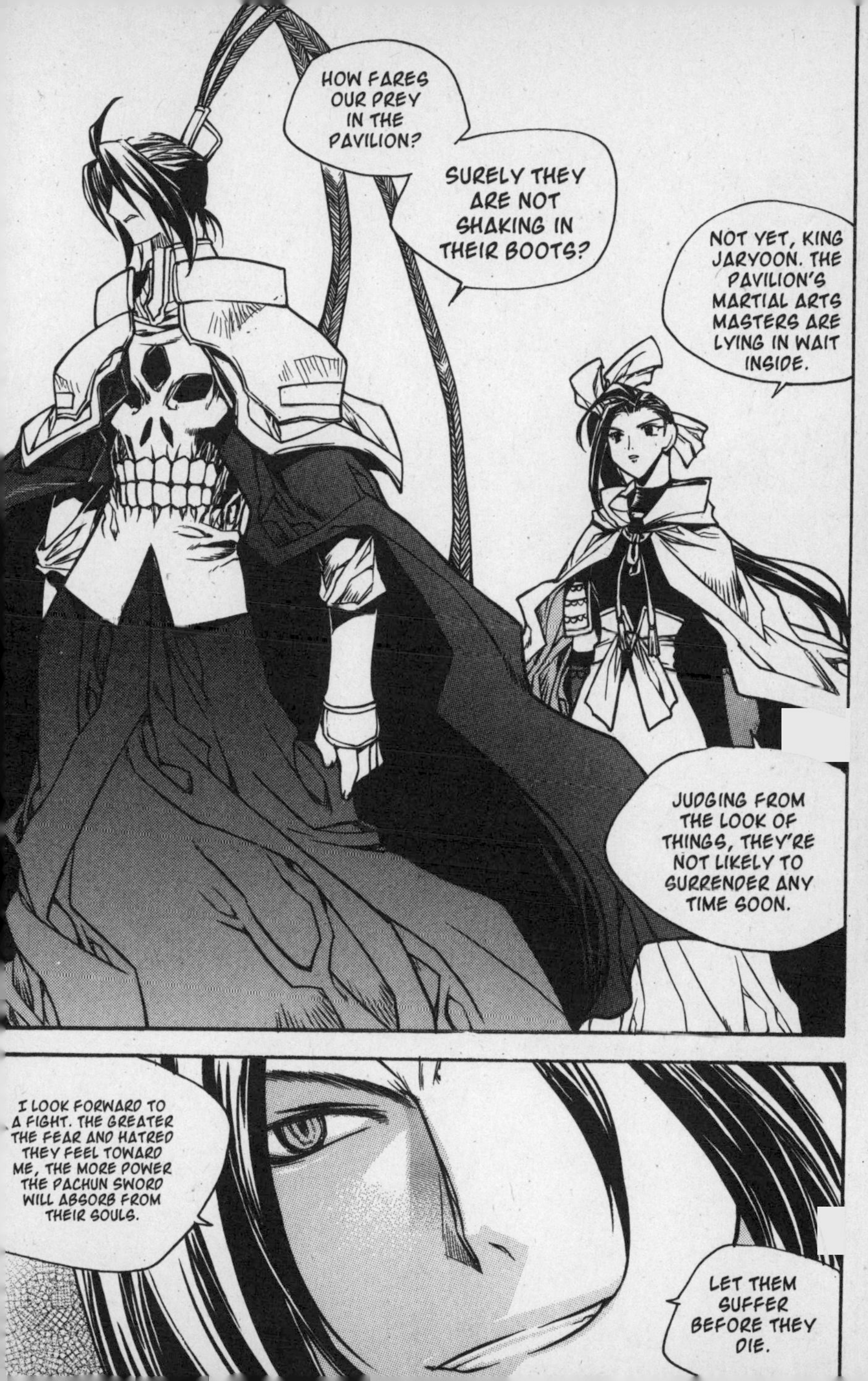
HOW FARES OUR PREY IN THE PAVILION?
SURELY THEY ARE NOT SHAKING IN THEIR BOOTS?
NOT YET, KING JARYOON. THE PAVILION'S MARTIAL ARTS MASTERS ARE LYING IN WAIT INSIDE.
JUDGING FROM THE LOOK OF THINGS, THEY'RE NOT LIKELY TO SURRENDER ANY TIME SOON.
I LOOK FORWARD TO A FIGHT. THE GREATER THE FEAR AND HATRED THEY FEEL TOWARD ME, THE MORE POWER THE PACHUN SWORD WILL ABSORB FROM THEIR SOULS.
LET THEM SUFFER BEFORE THEY DIE.

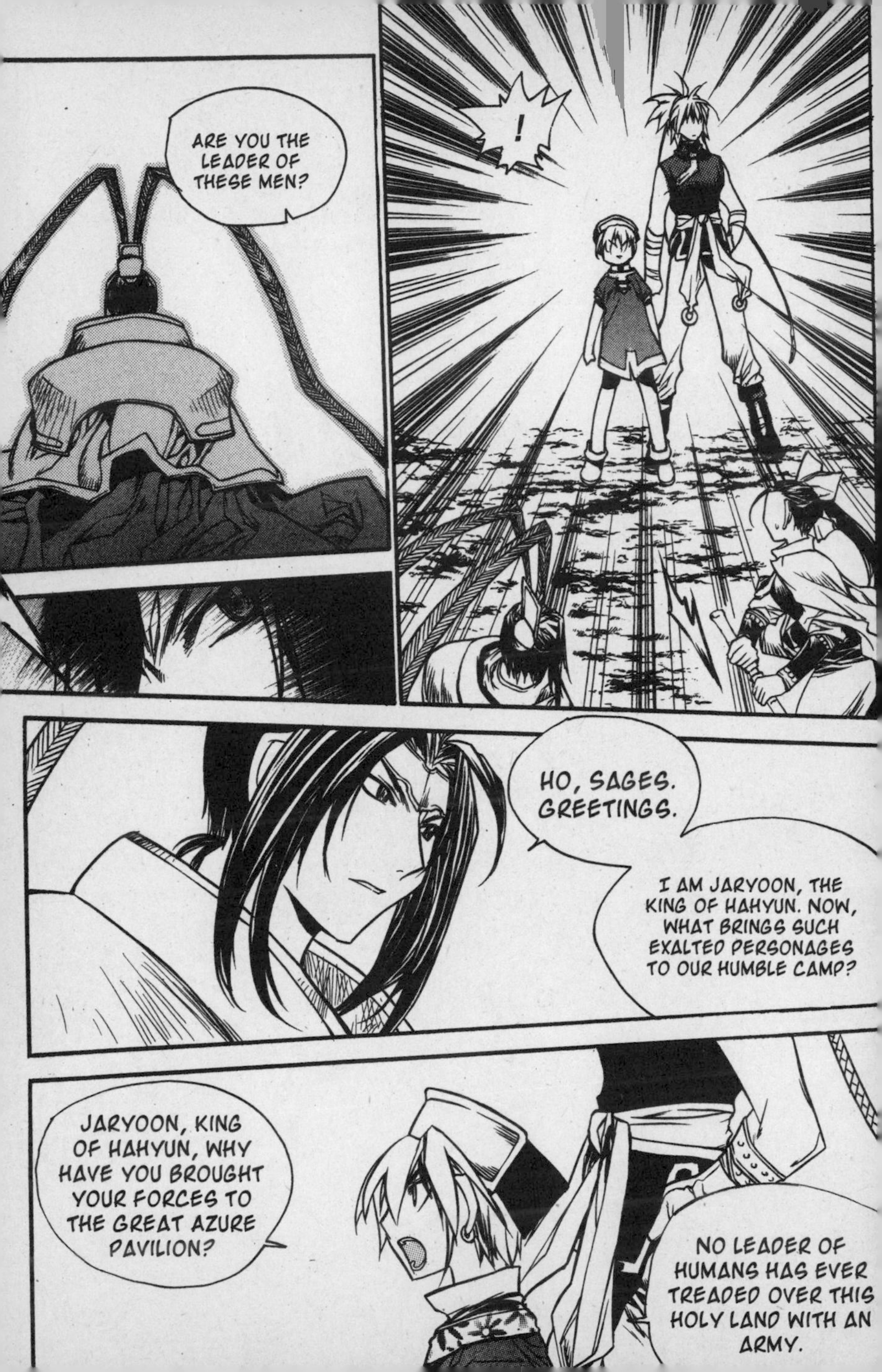
ARE YOU THE LEADER OF THESE MEN?
!
HO, SAGES. GREETINGS.
I AM JARYOON, THE KING OF HAHYUN. NOW, WHAT BRINGS SUCH EXALTED PERSONAGES TO OUR HUMBLE CAMP?
JARYOON, KING OF HAHYUN, WHY HAVE YOU BROUGHT YOUR FORCES TO THE GREAT AZURE PAVILION?
NO LEADER OF HUMANS HAS EVER TREADED OVER THIS HOLY LAND WITH AN ARMY.

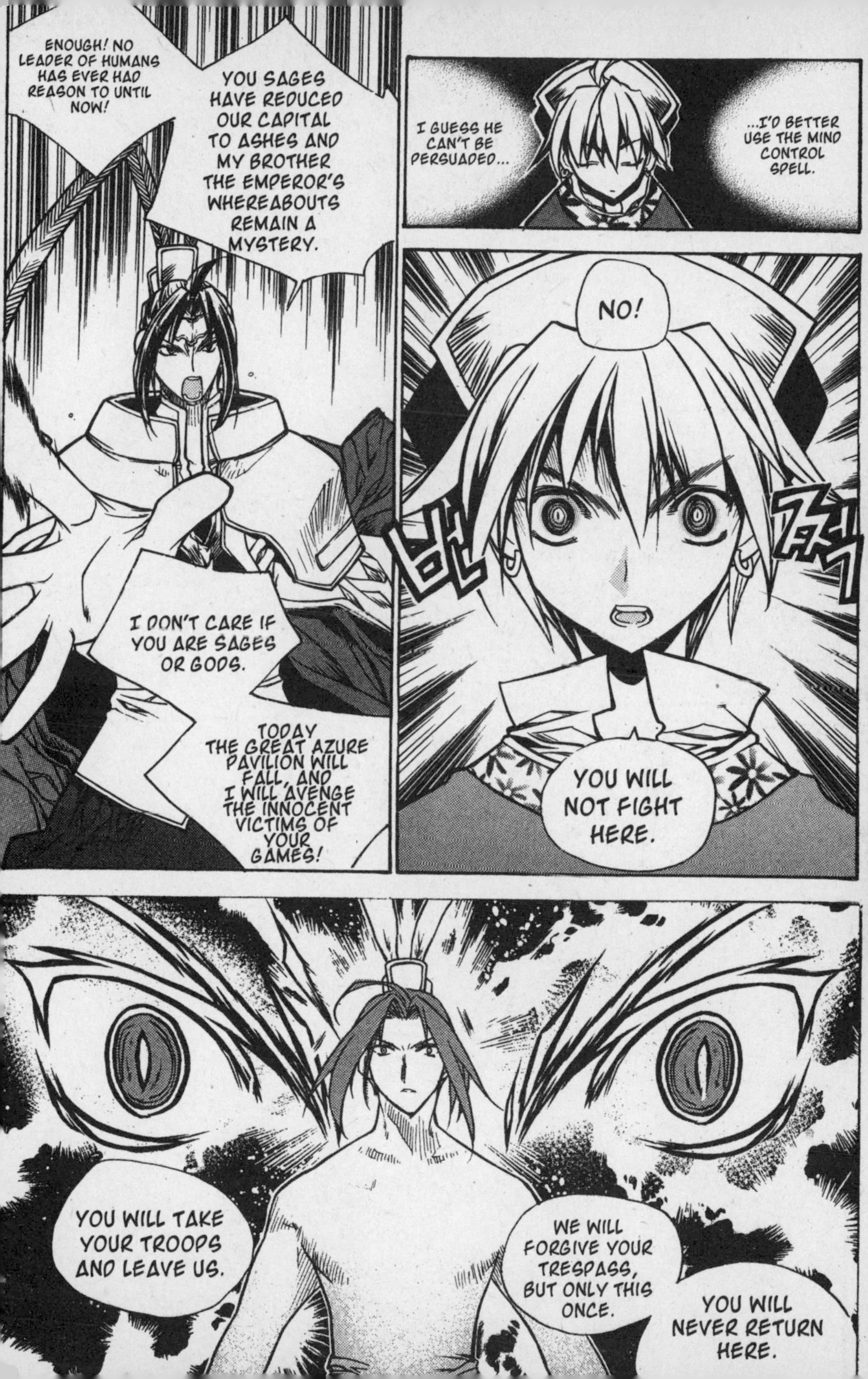
ENOUGH! NO LEADER OF HUMANS HAS EVER HAD REASON TO UNTIL NOW!
YOU SAGES HAVE REDUCED OUR CAPITAL TO ASHES AND MY BROTHER THE EMPEROR'S WHEREABOUTS REMAIN A MYSTERY.
I DON'T CARE IF YOU ARE SAGES OR GODS.
TODAY THE GREAT AZURE PAVILION WILL FALL, AND I WILL AVENGE THE INNOCENT VICTIMS OF YOUR GAMES!
I GUESS HE CAN'T BE PERSUADED...
...I'D BETTER USE THE MIND CONTROL SPELL.
NO!
YOU WILL NOT FIGHT HERE.
YOU WILL TAKE YOUR TROOPS AND LEAVE US.
WE WILL FORGIVE YOUR TRESPASS, BUT ONLY THIS ONCE.
YOU WILL NEVER RETURN HERE.

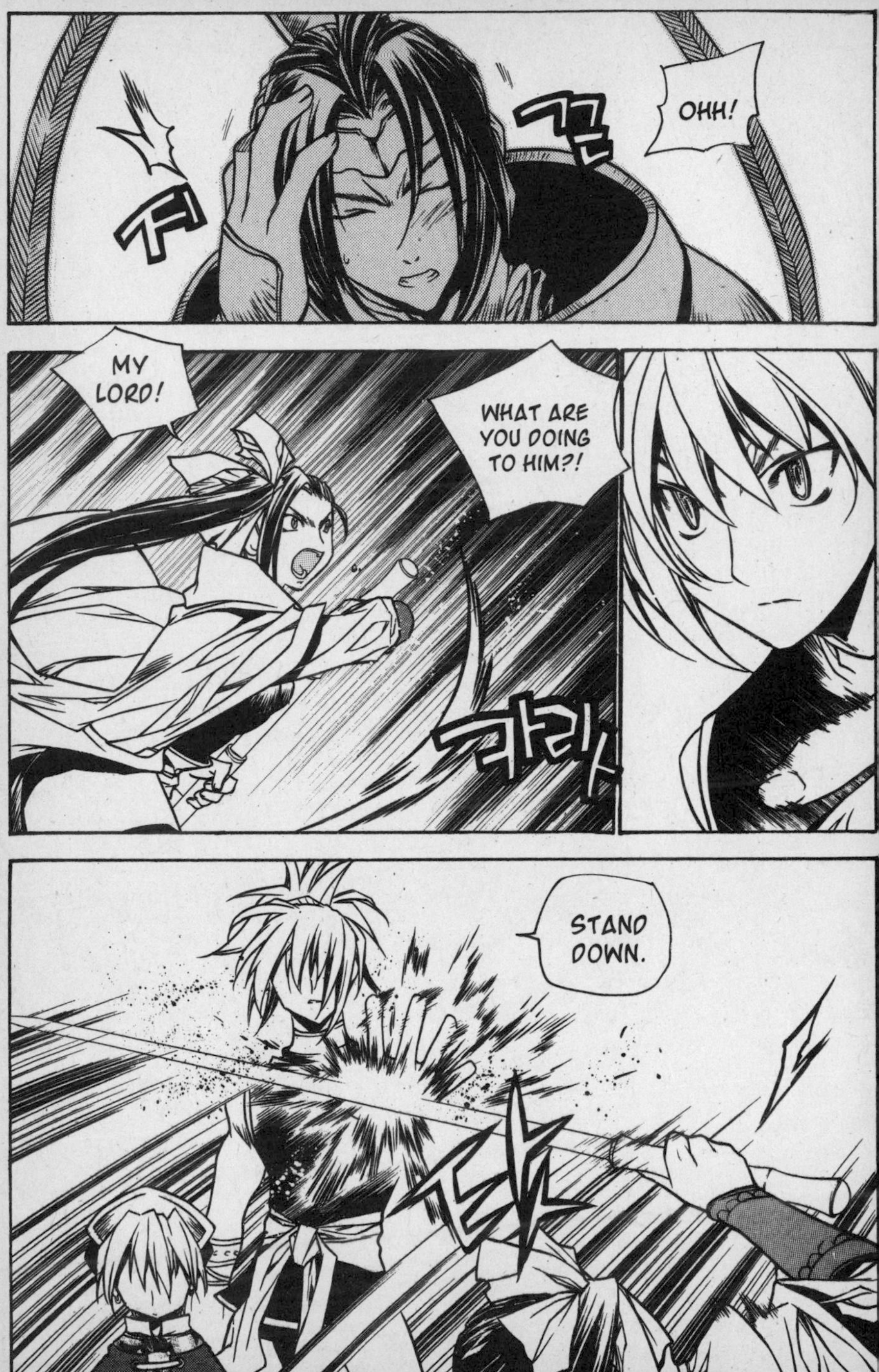
OHH!
MY LORD!
WHAT ARE YOU DOING TO HIM?!
STAND DOWN.

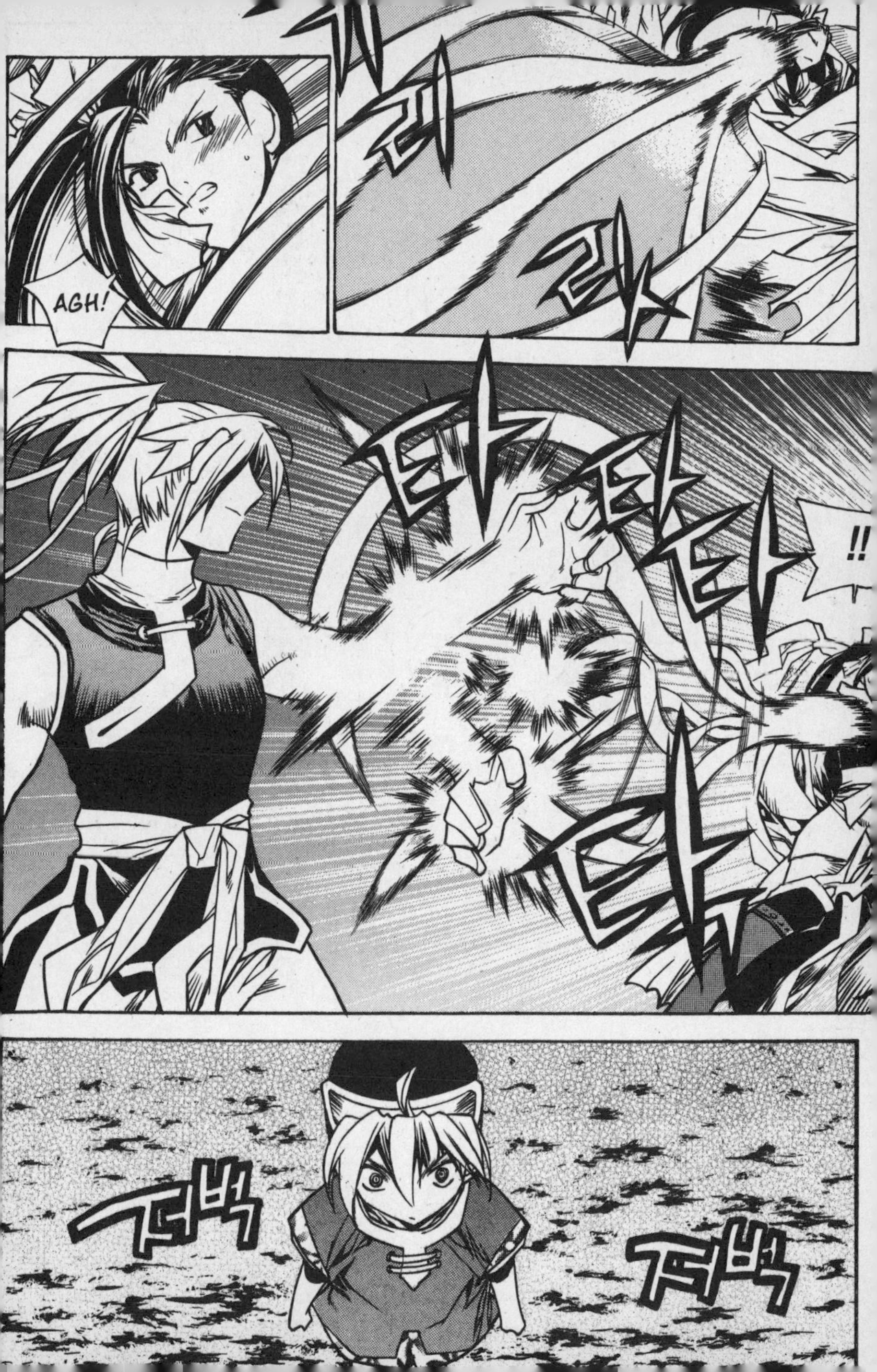
AGH!
!!

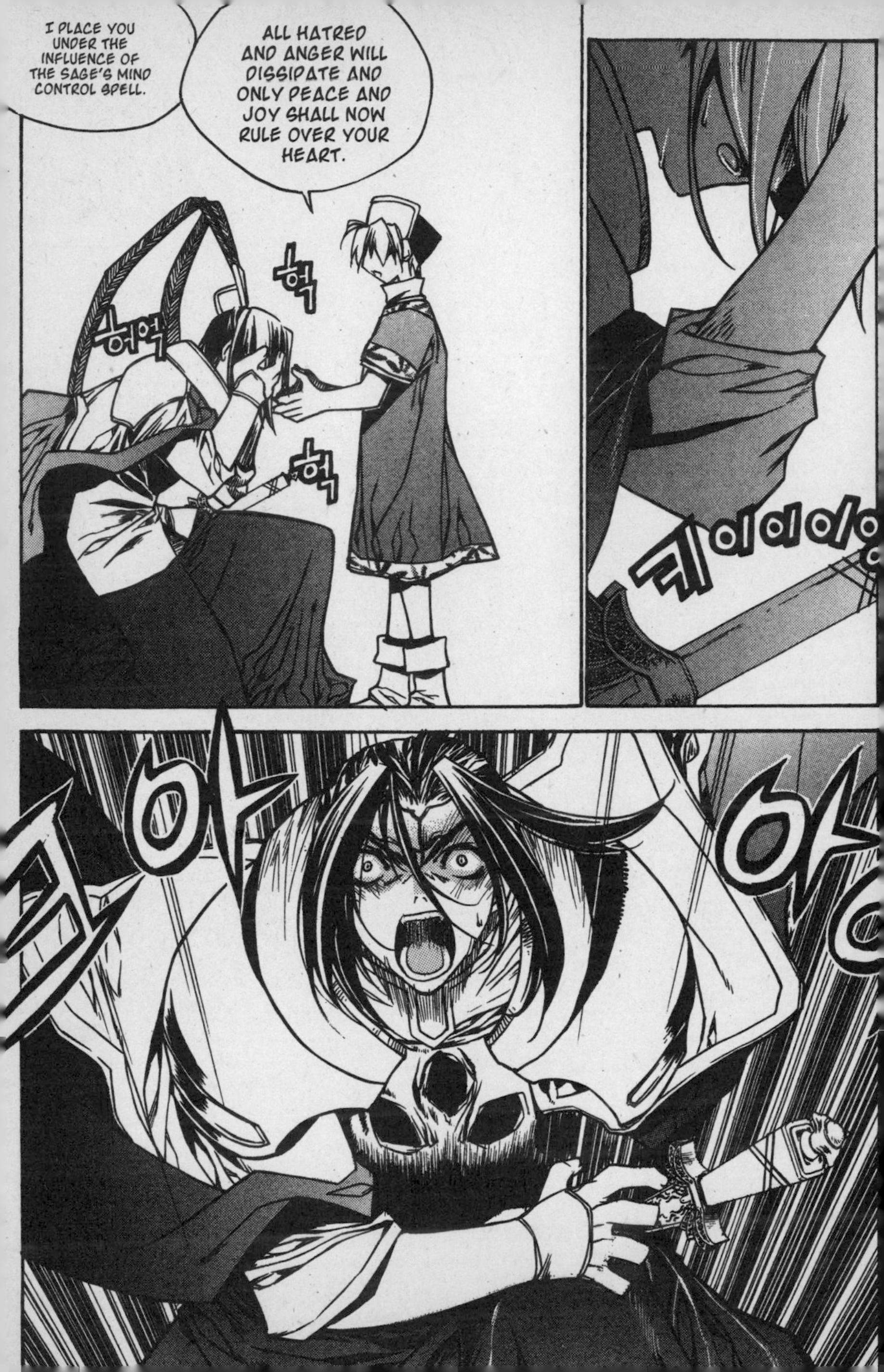
I PLACE YOU UNDER THE INFLUENCE OF THE SAGE'S MIND CONTROL SPELL.
ALL HATRED AND ANGER WILL DISSIPATE AND ONLY PEACE AND JOY SHALL NOW RULE OVER YOUR HEART.
헉
허억
헉
키이이이이
크아
아

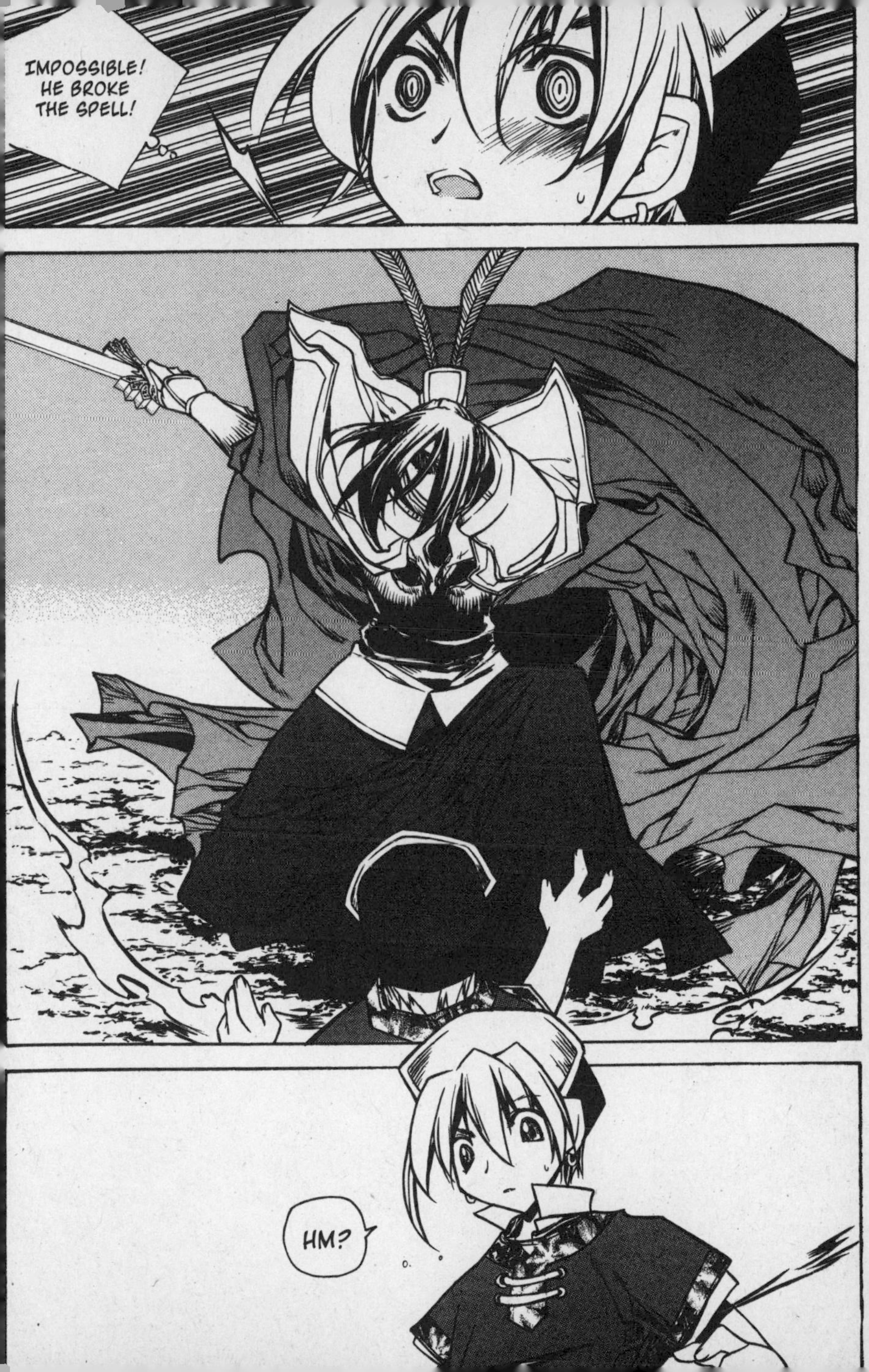
IMPOSSIBLE! HE BROKE THE SPELL!
HM?

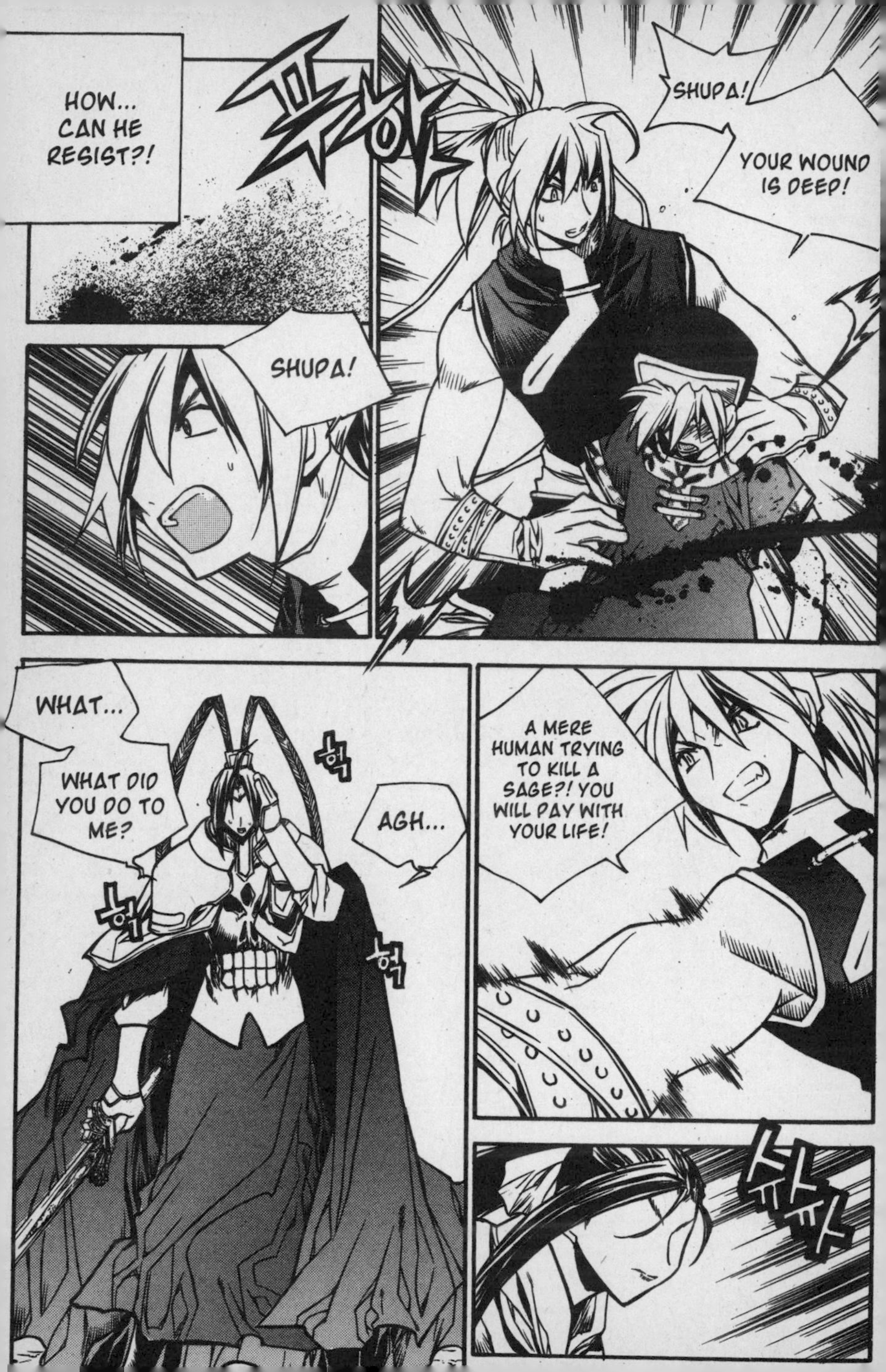
HOW... CAN HE RESIST?!
SHUPA!
SHUPA!
YOUR WOUND IS DEEP!
WHAT...
WHAT DID YOU DO TO ME?
헉
AGH...
헉
헉
A MERE HUMAN TRYING TO KILL A SAGE?! YOU WILL PAY WITH YOUR LIFE!

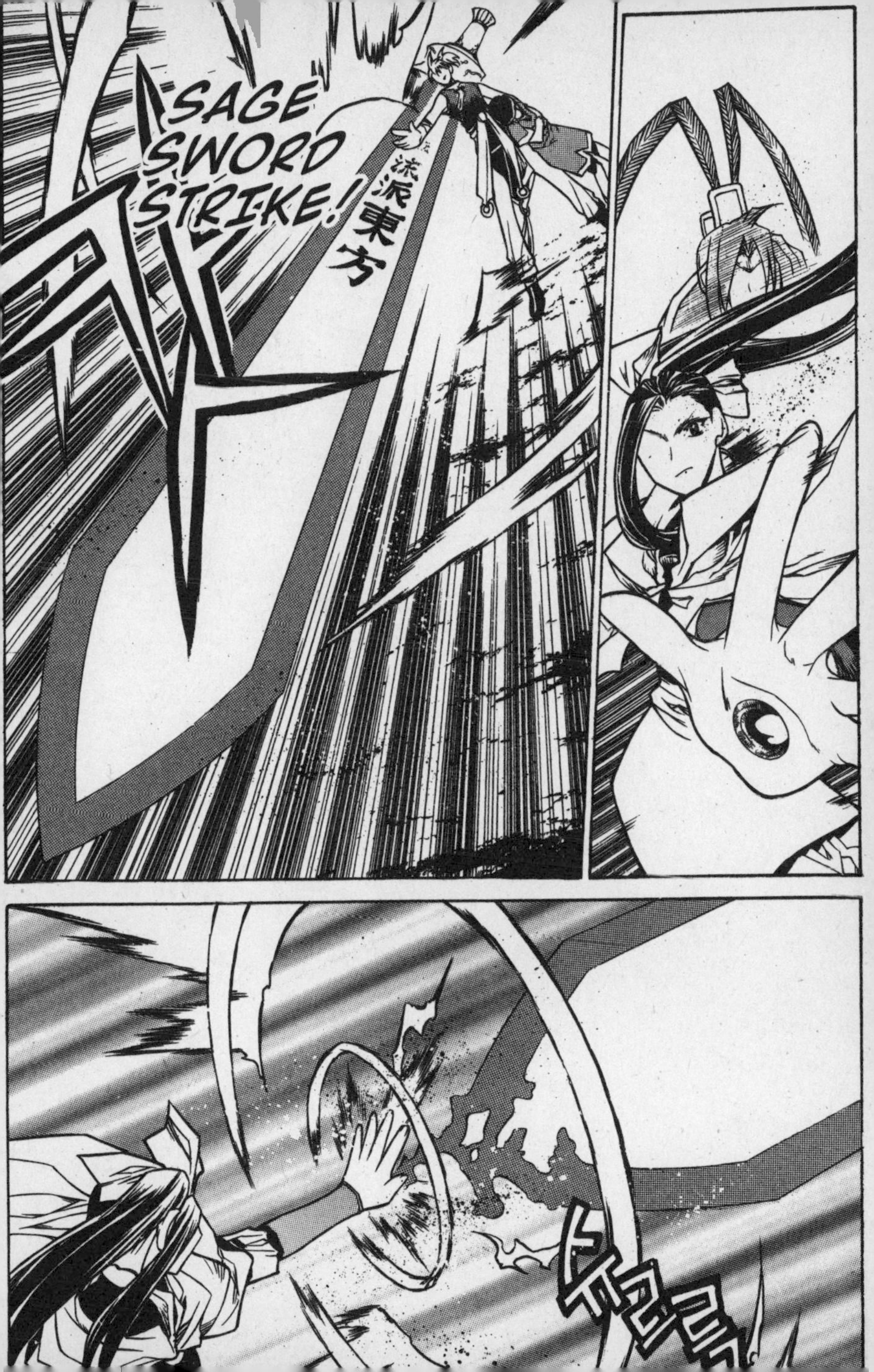
SAGE SWORD STRIKE!
流派東方

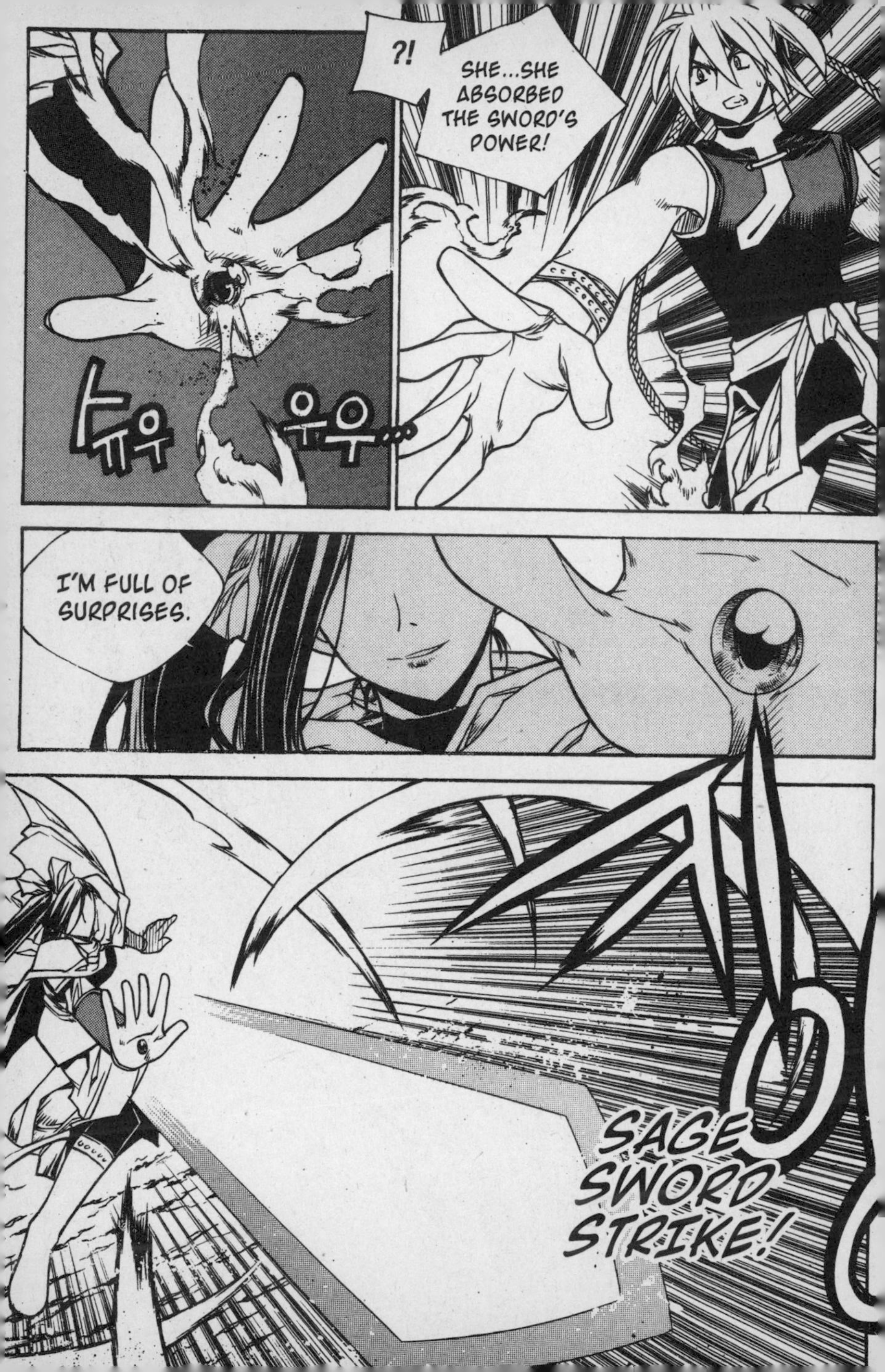
뉴우 우우...
?!
SHE...SHE ABSORBED THE SWORD'S POWER!
I'M FULL OF SURPRISES.
SAGE SWORD STRIKE!

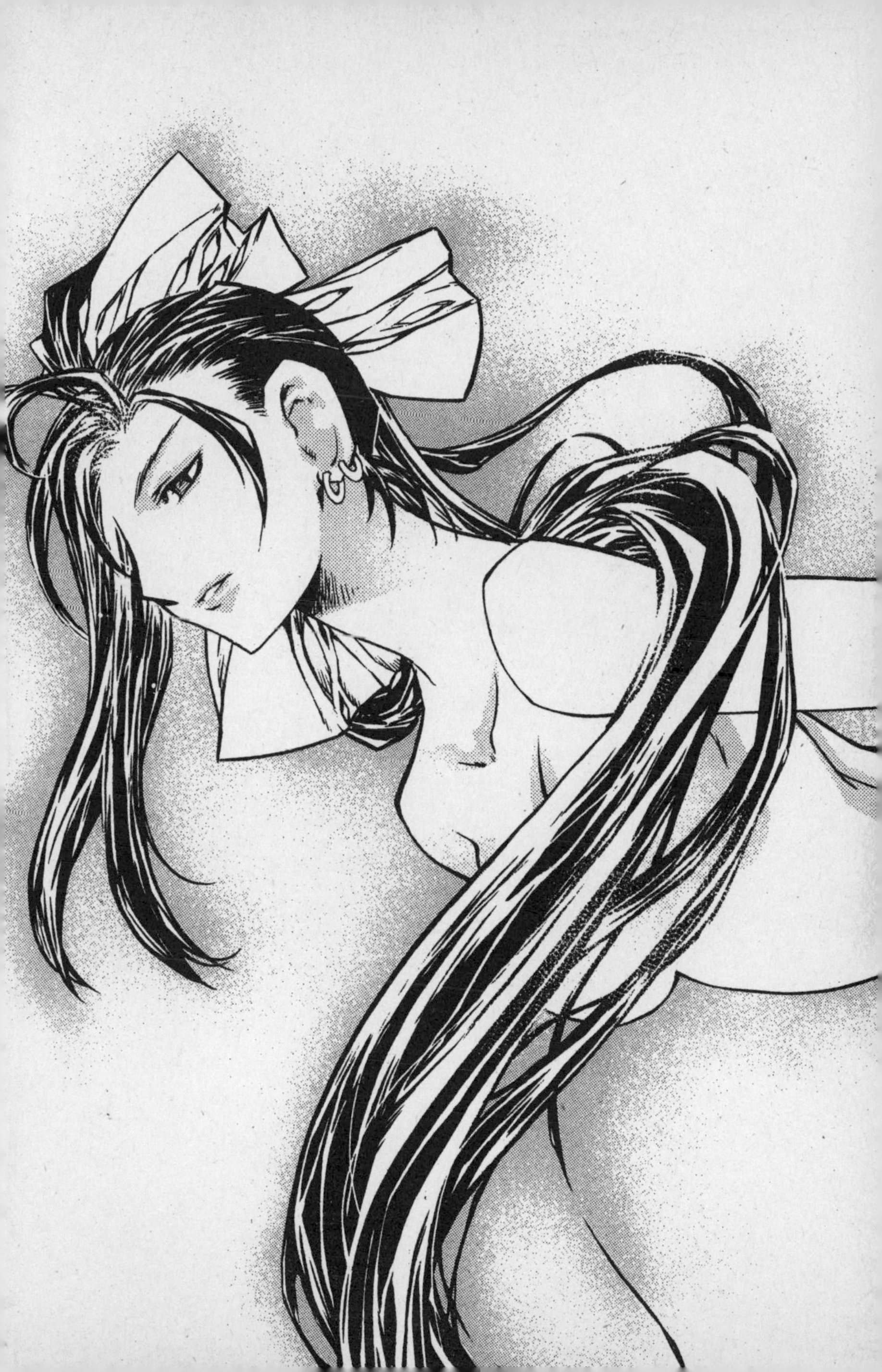

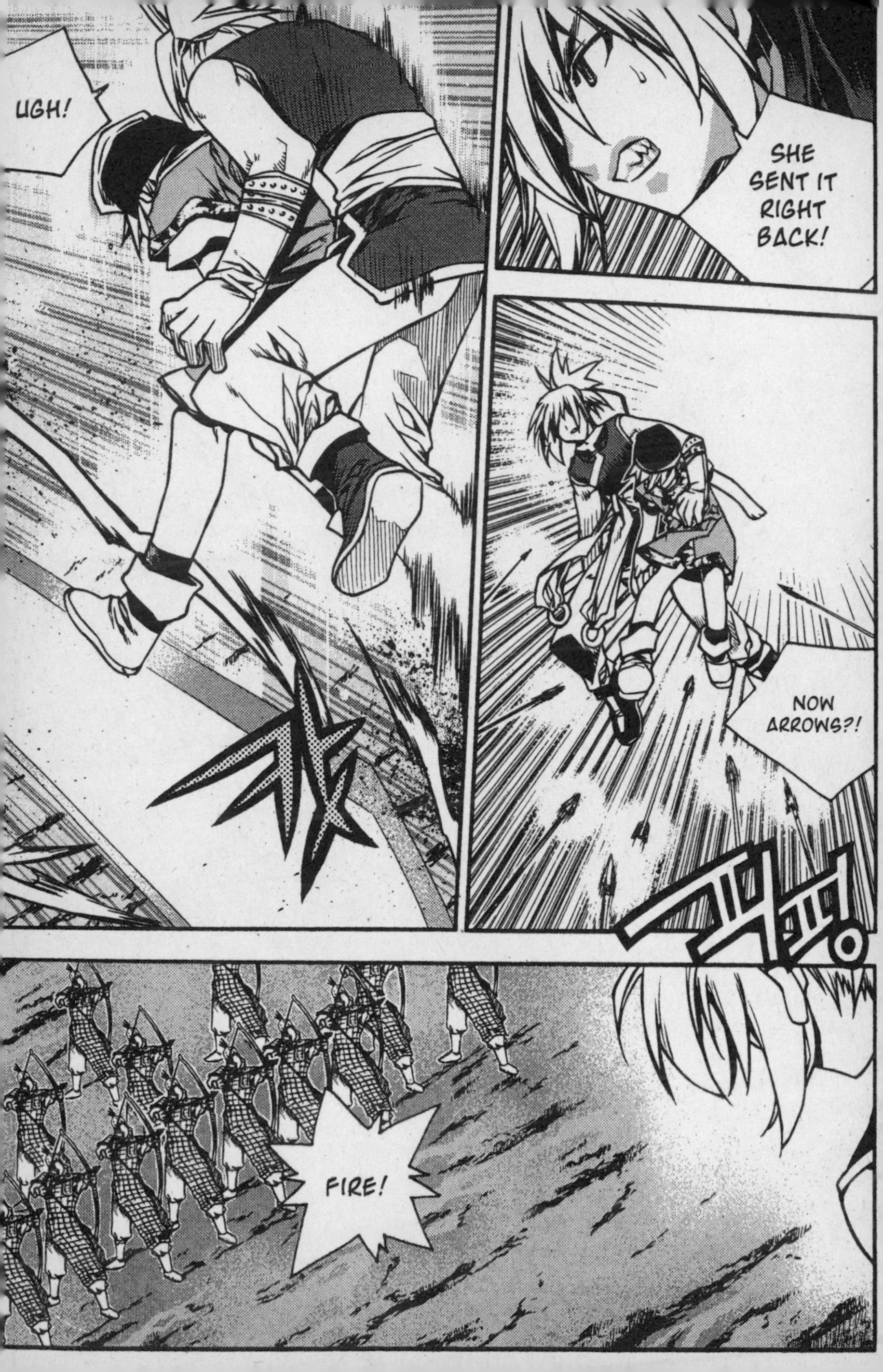
UGH!
SHE SENT IT RIGHT BACK!
NOW ARROWS?!
FIRE!

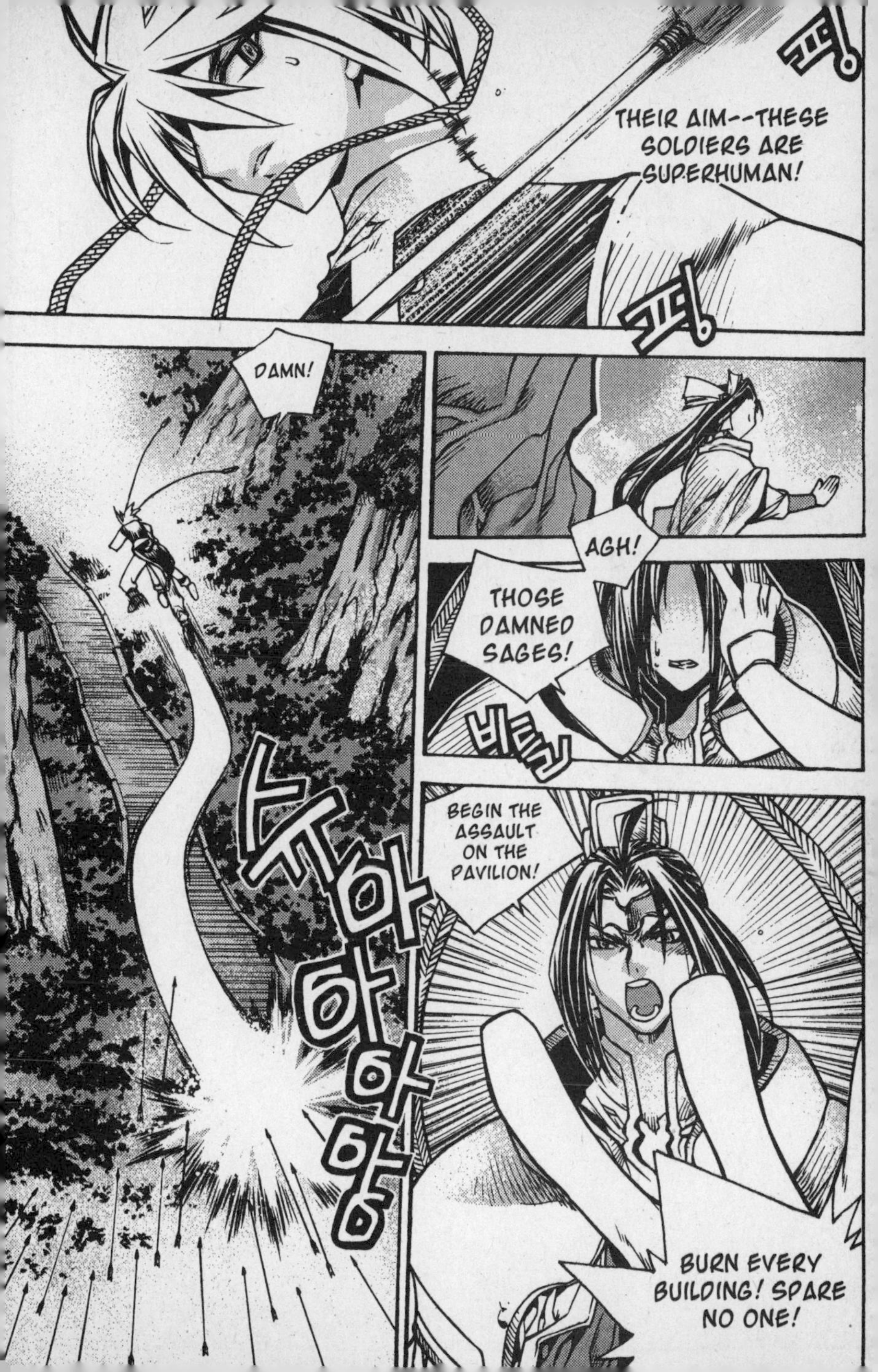
THEIR AIM--THESE SOLDIERS ARE SUPERHUMAN!
DAMN!
AGH!
THOSE DAMNED SAGES!
BEGIN THE ASSAULT ON THE PAVILION!
BURN EVERY BUILDING! SPARE NO ONE!

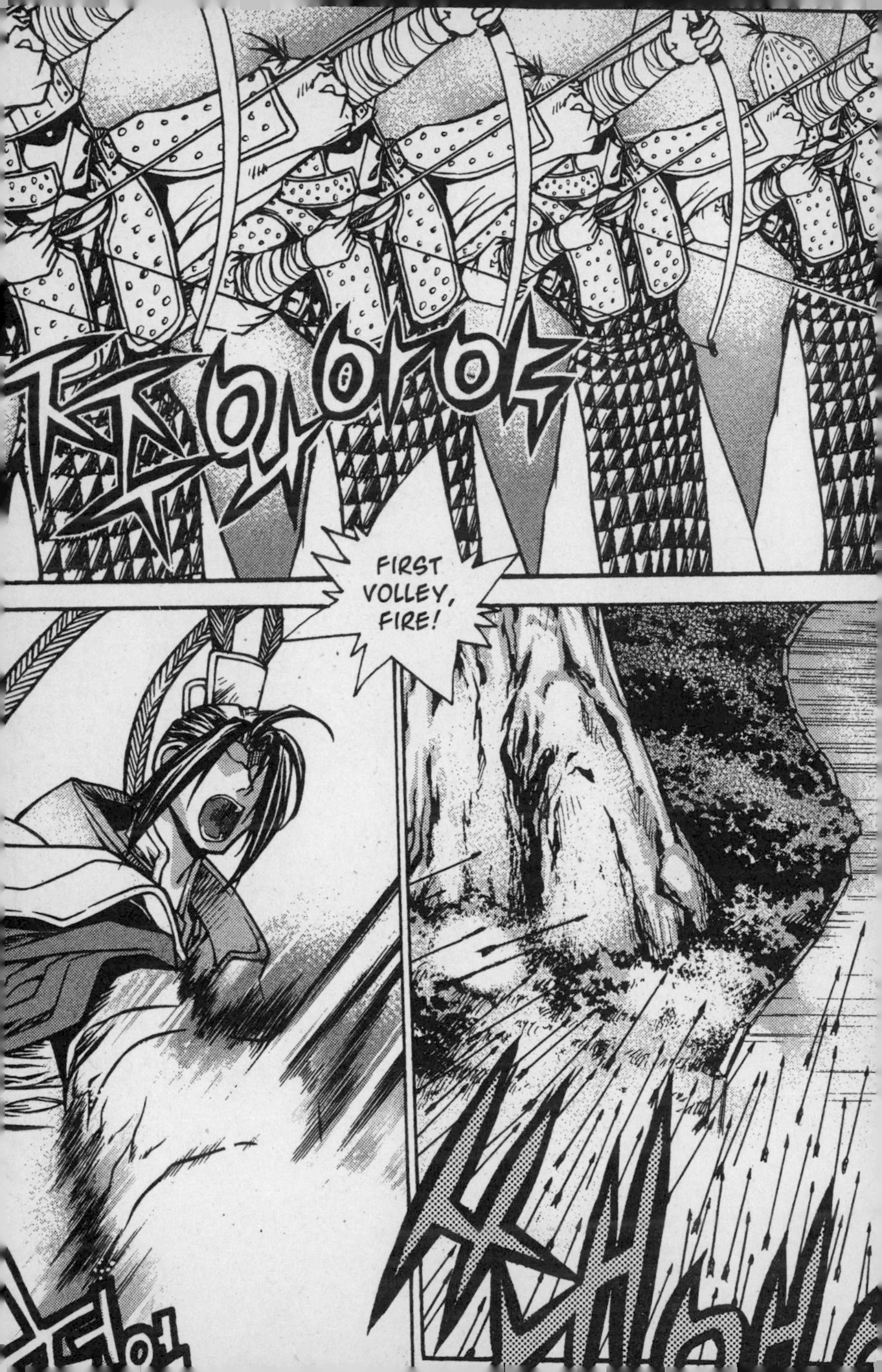
FIRST VOLLEY, FIRE!

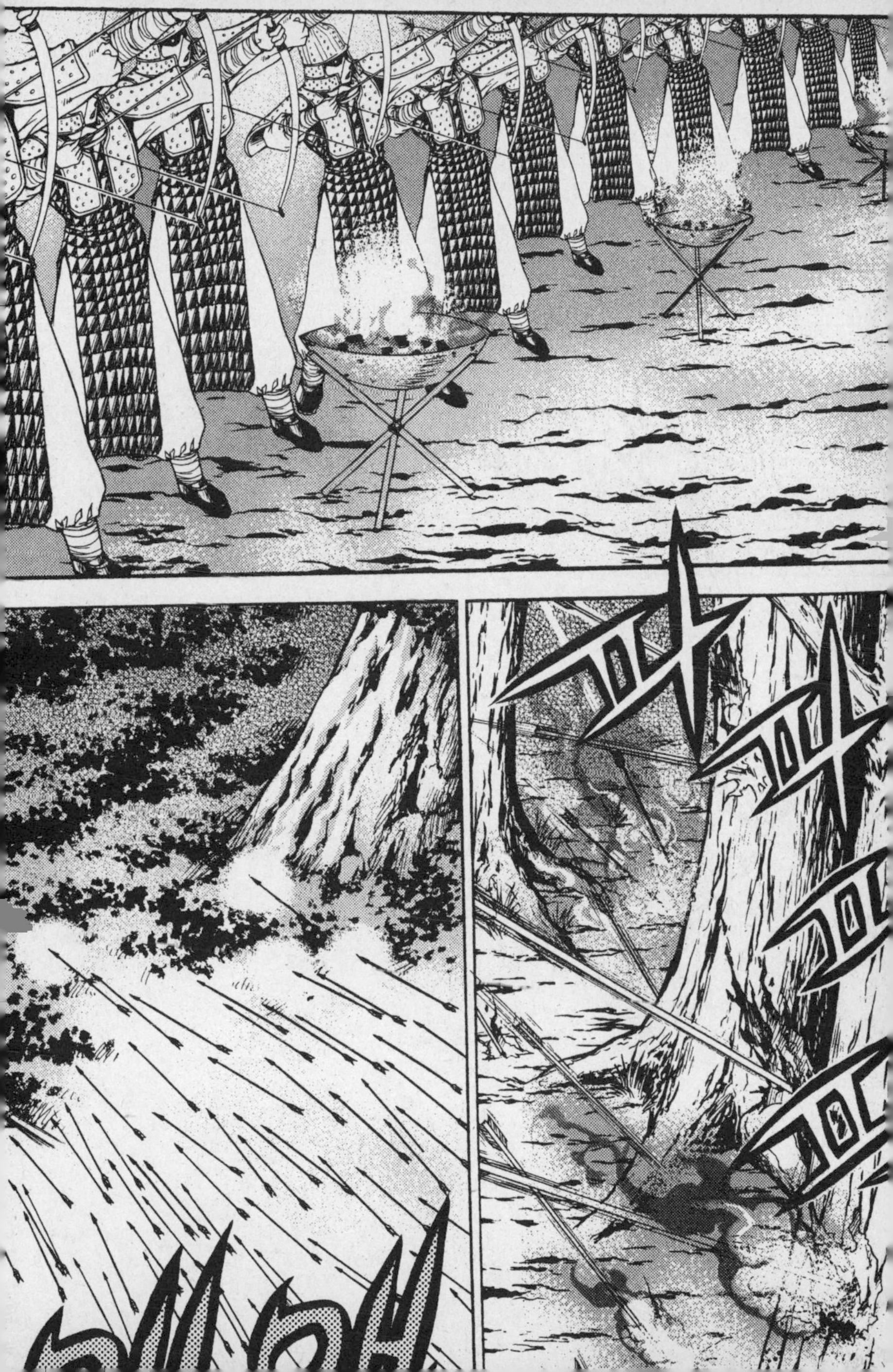

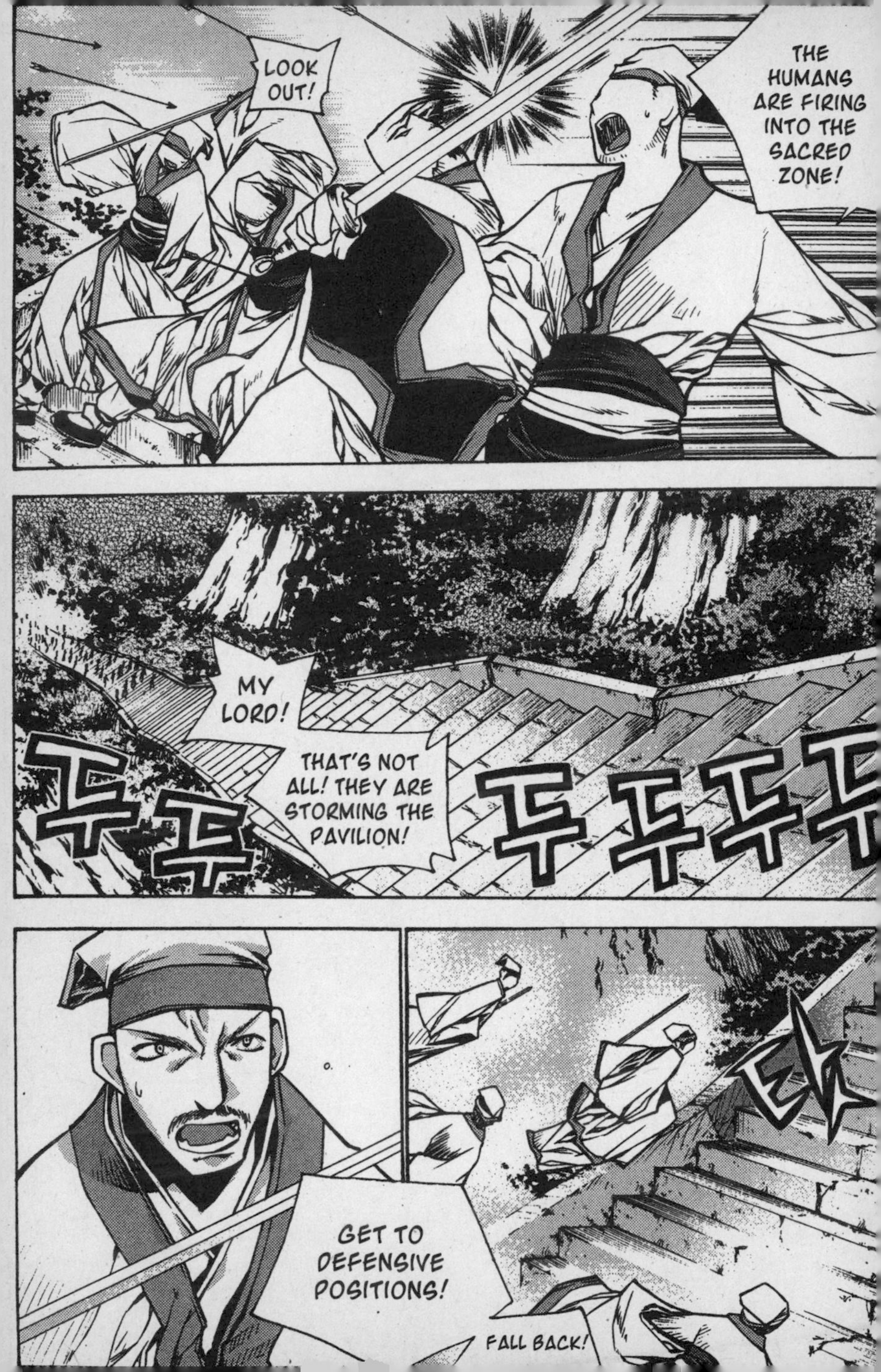
LOOK OUT!
THE HUMANS ARE FIRING INTO THE SACRED ZONE!
MY LORD!
THAT'S NOT ALL! THEY ARE STORMING THE PAVILION!
GET TO DEFENSIVE POSITIONS!
FALL BACK!

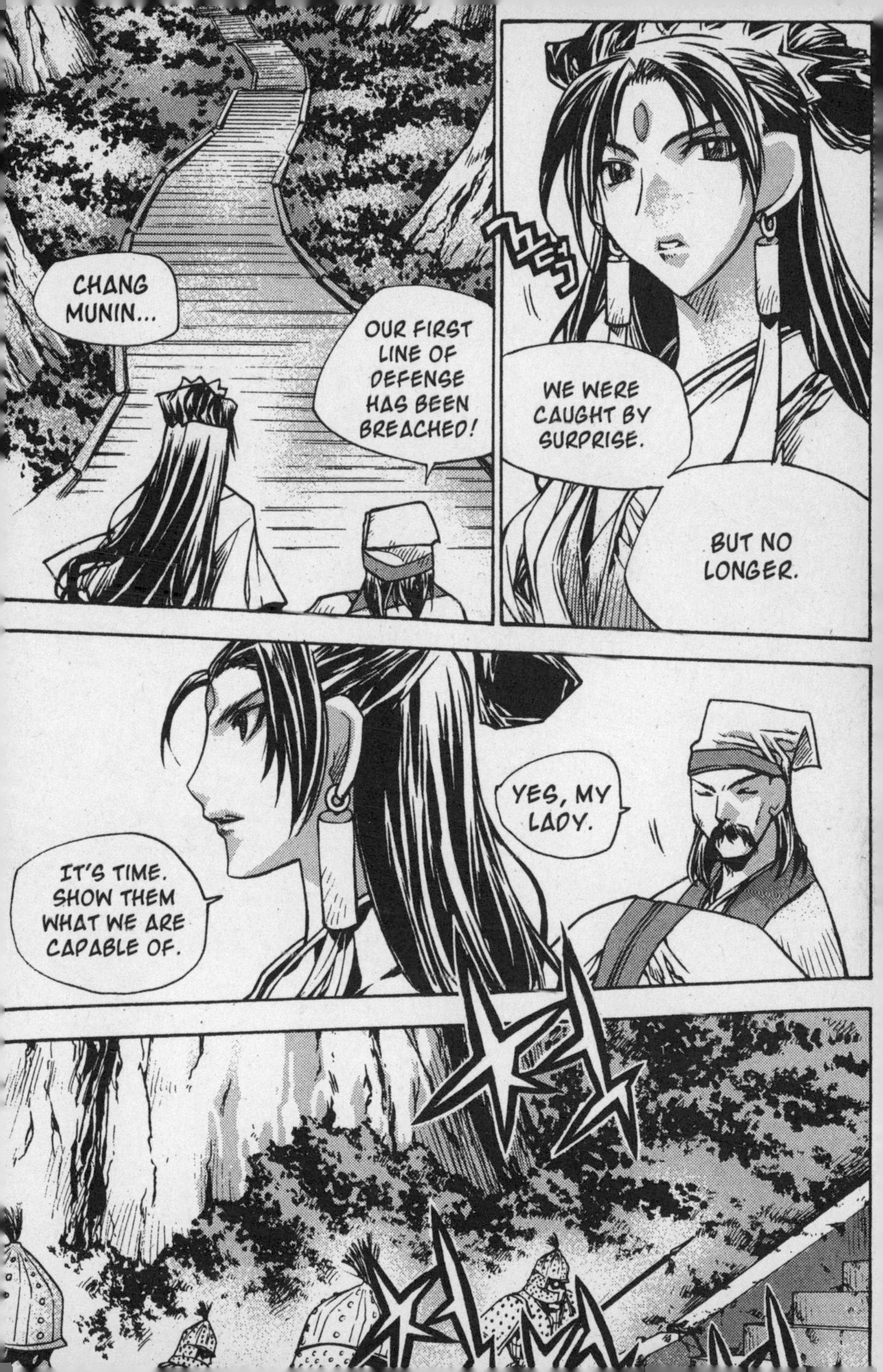
CHANG MUNIN...
OUR FIRST LINE OF DEFENSE HAS BEEN BREACHED!
WE WERE CAUGHT BY SURPRISE.
BUT NO LONGER.
IT'S TIME. SHOW THEM WHAT WE ARE CAPABLE OF.
YES, MY LADY.

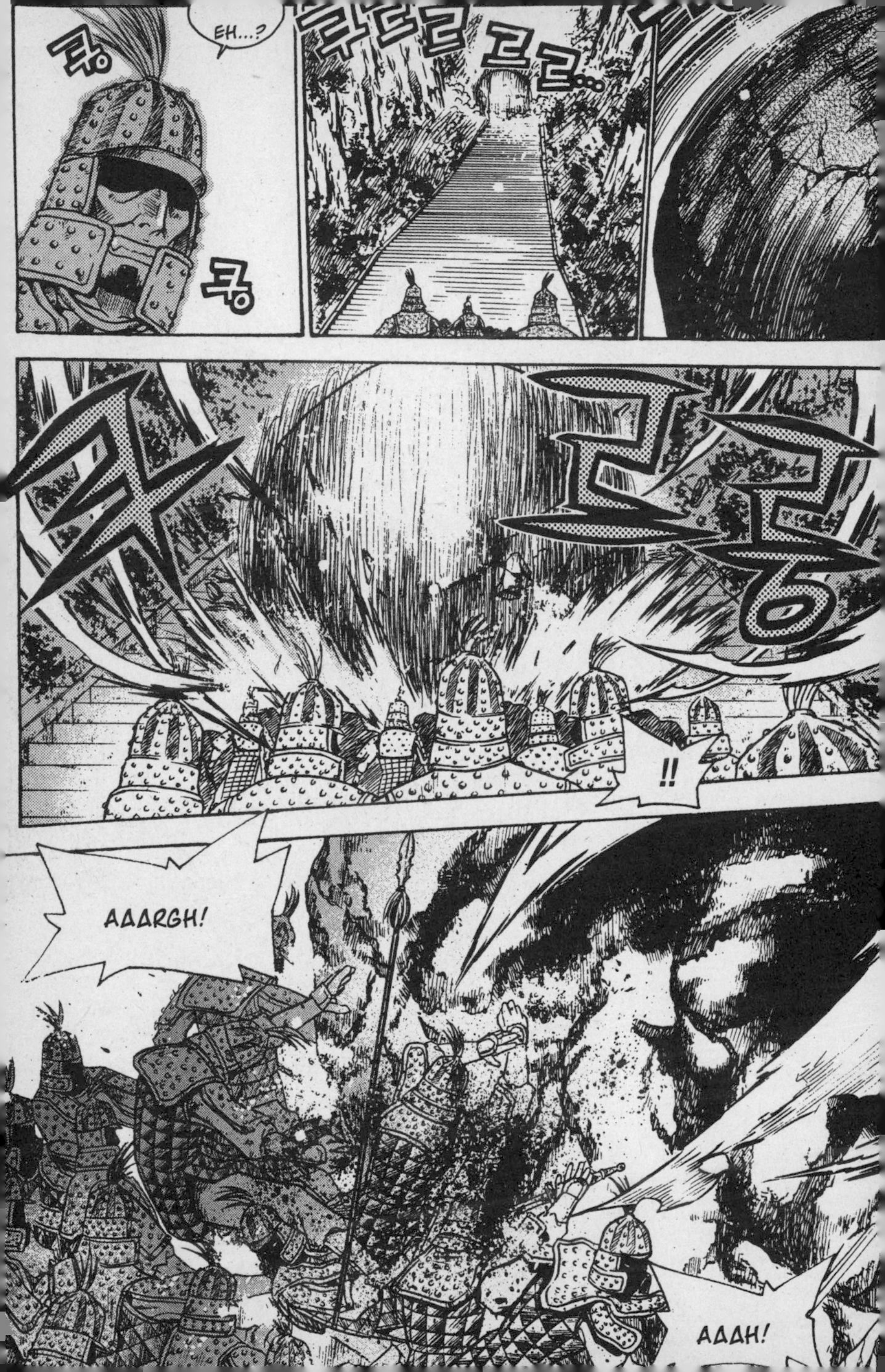
쿵
EH...?
쿵
쿠드르르르...
콰쾅
!!
AAARGH!
AAAH!

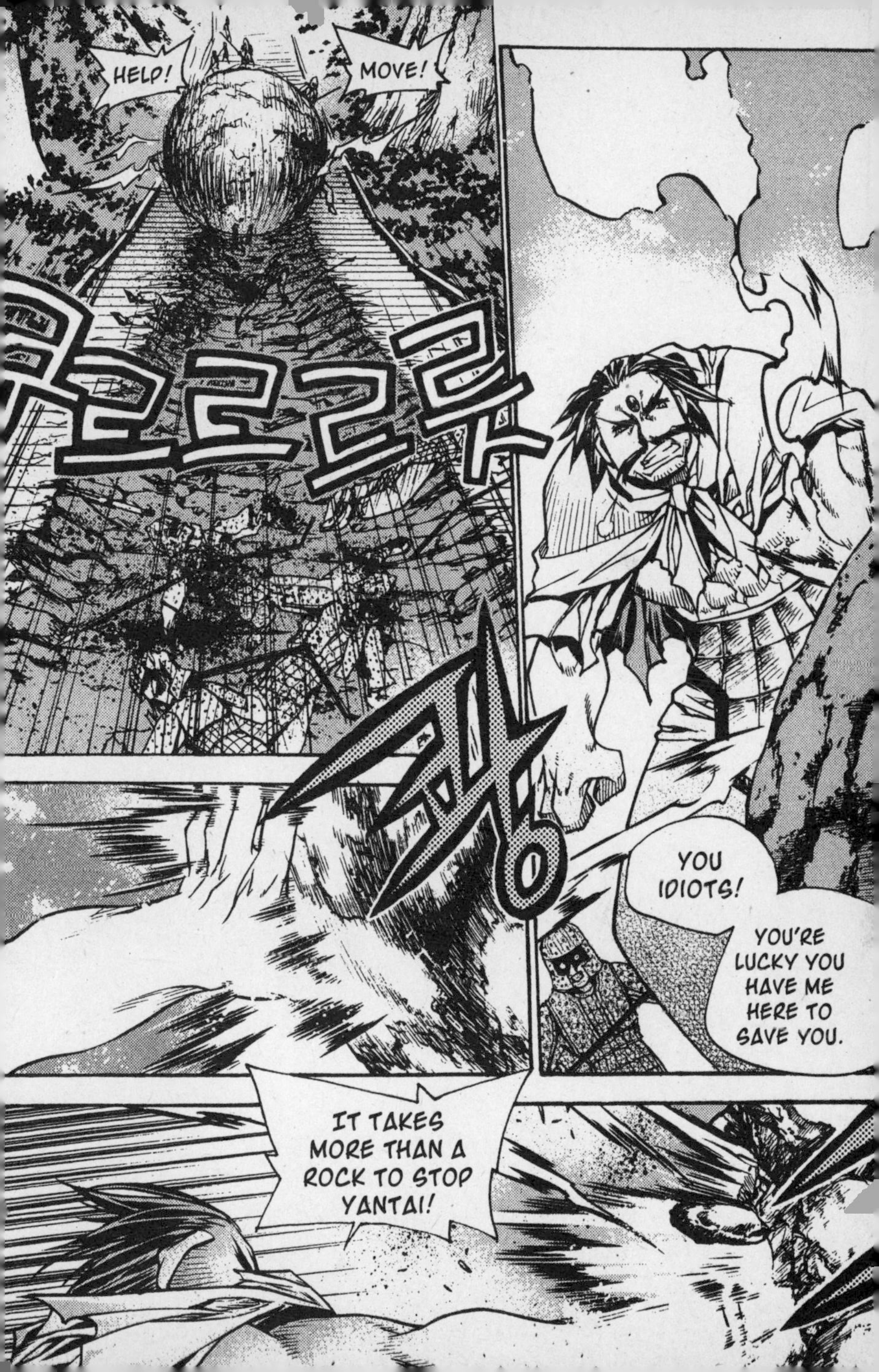
HELP!
MOVE!
YOU IDIOTS!
YOU'RE LUCKY YOU HAVE ME HERE TO SAVE YOU.
IT TAKES MORE THAN A ROCK TO STOP YANTAI!

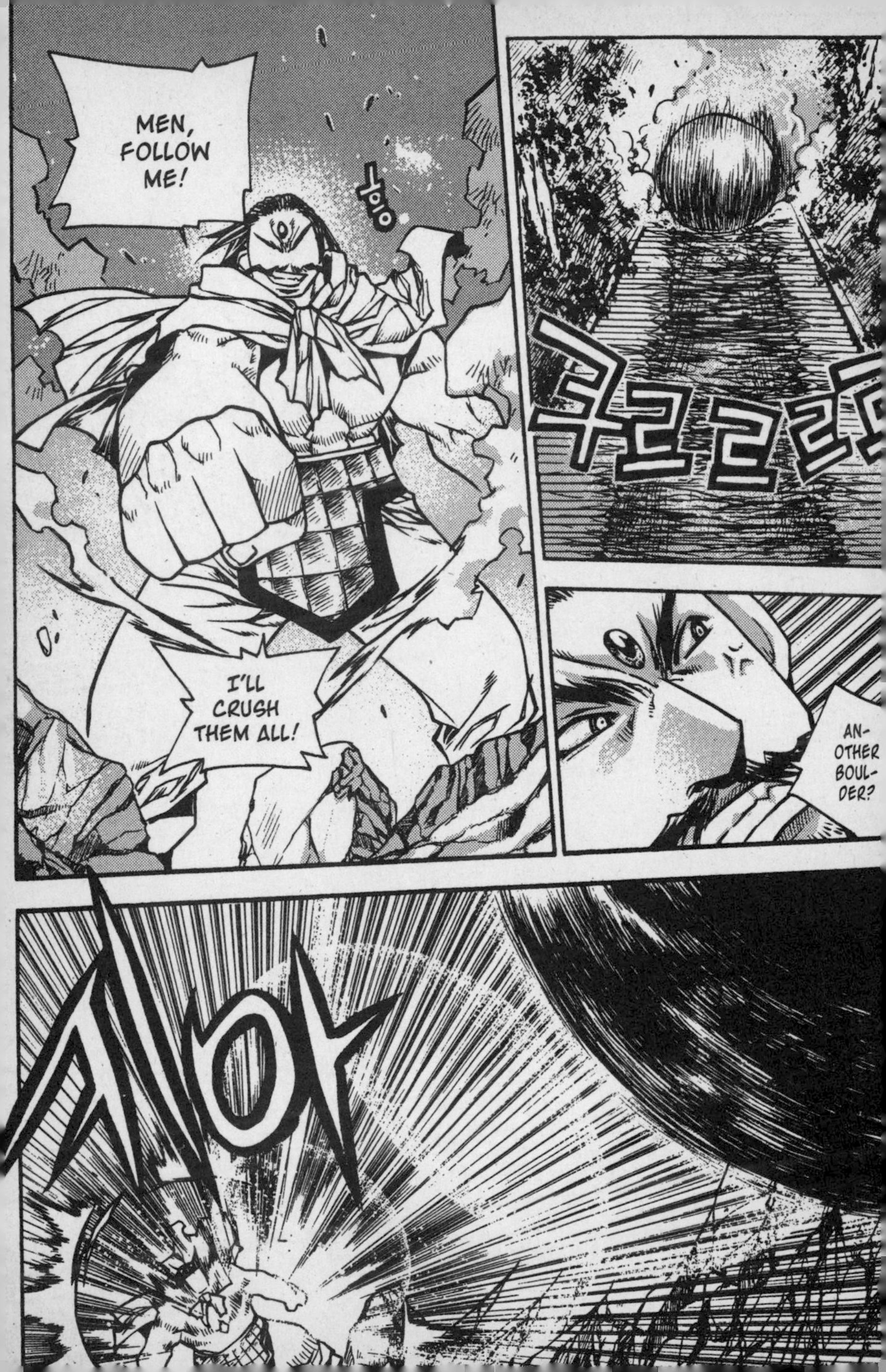
MEN, FOLLOW ME!
I'LL CRUSH THEM ALL!
AN-OTHER BOUL-DER?

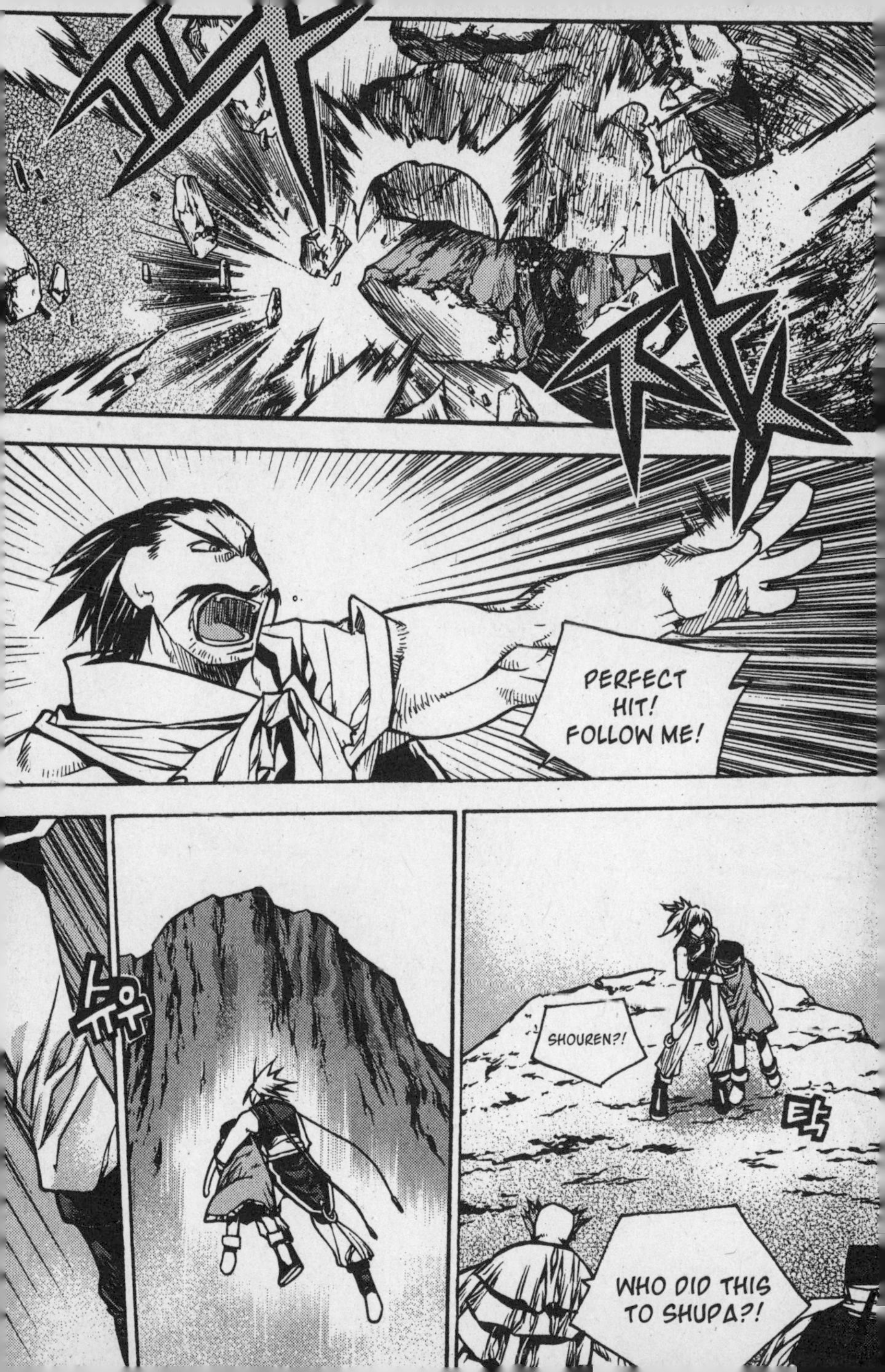
PERFECT HIT! FOLLOW ME!
SHOUREN?!
탁
WHO DID THIS TO SHUPA?!

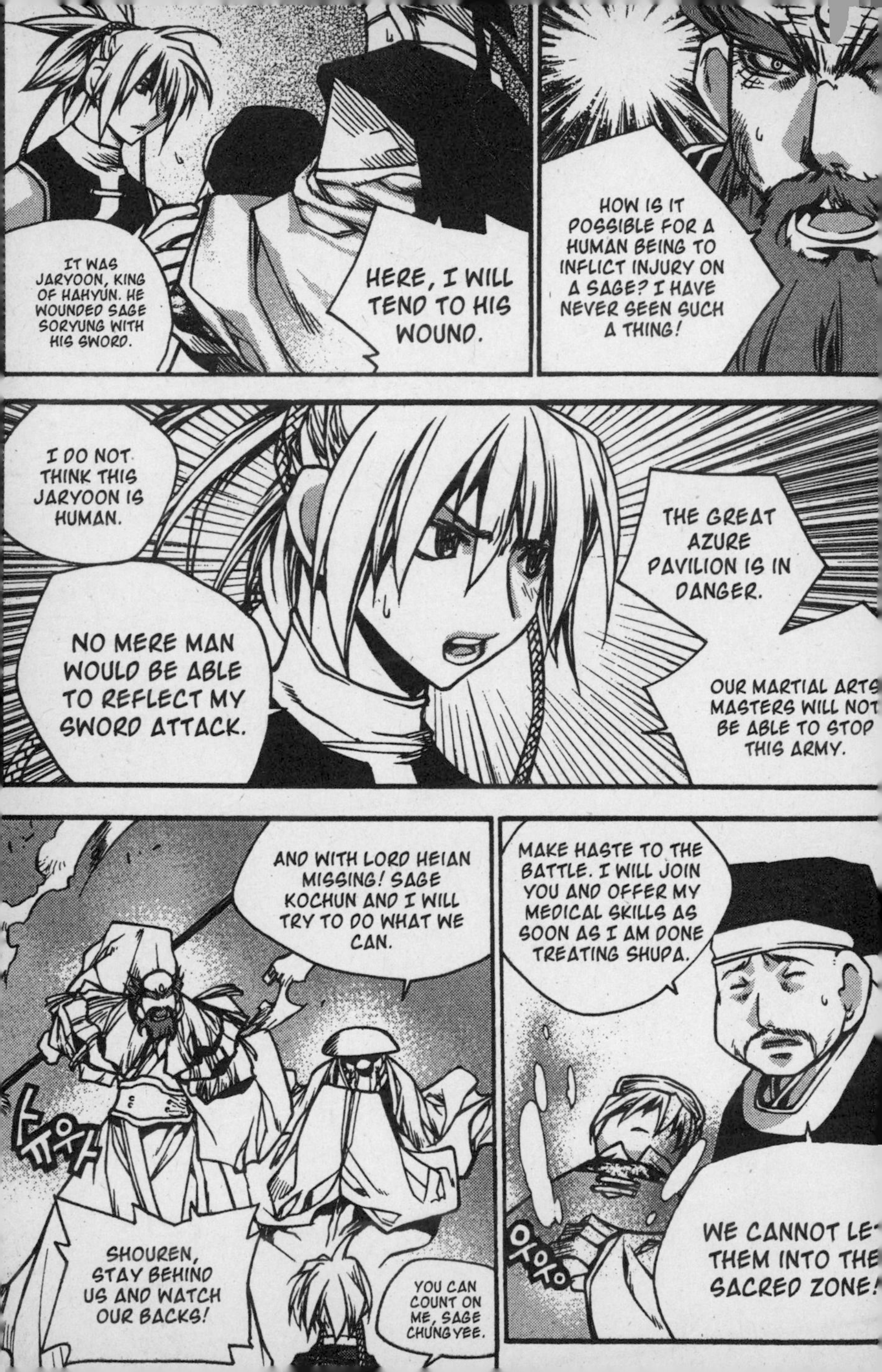
IT WAS JARYOON, KING OF HAHYUN. HE WOUNDED SAGE SORYUNG WITH HIS SWORD.
HERE, I WILL TEND TO HIS WOUND.
HOW IS IT POSSIBLE FOR A HUMAN BEING TO INFLICT INJURY ON A SAGE? I HAVE NEVER SEEN SUCH A THING!
I DO NOT THINK THIS JARYOON IS HUMAN.
NO MERE MAN WOULD BE ABLE TO REFLECT MY SWORD ATTACK.
THE GREAT AZURE PAVILION IS IN DANGER.
OUR MARTIAL ARTS MASTERS WILL NOT BE ABLE TO STOP THIS ARMY.
AND WITH LORD HEIAN MISSING! SAGE KOCHUN AND I WILL TRY TO DO WHAT WE CAN.
SHOUREN, STAY BEHIND US AND WATCH OUR BACKS!
YOU CAN COUNT ON ME, SAGE CHUNGYEE.
MAKE HASTE TO THE BATTLE. I WILL JOIN YOU AND OFFER MY MEDICAL SKILLS AS SOON AS I AM DONE TREATING SHUPA.
WE CANNOT LET THEM INTO THE SACRED ZONE!

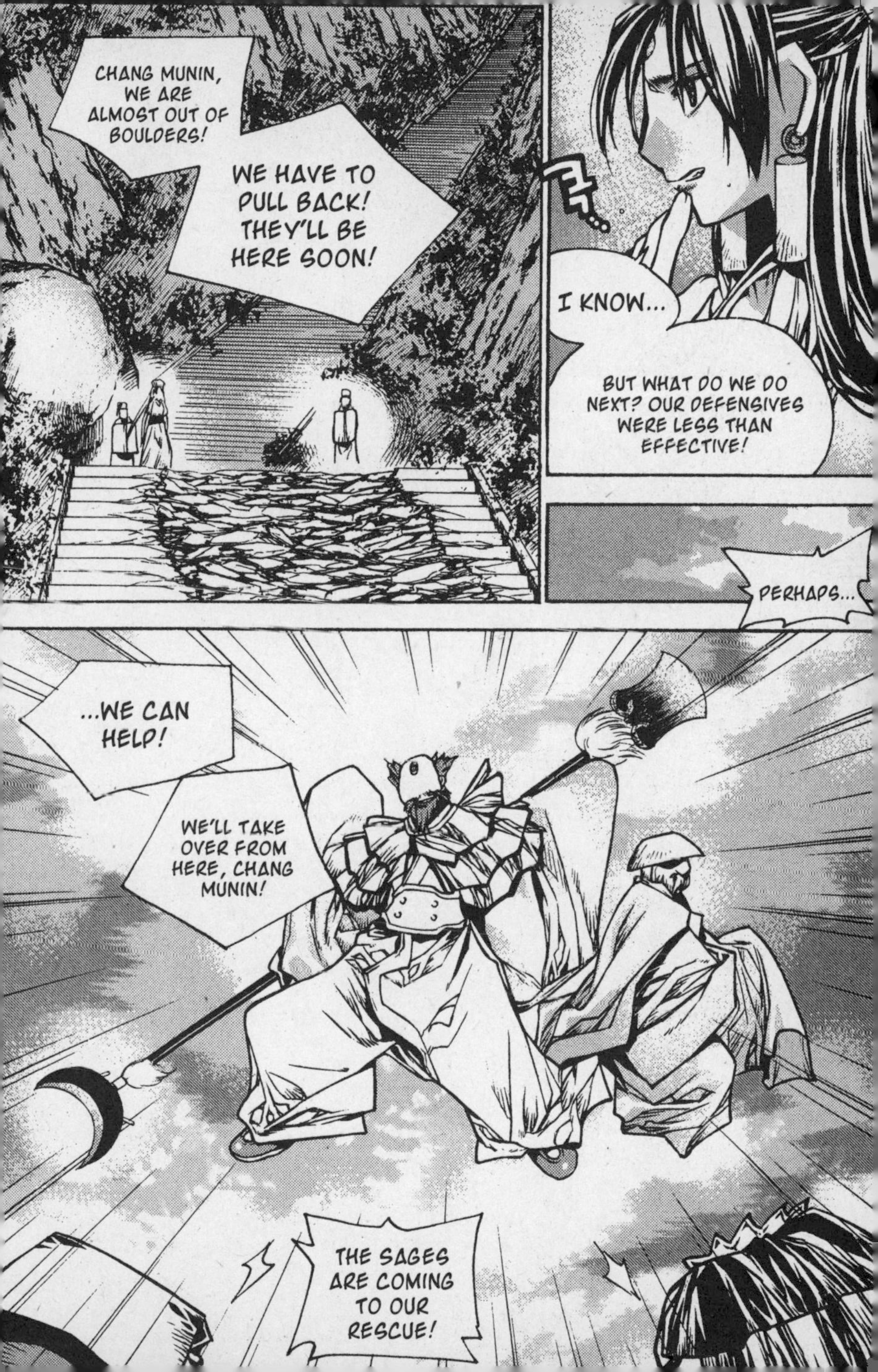
CHANG MUNIN, WE ARE ALMOST OUT OF BOULDERS!
WE HAVE TO PULL BACK! THEY'LL BE HERE SOON!
I KNOW...
BUT WHAT DO WE DO NEXT? OUR DEFENSIVES WERE LESS THAN EFFECTIVE!
PERHAPS...
...WE CAN HELP!
WE'LL TAKE OVER FROM HERE, CHANG MUNIN!
THE SAGES ARE COMING TO OUR RESCUE!

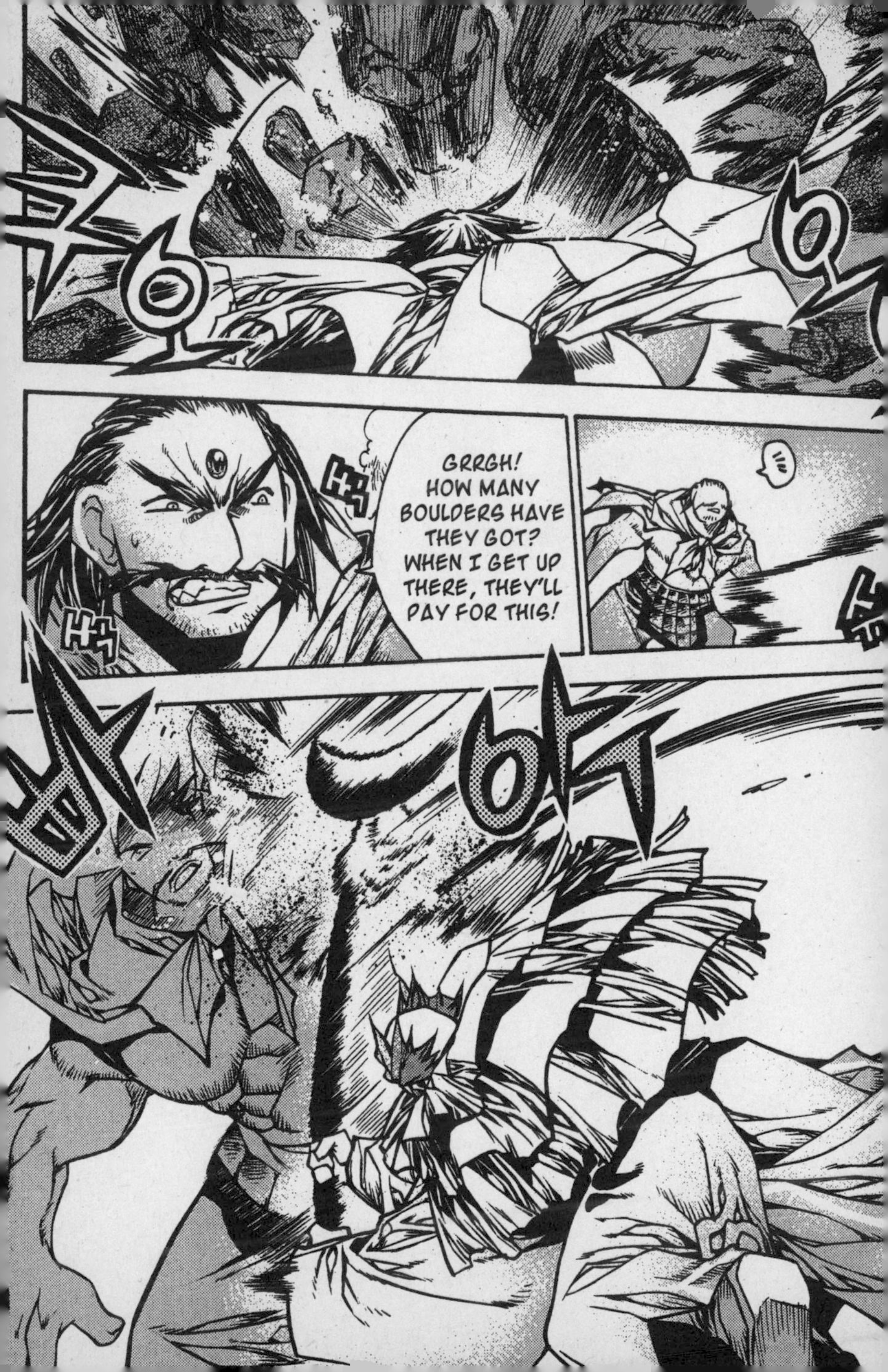
GRRGH!
HOW MANY BOULDERS HAVE THEY GOT? WHEN I GET UP THERE, THEY'LL PAY FOR THIS!

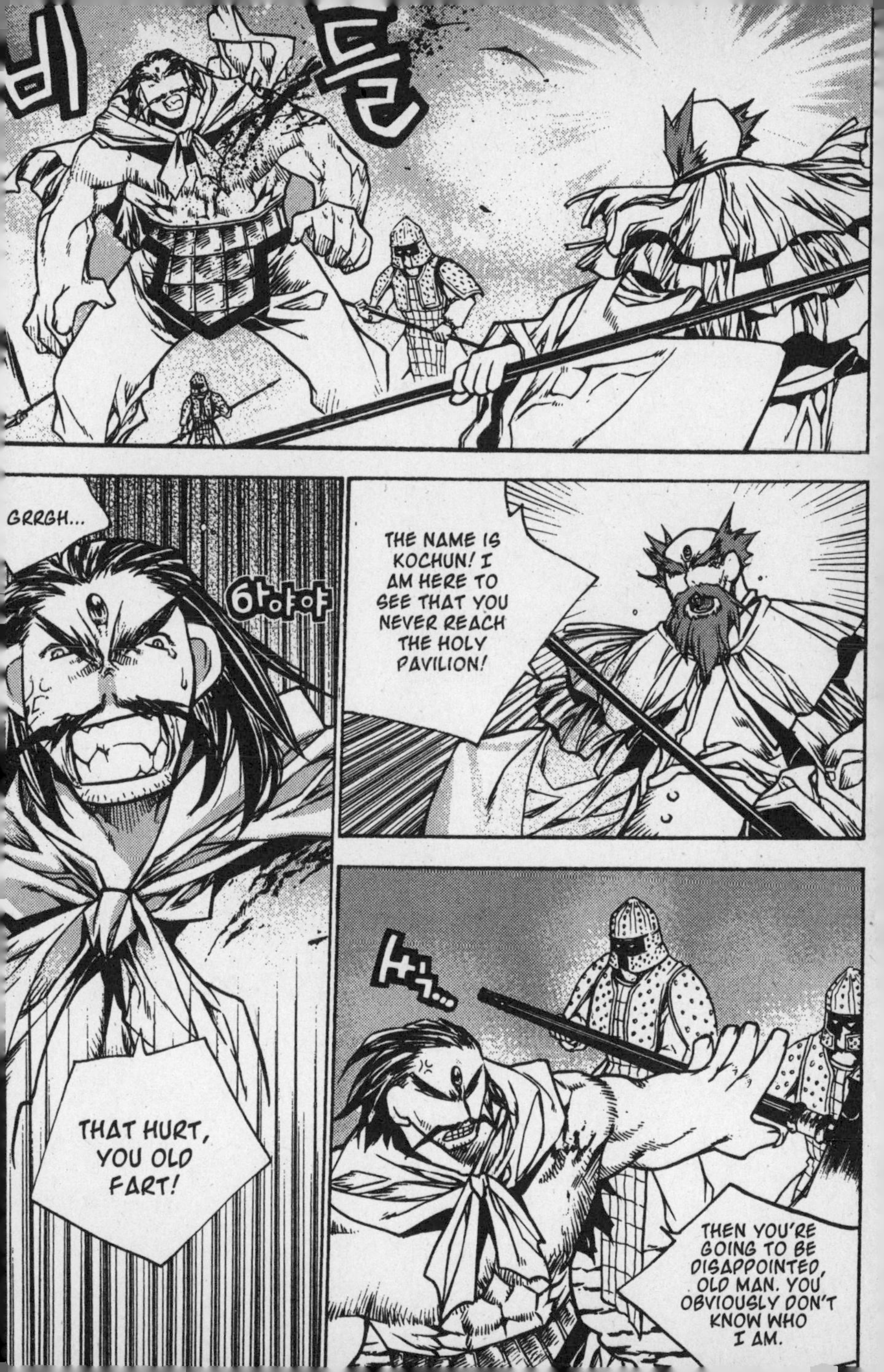
GRRGH...
THAT HURT, YOU OLD FART!
THE NAME IS KOCHUN! I AM HERE TO SEE THAT YOU NEVER REACH THE HOLY PAVILION!
THEN YOU'RE GOING TO BE DISAPPOINTED, OLD MAN. YOU OBVIOUSLY DON'T KNOW WHO I AM.

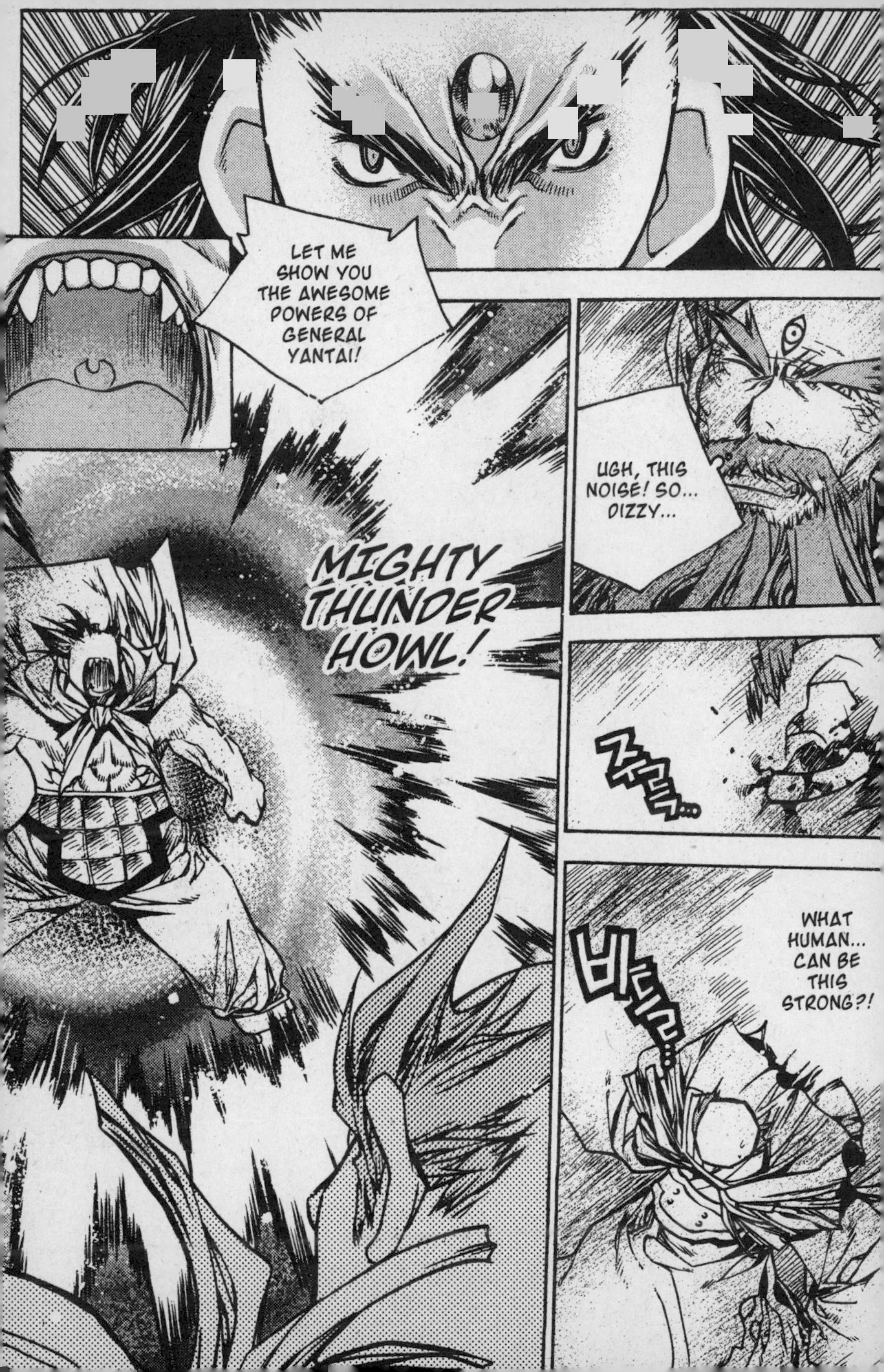
LET ME SHOW YOU THE AWESOME POWERS OF GENERAL YANTAI!
MIGHTY THUNDER HOWL!
UGH, THIS NOISE! SO... DIZZY...
WHAT HUMAN... CAN BE THIS STRONG?!

Chapter 65: Incantation to Dispel Demon Souls

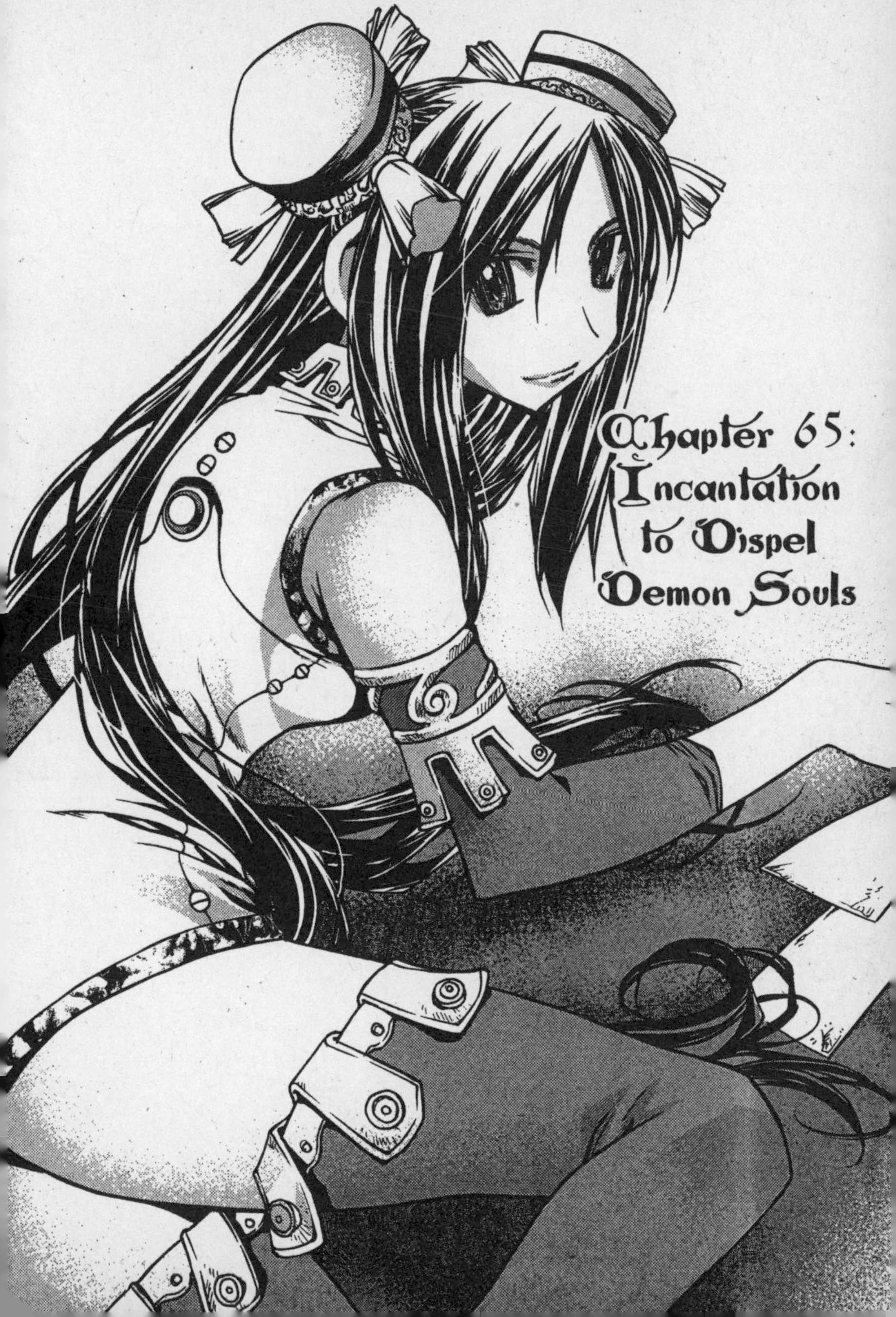

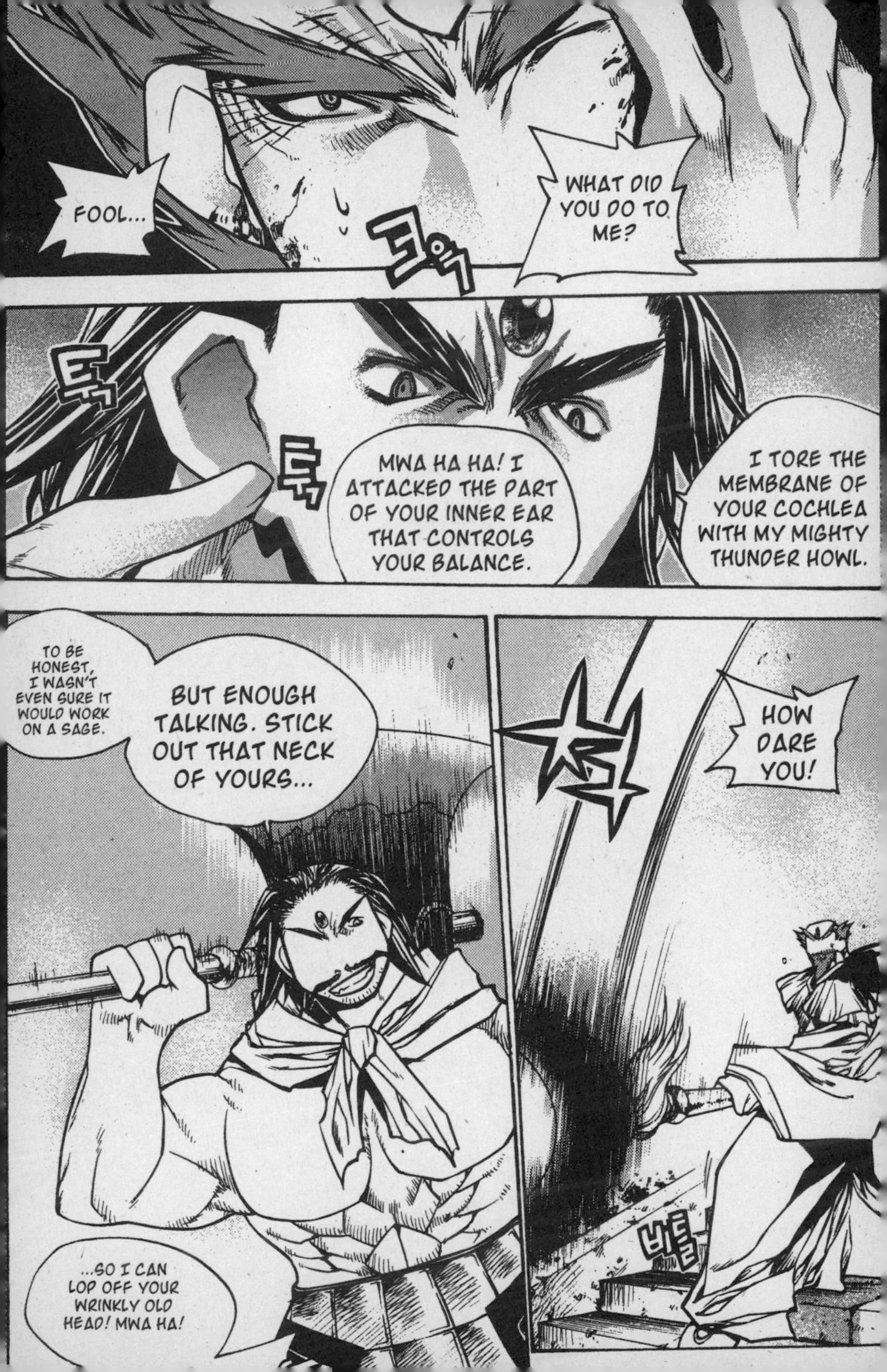
FOOL...
WHAT DID YOU DO TO ME?
MWA HA HA! I ATTACKED THE PART OF YOUR INNER EAR THAT CONTROLS YOUR BALANCE.
I TORE THE MEMBRANE OF YOUR COCHLEA WITH MY MIGHTY THUNDER HOWL.
TO BE HONEST, I WASN'T EVEN SURE IT WOULD WORK ON A SAGE.
BUT ENOUGH TALKING. STICK OUT THAT NECK OF YOURS...
...SO I CAN LOP OFF YOUR WRINKLY OLD HEAD! MWA HA!
HOW DARE YOU!

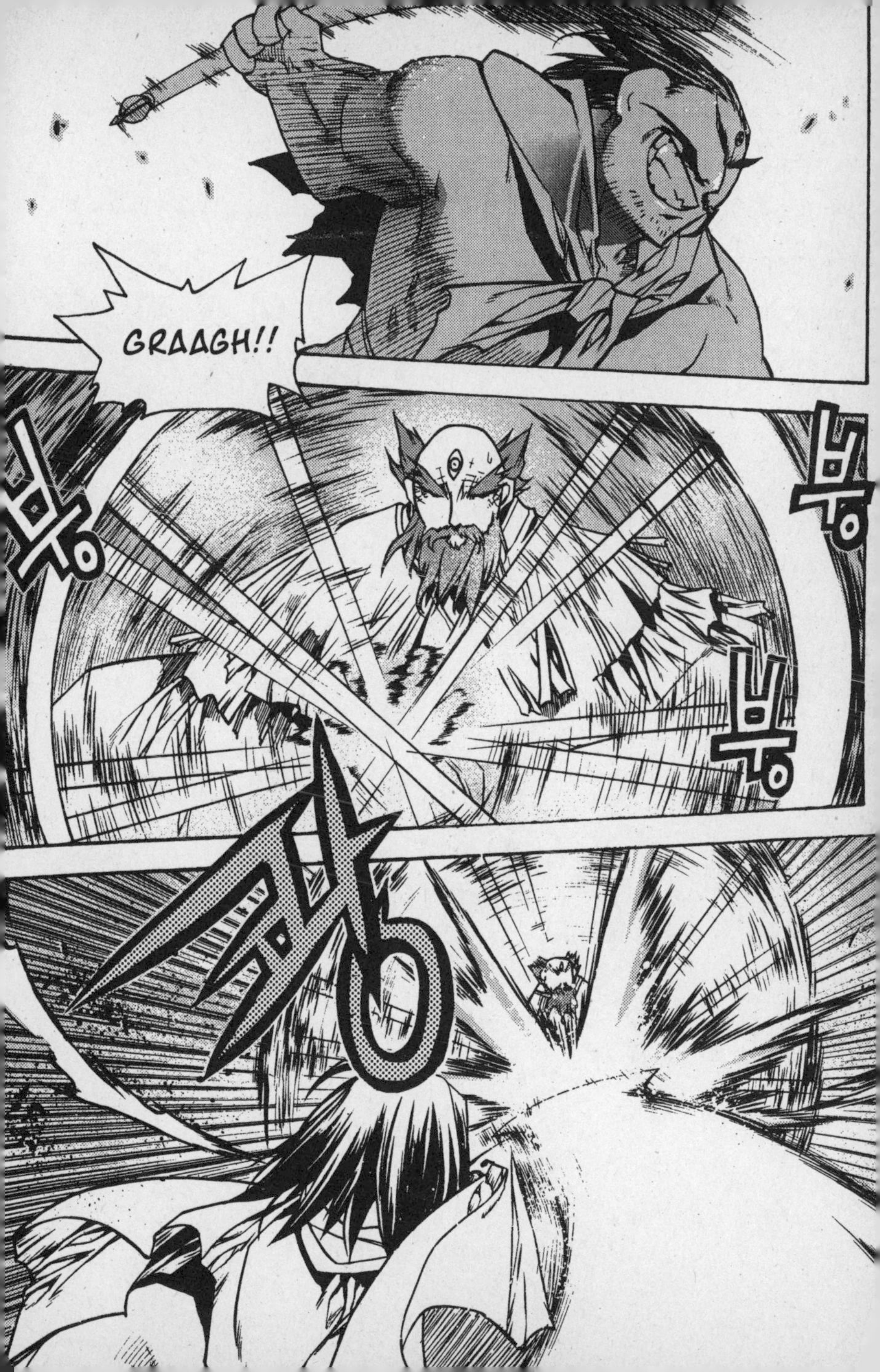
GRAAGH!!

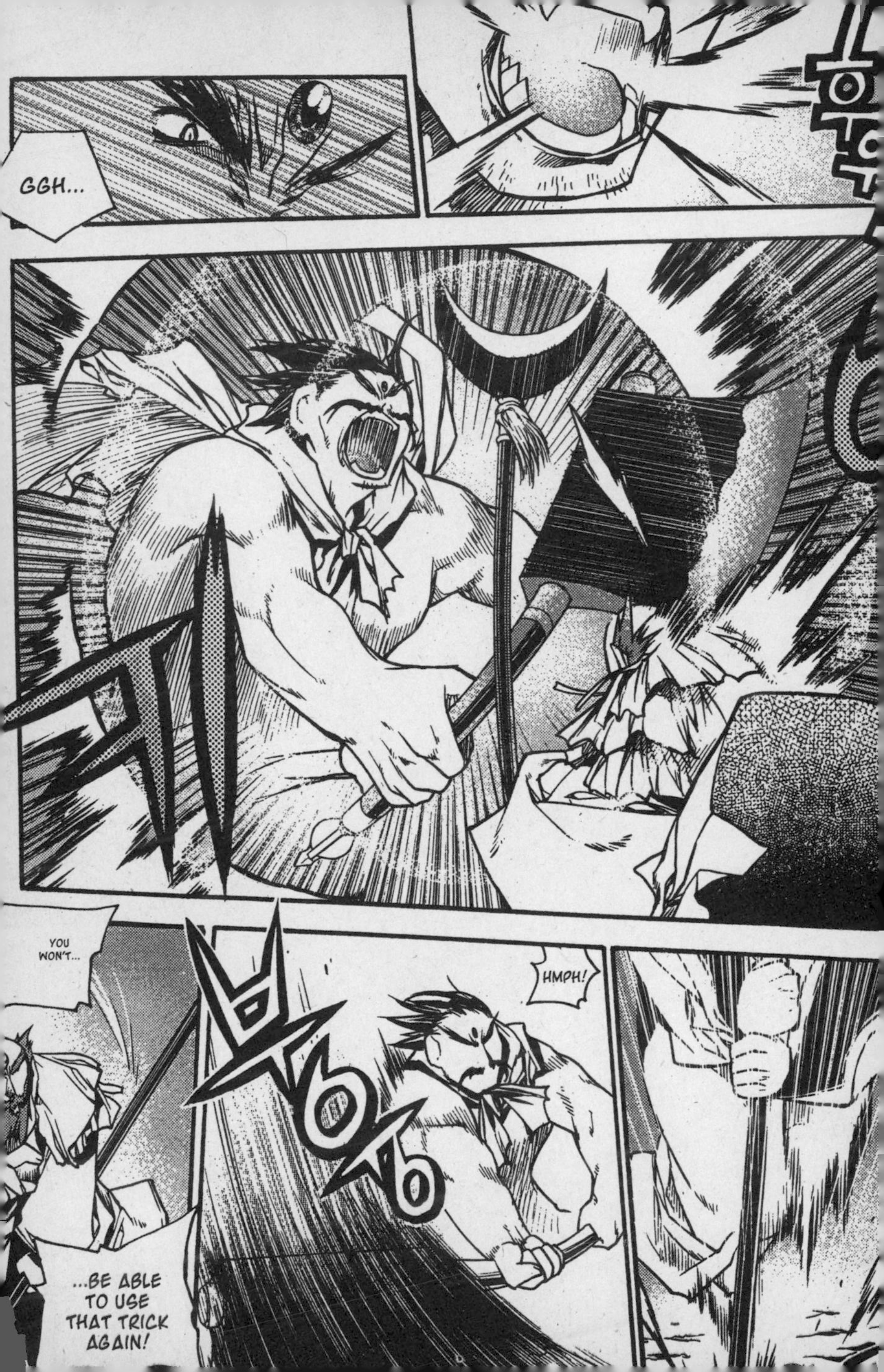
GGH...
YOU WON'T...
HMPH!
...BE ABLE TO USE THAT TRICK AGAIN!

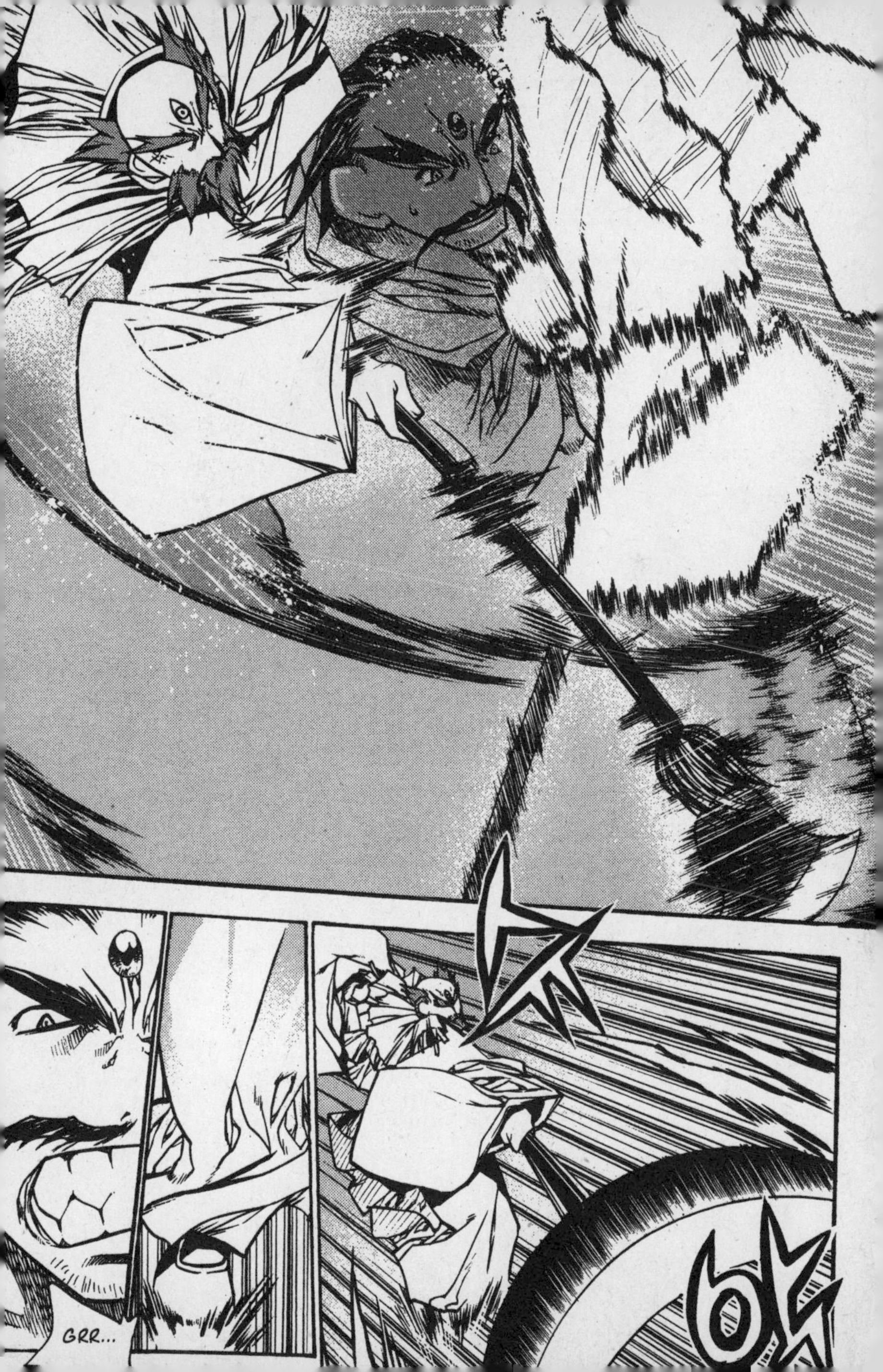
GRR...

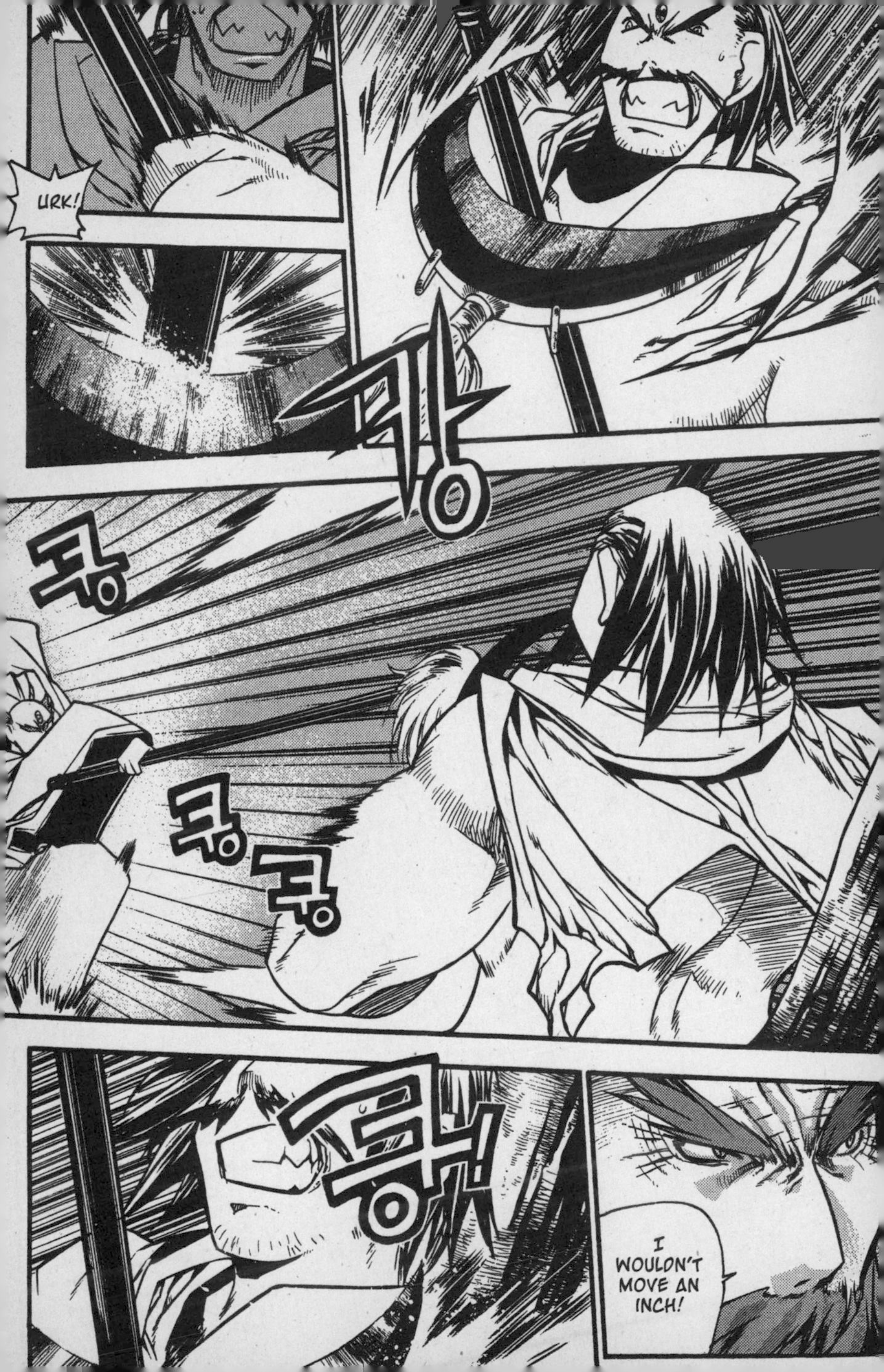
URK!
캉
쿵
쿵
쿵
쾅!
I WOULDN'T MOVE AN INCH!

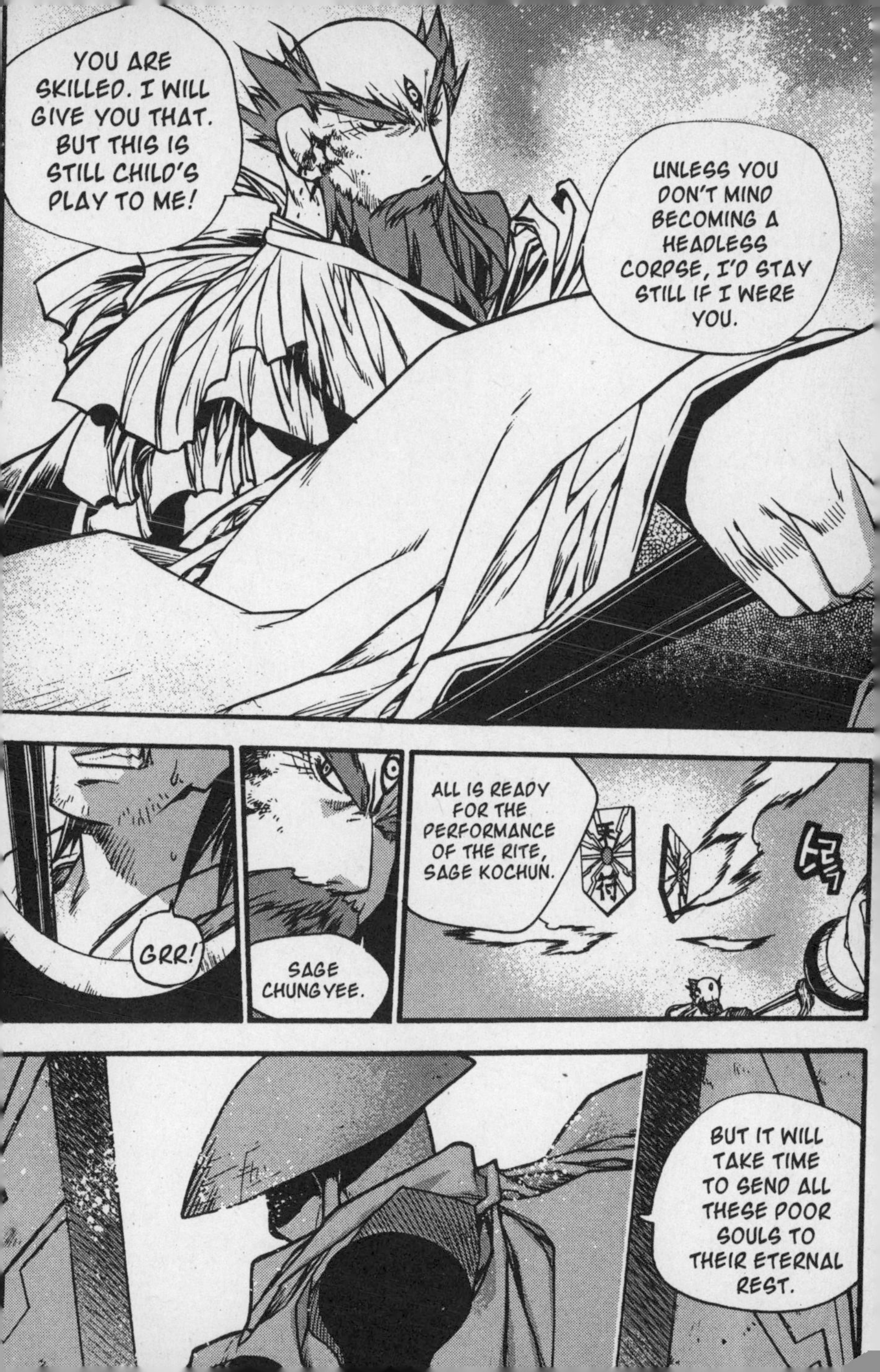
YOU ARE SKILLED. I WILL GIVE YOU THAT. BUT THIS IS STILL CHILD'S PLAY TO ME!
UNLESS YOU DON'T MIND BECOMING A HEADLESS CORPSE, I'D STAY STILL IF I WERE YOU.
GRR!
SAGE CHUNGYEE.
ALL IS READY FOR THE PERFORMANCE OF THE RITE, SAGE KOCHUN.
BUT IT WILL TAKE TIME TO SEND ALL THESE POOR SOULS TO THEIR ETERNAL REST.

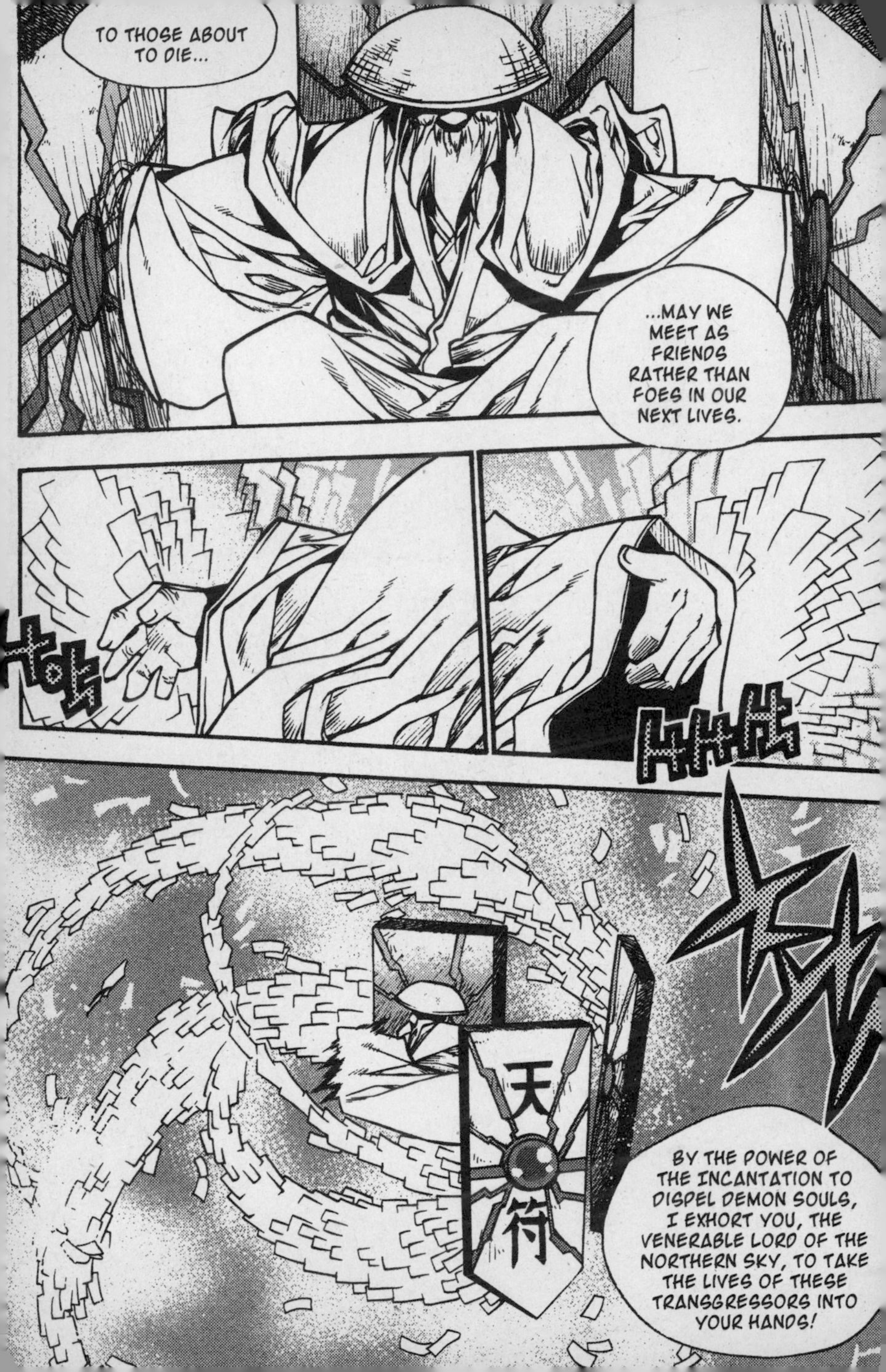
TO THOSE ABOUT TO DIE...
...MAY WE MEET AS FRIENDS RATHER THAN FOES IN OUR NEXT LIVES.
天
符
BY THE POWER OF THE INCANTATION TO DISPEL DEMON SOULS, I EXHORT YOU, THE VENERABLE LORD OF THE NORTHERN SKY, TO TAKE THE LIVES OF THESE TRANSGRESSORS INTO YOUR HANDS!

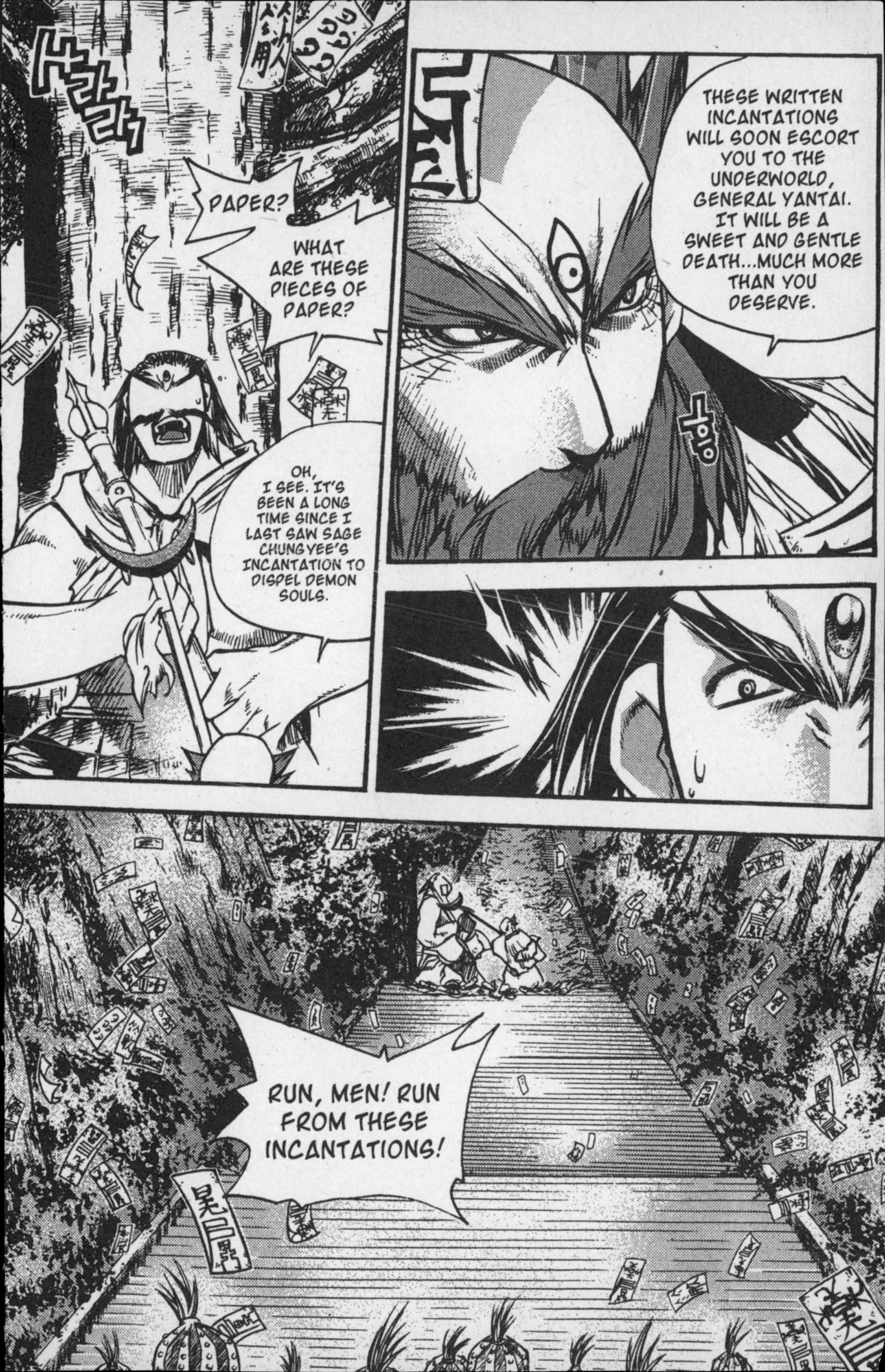
PAPER?
WHAT ARE THESE PIECES OF PAPER?
OH, I SEE. IT'S BEEN A LONG TIME SINCE I LAST SAW SAGE CHUNGYEE'S INCANTATION TO DISPEL DEMON SOULS.
THESE WRITTEN INCANTATIONS WILL SOON ESCORT YOU TO THE UNDERWORLD, GENERAL YANTAI. IT WILL BE A SWEET AND GENTLE DEATH...MUCH MORE THAN YOU DESERVE.
RUN, MEN! RUN FROM THESE INCANTATIONS!

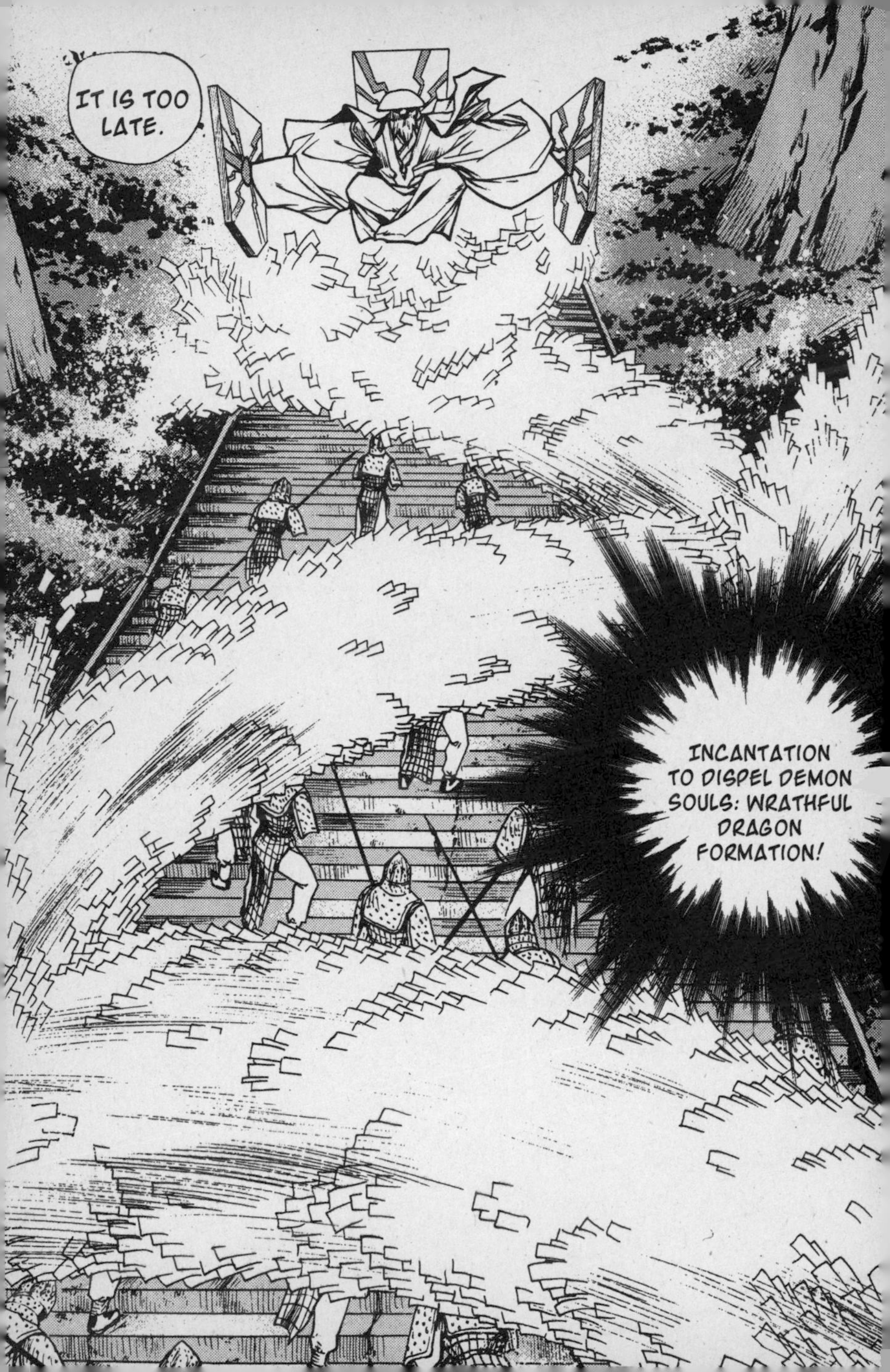
IT IS TOO LATE.
INCANTATION TO DISPEL DEMON SOULS: WRATHFUL DRAGON FORMATION!

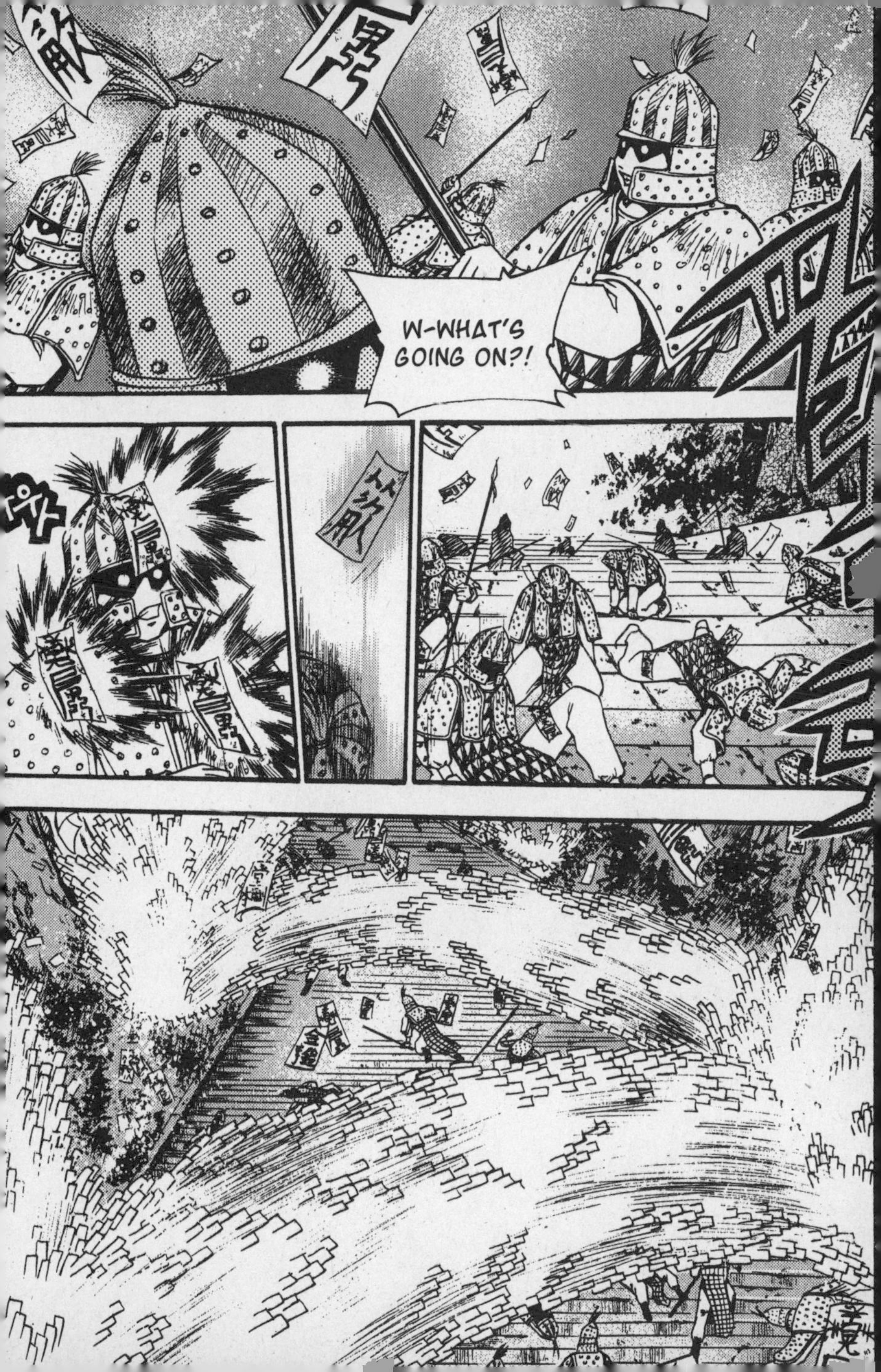
W-WHAT'S GOING ON?!

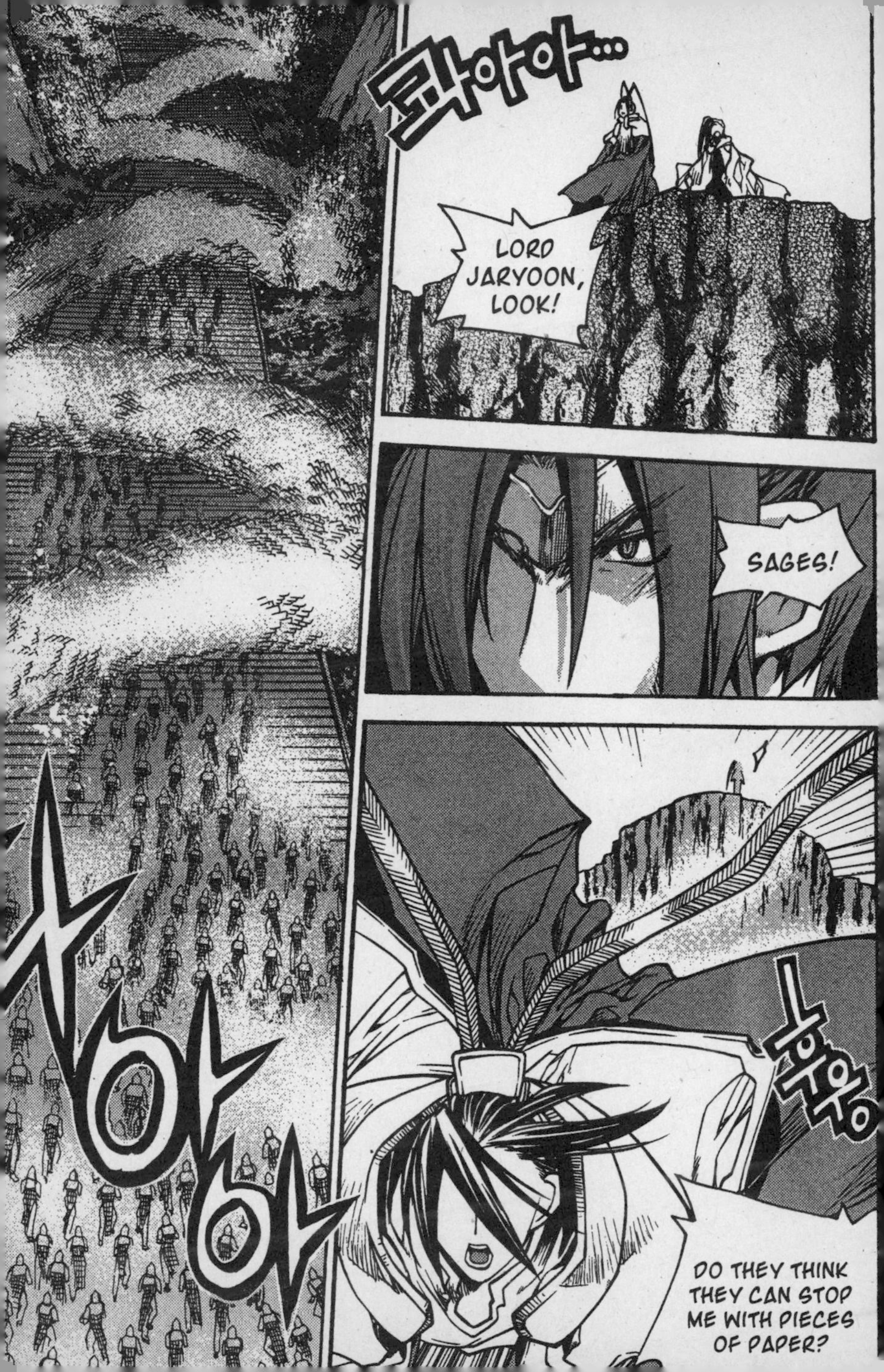

콰아아...
LORD JARYOON, LOOK!
SAGES!
DO THEY THINK THEY CAN STOP ME WITH PIECES OF PAPER?

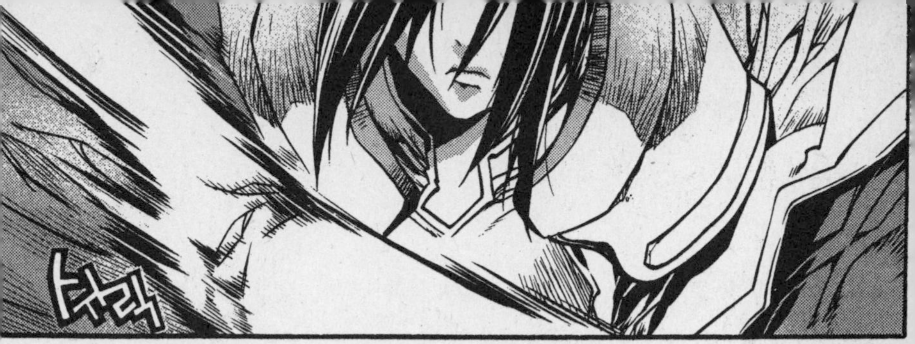

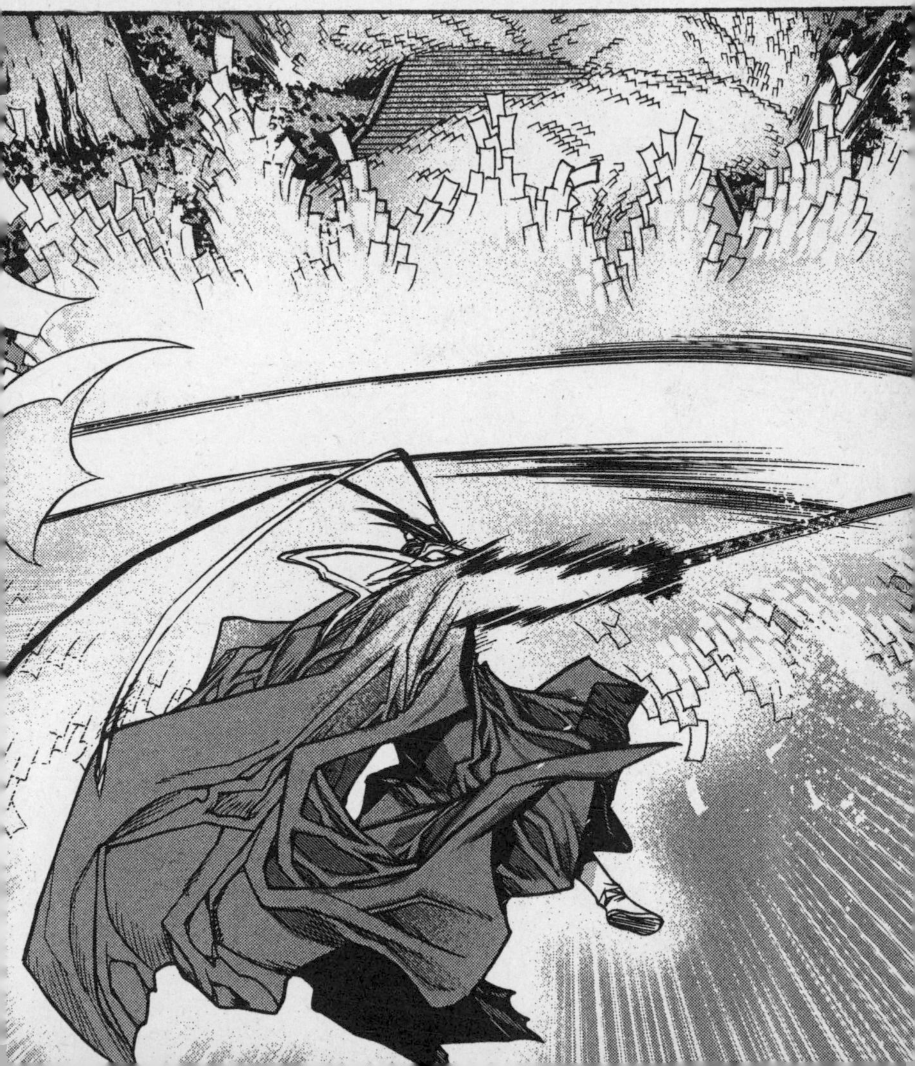

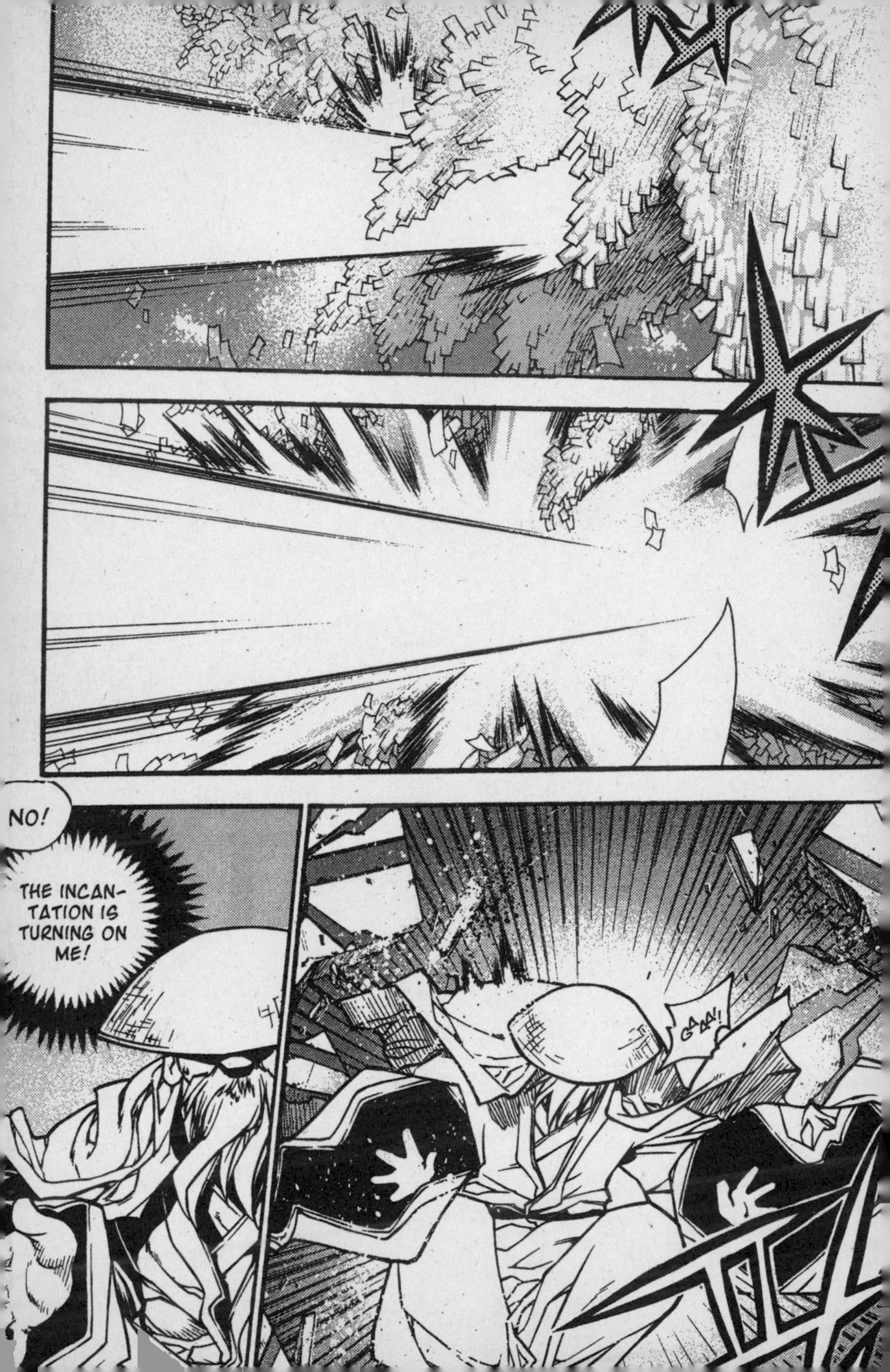
NO!
THE INCANTATION IS TURNING ON ME!
GAAA!

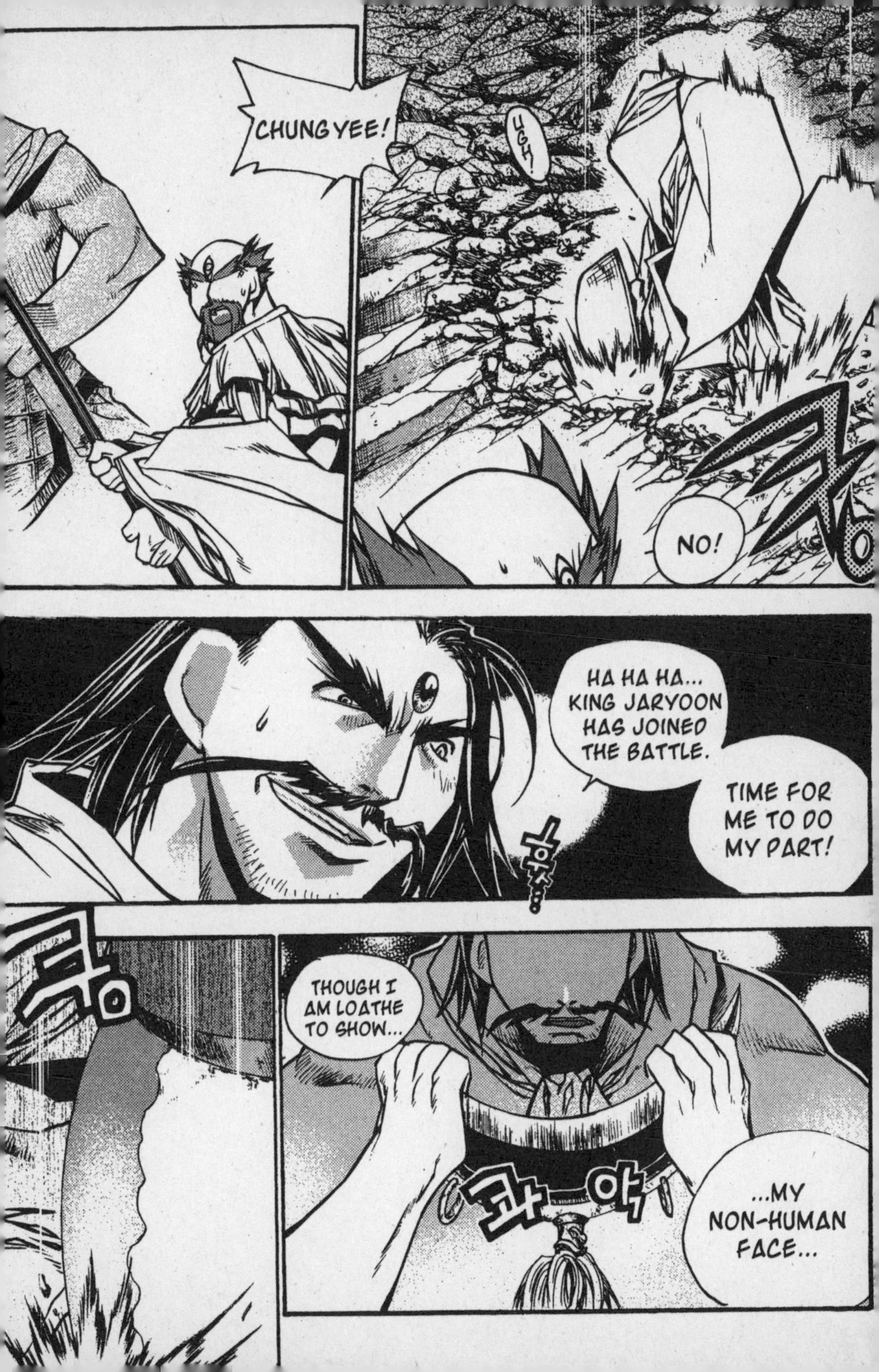
CHUNGYEE!
UGH!
NO!
HA HA HA... KING JARYOON HAS JOINED THE BATTLE.
TIME FOR ME TO DO MY PART!
THOUGH I AM LOATHE TO SHOW...
...MY NON-HUMAN FACE...

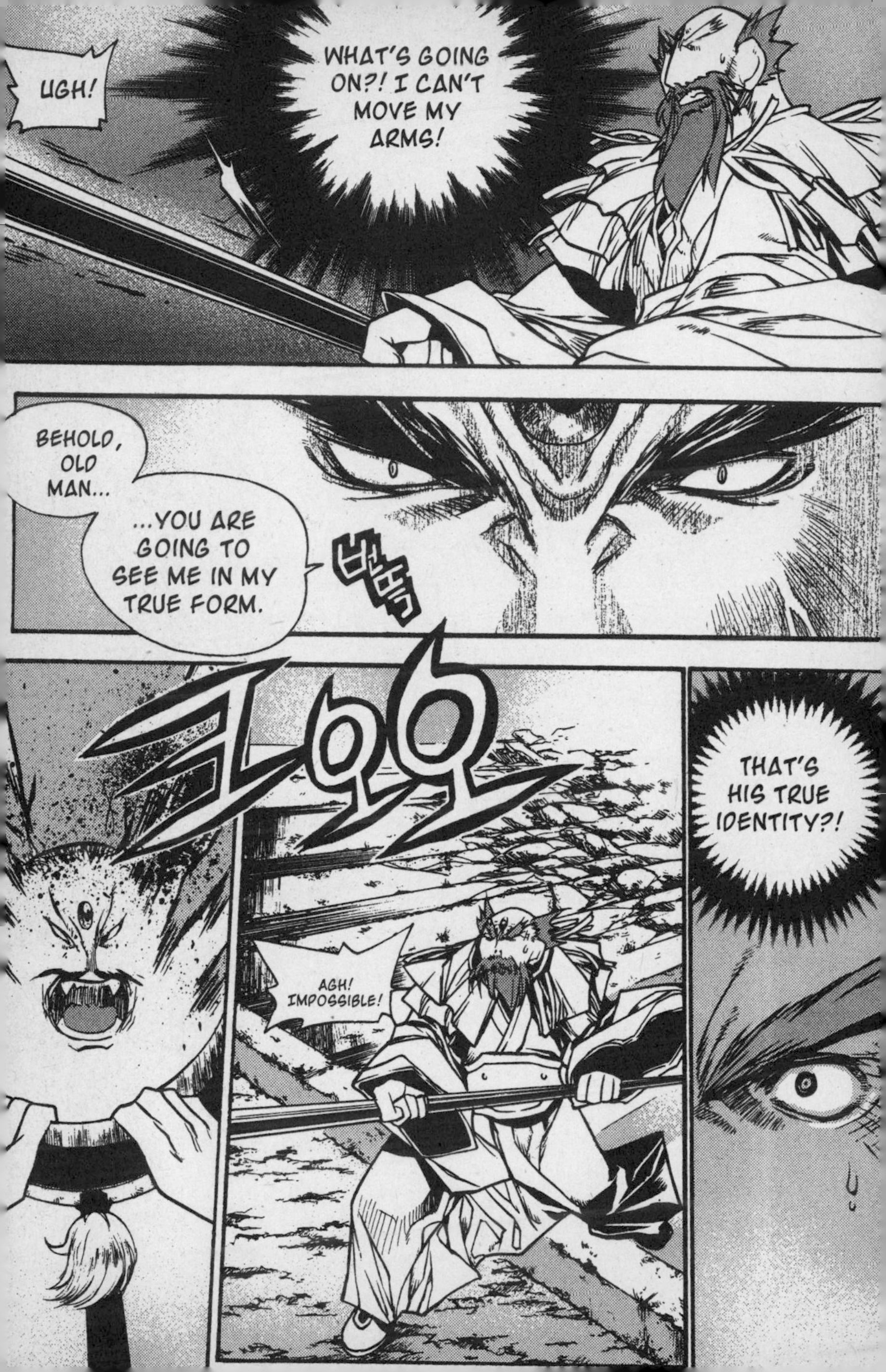
UGH!
WHAT'S GOING ON?! I CAN'T MOVE MY ARMS!
BEHOLD, OLD MAN...
...YOU ARE GOING TO SEE ME IN MY TRUE FORM.
AGH! IMPOSSIBLE!
THAT'S HIS TRUE IDENTITY?!

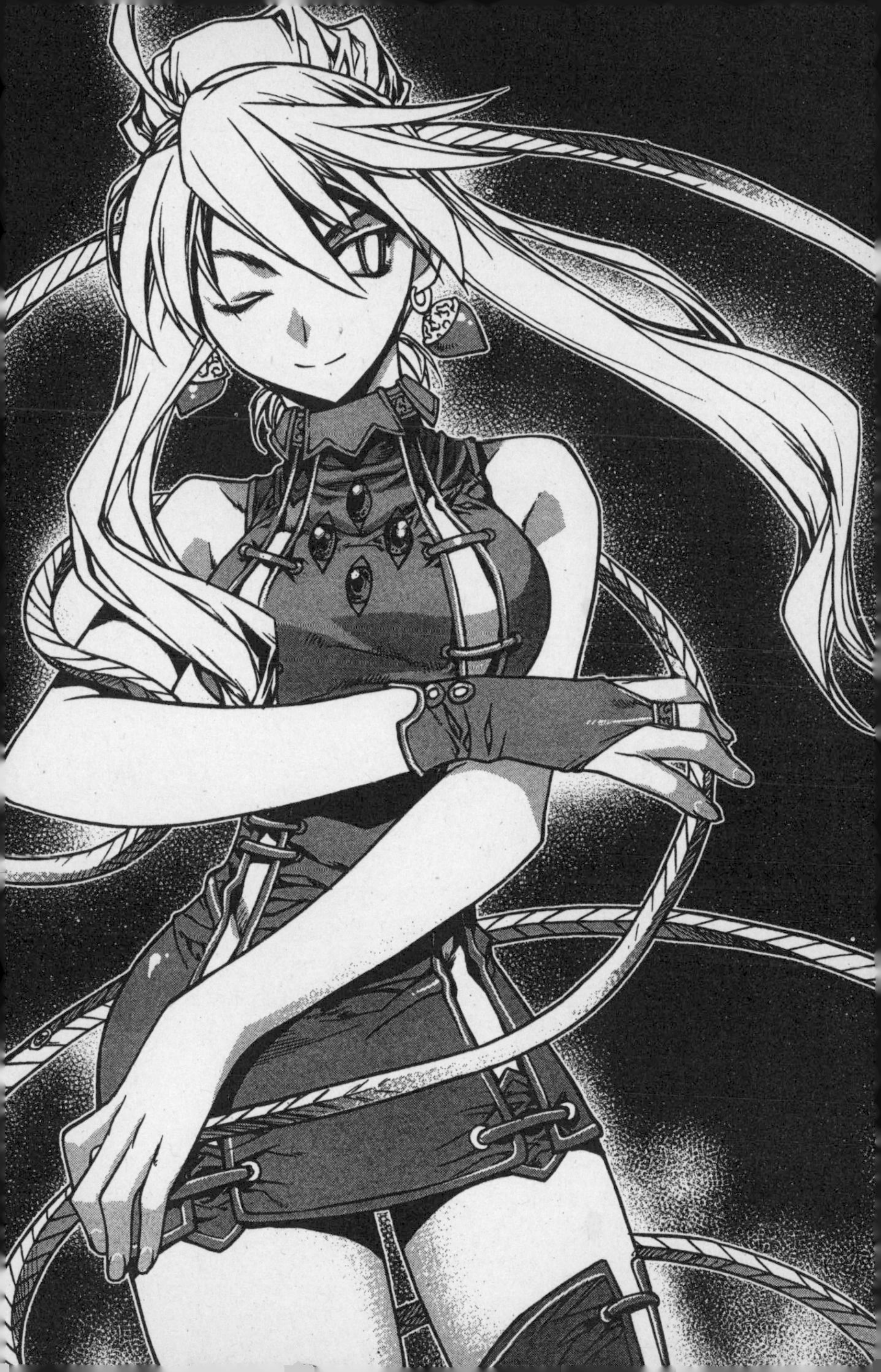

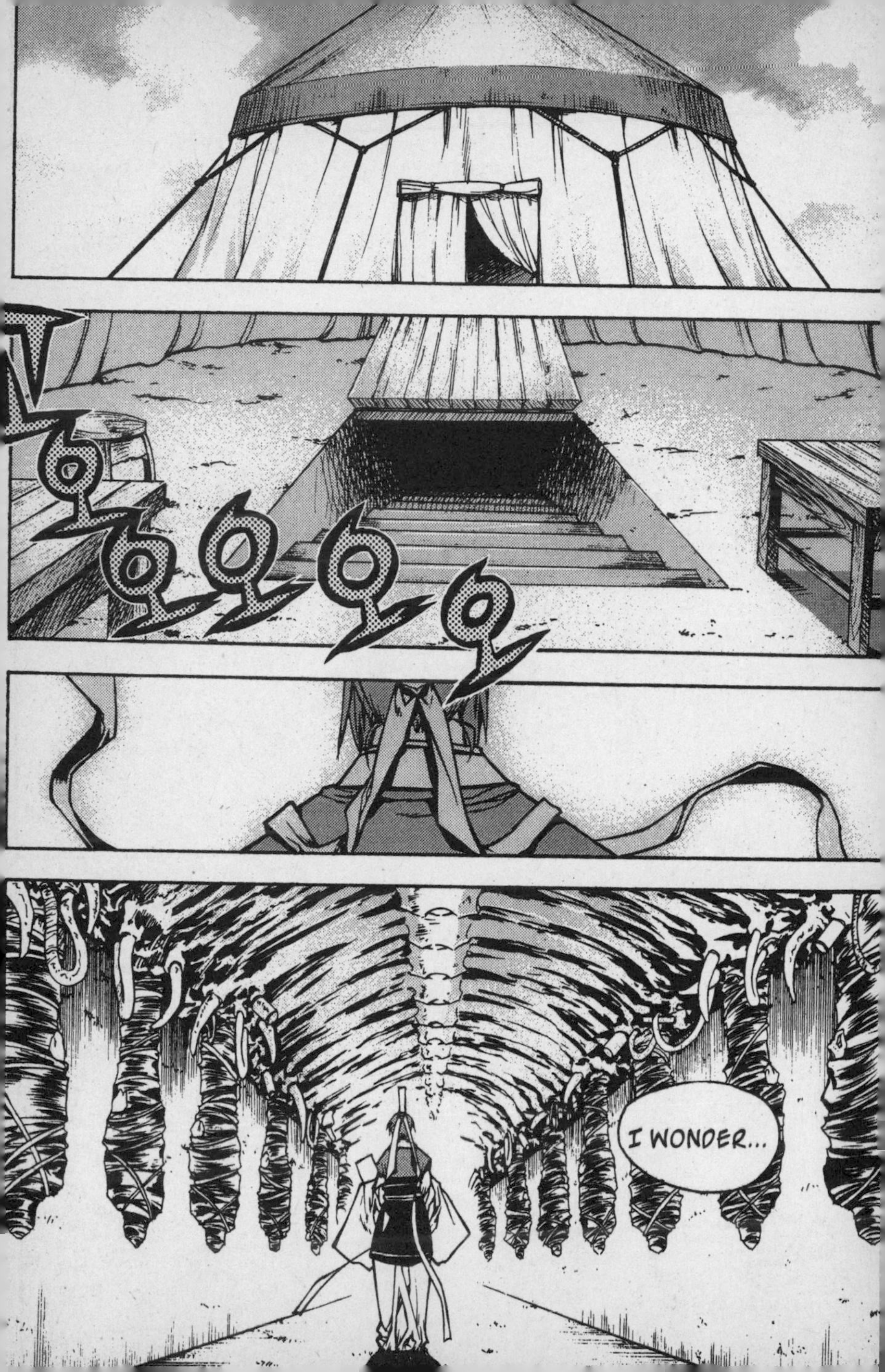
I WONDER...

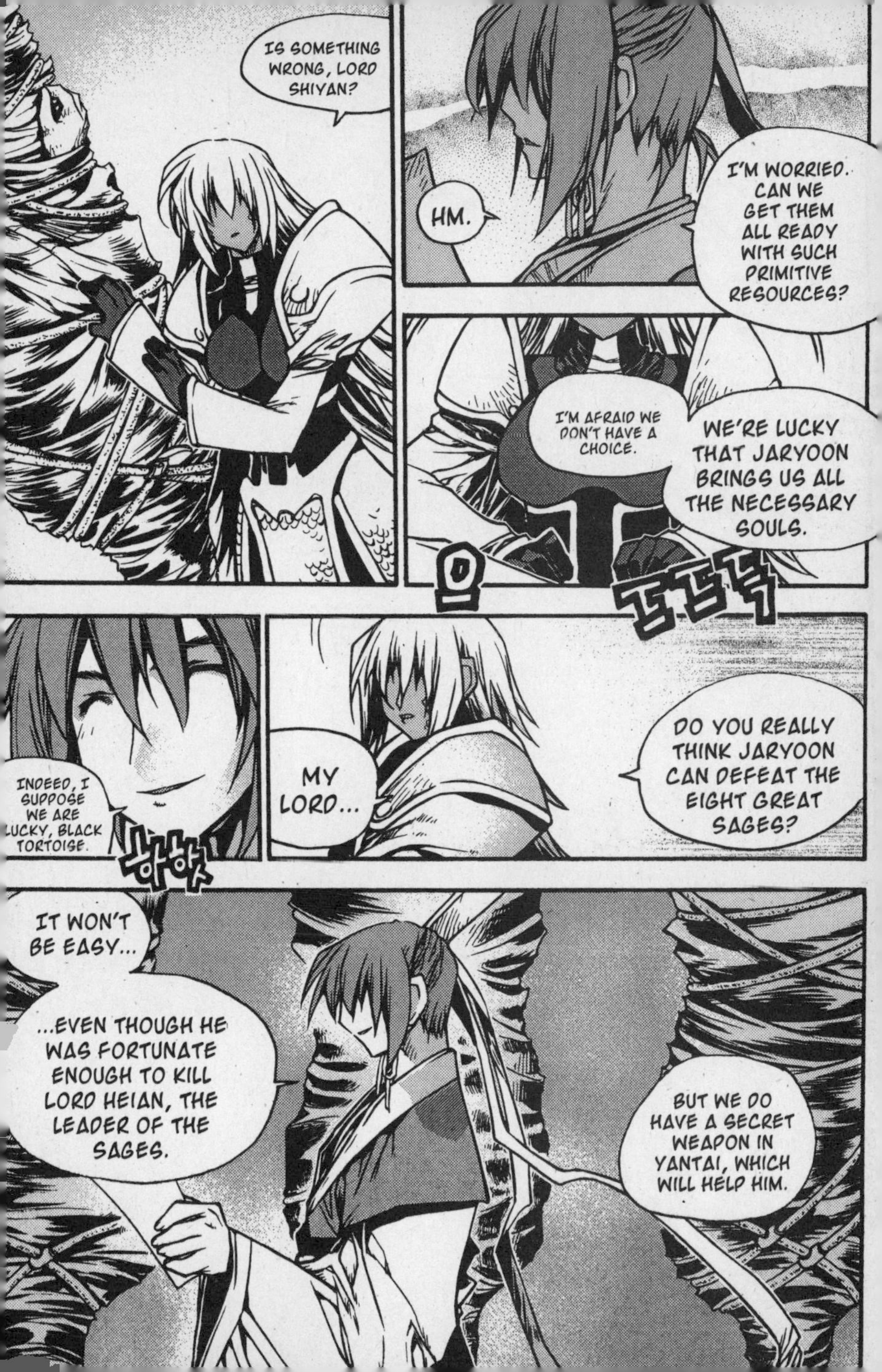
IS SOMETHING WRONG, LORD SHIYAN?
HM.
I'M WORRIED. CAN WE GET THEM ALL READY WITH SUCH PRIMITIVE RESOURCES?
I'M AFRAID WE DON'T HAVE A CHOICE.
WE'RE LUCKY THAT JARYOON BRINGS US ALL THE NECESSARY SOULS.
INDEED, I SUPPOSE WE ARE LUCKY, BLACK TORTOISE.
MY LORD...
DO YOU REALLY THINK JARYOON CAN DEFEAT THE EIGHT GREAT SAGES?
IT WON'T BE EASY...
...EVEN THOUGH HE WAS FORTUNATE ENOUGH TO KILL LORD HEIAN, THE LEADER OF THE SAGES.
BUT WE DO HAVE A SECRET WEAPON IN YANTAI, WHICH WILL HELP HIM.

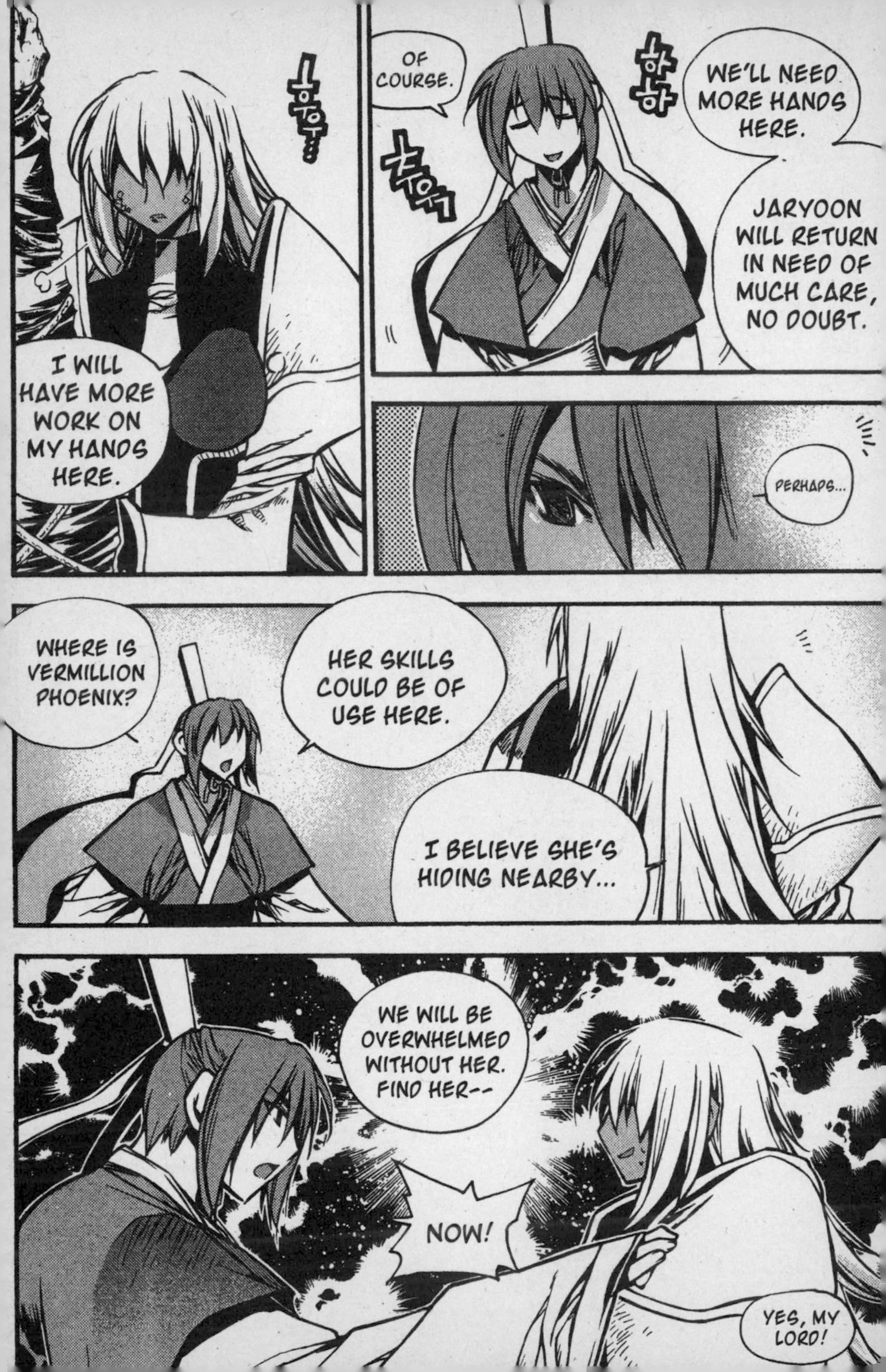
I WILL HAVE MORE WORK ON MY HANDS HERE.
OF COURSE.
하하
WE'LL NEED MORE HANDS HERE.
JARYOON WILL RETURN IN NEED OF MUCH CARE, NO DOUBT.
PERHAPS...
WHERE IS VERMILLION PHOENIX?
HER SKILLS COULD BE OF USE HERE.
I BELIEVE SHE'S HIDING NEARBY...
WE WILL BE OVERWHELMED WITHOUT HER. FIND HER--
NOW!
YES, MY LORD!

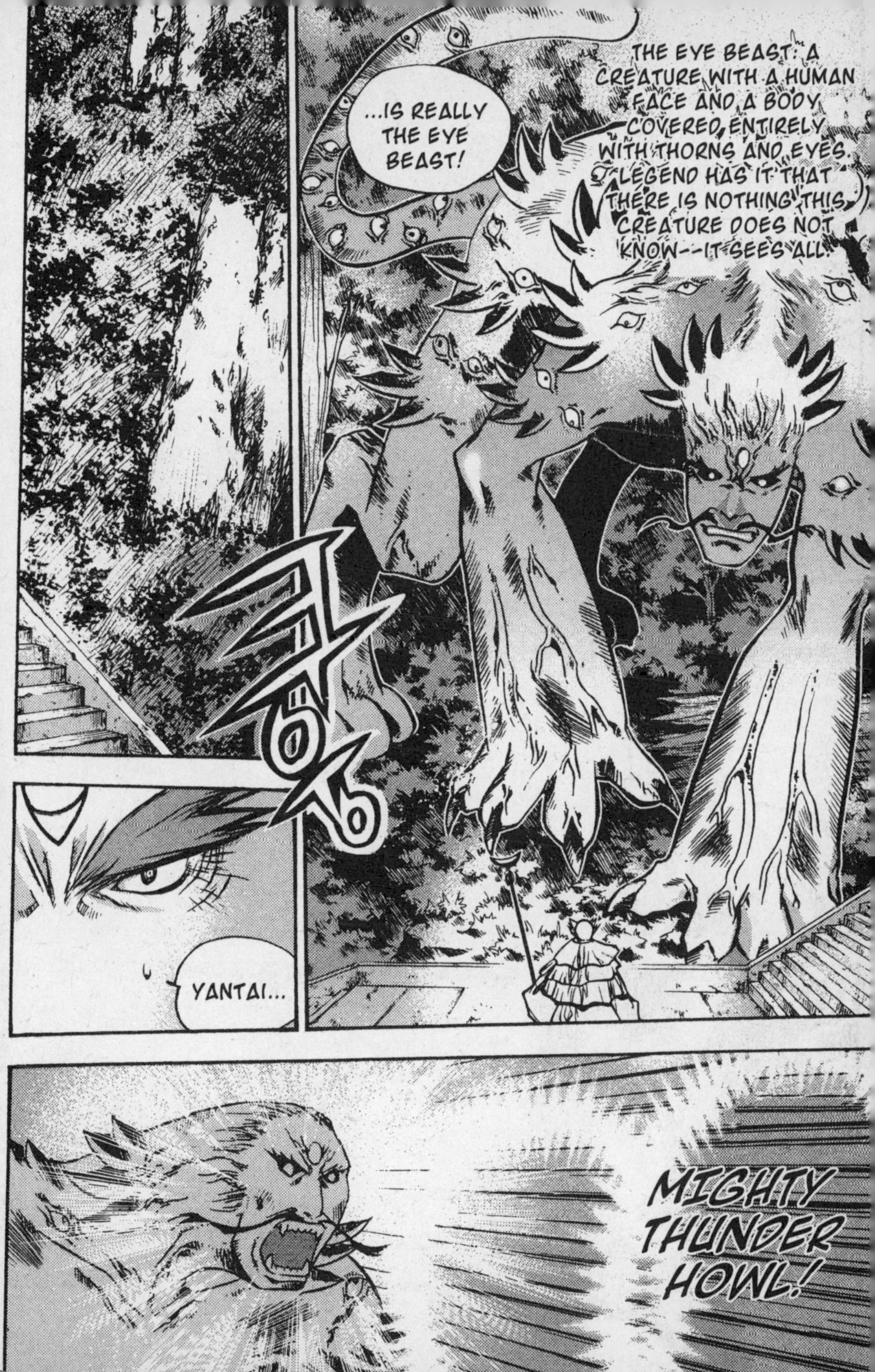
YANTAI...
...IS REALLY THE EYE BEAST!
THE EYE BEAST: A CREATURE WITH A HUMAN FACE AND A BODY COVERED ENTIRELY WITH THORNS AND EYES. LEGEND HAS IT THAT THERE IS NOTHING THIS CREATURE DOES NOT KNOW--IT SEES ALL.
MIGHTY THUNDER HOWL!

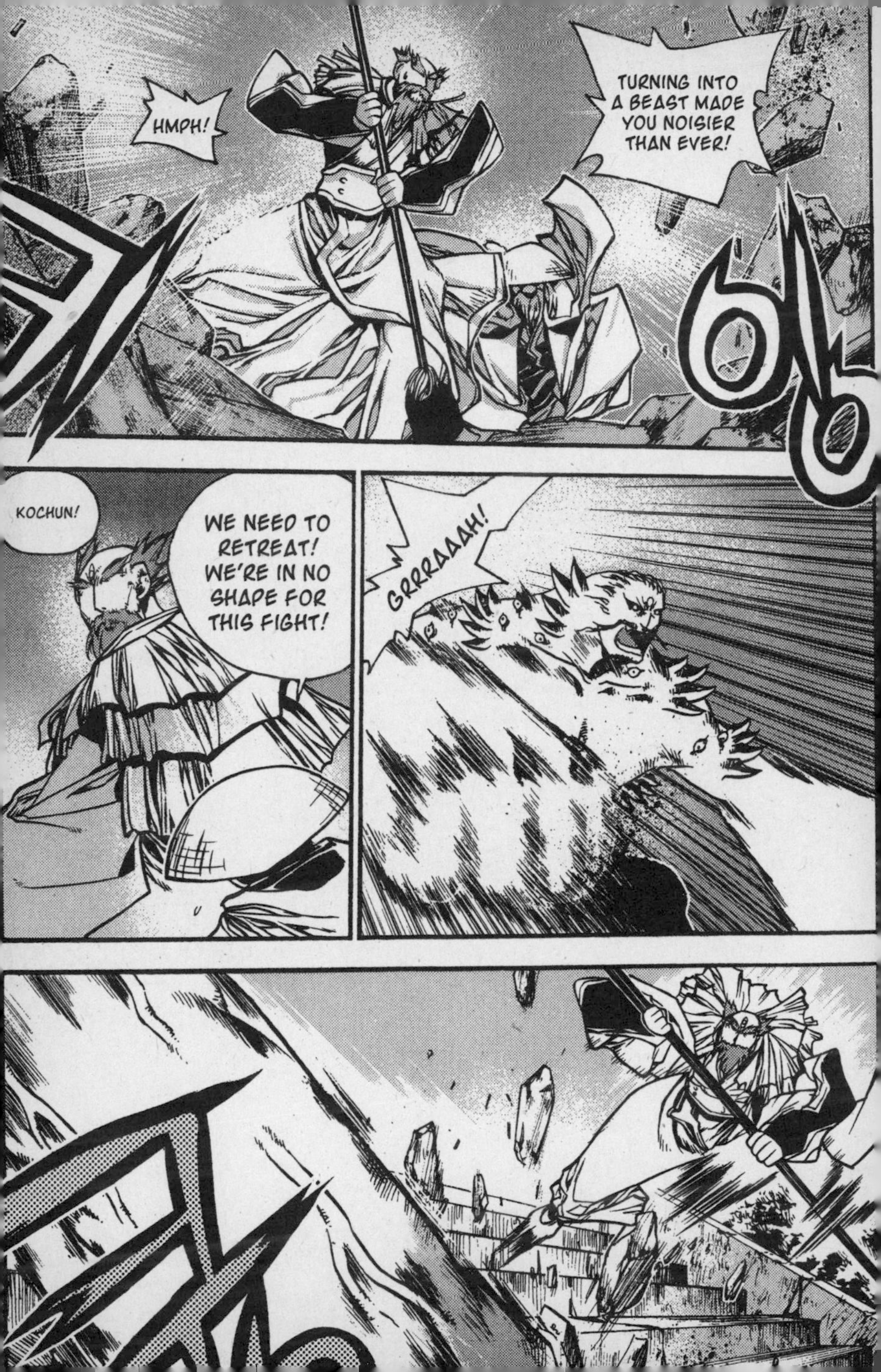
HMPH!
TURNING INTO A BEAST MADE YOU NOISIER THAN EVER!
KOCHUN!
WE NEED TO RETREAT! WE'RE IN NO SHAPE FOR THIS FIGHT!
GRRRAAAH!

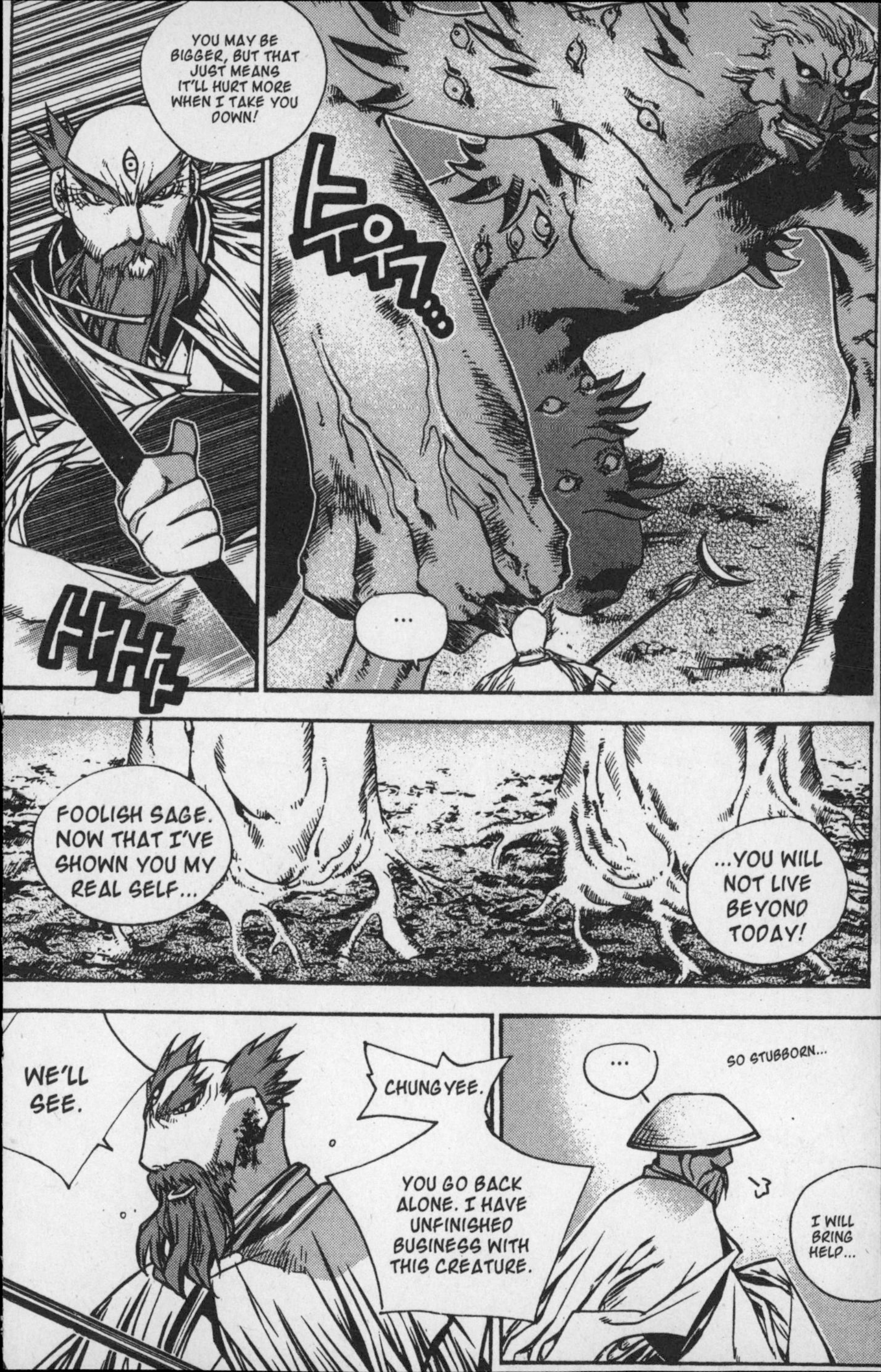
YOU MAY BE BIGGER, BUT THAT JUST MEANS IT'LL HURT MORE WHEN I TAKE YOU DOWN!
...
FOOLISH SAGE. NOW THAT I'VE SHOWN YOU MY REAL SELF...
...YOU WILL NOT LIVE BEYOND TODAY!
WE'LL SEE.
CHUNGYEE.
YOU GO BACK ALONE. I HAVE UNFINISHED BUSINESS WITH THIS CREATURE.
...
SO STUBBORN...
I WILL BRING HELP...

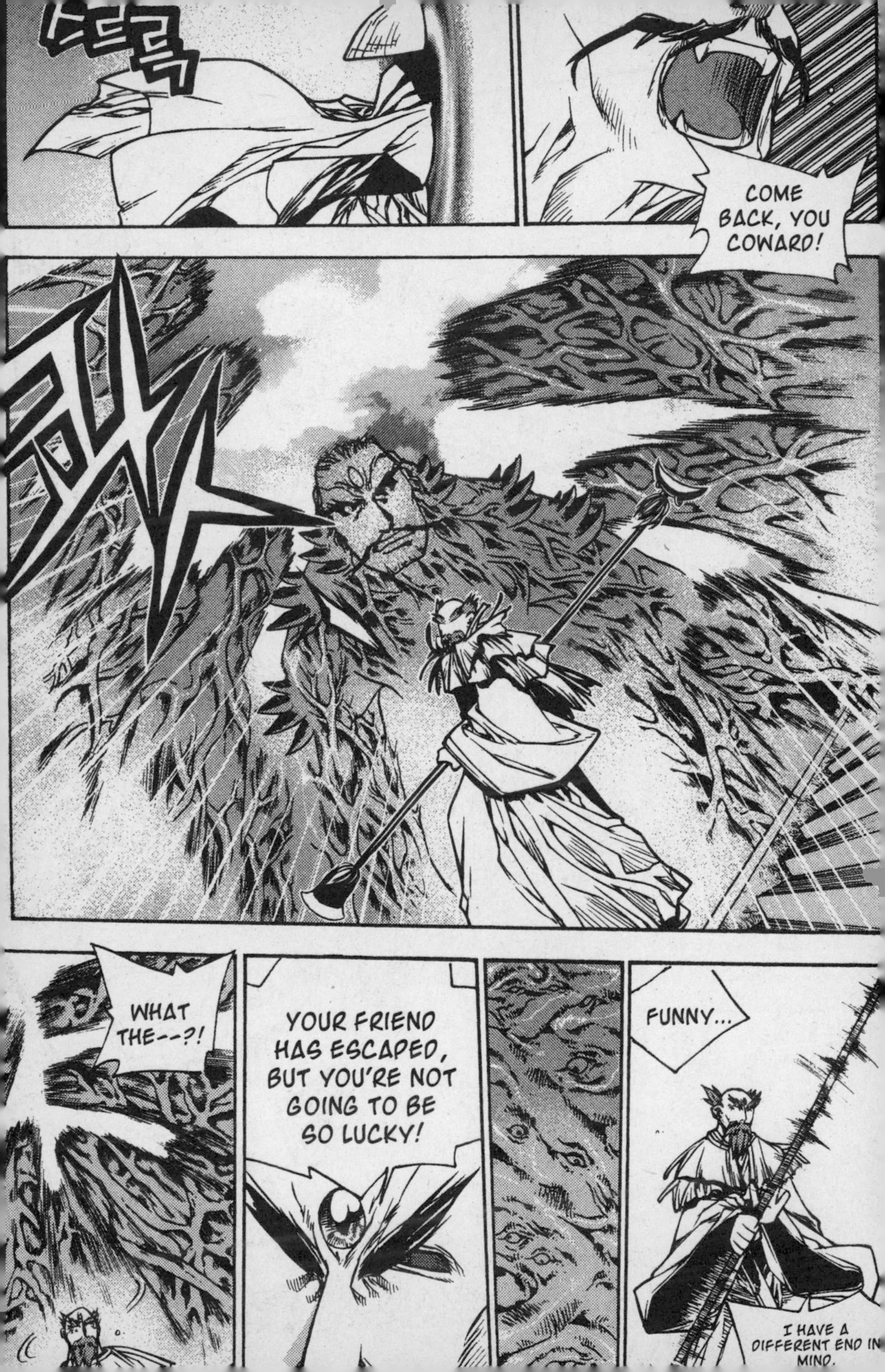
COME BACK, YOU COWARD!
WHAT THE--?!
YOUR FRIEND HAS ESCAPED, BUT YOU'RE NOT GOING TO BE SO LUCKY!
FUNNY...
I HAVE A DIFFERENT END IN MIND.

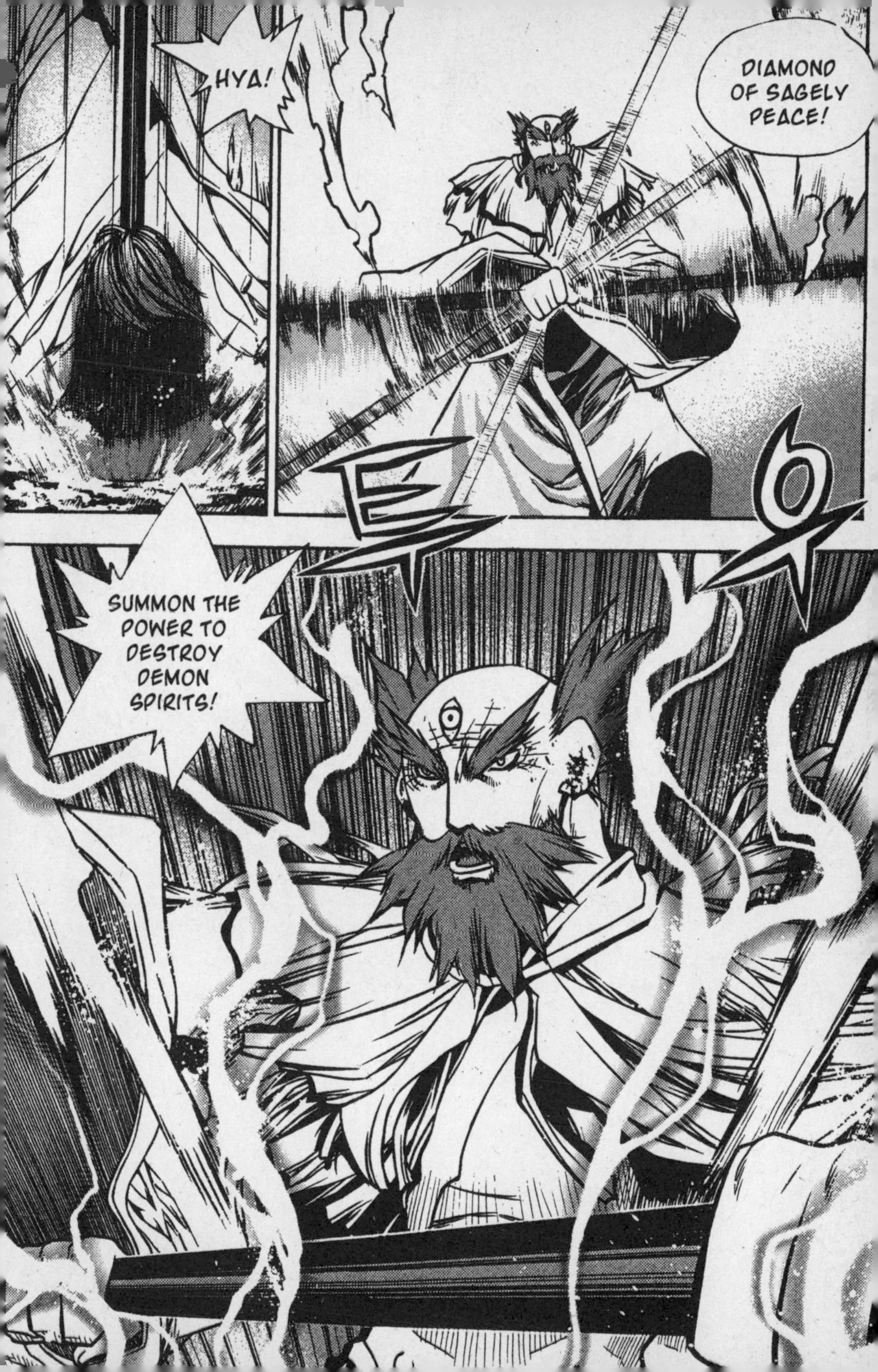
HYA!
DIAMOND OF SAGELY PEACE!
SUMMON THE POWER TO DESTROY DEMON SPIRITS!

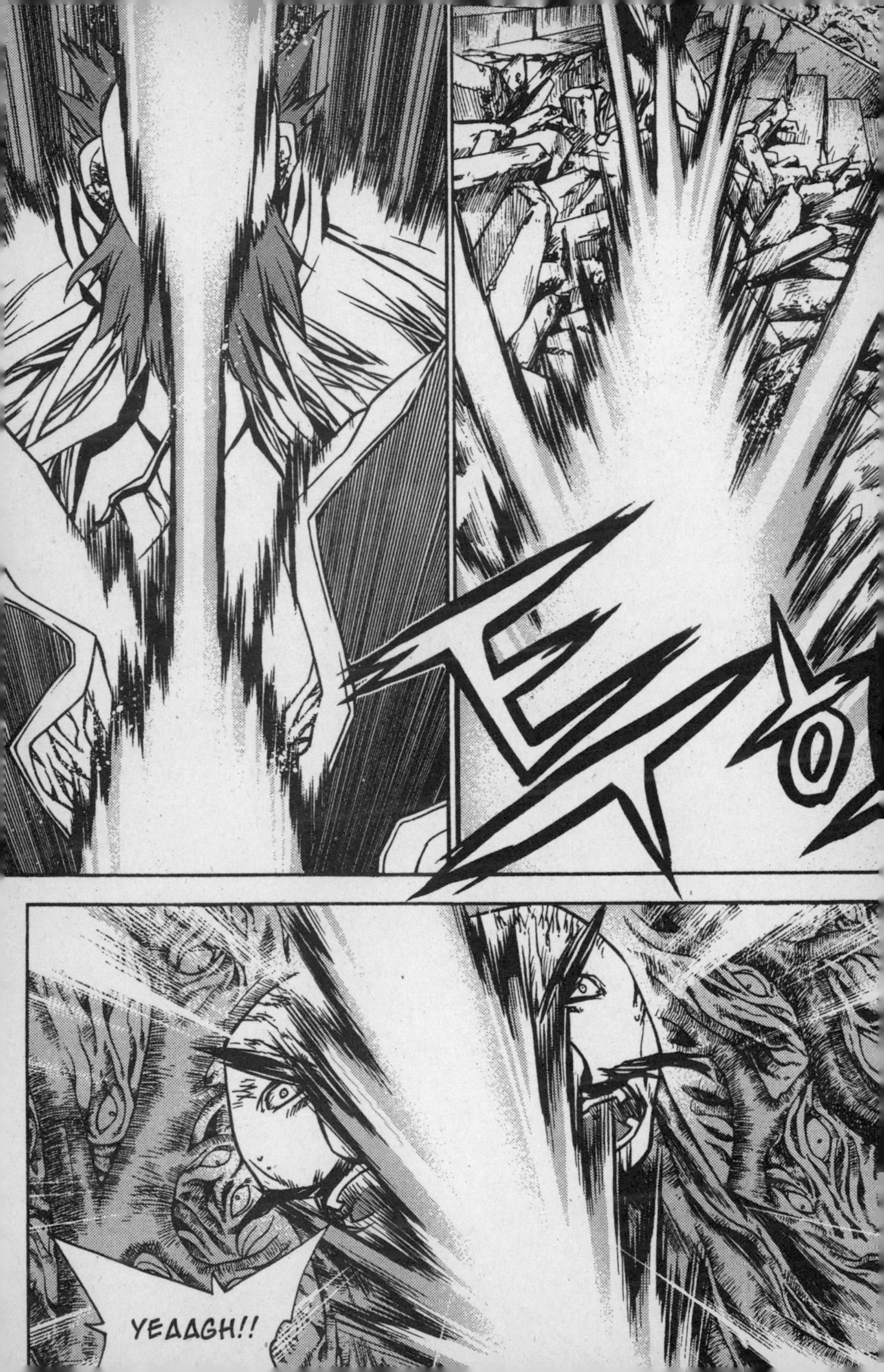
YEAAGH!!

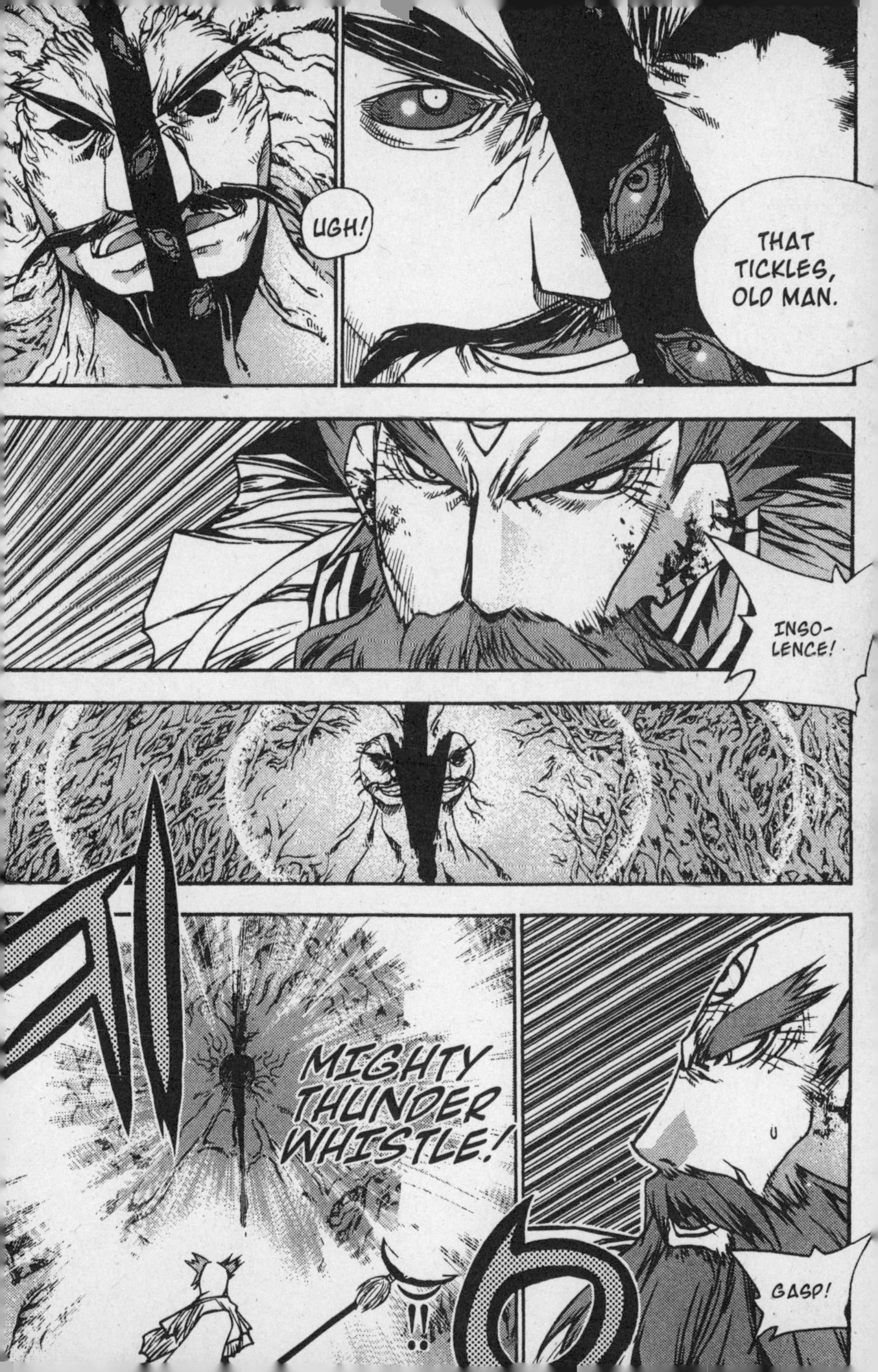
UGH!
THAT TICKLES, OLD MAN.
INSO-LENCE!
MIGHTY THUNDER WHISTLE!
!!
GASP!

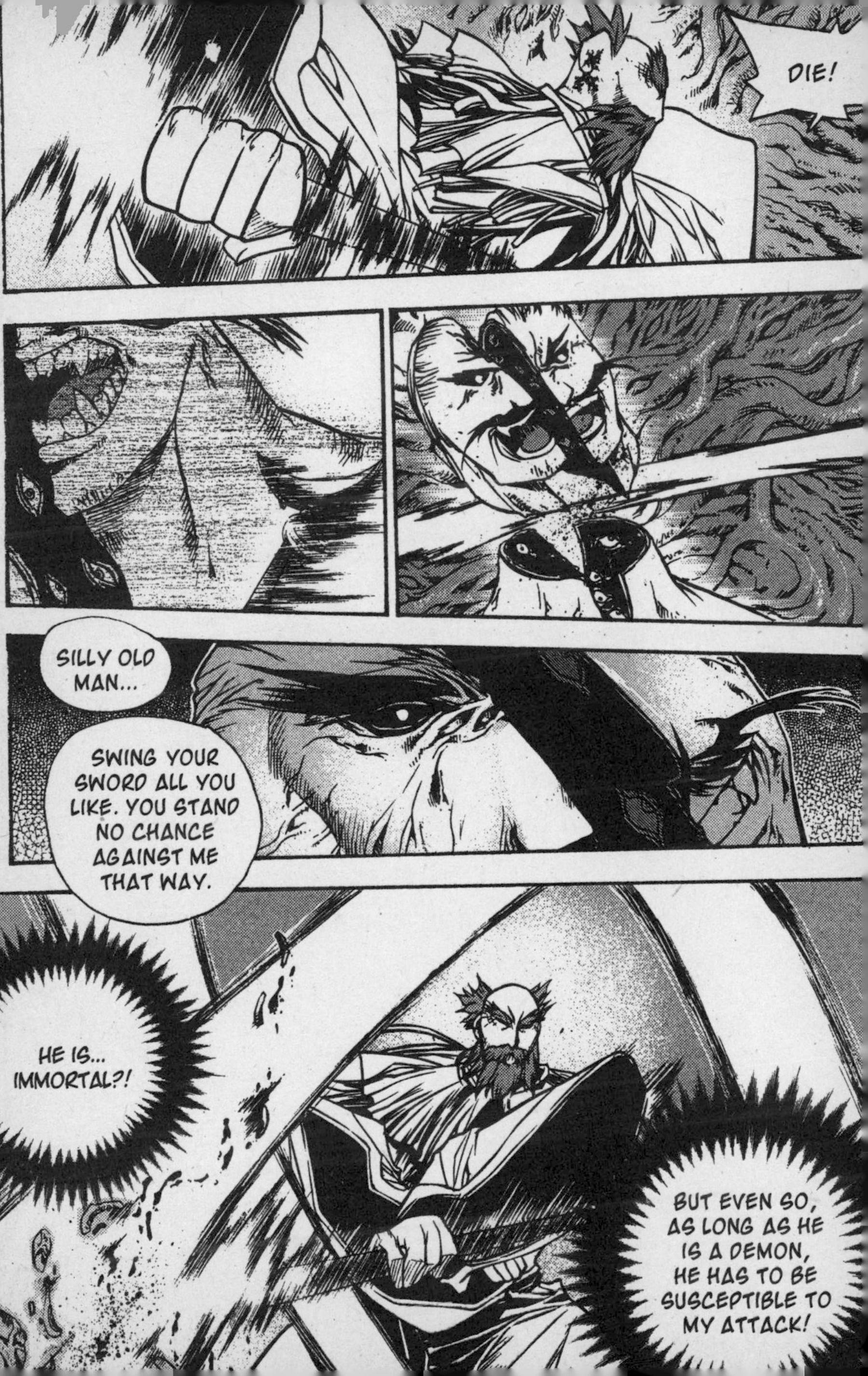
DIE!
SILLY OLD MAN...
SWING YOUR SWORD ALL YOU LIKE. YOU STAND NO CHANCE AGAINST ME THAT WAY.
HE IS... IMMORTAL?!
BUT EVEN SO, AS LONG AS HE IS A DEMON, HE HAS TO BE SUSCEPTIBLE TO MY ATTACK!

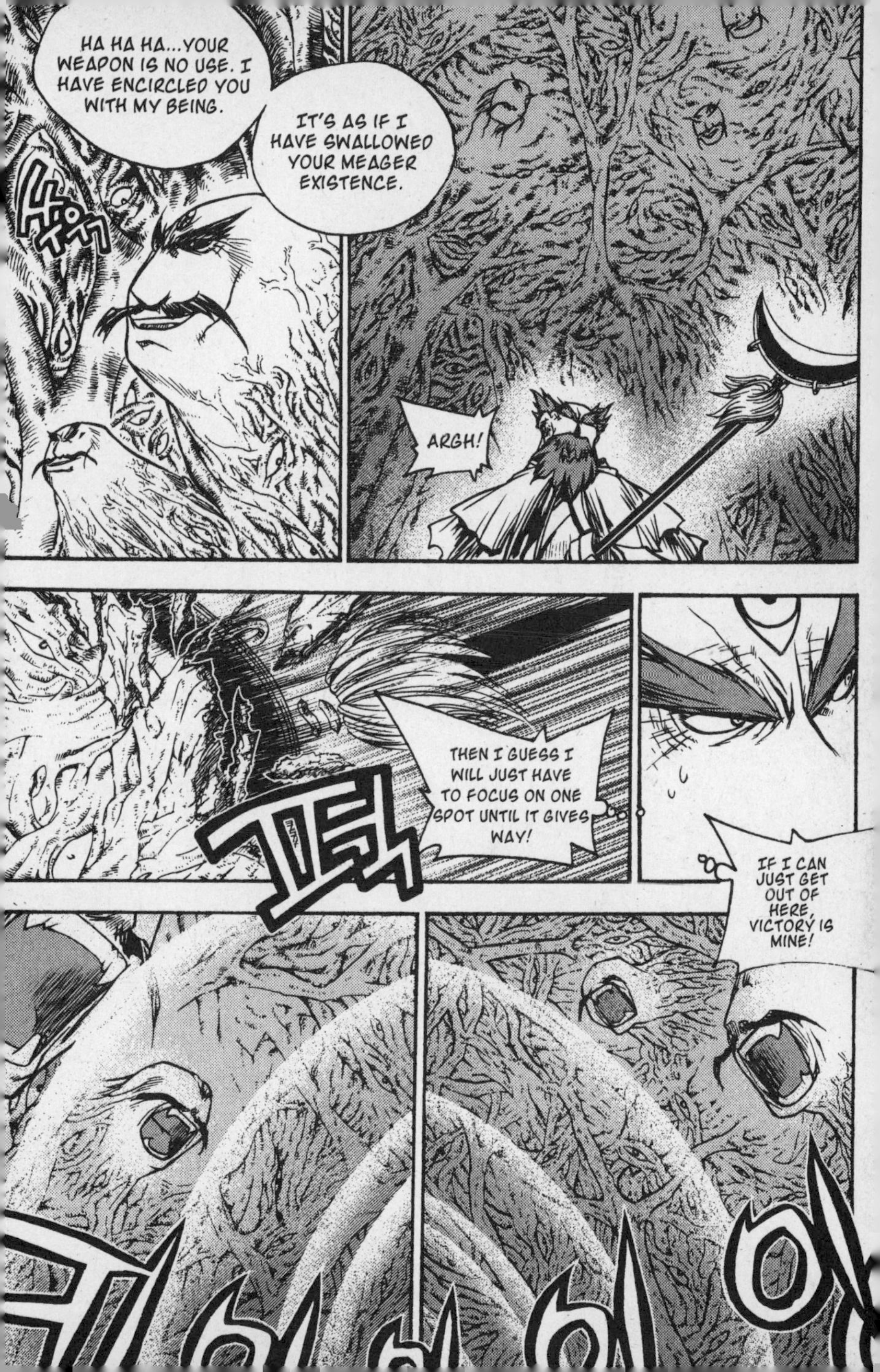
HA HA HA...YOUR WEAPON IS NO USE. I HAVE ENCIRCLED YOU WITH MY BEING.
IT'S AS IF I HAVE SWALLOWED YOUR MEAGER EXISTENCE.
ARGH!
THEN I GUESS I WILL JUST HAVE TO FOCUS ON ONE SPOT UNTIL IT GIVES WAY!
IF I CAN JUST GET OUT OF HERE, VICTORY IS MINE!

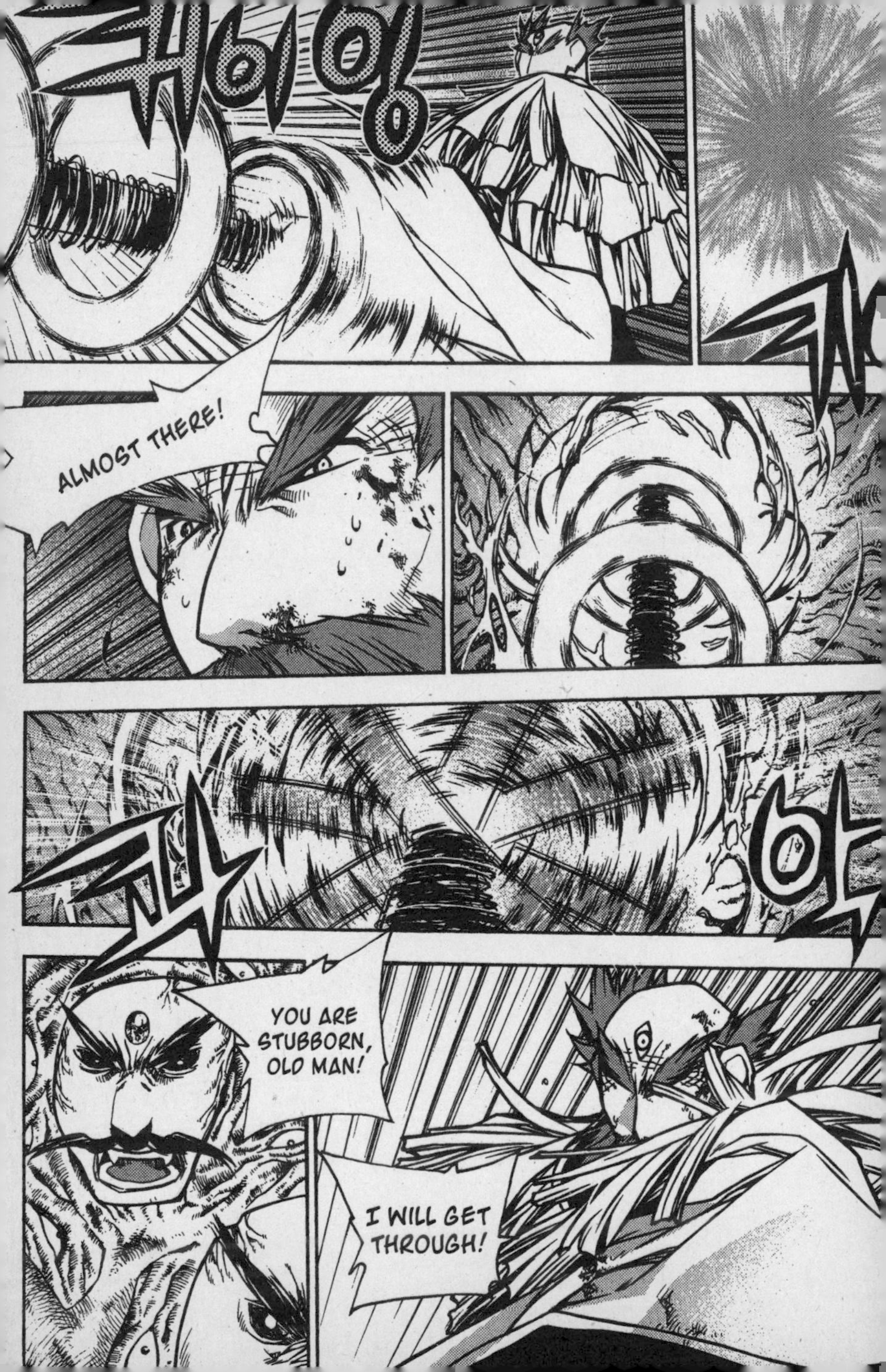
ALMOST THERE!
YOU ARE STUBBORN, OLD MAN!
I WILL GET THROUGH!

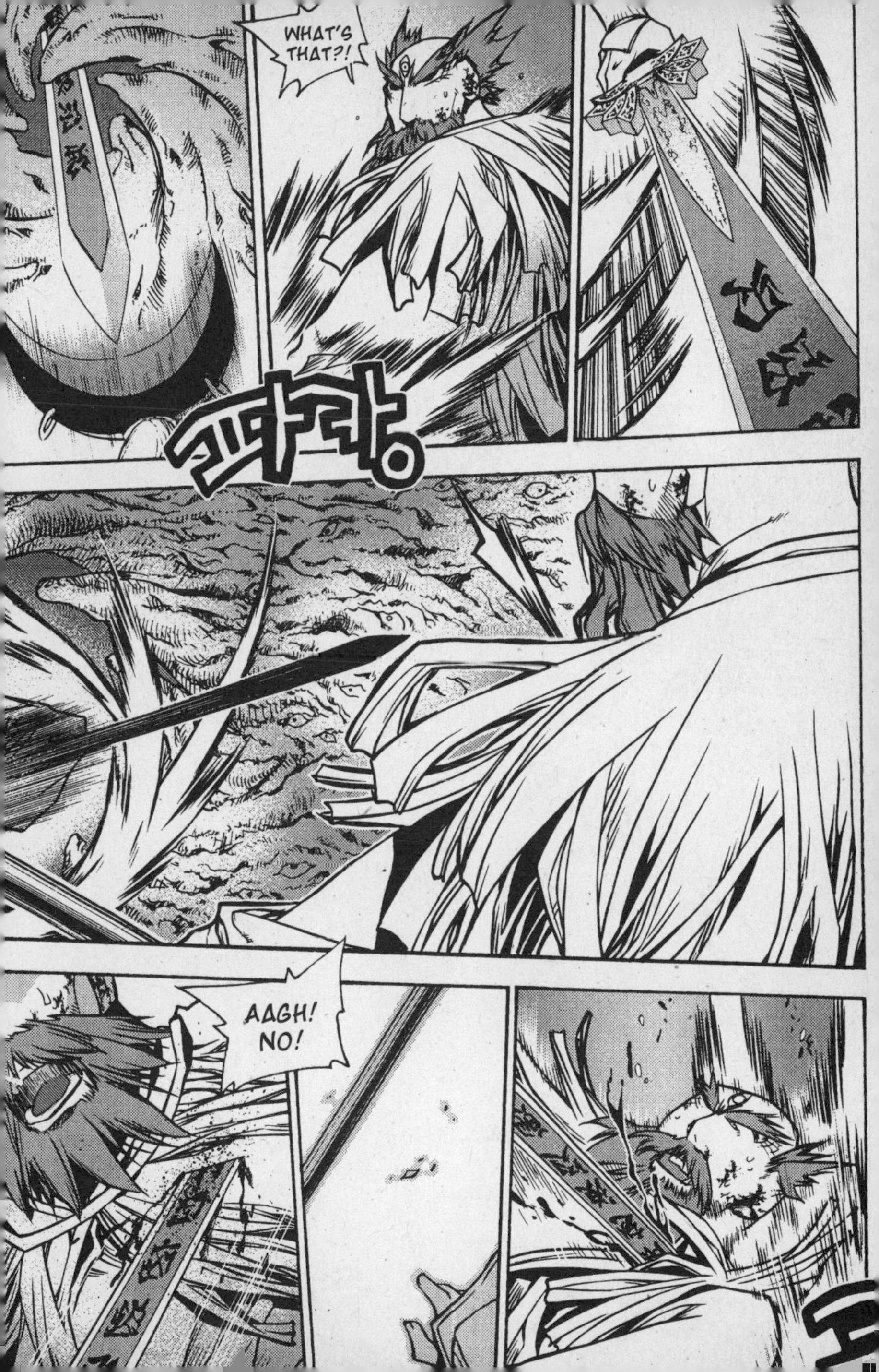
WHAT'S THAT?!
AAGH! NO!

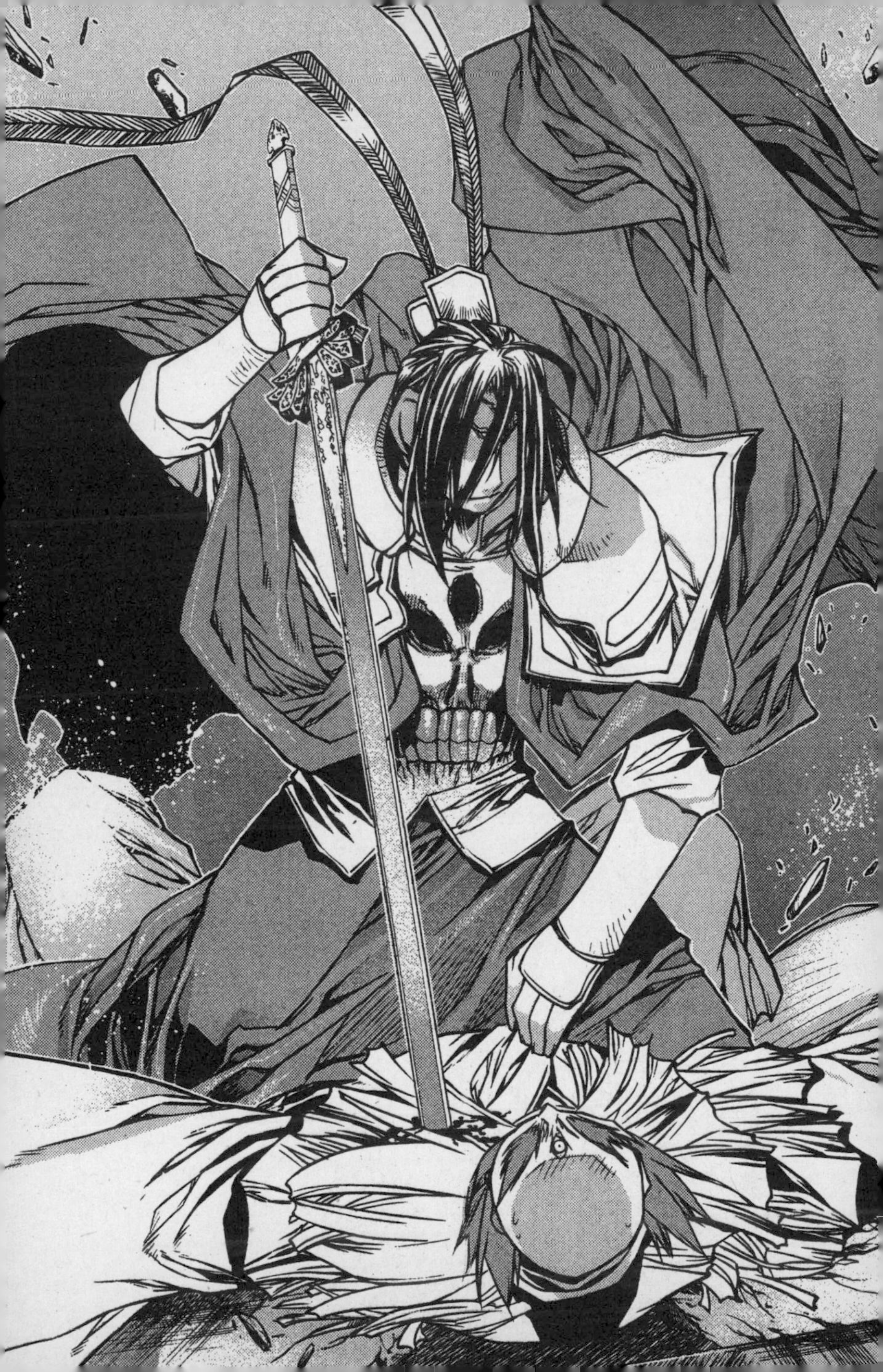

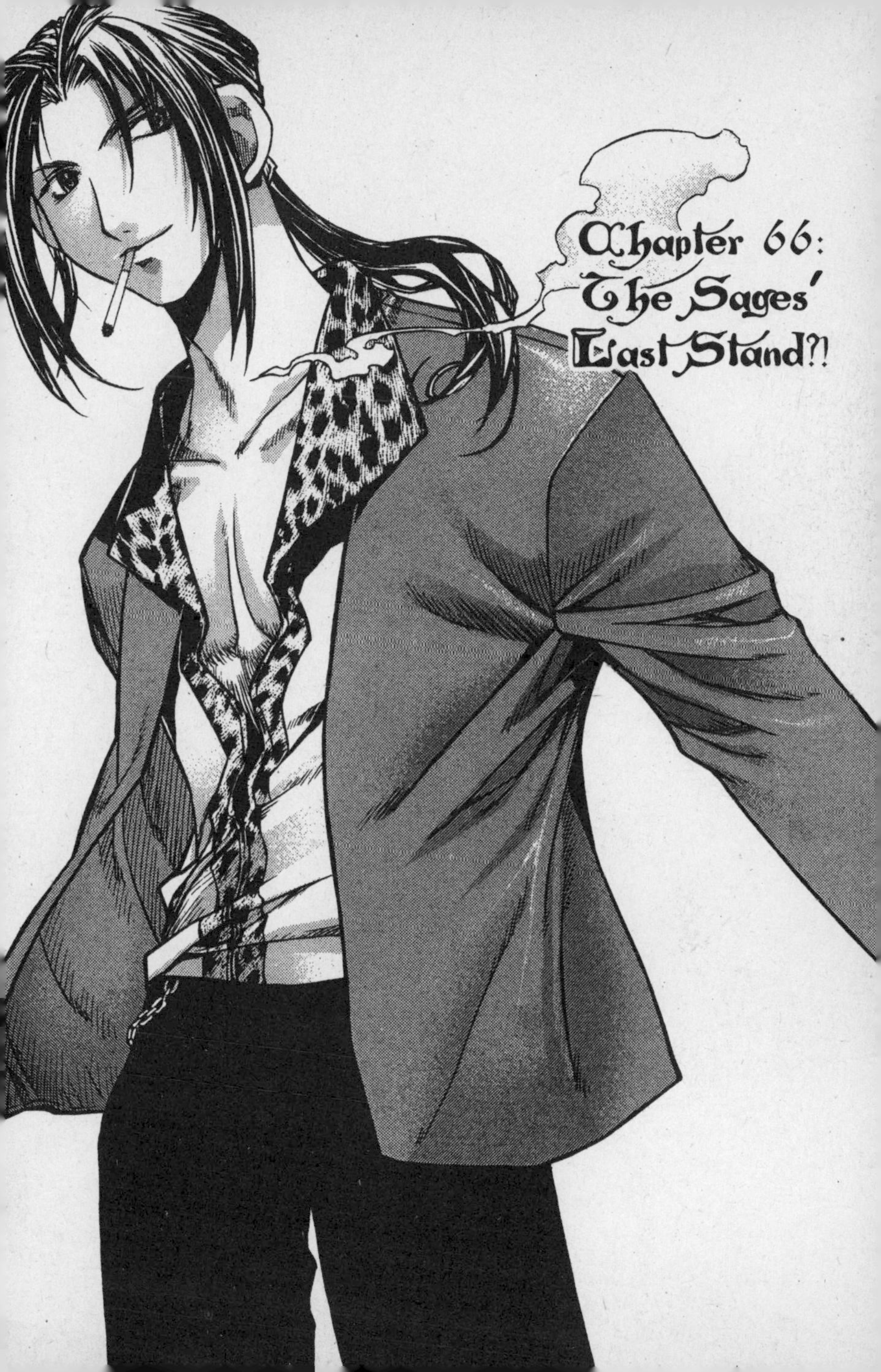
Chapter 66:
The Sages'
Last Stand?!

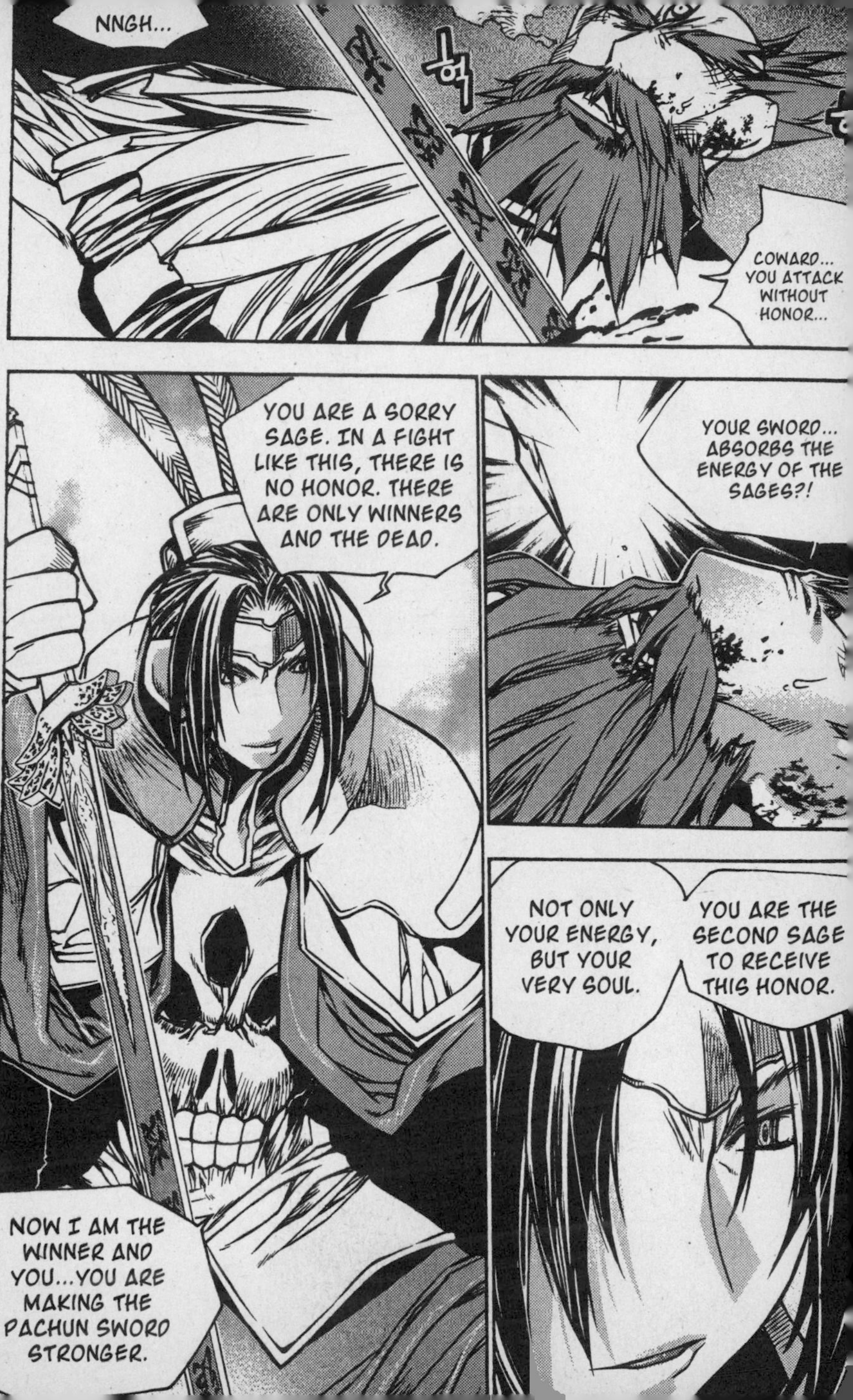

NNGH...
헉
COWARD... YOU ATTACK WITHOUT HONOR...
YOU ARE A SORRY SAGE. IN A FIGHT LIKE THIS, THERE IS NO HONOR. THERE ARE ONLY WINNERS AND THE DEAD.
NOW I AM THE WINNER AND YOU...YOU ARE MAKING THE PACHUN SWORD STRONGER.
YOUR SWORD... ABSORBS THE ENERGY OF THE SAGES?!
NOT ONLY YOUR ENERGY, BUT YOUR VERY SOUL.
YOU ARE THE SECOND SAGE TO RECEIVE THIS HONOR.

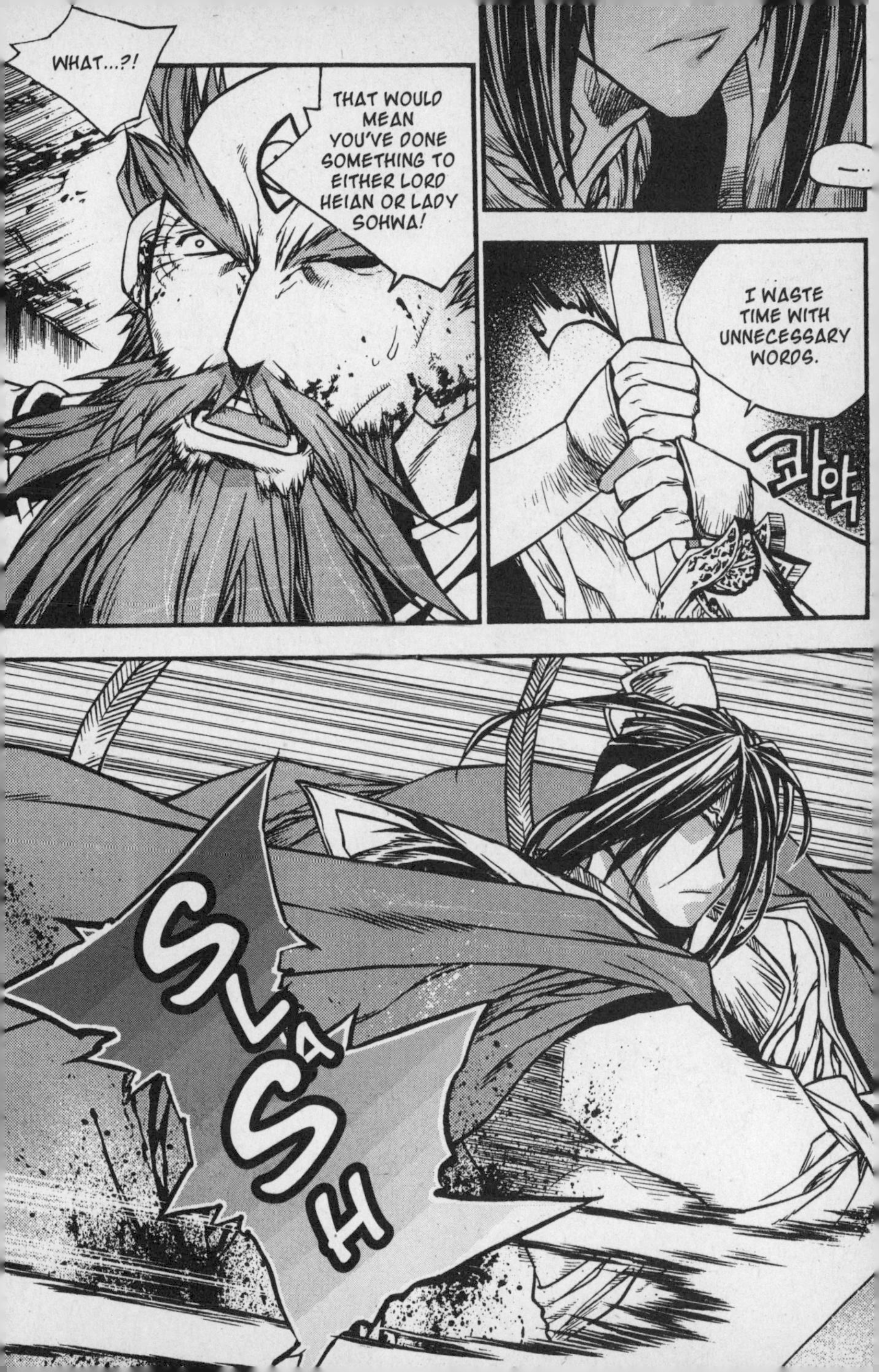
WHAT...?!
THAT WOULD MEAN YOU'VE DONE SOMETHING TO EITHER LORD HEIAN OR LADY SOHWA!
...
I WASTE TIME WITH UNNECESSARY WORDS.
콰악
SLASH

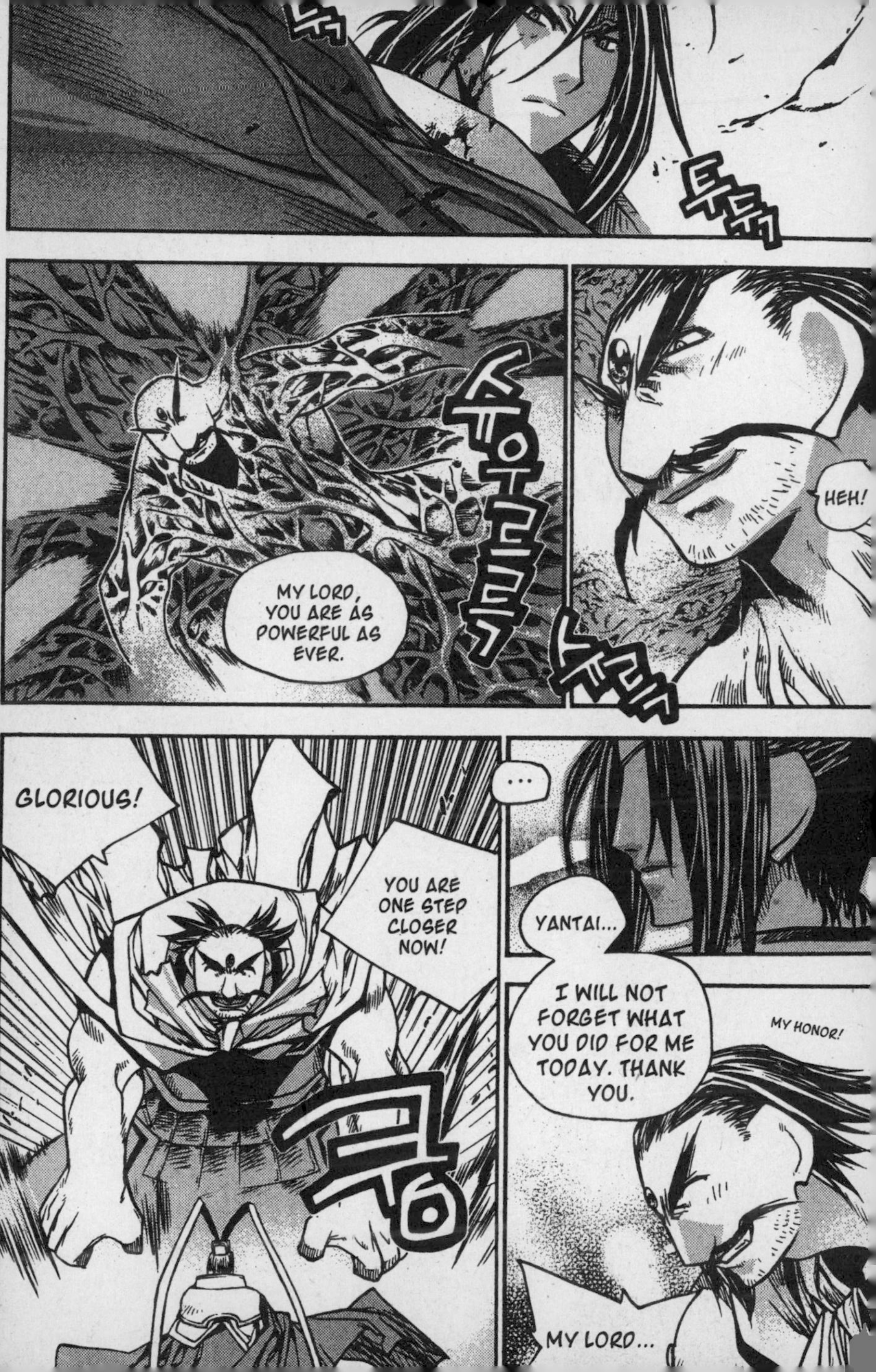
MY LORD, YOU ARE AS POWERFUL AS EVER.
HEH!
GLORIOUS!
YOU ARE ONE STEP CLOSER NOW!
...
YANTAI...
I WILL NOT FORGET WHAT YOU DID FOR ME TODAY. THANK YOU.
MY HONOR!
MY LORD...

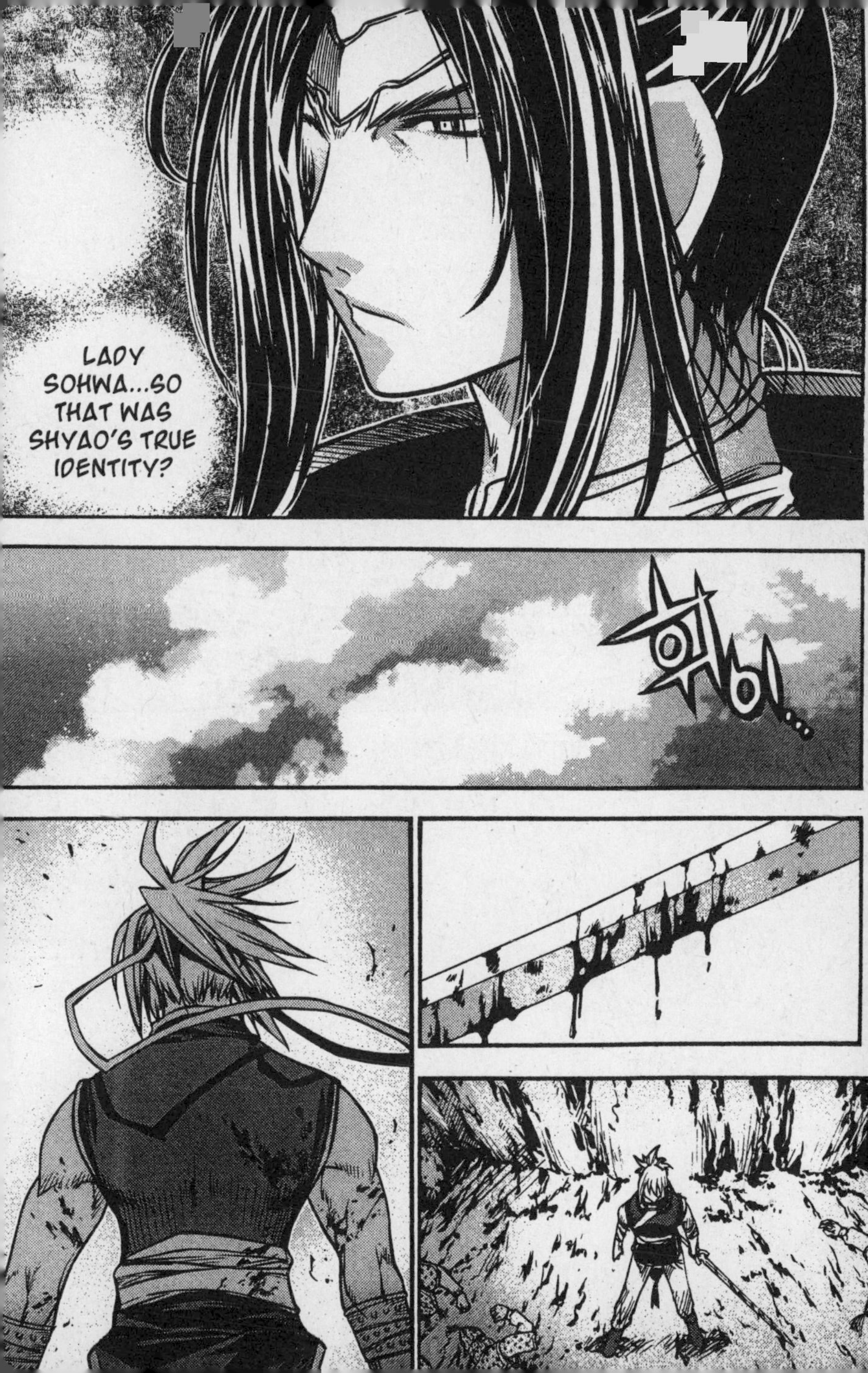
LADY SOHWA...SO THAT WAS SHYAO'S TRUE IDENTITY?

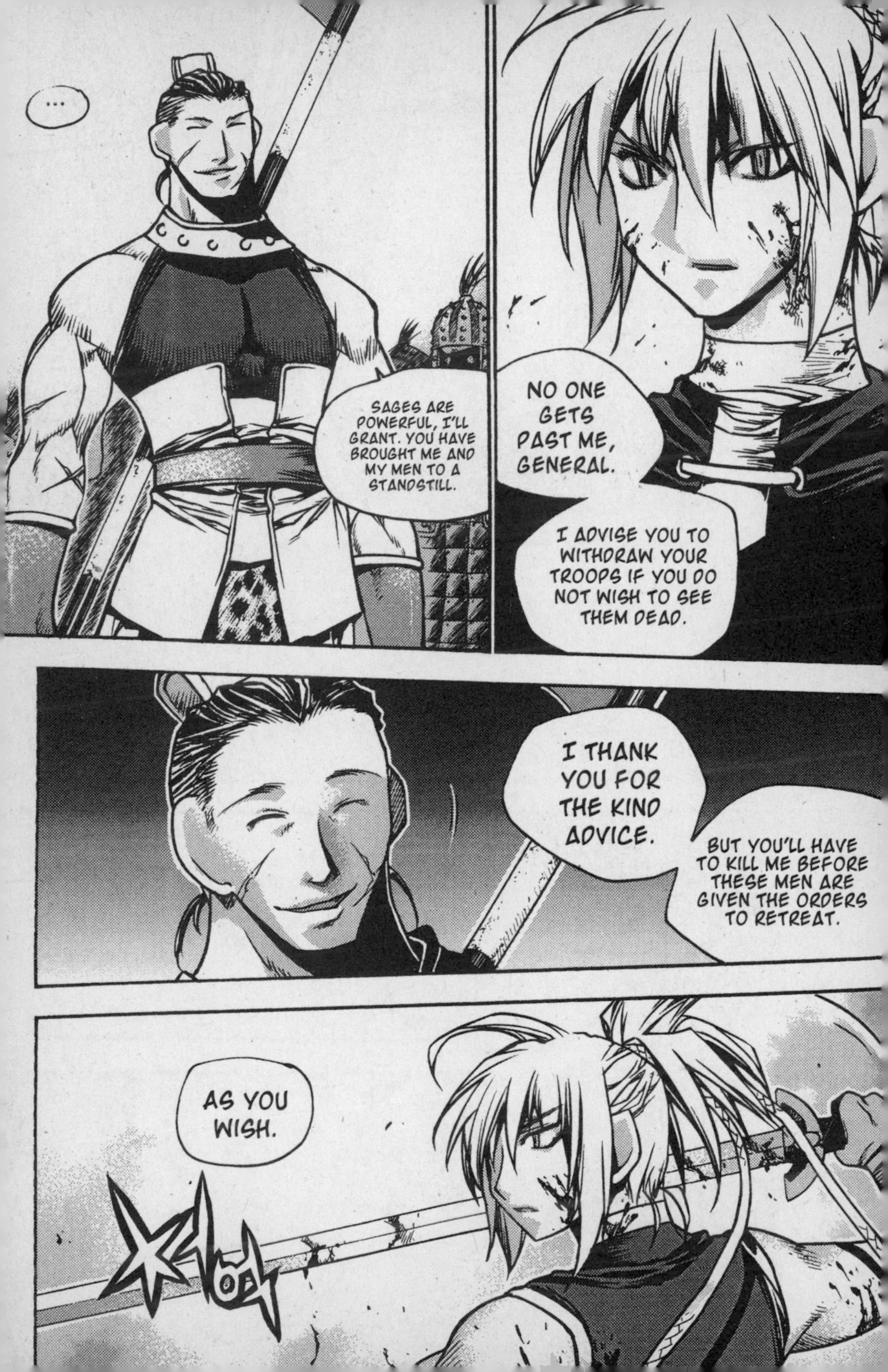
...
SAGES ARE POWERFUL, I'LL GRANT. YOU HAVE BROUGHT ME AND MY MEN TO A STANDSTILL.
NO ONE GETS PAST ME, GENERAL.
I ADVISE YOU TO WITHDRAW YOUR TROOPS IF YOU DO NOT WISH TO SEE THEM DEAD.
I THANK YOU FOR THE KIND ADVICE.
BUT YOU'LL HAVE TO KILL ME BEFORE THESE MEN ARE GIVEN THE ORDERS TO RETREAT.
AS YOU WISH.

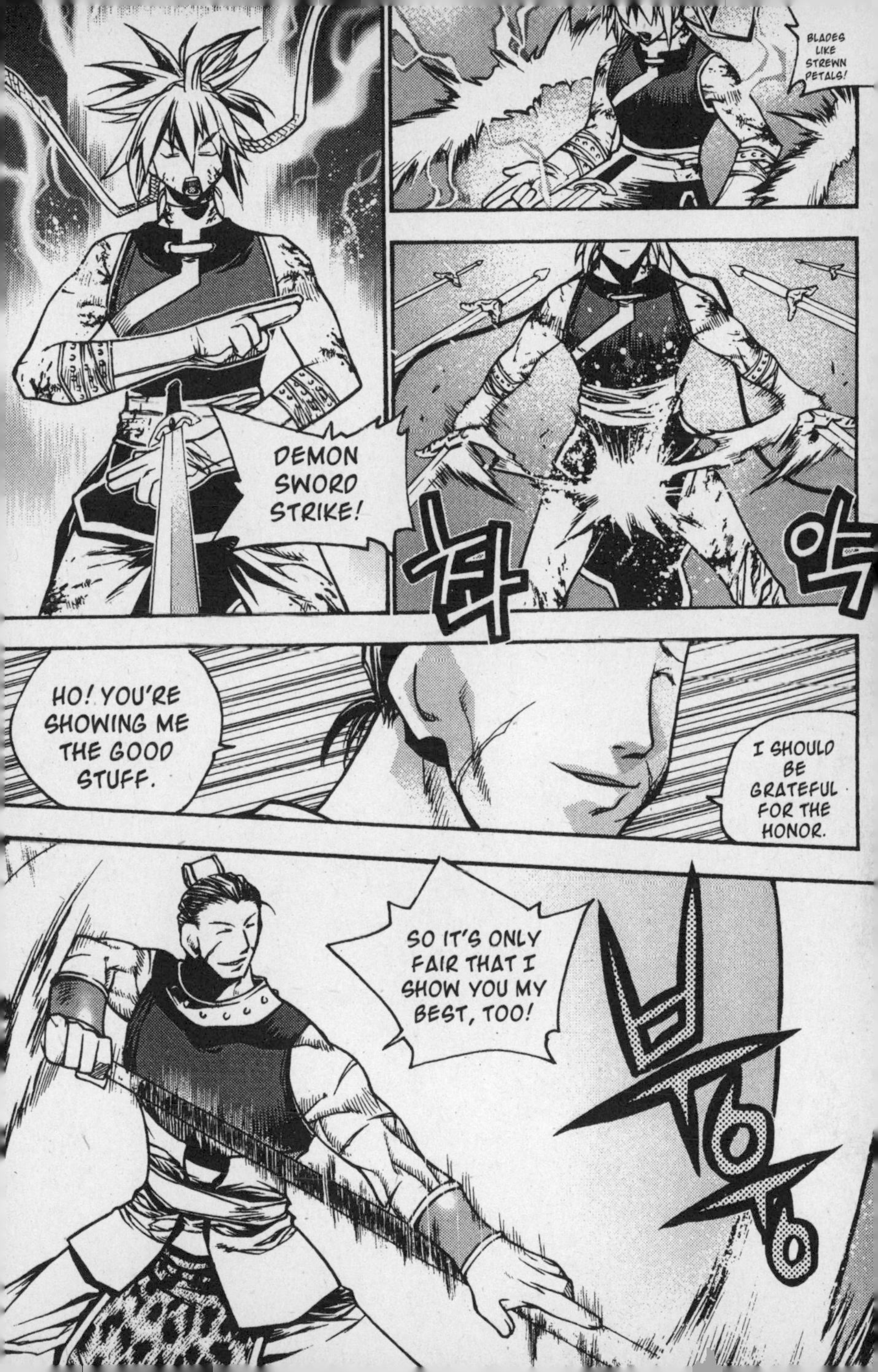
DEMON SWORD STRIKE!
BLADES LIKE STREWN PETALS!
HO! YOU'RE SHOWING ME THE GOOD STUFF.
I SHOULD BE GRATEFUL FOR THE HONOR.
SO IT'S ONLY FAIR THAT I SHOW YOU MY BEST, TOO!

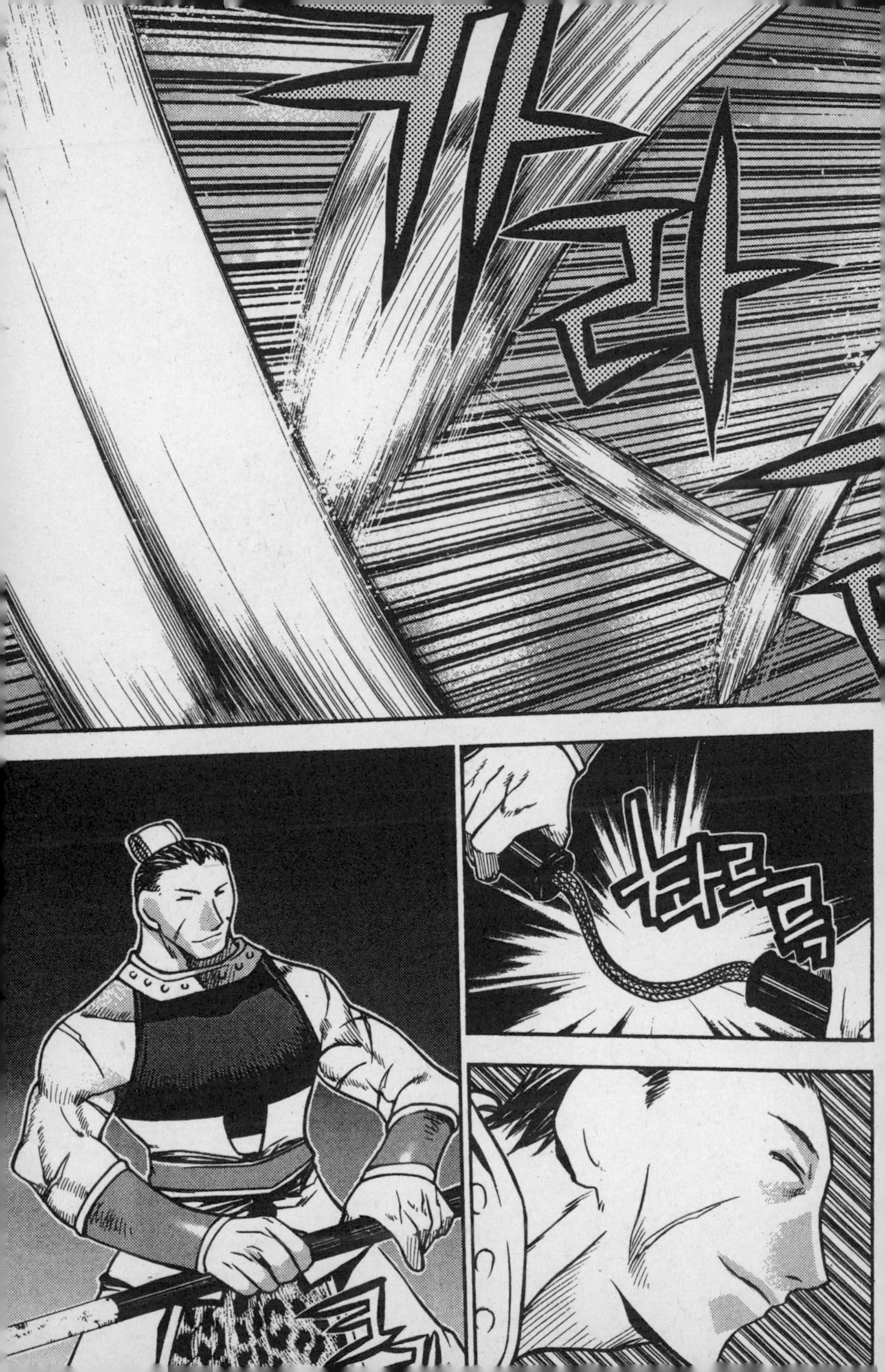

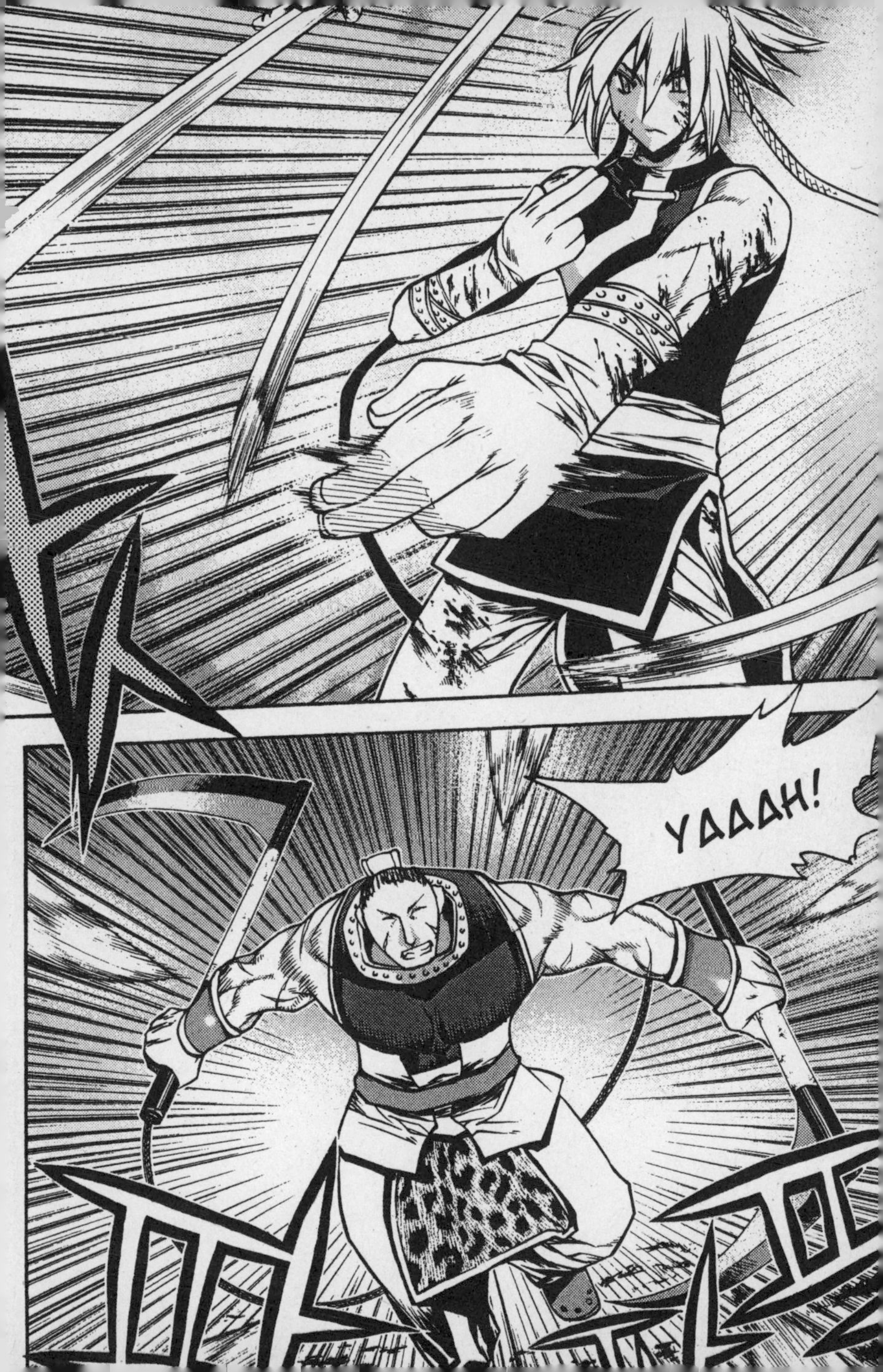
YAAAH!

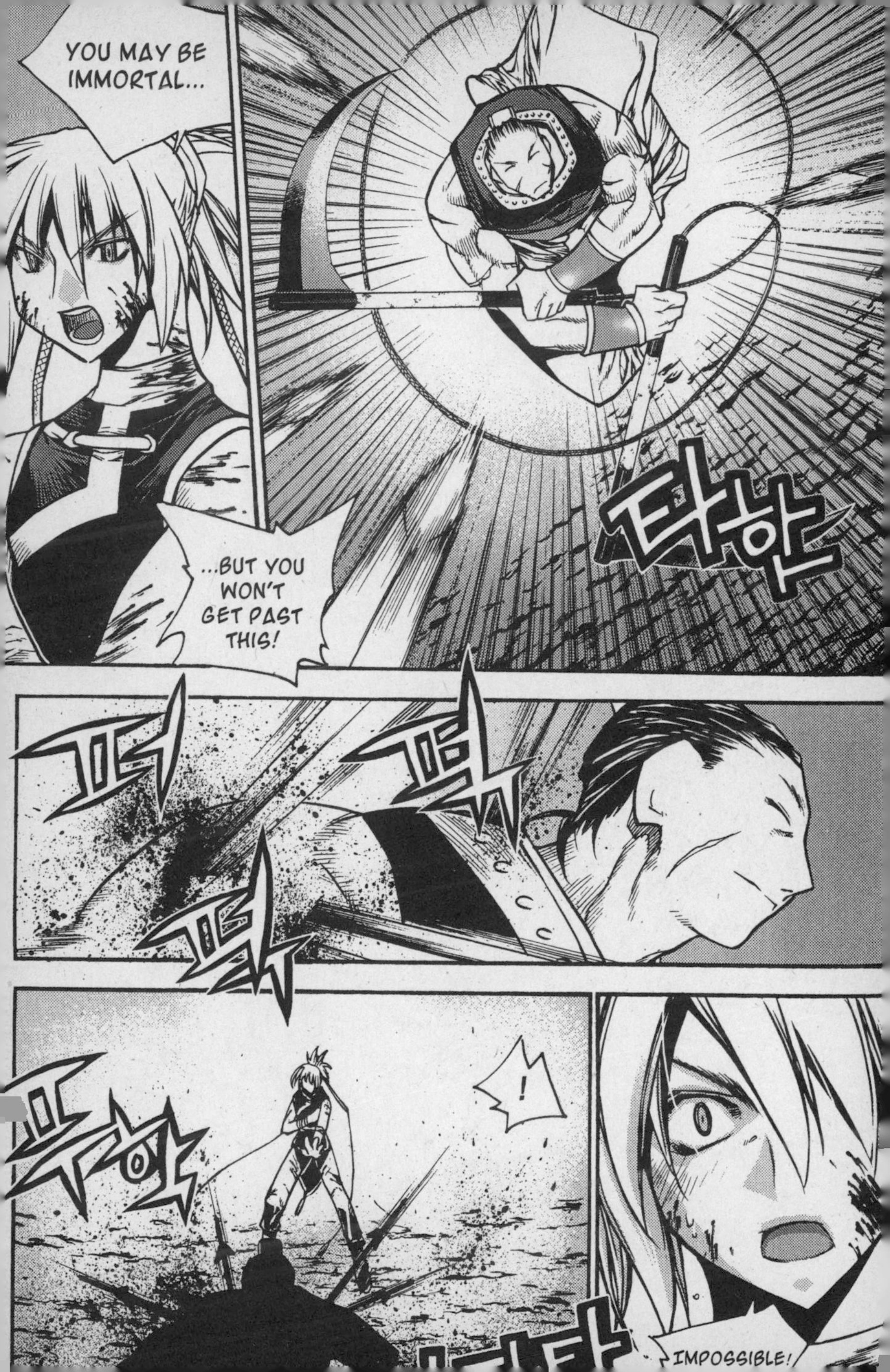
YOU MAY BE IMMORTAL...
...BUT YOU WON'T GET PAST THIS!
!
IMPOSSIBLE!

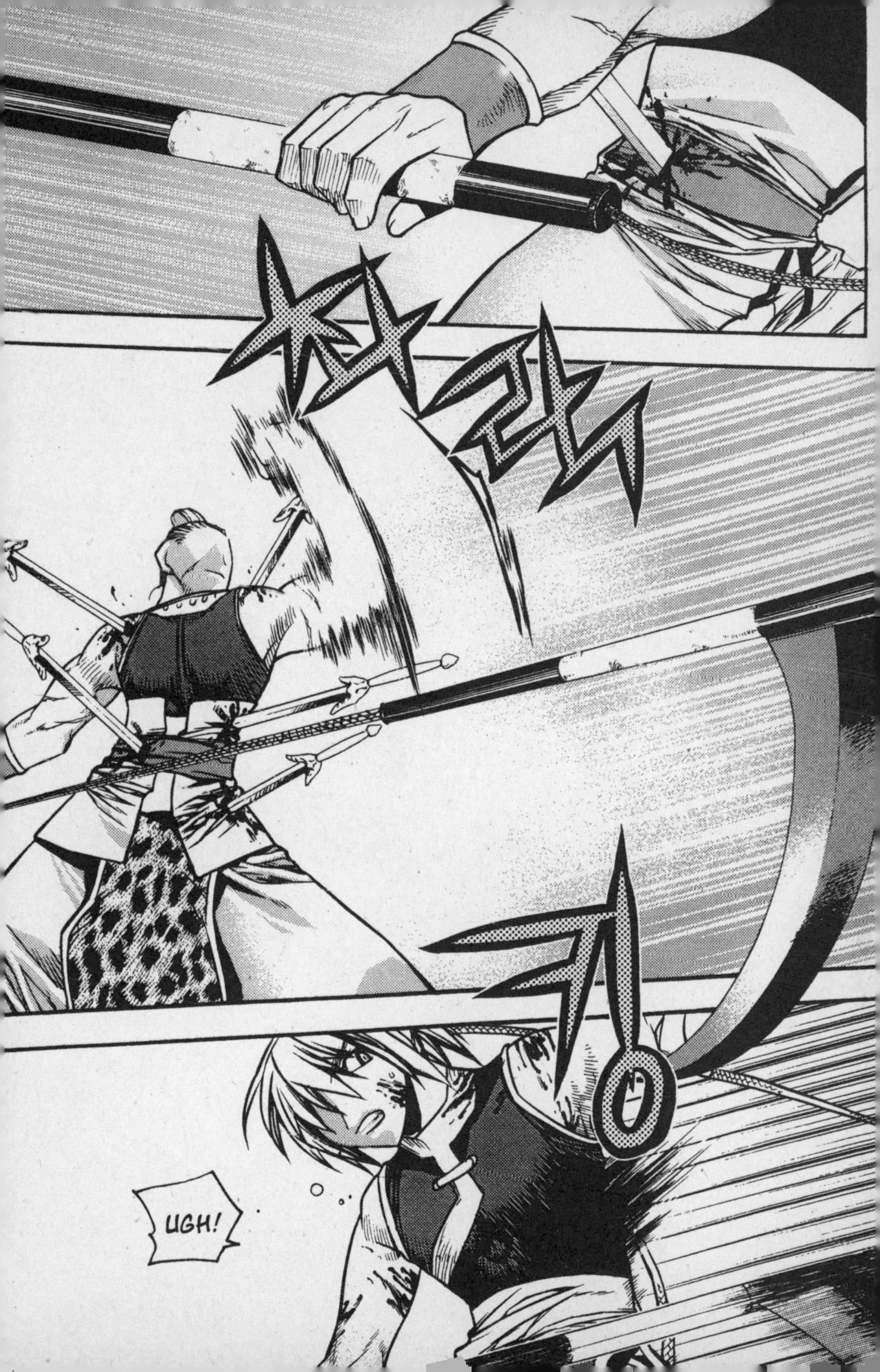
UGH!

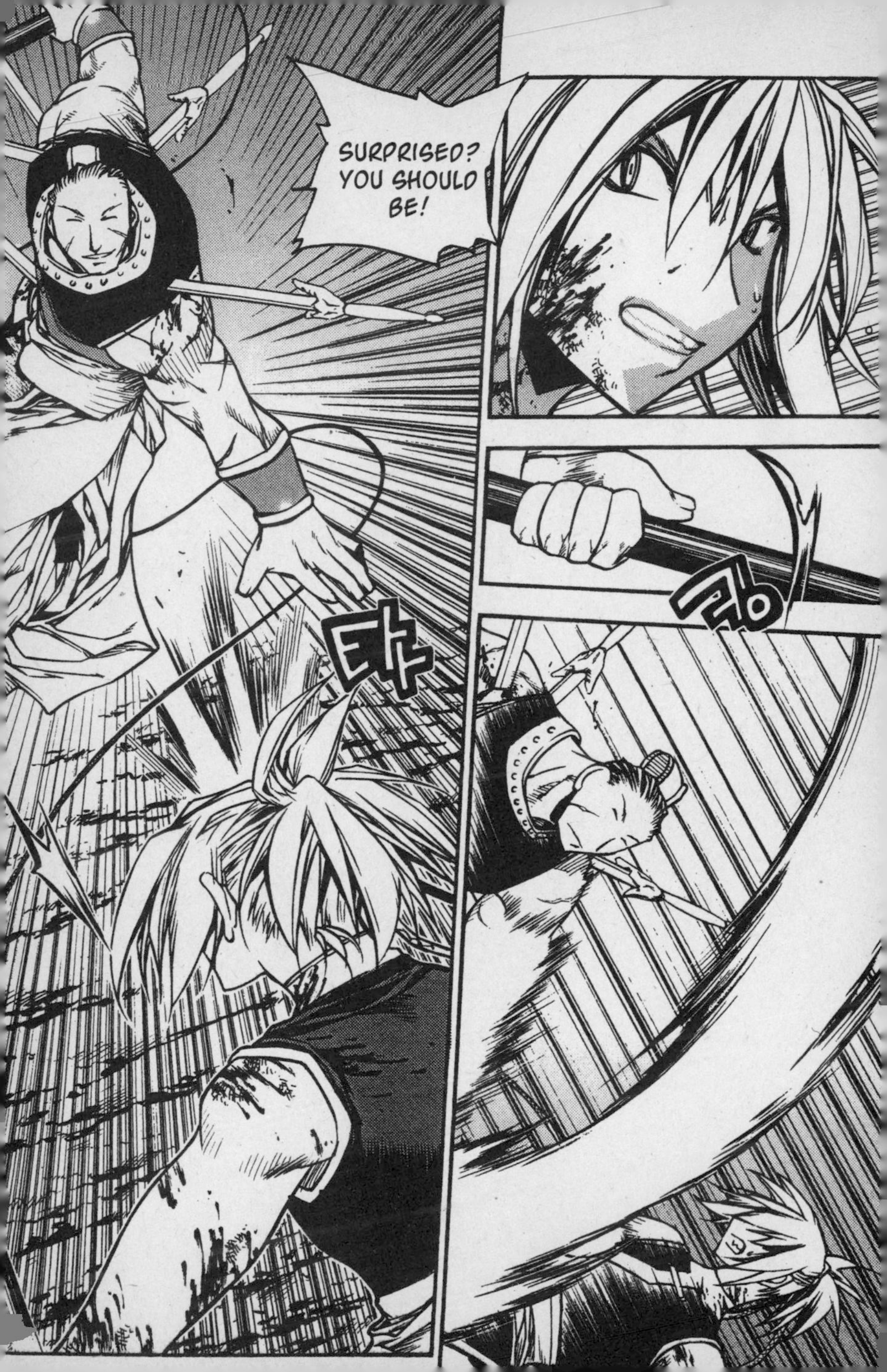
SURPRISED? YOU SHOULD BE!

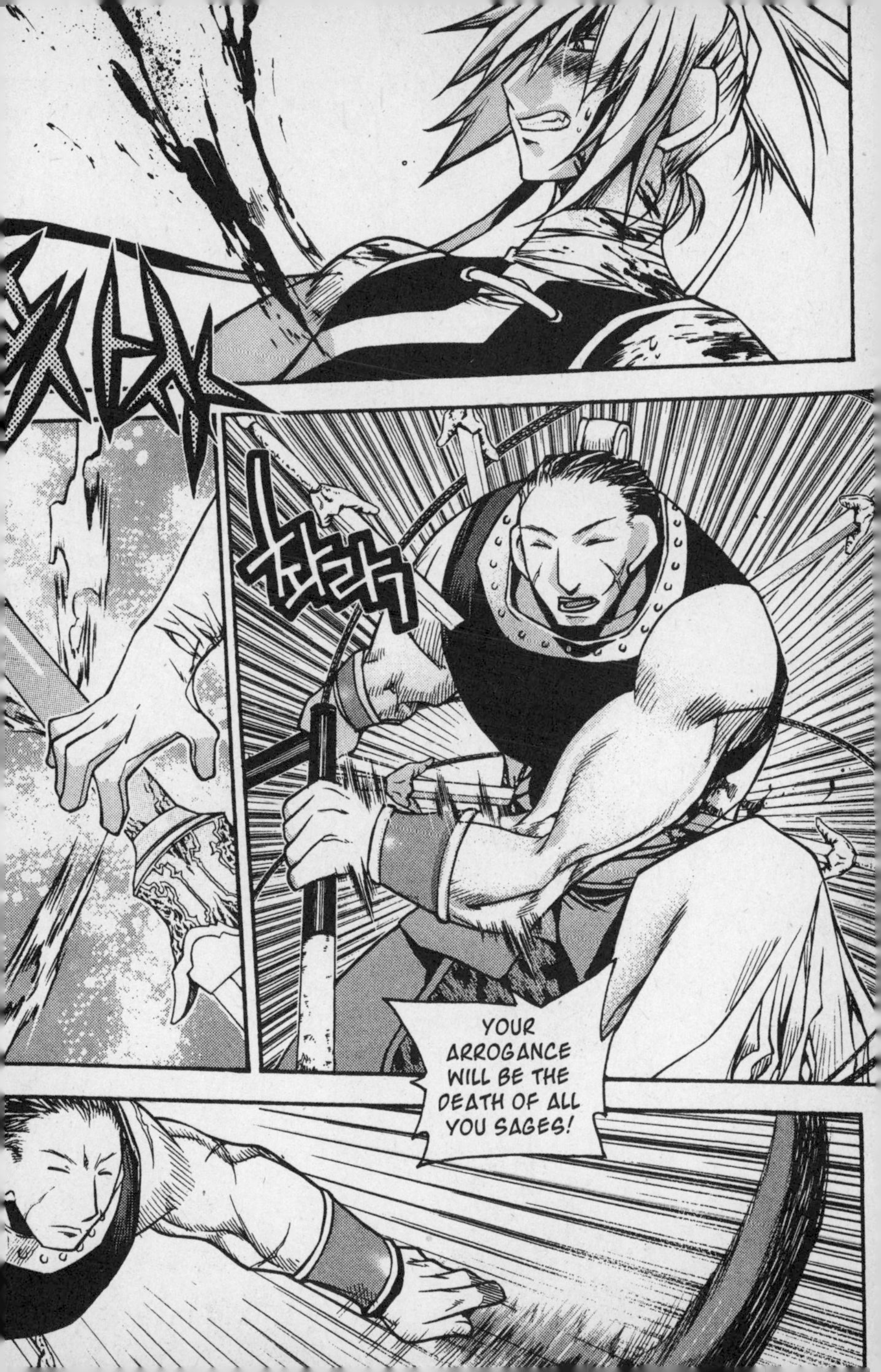
YOUR ARROGANCE WILL BE THE DEATH OF ALL YOU SAGES!

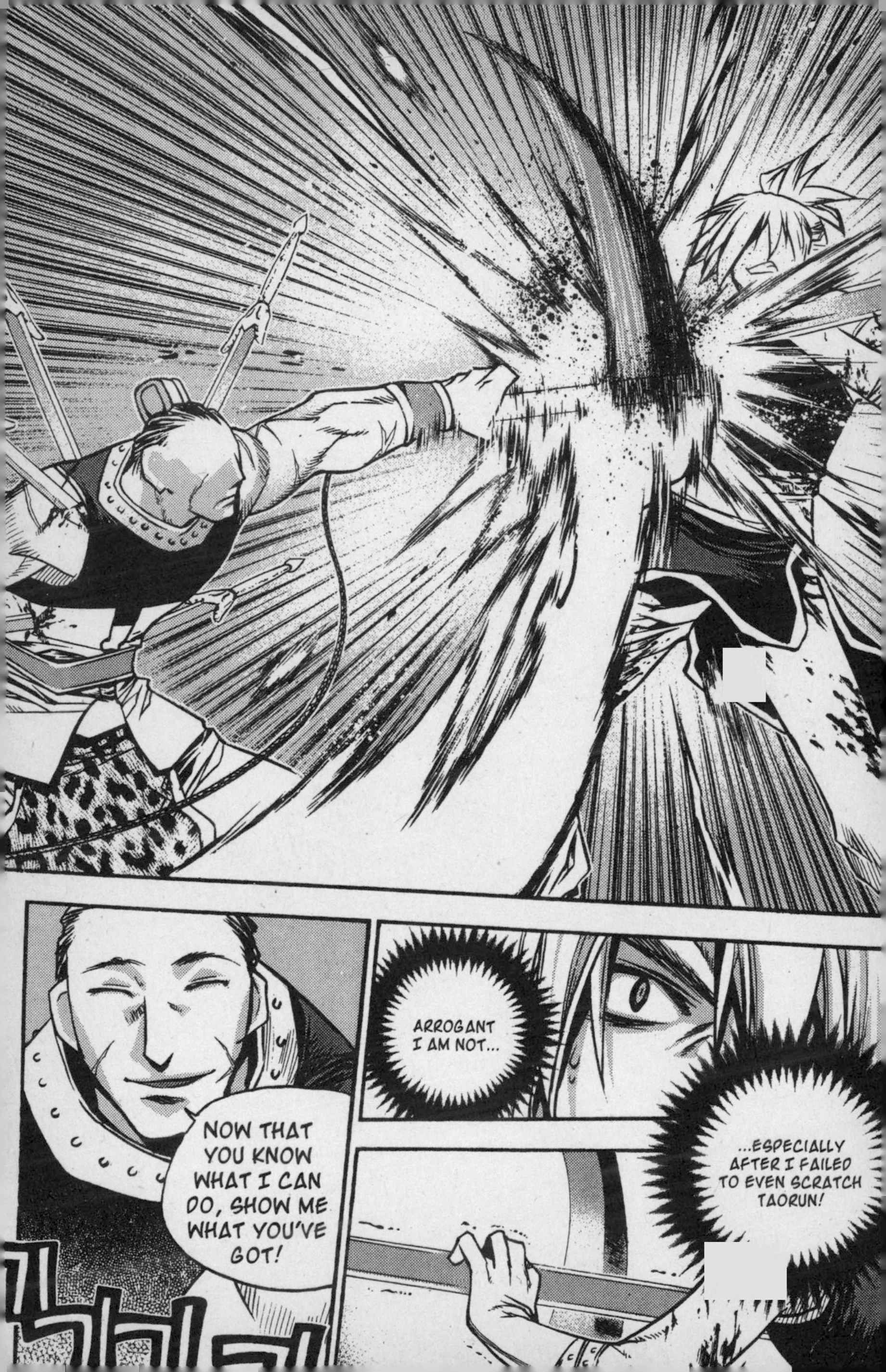
NOW THAT YOU KNOW WHAT I CAN DO, SHOW ME WHAT YOU'VE GOT!
ARROGANT I AM NOT...
...ESPECIALLY AFTER I FAILED TO EVEN SCRATCH TAORUN!

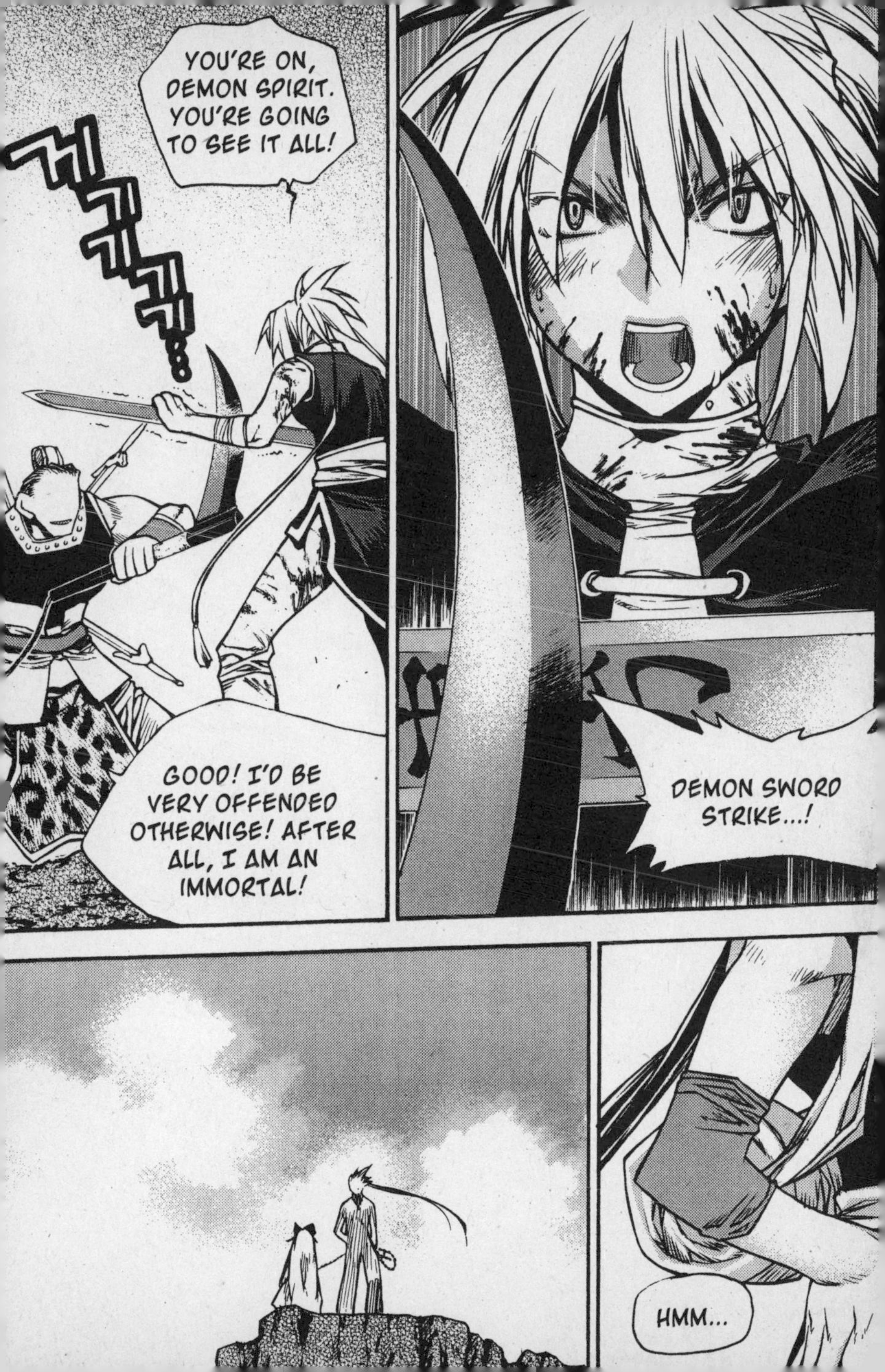

YOU'RE ON, DEMON SPIRIT. YOU'RE GOING TO SEE IT ALL!
GOOD! I'D BE VERY OFFENDED OTHERWISE! AFTER ALL, I AM AN IMMORTAL!
DEMON SWORD STRIKE...!
HMM...

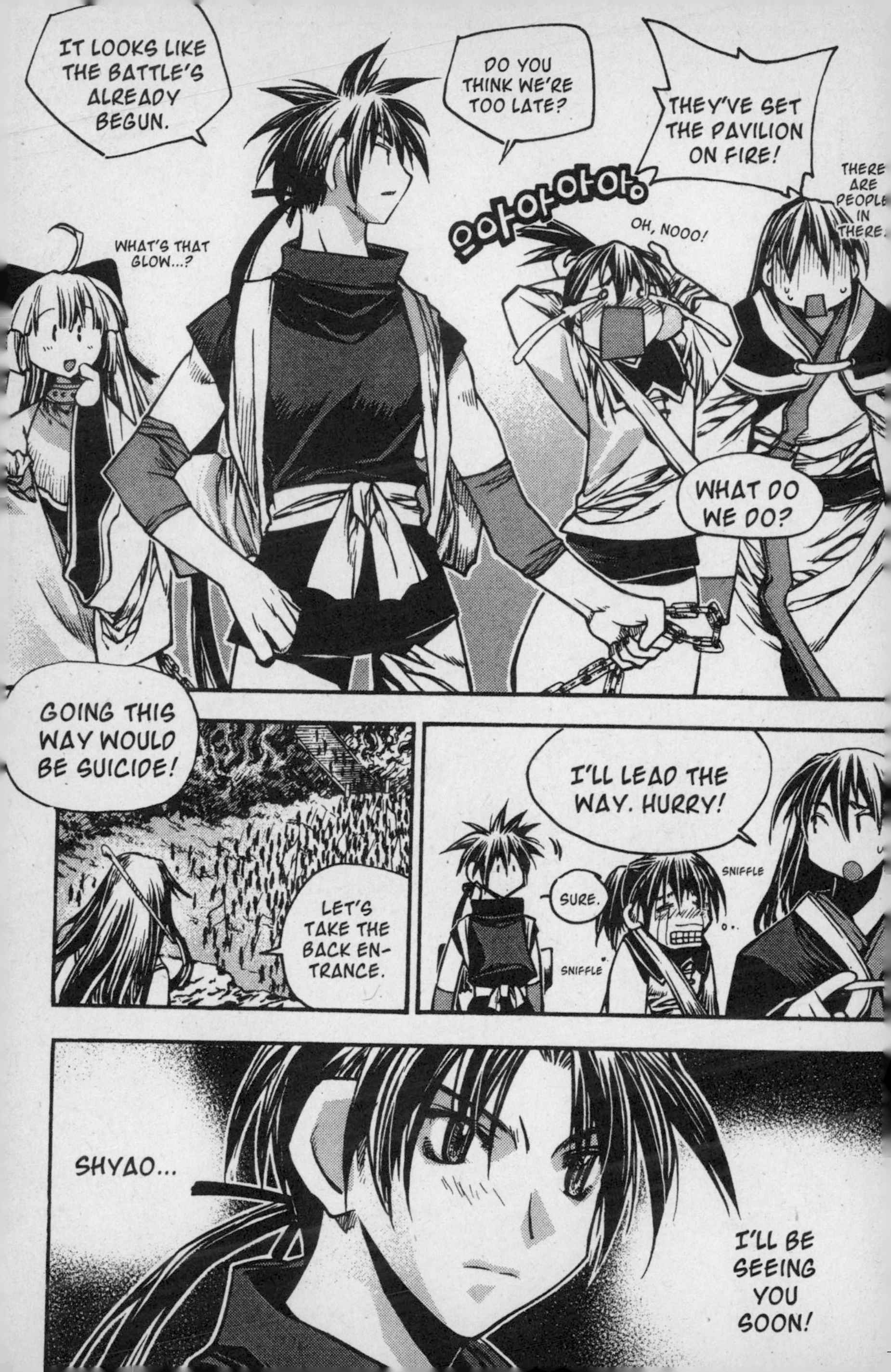
IT LOOKS LIKE THE BATTLE'S ALREADY BEGUN.
DO YOU THINK WE'RE TOO LATE?
THEY'VE SET THE PAVILION ON FIRE!
WHAT'S THAT GLOW...?
으아아아앙
OH, NOOO!
THERE ARE PEOPLE IN THERE.
WHAT DO WE DO?
GOING THIS WAY WOULD BE SUICIDE!
LET'S TAKE THE BACK EN-TRANCE.
I'LL LEAD THE WAY. HURRY!
SURE.
SNIFFLE
SNIFFLE
SHYAO...
I'LL BE SEEING YOU SOON!

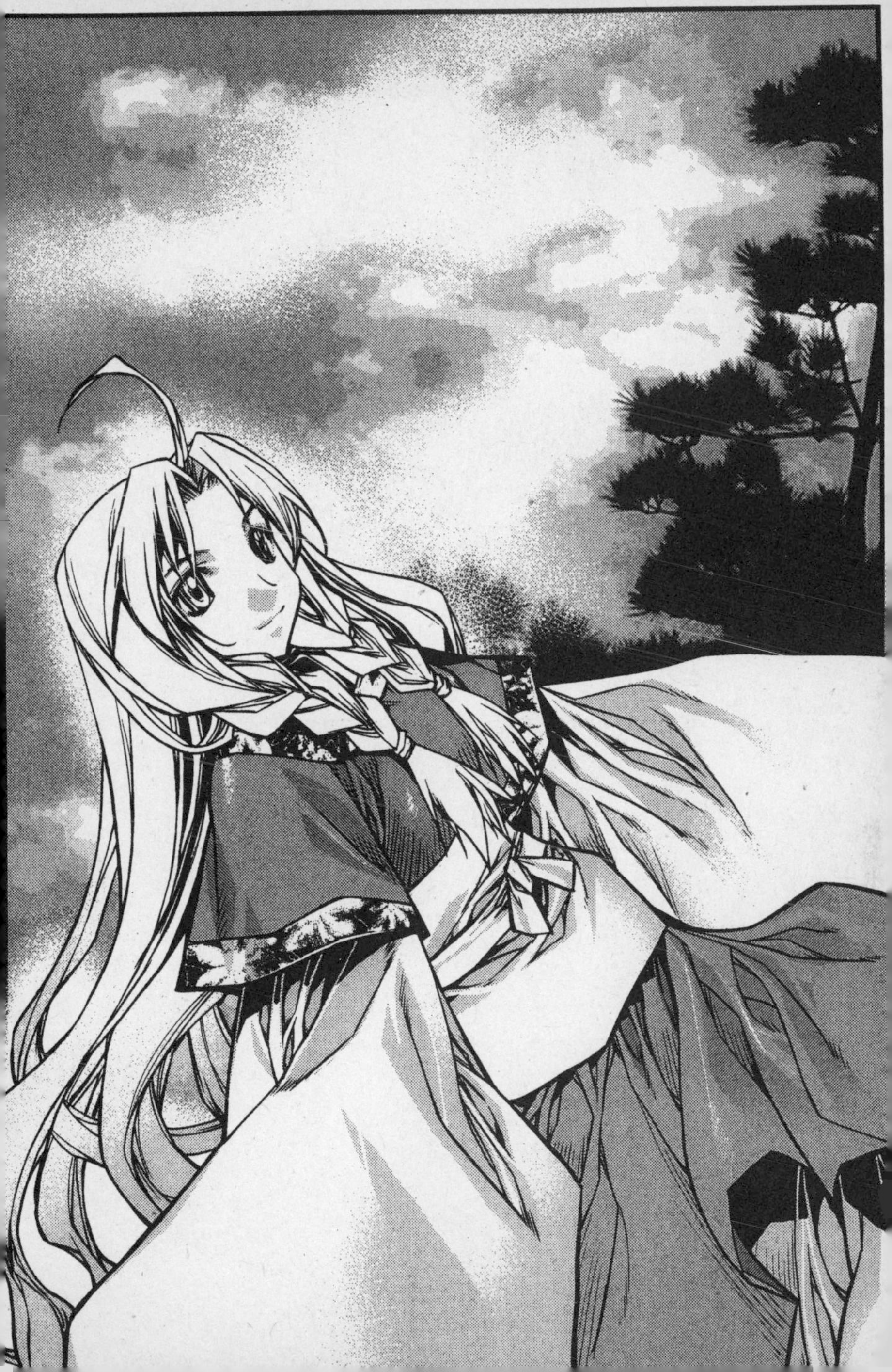

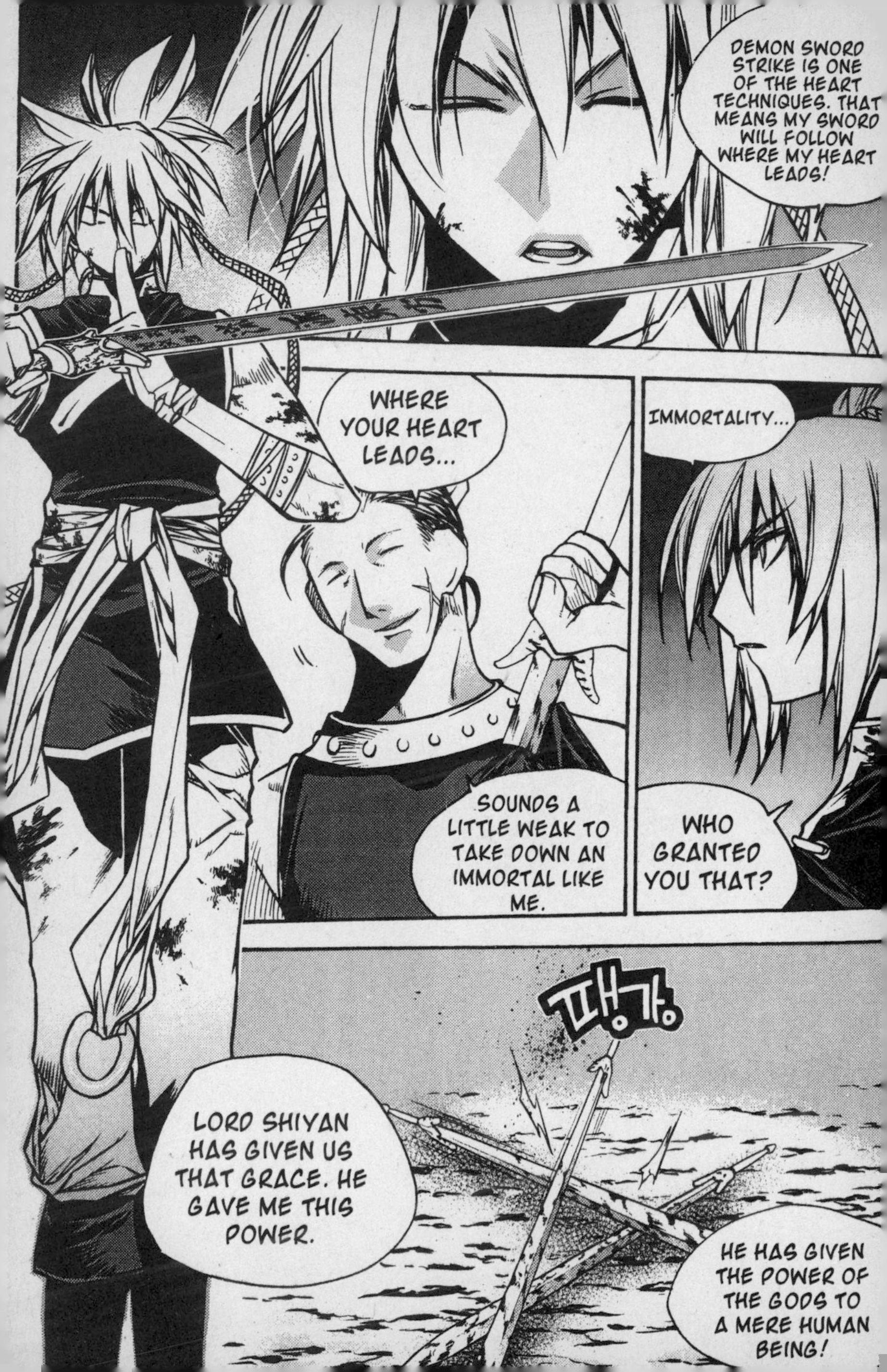
DEMON SWORD STRIKE IS ONE OF THE HEART TECHNIQUES. THAT MEANS MY SWORD WILL FOLLOW WHERE MY HEART LEADS!
WHERE YOUR HEART LEADS...
SOUNDS A LITTLE WEAK TO TAKE DOWN AN IMMORTAL LIKE ME.
IMMORTALITY...
WHO GRANTED YOU THAT?
패앵가
LORD SHIYAN HAS GIVEN US THAT GRACE. HE GAVE ME THIS POWER.
HE HAS GIVEN THE POWER OF THE GODS TO A MERE HUMAN BEING!

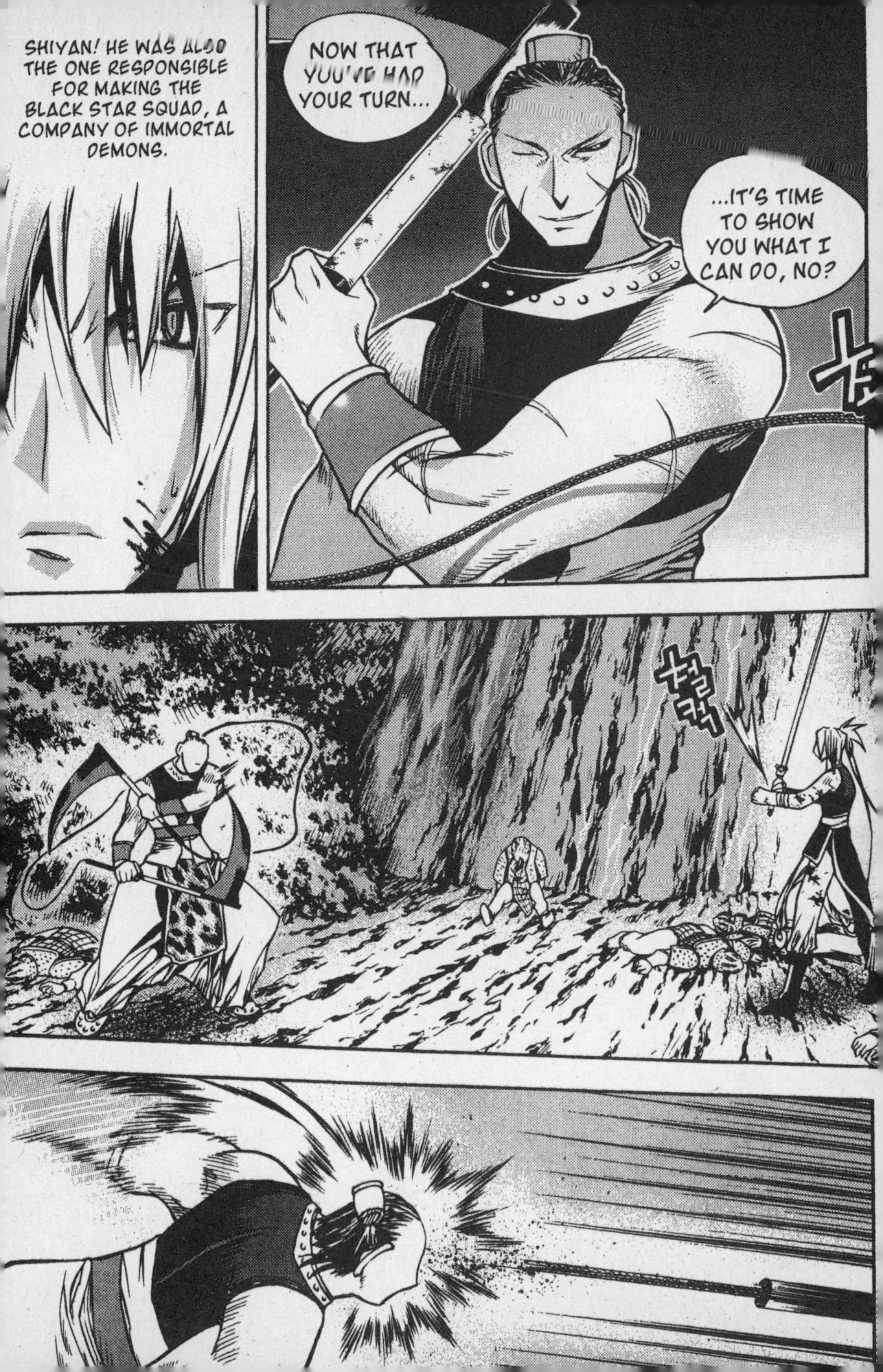
SHIYAN! HE WAS ALSO THE ONE RESPONSIBLE FOR MAKING THE BLACK STAR SQUAD, A COMPANY OF IMMORTAL DEMONS.
NOW THAT YOU'VE HAD YOUR TURN...
...IT'S TIME TO SHOW YOU WHAT I CAN DO, NO?

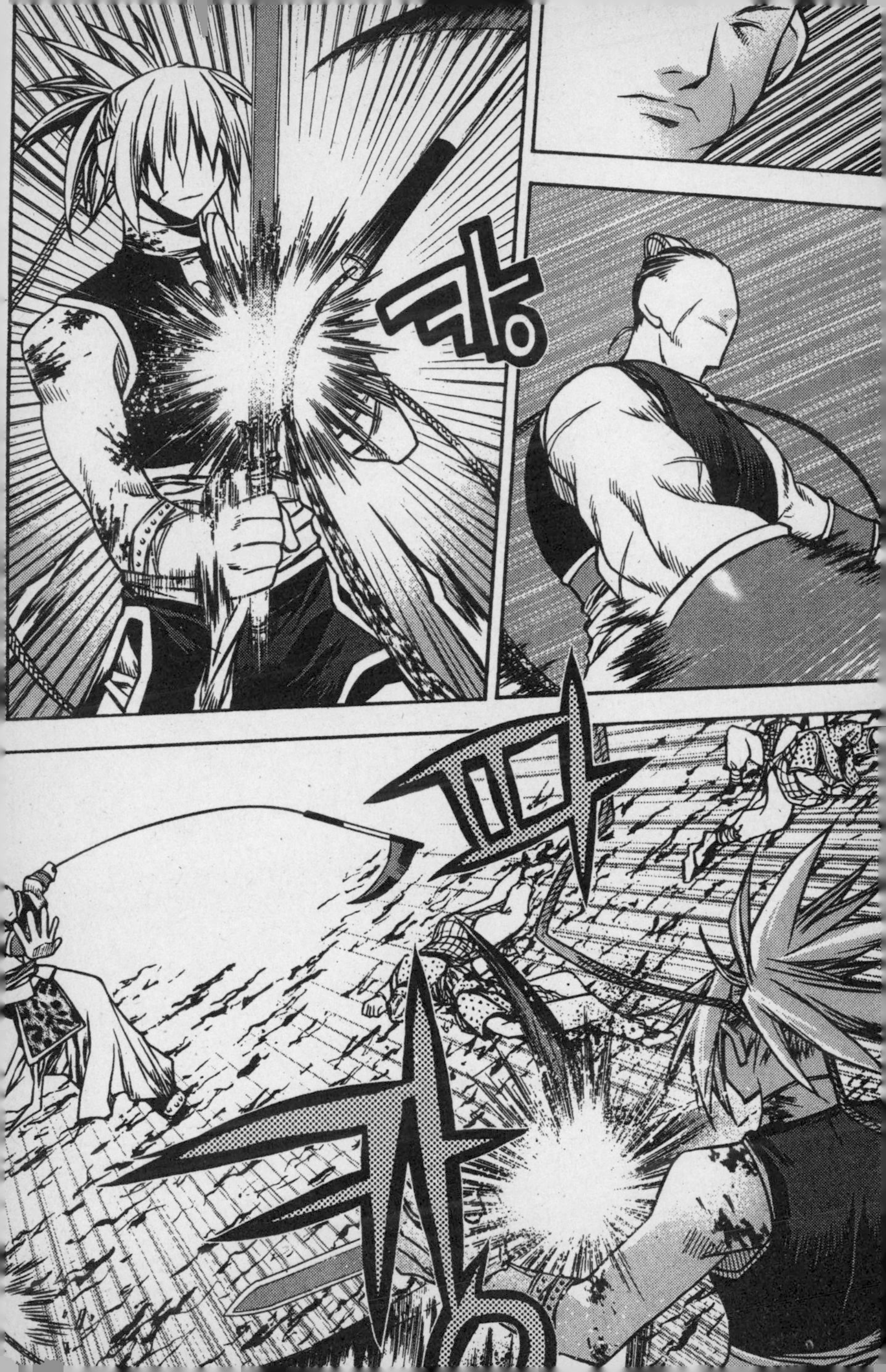
캉
파

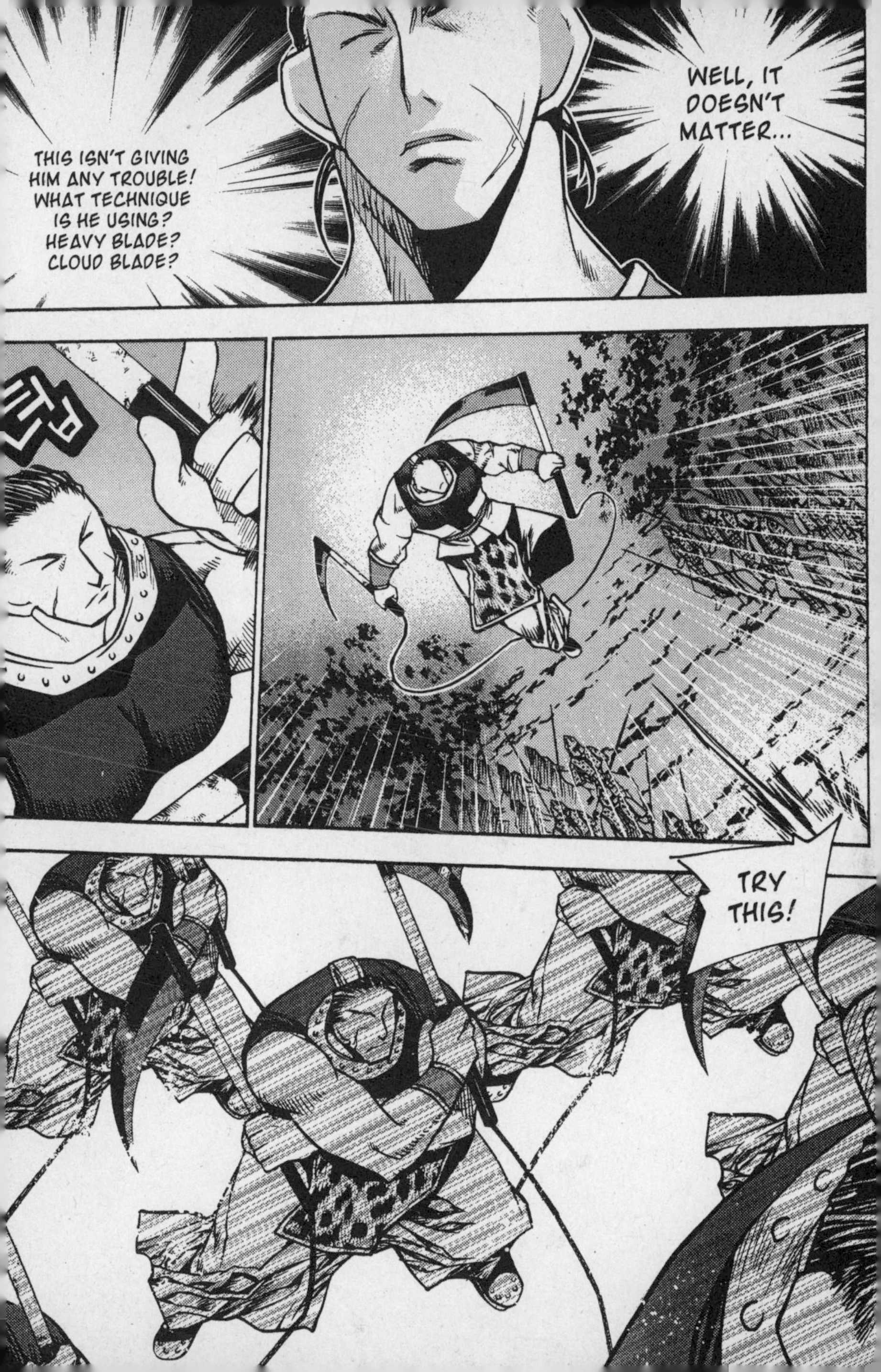
THIS ISN'T GIVING HIM ANY TROUBLE! WHAT TECHNIQUE IS HE USING? HEAVY BLADE? CLOUD BLADE?
WELL, IT DOESN'T MATTER...
TRY THIS!

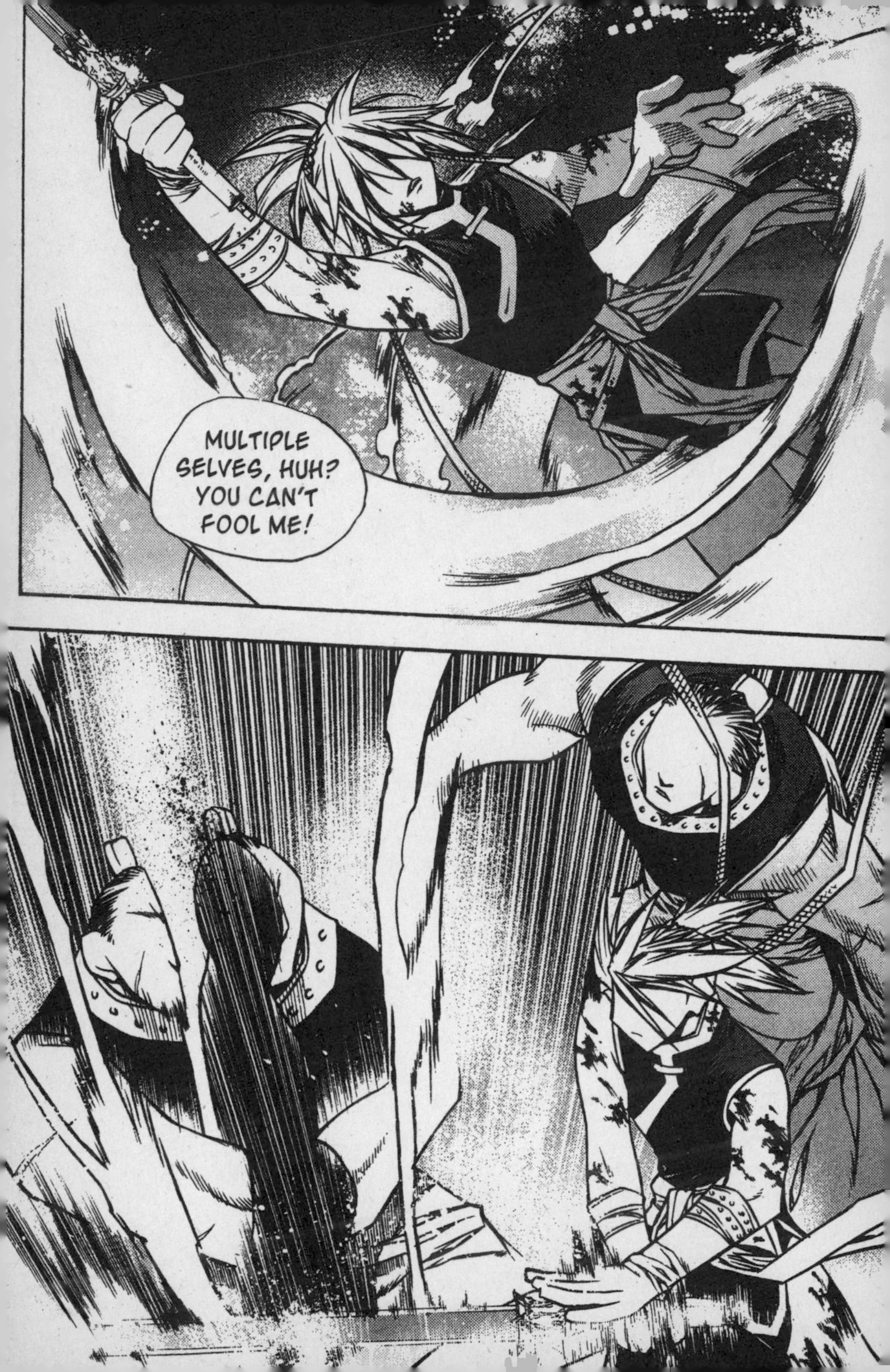
MULTIPLE SELVES, HUH? YOU CAN'T FOOL ME!

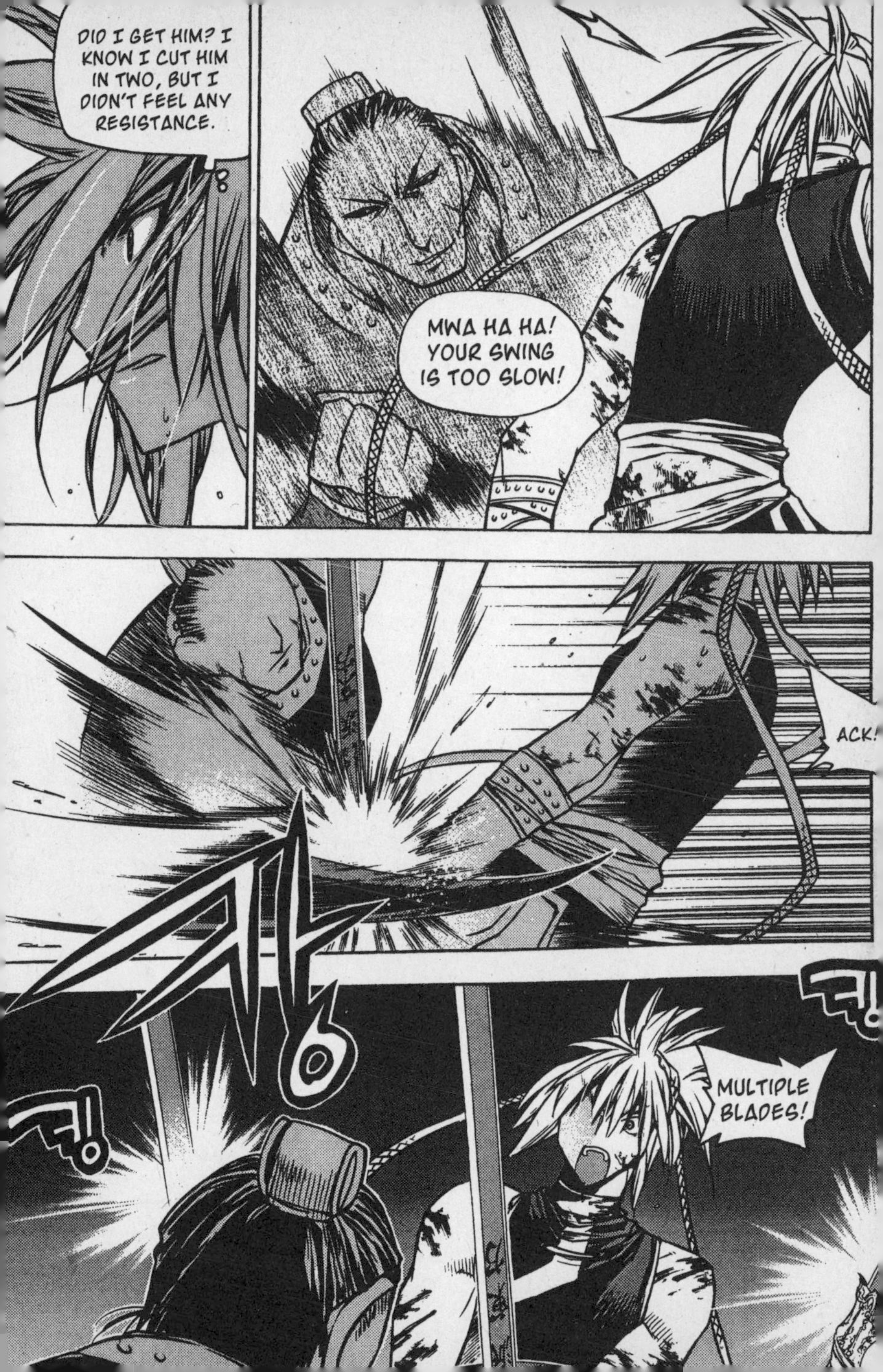
DID I GET HIM? I KNOW I CUT HIM IN TWO, BUT I DIDN'T FEEL ANY RESISTANCE.
MWA HA HA! YOUR SWING IS TOO SLOW!
ACK!
MULTIPLE BLADES!

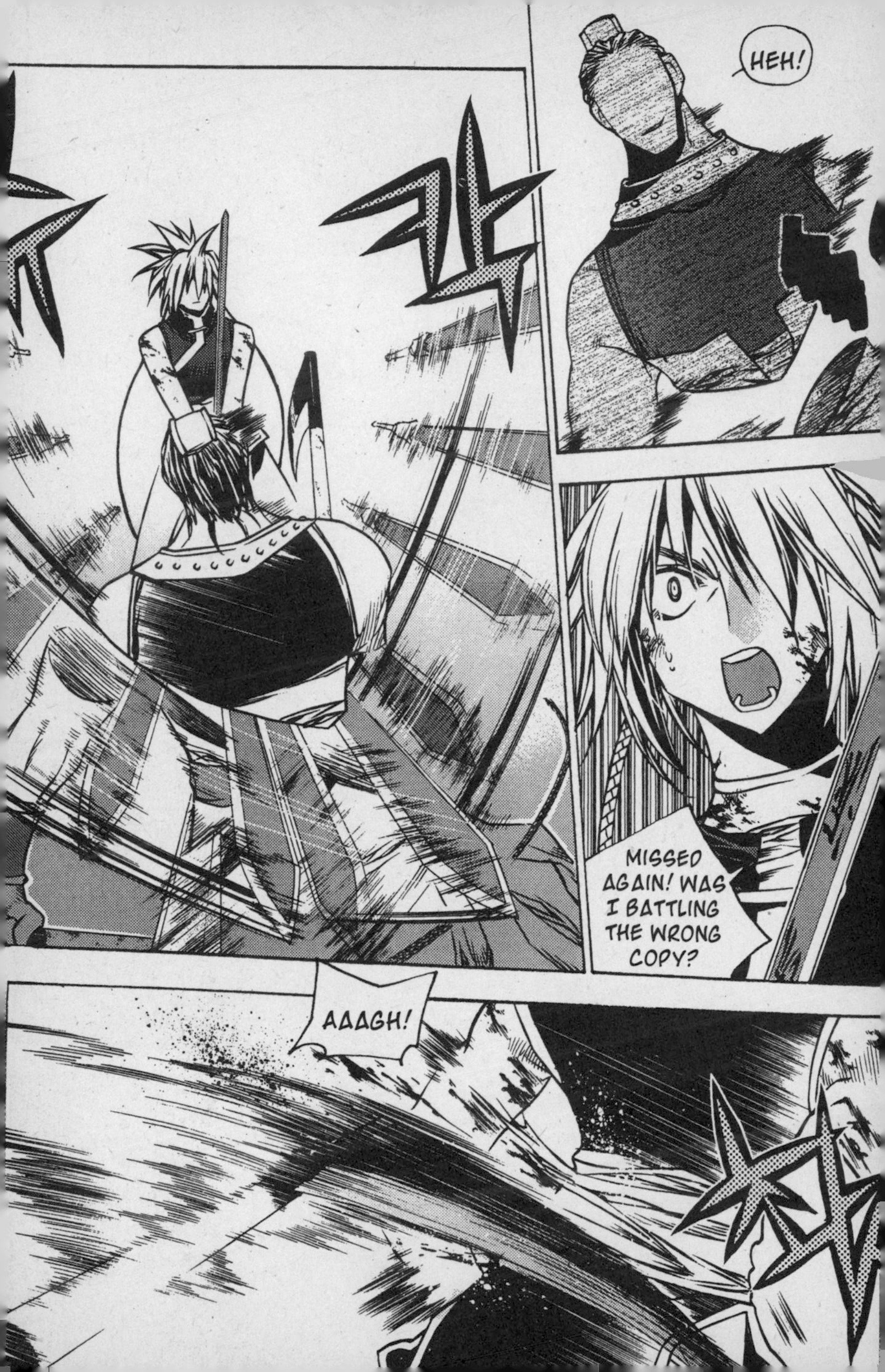
HEH!
MISSED AGAIN! WAS I BATTLING THE WRONG COPY?
AAAGH!

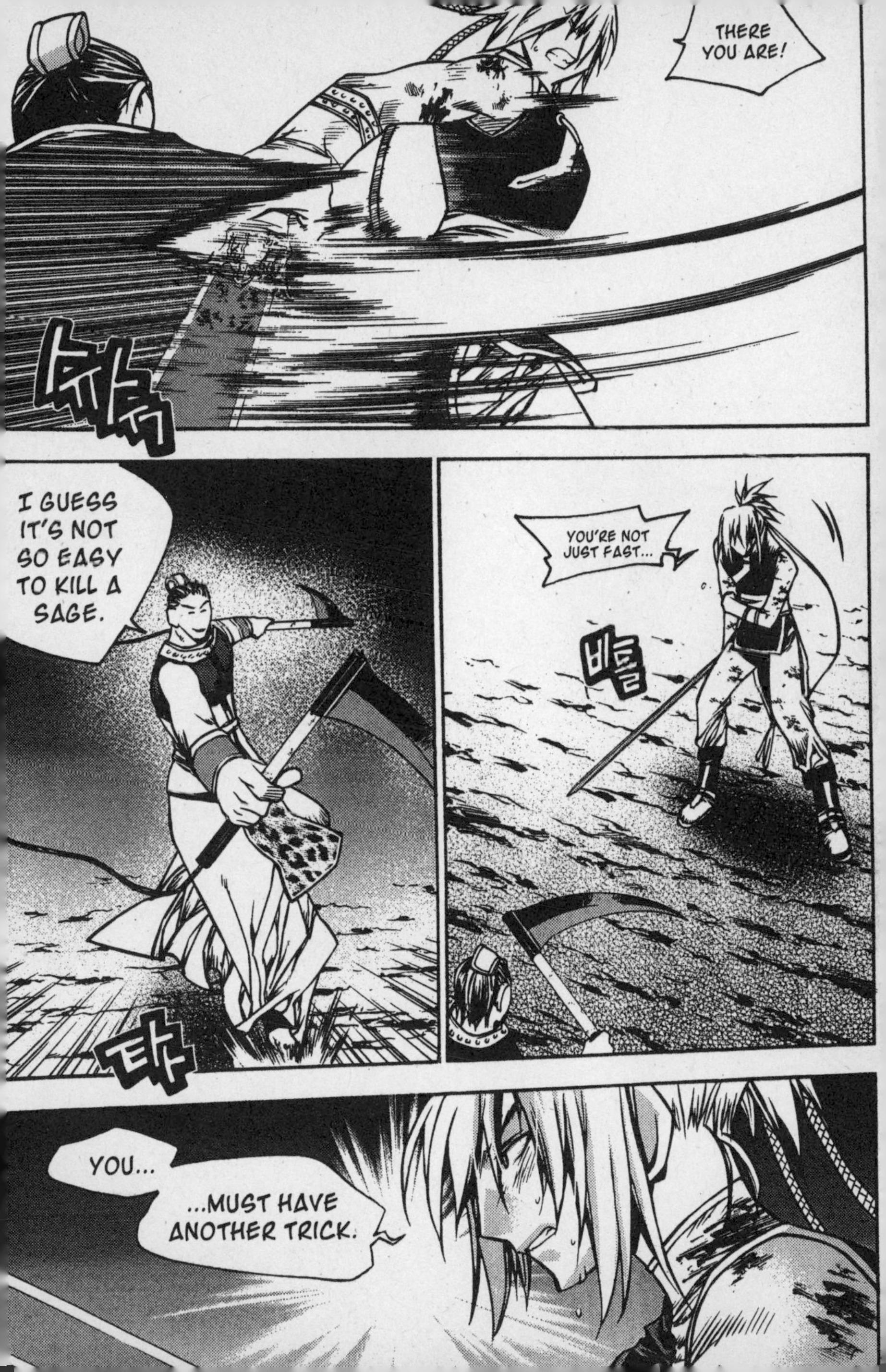
THERE YOU ARE!
I GUESS IT'S NOT SO EASY TO KILL A SAGE.
YOU'RE NOT JUST FAST...
비틀
YOU...
...MUST HAVE ANOTHER TRICK.

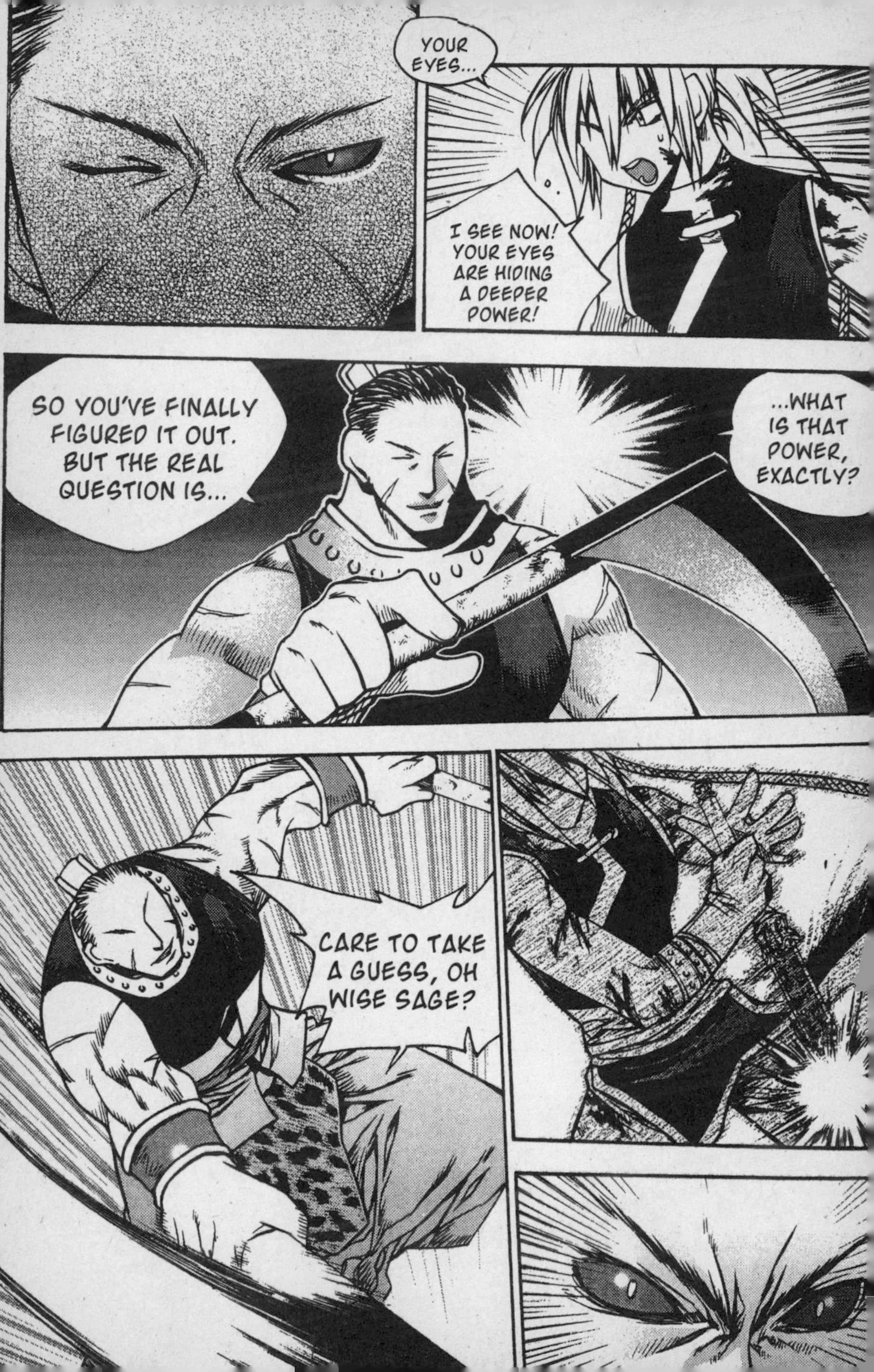
YOUR EYES...
I SEE NOW! YOUR EYES ARE HIDING A DEEPER POWER!
SO YOU'VE FINALLY FIGURED IT OUT. BUT THE REAL QUESTION IS...
...WHAT IS THAT POWER, EXACTLY?
CARE TO TAKE A GUESS, OH WISE SAGE?

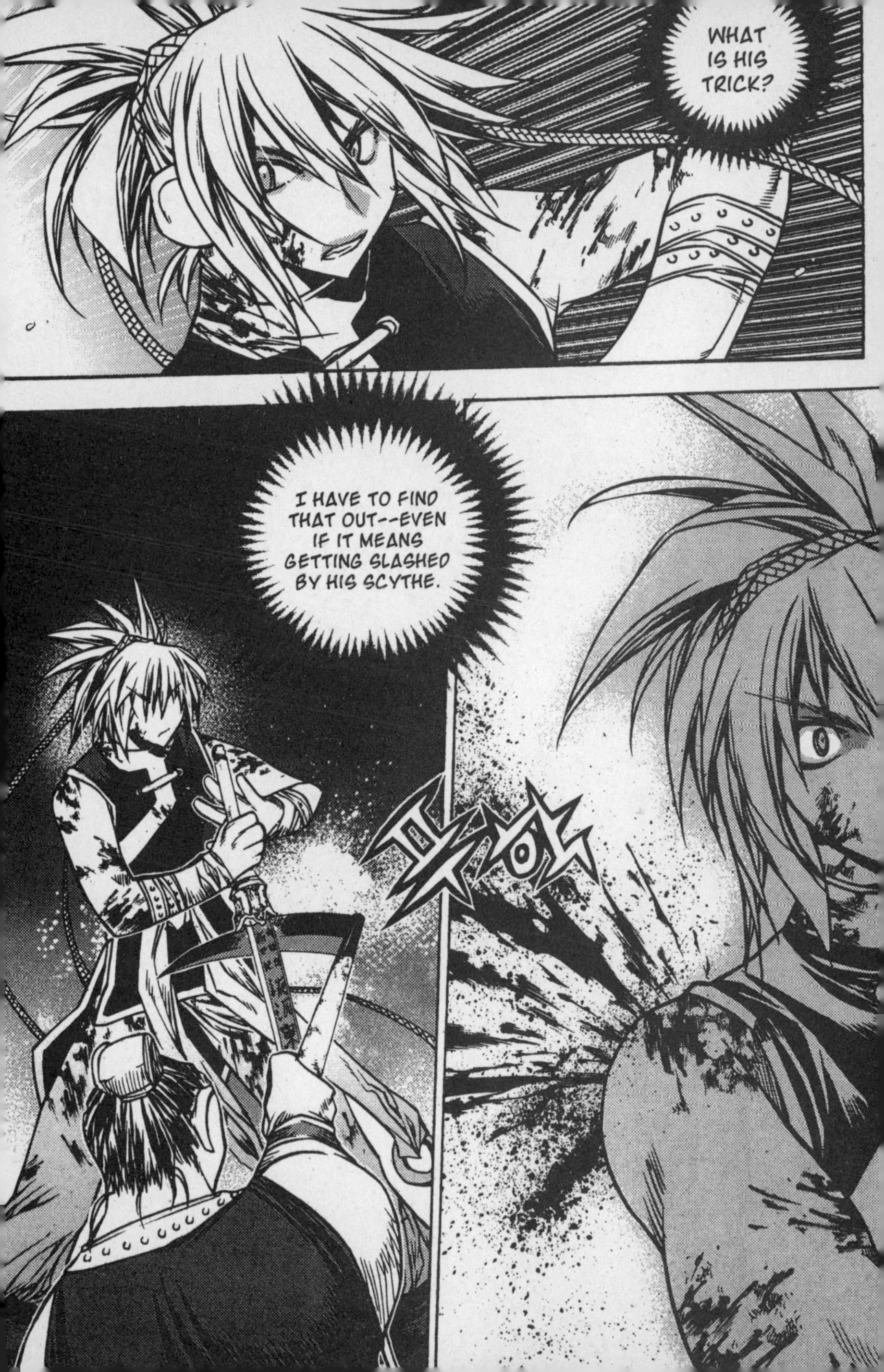
WHAT IS HIS TRICK?
I HAVE TO FIND THAT OUT--EVEN IF IT MEANS GETTING SLASHED BY HIS SCYTHE.

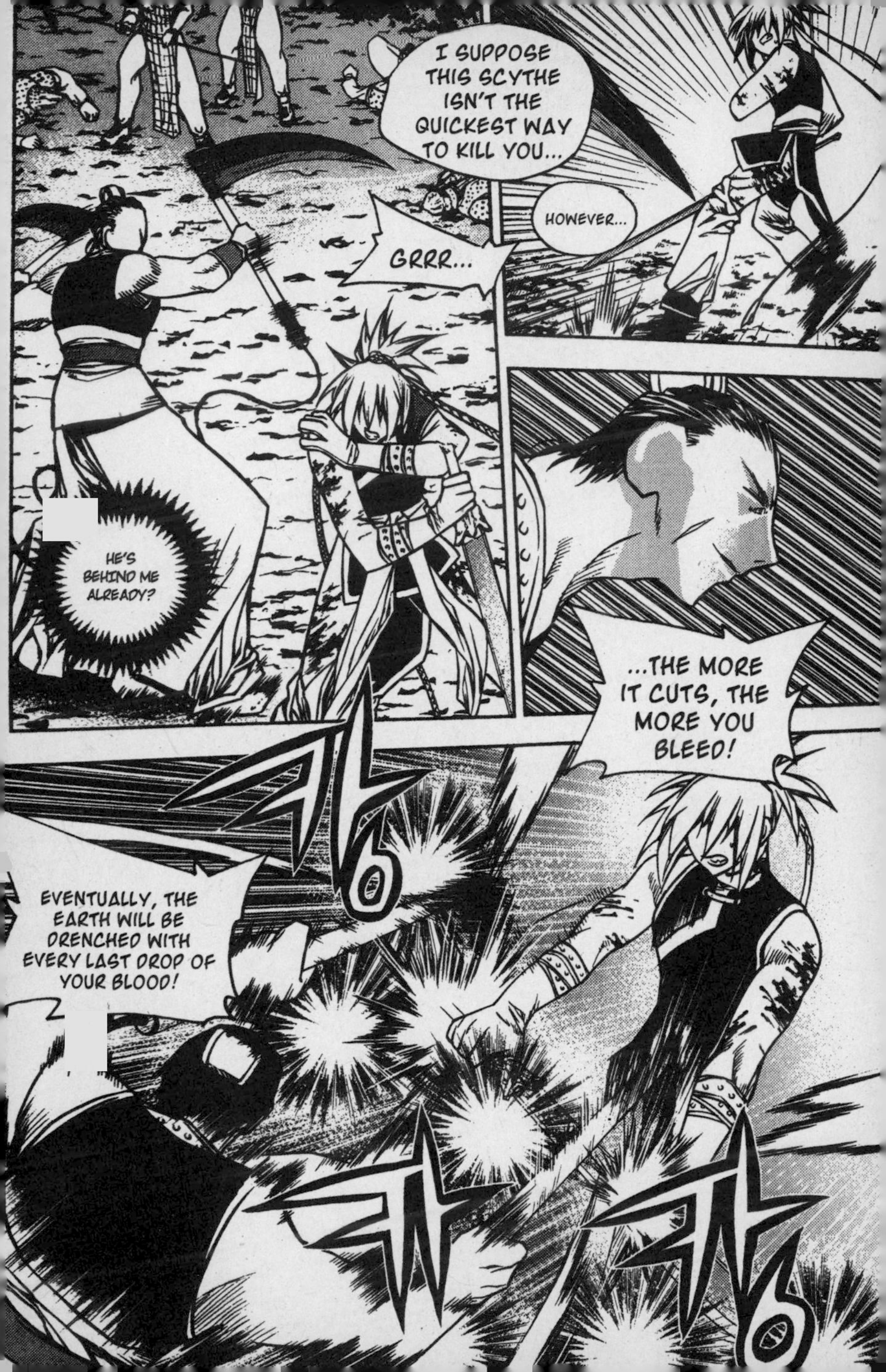
I SUPPOSE THIS SCYTHE ISN'T THE QUICKEST WAY TO KILL YOU...
GRRR...
HOWEVER...
HE'S BEHIND ME ALREADY?
...THE MORE IT CUTS, THE MORE YOU BLEED!
EVENTUALLY, THE EARTH WILL BE DRENCHED WITH EVERY LAST DROP OF YOUR BLOOD!

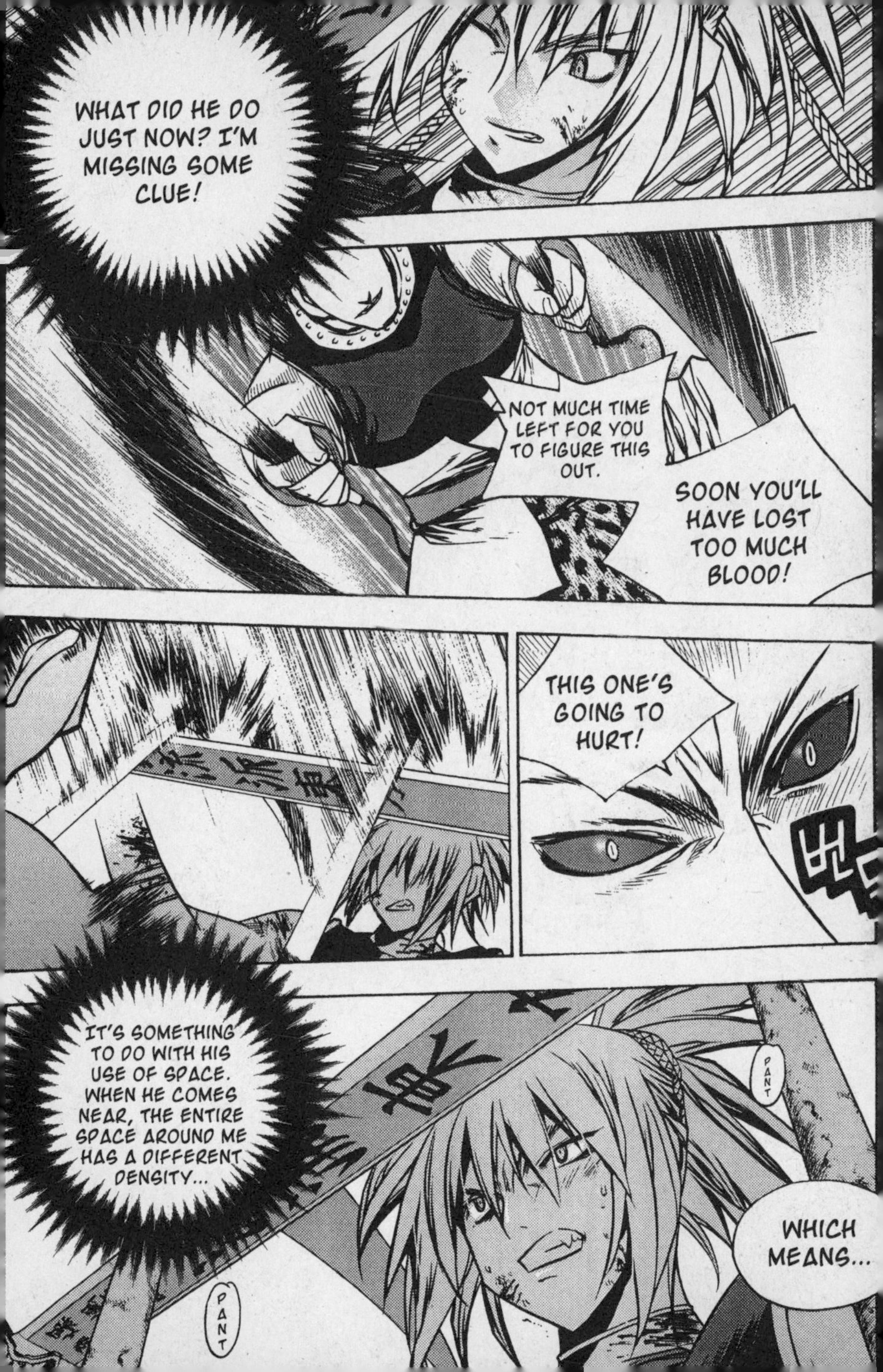
WHAT DID HE DO JUST NOW? I'M MISSING SOME CLUE!
NOT MUCH TIME LEFT FOR YOU TO FIGURE THIS OUT.
SOON YOU'LL HAVE LOST TOO MUCH BLOOD!
THIS ONE'S GOING TO HURT!
IT'S SOMETHING TO DO WITH HIS USE OF SPACE. WHEN HE COMES NEAR, THE ENTIRE SPACE AROUND ME HAS A DIFFERENT DENSITY...
PANT
WHICH MEANS...
PANT

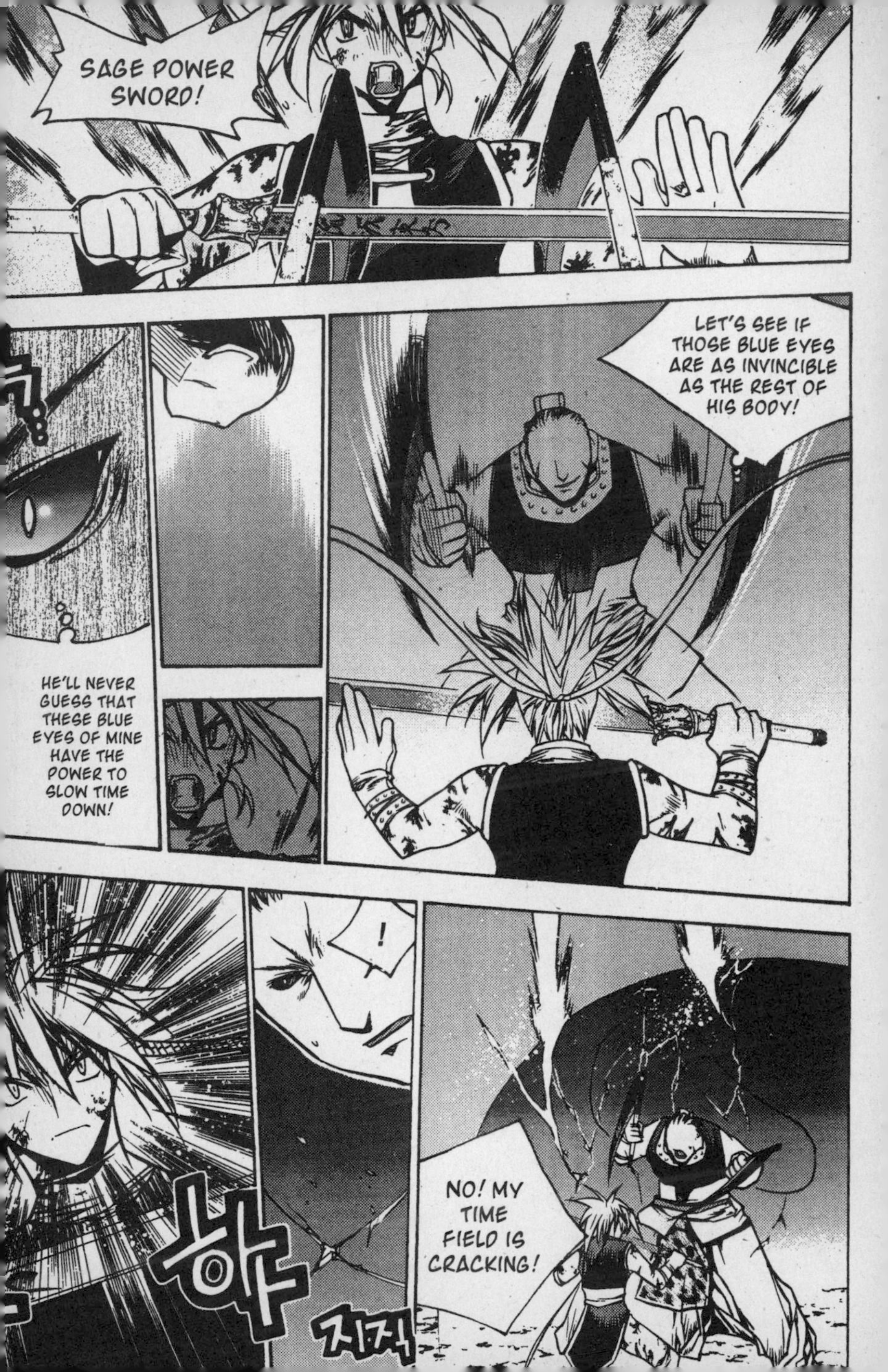
SAGE POWER SWORD!
HE'LL NEVER GUESS THAT THESE BLUE EYES OF MINE HAVE THE POWER TO SLOW TIME DOWN!
LET'S SEE IF THOSE BLUE EYES ARE AS INVINCIBLE AS THE REST OF HIS BODY!
하
!
NO! MY TIME FIELD IS CRACKING!

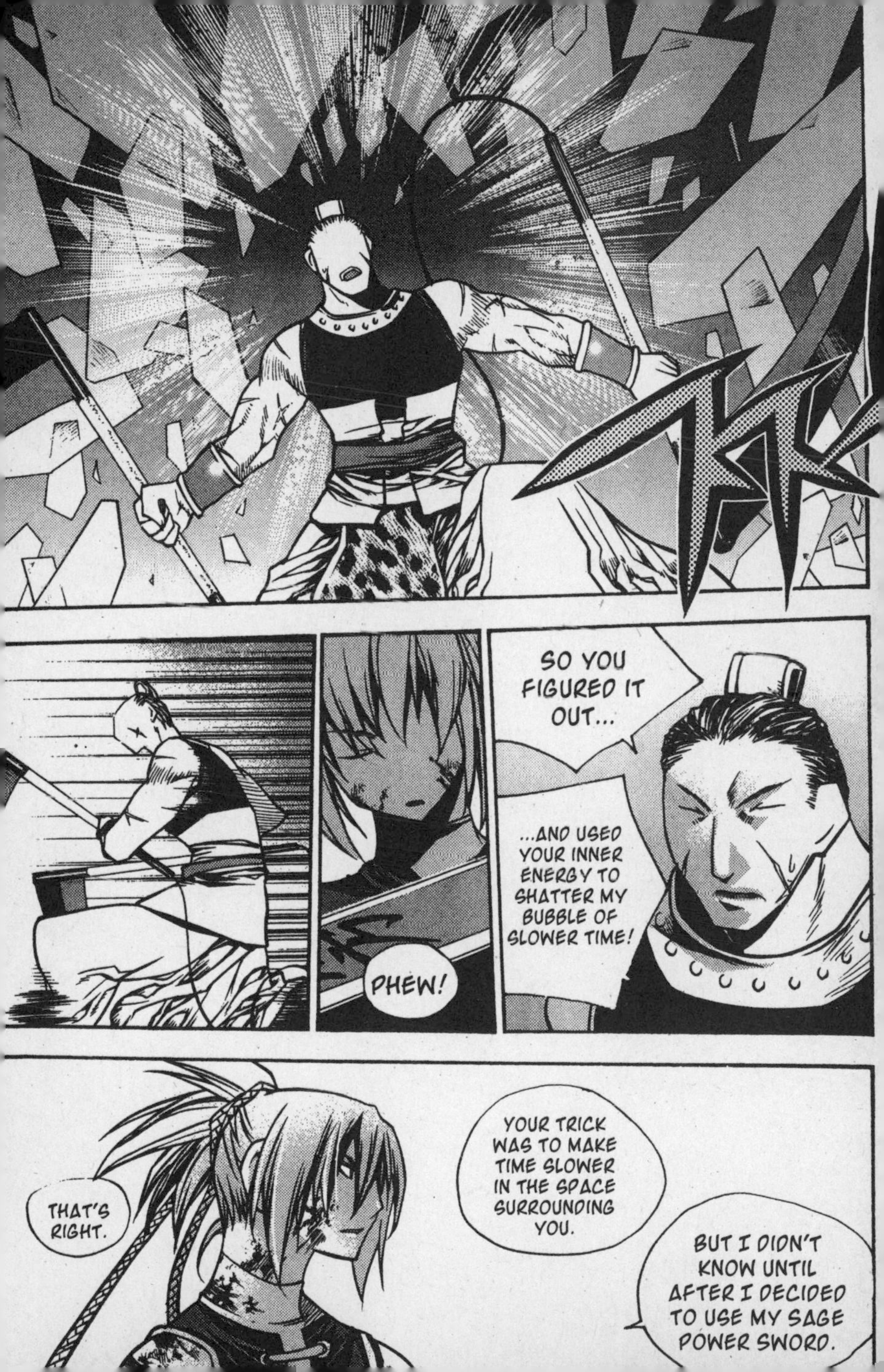
SO YOU FIGURED IT OUT...
PHEW!
...AND USED YOUR INNER ENERGY TO SHATTER MY BUBBLE OF SLOWER TIME!
THAT'S RIGHT.
YOUR TRICK WAS TO MAKE TIME SLOWER IN THE SPACE SURROUNDING YOU.
BUT I DIDN'T KNOW UNTIL AFTER I DECIDED TO USE MY SAGE POWER SWORD.

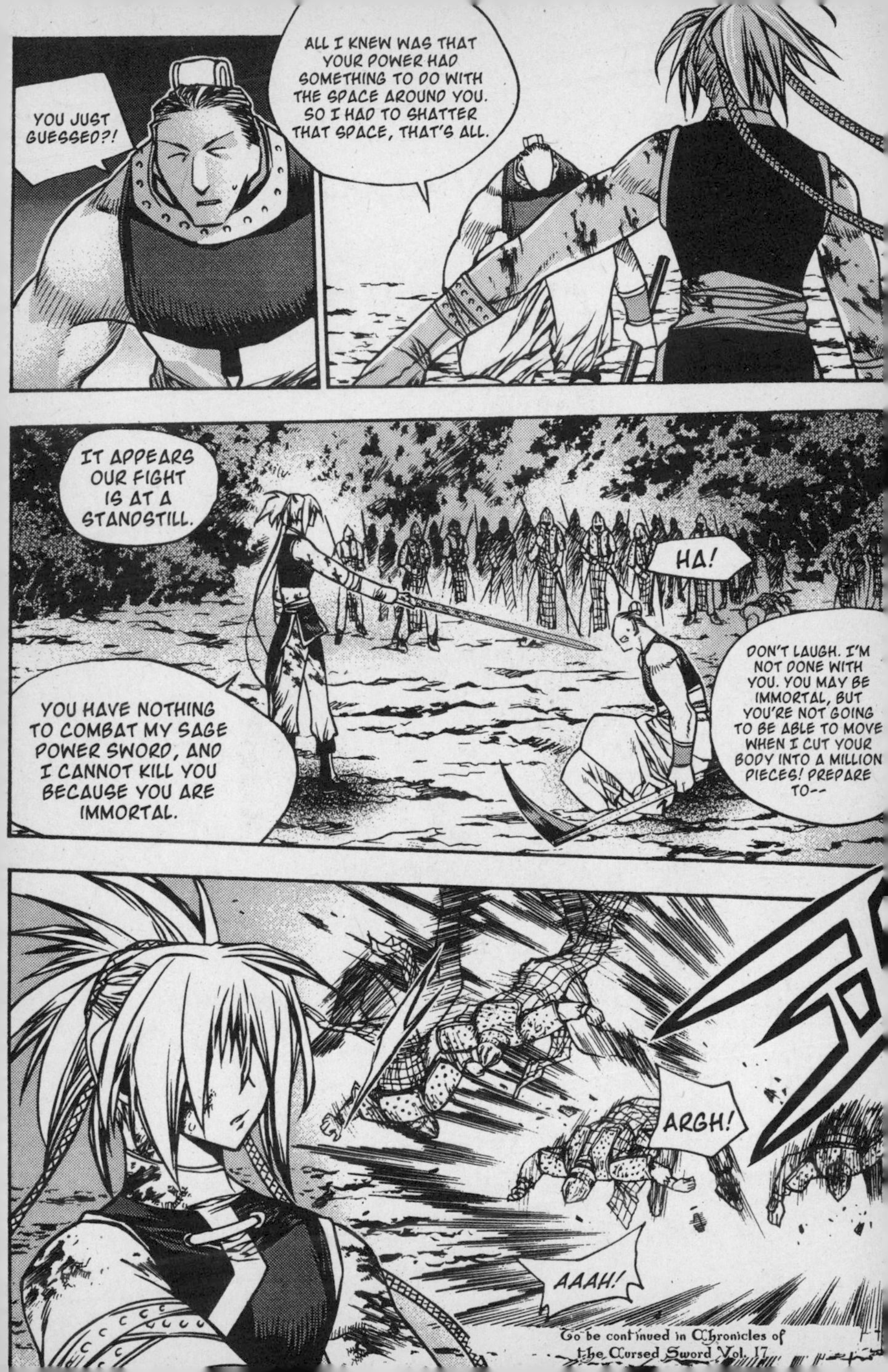
YOU JUST GUESSED?!
ALL I KNEW WAS THAT YOUR POWER HAD SOMETHING TO DO WITH THE SPACE AROUND YOU. SO I HAD TO SHATTER THAT SPACE, THAT'S ALL.
IT APPEARS OUR FIGHT IS AT A STANDSTILL.
YOU HAVE NOTHING TO COMBAT MY SAGE POWER SWORD, AND I CANNOT KILL YOU BECAUSE YOU ARE IMMORTAL.
HA!
DON'T LAUGH. I'M NOT DONE WITH YOU. YOU MAY BE IMMORTAL, BUT YOU'RE NOT GOING TO BE ABLE TO MOVE WHEN I CUT YOUR BODY INTO A MILLION PIECES! PREPARE TO--
ARGH!
AAAH!
To be continued in Chronicles of the Cursed Sword Vol. 17

Next Volume:

TOKYOPOP
CHRONICLES OF THE
CURSED SWORD
AUTHOR: YEO BEOP-RYONG
ILLUSTRATOR: PARK HUI-JIN
17

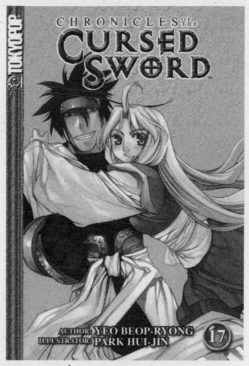

Jargoon's destruction awakens the displeasure of the heavenly god, who threatens to cut off the heavenly realm from the human realm--thereby killing every living being on earth. With no other options left, Rey plans to fight the god with his own godlike powers!

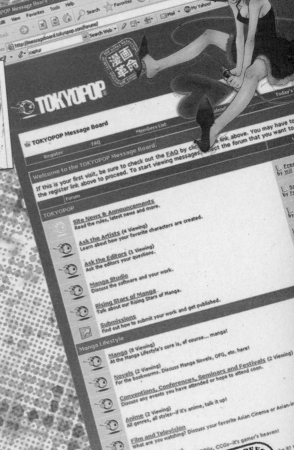